Constitutional Theory: Schmitt after Derrida

This book advances a new reading of the central works of Carl Schmitt and, in so doing, rethinks the primary concepts of constitutional theory. In this book, Jacques de Ville engages in a close analysis of a number of Schmitt's texts, including *Dictatorship* (1921), *The Concept of the Political* (1927), *Constitutional Theory* (1928), *Land and Sea* (1942), *Ex Captivitate Salus* (1950), *The Nomos of the Earth* (1950) and *The Theory of the Partisan* (1963). This engagement takes place from the perspective of constitutional theory and focuses specifically on concepts or themes such as sovereignty, the state, the political, constituent power, democracy, representation, the constitution and human rights. The book seeks to rethink the structure of these concepts in line with Derrida's analysis of Schmitt's texts on the concept of the political in *Politics of Friendship* (1993). This happens by way of an analysis of Derrida's engagement with Freud and other psychoanalysts. Although the main focus in the book is on Schmitt's texts, it further examines two texts of Derrida (*Khōra* (1993) and *Fors: The Anglish Words of Nicholas Abraham and Maria Torok* (1976)), by reading these alongside Schmitt's own reflections on the positive concept of the constitution.

Jacques de Ville is Professor of Law at the University of the Western Cape, South Africa.

Constitutional Theory: Schmitt after Derrida

Jacques de Ville

Birkbeck LAW PRESS

First published 2017
by Birkbeck Law Press

2 Park Square, Milton Park, Abingdon, Oxfordshire OX14 4RN
711 Third Avenue, New York, NY 10017

Birkbeck Law Press is an imprint of the Taylor & Francis Group, an informa business

First issued in paperback 2018

British Library Cataloguing in Publication Data
A catalogue record for this book is available from the British Library

Library of Congress Cataloging in Publication Data
Names: De Ville, Jacques, author.
Title: Constitutional theory : Schmitt after Derrida / Jacques de Ville.
Description: Abingdon, Oxon [UK]; New York : Routledge, 2017. |
Includes bibliographical references and index.
Identifiers: LCCN 2016044265| ISBN 9781138293786 (hardback) |
ISBN 9781351866408 (adobe reader) | ISBN 9781351866392 (epub3) | ISBN 9781351866385 (mobipocket)
Subjects: LCSH: State, The. | Constitutional law—Philosophy. | Constituent power. | Constitution (Philosophy) | Human rights. | Derrida, Jacques. Politiques de l'amitié. English. | Schmitt, Carl, 1888–1985.
Classification: LCC K3165. D425 2017 | DDC 342.001—dc23
LC record available at https://lccn.loc.gov/2016044265

ISBN: 978-1-138-29378-6 (hbk)
ISBN: 978-0-367-02414-7 (pbk)

Typeset in Times New Roman
by Keystroke, Neville Lodge, Tettenhall, Wolverhampton

For Zanél, Chloé and Kelsey

Contents

Acknowledgements

A few people deserve special mention here for their sharing of insights and providing support and assistance to me over the years leading to the present publication. These include Jaco Barnard-Naudé, Henk Botha, Cosmin Cercel, Julia Chryssostalis, Wessel le Roux, Susanna Lindroos-Hovinheimo, Panu Minkkinen, Stewart Motha, Kessler Perumalsamy, Nico Steytler and Philippe van Haute.

Lynn Thomas and Hazel Jeftha are thanked for providing administrative support, as well as the personnel at the University of the Western Cape library, specifically Messrs Fortune and Tarkey and Mmes Moon, Mpandle and Primo.

Costas Douzinas, Fiona Macmillan and the rest of the editorial board of Birkbeck Law Press, as well as Colin Perrin, are thanked for their support of this project.

I would also like to express my thanks to the two anonymous reviewers for their comments.

Earlier versions of most of the chapters included in the present publication have been presented at conferences and some have appeared in print before. Each of these papers, articles and chapters were thoroughly reworked for the present publication: Chapter 2, Section A was presented at the International Symposium for Phenomenology, 8–13 July 2013, held in Perugia, Italy, and was published in 2015 as 'The foreign body within the body politic: Derrida, Schmitt and the concept of the political', *Law and Critique*, 26(1): 45–63. Chapter 2, Section B was presented at a Swedish-Finnish workshop 'Friend or Foe? The Contemporary Relevance of Carl Schmitt', 17–18 June 2013 at the Faculty of Law, University of Helsinki, Finland and was published in 2016 as 'Rethinking the concept of the political: Derrida's reading of Schmitt's "The Theory of the Partisan"', pp. 134–46, in M. Arvidsson, L. Brännström and P. Minkkinen (eds), *The Contemporary Relevance of Carl Schmitt: Law, Politics, Theology*, Abingdon and New York: Routledge. Chapter 2, Section C was presented at the Critical Legal Conference, 5–7 September 2013, held at the Queen's University Belfast, Northern Ireland and was published in 2016 as 'Schmitt's *Weisheit der Zelle*: rethinking the concept of the political', pp. 215–31, in S. Motha and H. van Rijswijk (eds), *Law, Violence, Memory: Uncovering the Counter-Archive*, Abingdon and New York: Routledge.

Chapter 3 was presented at the Derrida Today Conference, 8–11 June 2016, held at Goldsmiths, University of London. Chapter 4 was presented at the Critical Legal Conference, 1–3 September 2016, held at the University of Kent, UK. Chapter 5(a) was presented at the International Summer School on Religion, Law and Justice, 24–26 February 2015, University of the Western Cape, South Africa, and at the conference Law in Crisis: New Developments, 25 September 2015, Potchefstroom, North-West University, South Africa. Chapter 5, Section B was presented at the International Symposium for Phenomenology, 6–11 July 2015, held in Perugia, Italy. Chapter 7 was presented at the Critical Legal Conference, 3–5 September 2015, held at the University of Wrocław, Poland. Chapter 2, Section C, Chapter 5, Section A and Chapter 6 were (also) presented at Faculty and Departmental Seminars of the University of the Western Cape. I would like to express my thanks to all the participants in these seminars, workshops, conferences and symposia for their useful comments, as well as to the publishers for permission to include the material previously published, in the present publication.

Note on translations and references

In the chapters that follow, reference will as a rule be made only to the English version where a translation of a specific text of Schmitt and Derrida is available. If a quotation is at stake or where the wording of the original French (in the case of Derrida) or German (in the case of Schmitt) is a central issue, reference will be made to both the translation and the original, where the latter was available to me. The same applies to the translated texts of other authors. Reference to the original text is essential for purposes of the close reading of Schmitt, and to some extent of Derrida, undertaken here.

Where no reference is made to a specific English translation of a text in the original French and German by Derrida, Schmitt or another author, the translation is my own.

English translations have in many cases been modified. This will not be specifically indicated in respect of each translation so modified.

List of abbreviations

For ease of reference, the following abbreviations are used for the most frequently cited texts of Derrida and of Schmitt. Full references are given in the Bibliography.

Adieu	*Adieu: to Emmanuel Levinas* (Derrida 1999b)
AR	*Acts of Religion* (Derrida 2002a)
'Auto'	'Autoimmunity: real and symbolic suicides – a dialogue with Jacques Derrida', in *Philosophy in a Time of Terror: Dialogues with Jürgen Habermas and Jacques Derrida* (Derrida 2003a)
BdP	*Der Begriff des Politischen* (Schmitt 2002a)
B&S I	*The Beast & the Sovereign,* vol. I (Derrida 2009)
B&S II	*The Beast & the Sovereign,* vol. II (Derrida 2011a)
CoP	*The Concept of the Political* (Schmitt 2007a)
CP	*La Carte Postale: de Socrate à Freud et au-delà* (Derrida 1980)
CPD	*The Crisis of Parliamentary Democracy* (Schmitt 1988a)
CT	*Constitutional Theory* (Schmitt 2008a)
CW	*Chora L Works* (Derrida and Eisenman 1997)
D	*Dictatorship: From the Origin of the Modern Concept of Sovereignty to Proletarian Class Struggle* (Schmitt 2014a)
DARD	*Über die drei Arten des rechtswissenschaftlichen Denkens* (Schmitt 2006c)
DC	*Donoso Cortés in gesamteuropäischer Interpretation* (Schmitt 2009a)
DD	*Die Diktatur: Von den Anfängen des modernen Souveranitätsgedankens bis zum proletarischen Klassenkampf* (Schmitt 2006b)
Dis	*Dissemination* (Derrida 2004a)
Diss	*La Dissémination* (Derrida 1972b)
DJ	'Eröffnung' and 'Schlußwort' in *Das Judentum in der Rechtswissenschaft* (Schmitt 1936a and b)
DL	*Der Leviathan in der Staatslehre des Thomas Hobbes: Sinn und Fehlschlag eines politischen Symbols* (Schmitt 2012a)
DPS	*Dialogues on Power and Space* (Schmitt 2015)
DT	*Donner le Temps* (Derrida 1991)

ECS	*Ex Captivitate Salus: Erfahrungen der Zeit 1945/47* (Schmitt 2010c)
É&D	*L'Écriture et la Différence* (Derrida 1967)
EO	*The Ear of the Other* (Derrida 1988c)
ET	*Echographies of Television* (Derrida and Stiegler 2002)
FA	*Four Articles: 1931–1938* (Schmitt 1999)
FdL	*Force de Loi* (Derrida 2005c)
'F&K'	'Faith and knowledge: the two sources of "religion" at the limits of reason alone' in *Religion* (Derrida 1998a)
'Fore'	'Foreword: *Fors*: the anglish words of Nicolas Abraham and Maria Torok', in *The Wolf Man's Magic Word: A Cryptonomy* (Derrida 1986b)
Fors	'Fors: Les mots anglés de Nicolas Abraham et Maria Torok' in *Cryptymie le Verbier de l'Homme aux Loups* (Derrida 1976b)
FP	*Frieden oder Pazifismus? Arbeiten zum Volkerrecht und zur internationalen Politik 1924–1978* (Schmitt 2005a)
F&S	*Foi et Savoir: Suivi de le Siècle et le Pardon* (Derrida 2001b)
FWT	*For What Tomorrow . . . A Dialogue* (Derrida and Roudinesco 2004)
'*Geschl* IV'	'Heidegger's ear: philopolemology (*Geschlecht* IV)', in *Reading Heidegger* (Derrida 1993a)
GL	*Glossarium: Aufzeichnungen der Jahre 1947–1951* (Schmitt 1991)
G&L	*The Gift of Death & Literature in Secret* (Derrida 2008a)
Glas	*Glas* (Derrida 1986a)
Glas (F)	*Glas* (Derrida 1974)
GLP	*Die geistesgeschichtliche Lage des heutigen Parlamentarismus* (Schmitt 2010d)
'GP'	'Gespräch über den Partisanen', in *Guerrilleros, Partisanen: Theorie und Praxis* (Schmitt and Schickel 1970)
GT	*Given Time: I. Counterfeit Money* (Derrida 1992a)
HdV	*Der Hüter der Verfassung* (Schmitt 1996a)
Khôra	*Khôra* (Derrida 1993d)
LL	*Legality and Legitimacy* (Schmitt 2004c)
L&L	*Legalität und Legitimität* (Schmitt 2012b)
L&M	*Land und Meer: Eine weltgeschichtliche Betrachtung* (Schmitt 2008e)
L&S	*Land and Sea* (Schmitt 1997)
Ltd	*Limited Inc* (Derrida 1988a)
NdE	*Der Nomos der Erde im Völkerrecht recht des Jus Publicum Europaeum* (Schmitt 2011a)
Neg	*Negotiations: Interventions and Interviews 1971–2001* (Derrida 2002b)
NoE	*The Nomos of the Earth in the International Law of the Jus Publicum Europaeum* (Schmitt 2006a)
OH	*Of Hospitality* (Derrida and Dufourmantelle 2000)

ON	*On the Name* (Derrida 1995c)
PA	*Politiques de l'amitié* (Derrida 1994)
PB	*Positionen und Begriffe im Kampf mit Weimar – Genf – Versailles 1923–1939* (Schmitt 1994)
PC	*The Post Card: From Socrates to Freud and Beyond* (Derrida 1987)
PdS	*Points de Suspension: Entretiens* (Derrida 1992c)
PoF	*Politics of Friendship* (Derrida 1997a)
Points	*Points . . . Interviews, 1974–1994* (Derrida 1995a)
Psy I	*Psyche: Inventions of the Other,* vol. I (Derrida 2007a)
Psy II	*Psyche: Inventions of the Other,* vol. II (Derrida 2008b)
Psy II (F)	*Psyché: Inventions de l'Autre,* vol. II (Derrida 2003c)
PT	*Political Theology: Four Chapters on the Concept of Sovereignty* (Schmitt 2005b)
PT (G)	*Politische Theologie: Vier Kapitel zur Lehre von der Souveränität* (Schmitt 2004d)
PT II	*Political Theology II: The Myth of the Closure of any Political Theology* (Schmitt 2008c)
PT II (G)	*Politische Theologie II: Die Legende von der Erledigung jeder Politischen Theologie* (Schmitt 2008b)
RC	*Roman Catholicism and Political Form* (Schmitt 1996b)
Res	*Resistances of Psychoanalysis* (Derrida 1998b)
RK	*Romischer Katholizismus und politische Form* (Schmitt 2008f)
Rog	*Rogues: Two Essays on Reason* (Derrida 2005b)
SB&S I	*Séminaire: La Bête et le Souverain,* vol. I (Derrida 2008d)
SB&S II	*Séminaire: La Bête et le Souverain,* vol. II (Derrida 2010)
SBV	*Staat, Bewegung, Volk: Die Dreigliederung der politischen Einheit* (Schmitt 1934)
SdM	*Spectres de Marx: l'État de la Dette, le Travail du Deuil et la Nouvelle Internationale* (Derrida 1993c)
SGN	*Staat, Großraum, Nomos: Arbeiten aus den Jahren 1916–1969* (Schmitt 1995)
SMP	*State, Movement, People: The Triadic Structure of the Political Unity* (Schmitt 2001)
SoM	*Specters of Marx: The State of Debt, the Work of Mourning, and the New International* (Derrida 2006a)
SP	*Speech and Phenomena and Other Essays on Husserl's Theory of Signs* (Derrida 1973)
SQ	*Sovereignties in Question: The Poetics of Paul Celan* (Derrida (2005a)
TdP	*Theorie des Partisanen: Zwischenbemerkungen zum Begriff des Politischen* (Schmitt 2010a)
TL	*The Leviathan in the State Theory of Thomas Hobbes: Meaning and Failure of a Political Symbol* (Schmitt 2008d)
TOH	*The Other Heading: Reflections on Today's Europe* (Derrida 1992b)

'TP'	'The Theory of the Partisan: a commentary/remark on the concept of the political' (Schmitt 2004a)
TTJT	*On the Three Types of Juristic Thought* (Schmitt 2004b)
VL	*Verfassungslehre* (Schmitt 2010b)
Voy	*Voyous: Deux Essais sur la Raison* (Derrida 2003b)
VRA	*Verfassungsrechtliche Aufsätze aus den Jahren 1924–1954: Materialien zu einer Verfassungslehre* (Schmitt 2003)
WD	*Writing and Difference* (Derrida 1978)
WM	*The Work of Mourning* (Derrida 2001a)
WoW	*Writings on War* (Schmitt 2011c)

Chapter 1

Introduction

Schmitt and Derrida

Despite their very pronounced political and theoretical differences, Jacques Derrida (1930–2004) devotes three chapters to the texts of Carl Schmitt (1888–1985) in his *Politics of Friendship* (1994), in seeking a beyond to the traditional conception of friendship in the metaphysical tradition. Here Derrida, different from other contemporary philosophers,[1] affirms in large part Schmitt's analysis of the enemy by exploring in detail *The Concept of the Political* (1927), 'The Theory of the Partisan' (1963) and 'Weisheit der Zelle' (1947).[2] Derrida's analysis of Schmitt's texts has thus far found little resonance with scholars within constitutional theory and other, related fields. The political-theological reading of Schmitt by Meier (1998), as well as the reading of Schmitt by Agamben (1998; 2005) with its emphasis on sovereignty and the exception, has thus far been much more influential. There is no doubt considerable value in the readings of Meier and Agamben as well as in the readings of their followers, which will be relied on in the analysis that follows, yet the present publication (hereafter '*SAD*') returns to Derrida's reading of Schmitt and gives it a certain preferential status. It specifically raises the question as to the implications for constitutional theory should one take seriously Derrida's deconstruction of Schmitt's concept of the political in *Politics of Friendship*. Can such a reading provide a foundation for constitutional discourse? The answer, which will be given in Chapter 8, will be an ambivalent yes *and* no.

Constitutional theory

Why *'constitutional theory'*? The latter is of course the title of the 2008 translation of Schmitt's highly acclaimed *Verfassungslehre* (1928). In this text, Schmitt spells

1 See e.g. Agamben (1998: 8): 'The fundamental categorical pair of Western politics is not that of friend/enemy but that of bare life/political existence, *zoē/bios*, exclusion/inclusion'.

2 Derrida also refers to Schmitt in a number of other texts, including *Rogues*, 'Autoimmunity' and *The Beast & the Sovereign*, vols I and II.

out the radical implications of his own analysis in *The Concept of the Political*, thereby dislocating the foundations of liberal constitutionalism. He argues in this respect that the political component of modern constitutions, which is repressed by liberal thinking through its privileging of the rule of law, separation of powers and freedom, is in fact the most important component of a constitution. In showing the priority of the political component, Schmitt insists on drawing a distinction between the constitution as such and constitutional laws; distinguishes between, yet shows the interdependence between, the two principles of political form, that is, identity and representation; resurrects the concept of sovereignty in the form of constituent power; understands equality as first of all and necessarily implying an inequality in respect of those who are excluded from the political unity; and subjects freedom to the political component of the constitution.

The focus in *SAD* will be on some of the main concepts and themes explored by Schmitt in *Constitutional Theory*, which intersect with the thinking of Derrida. These include: sovereignty; the state; the political; constituent power; democracy; representation; the constitution; human rights, specifically freedom and equality; as well as the international and transnational framework within which national constitutions operate.[3] *SAD* will closely analyse Schmitt's *Constitutional Theory* as well as a number of Schmitt's other texts, and will more specifically seek to reconceptualise the above-mentioned concepts in line with Derrida's thinking, whilst remaining faithful to Schmitt's texts. The forces at the origin of the modern constitution will be central to this analysis. This was also Schmitt's concern, and remains the concern today of constitutional theorists. A reading of Schmitt through a Derridean lens allows us to rethink such origin and, as we will see in what follows, makes it possible to view a constitution as a gift without return to the self.

Reading Schmitt

The first possible reading strategy in respect of Schmitt, that is, apart from agreeing with his analyses in all or most respects, would be to critically engage in refutation, and to seek rational and logical alternatives to the conservative and often authoritarian responses he gives to the burning questions of constitutional theory. This strategy will not be adopted here, at least not as a primary strategy, because refutation, as Derrida (2016: 2) points out, still belongs to metaphysics, and takes no step beyond it. A second possible strategy would be to simply ignore or disregard Schmitt because of his Nazi collaboration and anti-Semitism. Writing about him would, in the view of some, even make one complicit in these stances. In support of this reading strategy, and as set out in more detail in later chapters, there can be little doubt that Schmitt's anti-Semitism was pervasive, that is, not

3 Although Derrida explores all of these 'themes' in his texts, he does not necessarily do so with reference to Schmitt.

adopted by him simply in order to curry favour with the Nazis from 1933 to 1936. Are all his texts thereby tainted with anti-Semitism,[4] or is it possible, as a third possible reading strategy, to distinguish and separate Schmitt's political commitments from his thinking? A reductive reading of Schmitt as an anti-Semite fails to take account of the Freudian insight into the inevitable tensions and contradictions in a person's life and thinking. The consequential idea that Schmitt should because of his anti-Semitism be isolated and ignored, or that this can be done in respect of a certain part of his work, likewise fails to take account of Freud's insights regarding human nature.[5] As Malpas points out in respect of Heidegger's recently published *Black Notebooks, 1931–1941*:

> [t]here is surely nothing of which humans are capable that is not also a possibility to which we are ourselves connected just by virtue of our being human . . . . This is partly why the Holocaust is so horrific – it is a horror that proceeds, not from something that is *other* than human, nor from some *single person* (Hitler) or *exclusive group of persons* (the Nazis, the Germans, the Europeans) such that they could be set apart, excluded or quarantined from the rest of us, but from a possibility that belongs to human being itself.
>
> (Malpas 2016: 10–11)

The above passage is cited here because of the centrality of human nature and of psychoanalysis for the reading strategy or analysis that follows. This 'analysis' will not involve a psychoanalysis of Schmitt himself, though his texts will indeed be subjected to what can be called here a 'quasi-psychoanalysis', the nature of which will be clarified in what follows. Malpas in the above passage and in the rest of his chapter on Heidegger makes out a strong argument that there is indeed an obligation to seek to understand thinkers like Heidegger and Schmitt, specifically the relation between their anti-Semitism and their philosophical thinking. This is an obligation which Derrida took very seriously, especially in the case of Heidegger.[6] In the case of Schmitt, this obligation should arguably also involve an attempt to understand the seemingly important role of a certain political theology in his thinking,[7] though without ignoring the tensions and contradictions in his texts.

Derrida's reading of Schmitt in *Politics of Friendship* does not consist of a simple affirmation of Schmitt's contentions, a critique or an attempt to separate the 'good' from the 'bad'. This follows from what could in some sense be called Derrida's general 'project', that is, the deconstruction of the metaphysics of

4 See e.g. Gross (2015).
5 See e.g. Freud (2001, XIV: 281) on the impossibility of eradicating 'evil'.
6 See e.g. Derrida (1988b).
7 See in this respect, Meier (1998).

presence.[8] In brief, Derrida seeks to show that metaphysics has a (problematic) desire for presence as its founding principle, and he seeks a passage beyond this. This general project is 'executed' in a singular manner in respect of each text which Derrida reads, so that no 'method', which is applied in the same manner to all texts, can be said to be at stake here. Another text, another event in a sense announces itself through each reading, which cannot simply be traced back to the author and his work (Derrida 1988b: 91). In *Limited Inc*, where Derrida engages with the thinking of J. L. Austin and John Searle in their analyses of speech act theory, Derrida is very explicit about the 'strategy' that he follows, specifically in exposing the structural impossibility as well as illegitimate logic at stake in metaphysical thinking. It also gives us a foretaste of how Derrida will engage with Schmitt's texts in *Politics of Friendship*, and thus assists us in understanding Schmitt's own strategy as a metaphysical thinker in the construction of concepts. Schmitt was no doubt acutely aware of what was at stake in such construction, as appears for example from the essay 'Reich – Staat – Bund':

> In the political battle, concepts and conceptualised words are anything but empty sound. They are the expression of sharp and precisely elaborated oppositions and friend-enemy constellations. Understood thus, the content of world history which is accessible to our consciousness has at all times been a battle for words and concepts. These are of course not empty, but energy-laden words and concepts, and often very sharp weapons.
>
> (*PB* 218)

In view of Derrida's analysis in *Limited Inc*,[9] Schmitt's style of analysis can briefly be summarised as follows: Schmitt, in order to arrive at a pure concept, for example of the political, the partisan, constituent power, representation, the constitution, equality and freedom, as well as of *nomos*, engages in each instance in an idealisation, in the face of what he sometimes refers to as a certain 'conceptual dissolution' (for example in respect of the partisan), 'collapse' (for example in respect of the state) or boundless extension of a concept (for example of democracy and equality) which has taken place in the twentieth century. The conceptual extension, collapse or dissolution which Schmitt seeks to overcome is moreover regarded by him as something extrinsic, contingent, accidental or reducible, and the ideal is posited in a hierarchical opposition in relation thereto. The first term of the hierarchical opposition, for example the political/depoliticisation, the telluric partisan/the world revolutionary partisan, serves in each instance as a foundation or as a form of 'presence' (tied to the concrete, the earth and the home) and the second term in each instance represents a 'fall' from such presence or a

8 See in general De Ville (2011a: 1–42).
9 See especially *Ltd* 67–8, 70, 77–8, 85–6, 89–96, 115–19.

'corruption' of an essential purity (associated with the abstract, the normative, rootlessness and the sea).

Derrida's own stance in respect of this typical style of argument appears clearly from the following passage in *Limited Inc* where he points out in relation to Austin and Searle that the 'corruption' or 'fall' as referred to above

> cannot be a mere extrinsic accident supervening on a structure that is original and pure, one that can be purged of what thus happens to it. The purportedly 'ideal' structure must necessarily be such that this corruption will be 'always possible.' This *possibility* constitutes part of the *necessary* traits of the purportedly ideal structure. The ('ideal') description of this structure should thus include, and not exclude, this possibility.
>
> (*Ltd* 77)

The purity of the inside, as Derrida (*Ltd* 103) further points out, is constructed in metaphysics 'by *accusing* exteriority of being a supplement, something inessential and yet detrimental to that essence, an excess that *should not have been added* to the unadulterated plenitude of the within'. Derrida's contention in the passage quoted above is however that the 'impure' and the 'parasite' (*Ltd* 90),[10] in opposition to the essence or purity of the ideal, is 'by definition never simply external, never simply something that can be excluded from or kept outside of the body "proper," shut out from the "familial" table or house.' Instead, it functions as 'its internal and positive condition of possibility. . ., the very force and law of its emergence' (*Ltd* 17).

The metaphysical strategy as described above is, as Derrida further notes, not motivated by logic, but by something non- or a-logical (*Ltd* 92). This strategy can more particularly be explained by the relationship of metaphysics to death, which as Derrida suggests in *Limited Inc.*, but spells out in more detail elsewhere, is both feared and desired.[11] The latter 'desire' is however radically repressed, or rather, 'forgotten'. It nonetheless still determines the strategy of metaphysics. It namely appears intolerable for metaphysics that the auto-destruction or self-implosion of the pure concept, manifesting itself as dissolution, boundless extension, corruption, etc., can be lodged within the concept itself. An attempt is therefore made to expel the particular manifestation of death from the essence of the concept. In the case of ethical concepts the metaphysical strategy is furthermore to construct such concepts in terms of a circular return to the self. Only if this force of self-destruction is affirmed rather than cast out can metaphysics do the impossible and break with the circular return to the self. In reading Schmitt, Derrida seeks specifically to locate this disruptive force in his texts on the political, and *SAD* will seek to do

10 A term incidentally used by Schmitt to refer to 'the Jew', see further Chapter 6 below.
11 See e.g. *PC*.

something similar in respect of Schmitt's texts on constitutional theory. The concern in what follows will consequently not only be with Schmitt's conscious intention, but also with that which lies behind his intention in the construction and analysis of concepts.[12]

Sequence and overview of chapters

As indicated above, the main focus of the analysis in the chapters that follow will be on the origin of the modern constitution, not in a historical, but in a philosophical sense. This is also the main concern of Schmitt's *Constitutional Theory*, as appears specifically from his analysis of the political component of the constitution, constituent power, the concept of the constitution and of fundamental rights. Yet as indicated above, an attempt will also be made to look beyond Schmitt's conception of the origin.

Chapter 2, Sections A–C will engage in detail with Derrida's reading in *Politics of Friendship* of Schmitt's main texts on the concept of the political, that is, *The Concept of the Political*, 'The Theory of the Partisan', and 'Weisheit der Zelle' in *Ex Captivitate Salus* (1950). At stake in Derrida's engagement with Schmitt is, as noted earlier, not a critique, but a reading through which Derrida is seeking traces in Schmitt's texts of an uneconomic friendship, or what he refers to as 'lovence', beyond the political. In *The Concept of the Political* Schmitt laments the demise in the twentieth century of the concept of the political and seeks to reinvigorate this concept by way of a rigorous definition thereof.[13] In 'The Theory of the Partisan' Schmitt identifies the different forms of hostility (real and absolute), associated with the telluric and world-revolutionary partisan, as compared to the conventional hostility established by the *jus publicum Europaeum*, central to *The Concept of the Political*. In 'Weisheit der Zelle' Schmitt again returns to the enemy, and here concludes that the enemy is the one who can put me in question, and the only one who can do so is the self, or the brother. A different structure of the political vis-à-vis what would appear from a traditional reading of Schmitt comes to the fore in Derrida's reading of these texts, with the force of self-destruction – alluded to by Schmitt in identifying the self, or the brother as enemy – playing an important role: the age of neutralisation and depoliticisation with its paradoxical intensification of hostility, as explored by Schmitt in *The Concept of the Political* and elsewhere, as well as the absolute hostility of the revolutionary

12 The focus here will also not be on any linear developments in Schmitt's thinking, e.g. regarding decisionism and concrete order thinking, but rather with the tensions and contradictions within Schmitt's text as a whole.

13 One is inevitably reminded here of the claim by the Critical Legal Studies (CLS) movement in the United States that law is politics, though the exploration of the concept of the political by CLS scholars arguably remained somewhat on the surface, and the political in the thinking of CLS scholars appears to remain trapped within a circular economy.

partisan at stake in 'Theory of the Partisan', in Derrida's reading, does not (in line with the reading strategy elaborated on above) involve an accidental ruination or perversion of the political, but instead reveals its peculiar 'structure'. Schmitt's friend-enemy distinction, with war as the extreme possibility, can be said to be preceded by a 'pre-originary' form of friendship characterised by dissymmetry and the perfect gift.

Chapter 3 looks into the concept of constituent power as elaborated on by Schmitt in *Dictatorship* (1921) and *Constitutional Theory*. The main focus of this chapter will be the notion of the 'political unity of the people' or the state that appears from Schmitt's texts, and the link between the people and sovereignty. A close reading of Schmitt's texts shows that the *demos* appears in the first place as a formless and groundless force. At stake here is not a presence, a substance, an identity or ontology, but rather a certain 'hauntology' on the model of a dualist conception of God. The God at stake here consists of both a loving God of salvation and a just, creator-God, in a state of permanent war with each other. Chapter 4 enquires into the relation posited by Schmitt between identity and representation in *Constitutional Theory*, as well as in *Roman Catholicism and Political Form* (1923). This relation is important for constituent power (Chapter 3), but also for constituted powers. It will be shown that for Schmitt the two principles cannot operate in isolation of each other in the modern state and furthermore that the representation of the *demos*, whether under a state of exception or a state of normality, cannot be conceived as a weakened doubling of the thing itself. Representation instead bears the burden of the un-representable.

Chapter 5, Sections A and B deal with the essence or concept of the modern constitution. There is a slight change in cue here with the focus moving away from Schmitt towards two of Derrida's texts. Each of the sections takes as their point of departure Schmitt's positive concept of the constitution. Two alternative yet closely related conceptions of the constitution are then posited. Section A proceeds by way of an analysis of Derrida's *Khōra*, which engages in a detailed reading of Plato's *Timaeus*. *Khōra*, usually translated as space, place, country, field, land or region, is shown by Derrida to not simply involve a conception of place or space; it is instead the placeless place, which gives place, that is, 'spacing'. The question is then raised whether the function of a constitution is not ultimately also to give place, similar to *khōra*. The suggestion in other words is that a constitution has its 'origin' or pre-origin in *khōra*. From here issues a call for justice as gift without exchange, as absolute hospitality, that is, a justice irreducible to law. Section B explores the concept of the constitution via the notions of trauma and memory. The chapter proceeds by way of an analysis of the notion of the crypt as employed by Abraham and Torok in their reading of Freud's case study of the Wolf Man, and the reading of their text by Derrida. The chapter shows that in both the instance of a constitution and in the case of the Wolf Man, a singular trauma can be said to be at stake, which finds expression in the text produced by its authors. The chapter explores the ways in which this trauma is to be understood as well as the timing of its occurrence.

In Chapter 6 the foundation of human rights is reconsidered via Schmitt's analyses of freedom and equality in *Constitutional Theory*. Schmitt here couples freedom to the rule-of-law component of the constitution, whereas equality is regarded as part of the political component. It is shown that Schmitt finds it difficult to keep these components completely separate in his analysis of the fundamental rights and the distinction ultimately collapses under the weight of the political component. Yet in this collapse a force beyond the political component appears, which can in a way be said to lie at the 'foundation' of these rights. A certain 'radicalisation' of freedom and equality in other words appears from Schmitt's analysis, which no longer opposes equality and freedom in traditional fashion. They are both conceptualised as beyond subjectivity, mastery, autonomy and consciousness and as incorporating a certain unconditionality. Both concepts ultimately call for a welcome beyond the constraints of conditional hospitality.

Chapter 7 moves beyond Schmitt's *Constitutional Theory* and explores his later thinking in respect of the notion of *nomos*, specifically with reference to *Land and Sea* and *The Nomos of the Earth*. In these texts Schmitt sketches in broad terms the developments in international law through the millennia, that is, the movement from a first to a second and ultimately a new *nomos* of the earth in the twentieth century. According to Schmitt the word *nomos* is to be understood in its originary sense, that is, as an appropriation of land, along with its division and subsequent production. *Nomos* is thus to be understood as the foundational order, yet not only of a specific domestic legal order, but of the earth as a whole. A close analysis of Schmitt's texts nevertheless shows that *nomos* is already a reaction to a certain uncanniness, a pre-originary 'not-at-home-ness', a strangeness, which structures man and all living beings in general. Chapter 8 will conclude *SAD* by contrasting a reading of Schmitt 'before' and 'after' Derrida.

Chapter 2

The concept of the political

More than 20 years have passed since the publication of Derrida's *Politics of Friendship* (1993). The three chapters (4, 5 and 6) of Derrida's text that deal with Schmitt's analysis of the concept of the political have attracted relatively little interest in the English-speaking world. It has generated much more controversy in Schmitt's country of origin, Germany. As noted in Chapter 1 above, Derrida in *Politics of Friendship* not only engages with *The Concept of the Political* (1927), but also with other texts of Schmitt that touch on the 'theme' of the political, such as 'The Theory of the Partisan' (1963), *Political Theology II* (1970), the *Glossarium* (1991) and *Ex Captivitate Salus* (1950). In these texts, Schmitt appears to seek in typical metaphysical style, as elaborated on in Chapter 1 above, the essence of the political, with the latter appearing to be in decline in the twentieth century. In *The Concept of the Political*, the focus of Section A, he finds this essence or 'criterion' in the drawing of a distinction between friend and enemy, which in turn finds its limit or extreme case in war. In both *The Concept of the Political* and 'The Theory of the Partisan', the focus of Section B, Schmitt seeks to understand the nature of war, specifically in the modern era, by enquiring into different forms of enmity or hostility. In *The Concept of the Political* he identifies the enemy as *polémios* or *hostis* (and not *ekhthrós* or *inimicus*). In 'The Theory of the Partisan' he identifies the different forms of hostility (real and absolute) associated with respectively the telluric and world-revolutionary partisan, as compared to the conventional hostility established by the *jus publicum Europaeum*, at stake in *The Concept of the Political*. Going back in time, as Derrida does in *Politics of Friendship*, Section C follows Schmitt in *Ex Captivitate Salus* where he enquires into the enemy with reference to Stirner's *The Ego and Its Own* (1845) as well as Descartes' *Meditations* (1641) and concludes that the enemy is the one who can put me in question, and the only one who can do so is the self, or the brother. The concept of the political thus loses its essence and self-destructs.

The focus in the three sections that follow will be a somewhat neglected aspect in the reception of Derrida's engagement with Schmitt, that is, the role of psychoanalysis. Following the analysis set out in Chapter 1 above, Derrida is not engaging in the first place in a critique of Schmitt as has been assumed in much of the literature. A deconstructive reading of Schmitt is taking place here, with Derrida seeking a form of friendship, or what he refers to as 'lovence', beyond the political. Derrida finds traces in the texts of Schmitt referred to above of something beyond the political. Sections A–C undertake an analysis of the new 'structure' of the concept of the political which comes to the fore in Derrida's reading. This new structure must be at the heart of any attempt to rethink constitutional theory after Derrida, as the concept of the political is central to Schmitt's *Constitutional Theory*.

SECTION A *POLÉMIOS*

> Viele zitieren den Satz des Heraklit: Der Krieg ist der Vater aller Dinge. Wenige aber wagen es, dabei an den Bürgerkrieg zu denken.[1]
>
> (*ECS* 26)

> Der hier genannte *pólemos* ist ein vor allem Göttlichen und Menschlichen waltender Streit, kein Krieg nach menschlicher Weise.[2]
>
> (Heidegger 1983: 66)

Introduction

As noted above, Schmitt in *Constitutional Theory* seeks to spell out the implications of his analysis in *The Concept of the Political*. In the latter text he contends that the concept of the political is to be understood with reference to the potential of a friend-and-enemy grouping, with war as the most extreme consequence of this grouping (*CoP* 28, 33). The political has no domain of its own, unlike for example religion, morality, aesthetics or economics. It instead refers to the degree of intensity of an existential relationship, that is, of a union or a separation, association or disassociation (*CoP* 26; Herrero 2015: 103). The political can consequently be reached from any domain (*CoP* 62; Schmitt 2002d: 308). The political is moreover inescapable, due to the animality, drives and passions at the heart of human nature (*CoP* 58–68). Meaning itself is for Schmitt (*CoP* 35/*BdP* 36) dependent on this antithesis whereby men 'may be required to sacrifice their lives, and authorized to shed blood as well as kill other human beings'.

Schmitt's attempt at strictly defining the political in *The Concept of the Political* is motivated by the problem of depoliticisation, which he observes in the 'disappearance' of the enemy in the twentieth century. In *Constitutional Theory*, Schmitt expresses a similar concern about depoliticisation, specifically insofar as the conception of the modern liberal constitution is concerned. He argues in this respect that the political component of the modern constitution, which is repressed by liberal thinking through its privileging of the rule-of-law component (Chapter 5, Section B below), is the most important component of the constitution. In advocating the priority of the political component, Schmitt further insists on the recognition of sovereignty, not of the constitution, but of the people as constituent power (Chapter 3 below); on the acknowledgement of the positive concept of the

1 'Many cite the phrase of Heraclitus: war is the father of all things. Few however dare to think of it in terms of civil war.' The two preceding sentences in *ECS* 26 read as follows: 'Poets and philosophers, historians and soldiers have spoken about war. Unfortunately, everything one says about war, only receives its ultimate and grim significance in civil war.'

2 'The *pólemos* in question here is a conflict that prevails prior to all things divine and human, not war in the human sense' (Heidegger 2000: 65).

constitution (as opposed to the absolute, ideal and relative concepts), that is, understanding the constitution as a political decision by the people concerning the form and nature of the political unity; on understanding equality in relation to democracy as first of all and necessarily implying an inequality in respect of those who are excluded from the political unity, and on the subjection of freedom to the political component of the constitution (Chapter 6 below).

In *Politics of Friendship* Derrida engages in some detail with Schmitt's *Concept of the Political*,[3] through which a new structure of the concept of the political comes to the fore. The present chapter focuses on Derrida's analysis in arriving at this new structure. The chapter will proceed by first enquiring into Derrida's analysis of Schmitt's reading of Plato, with Derrida showing that *phûsis* (usually translated as 'nature'), which lies at the basis of the distinction which Schmitt seeks to draw between *pólemos* and *stásis* and the corresponding distinction between the public enemy and the private enemy, is divided in itself, that is, *phûsis* has an 'other', which however does not belong to it. Thereafter Derrida's positioning of Schmitt alongside Freud and Heidegger will be analysed, which will seek to clarify what this division in *phûsis* entails. Derrida shows, first, how Schmitt ultimately sees civil war and external war as manifestations of the same concept of war. Secondly, he shows that the distinction between private and public (or between self and other), which Schmitt desperately seeks to maintain, ultimately breaks down, as Schmitt himself acknowledges in *The Concept of the Political*. Thirdly, tying in closely with the second point, he shows that Schmitt in *Political Theology II* speaks of *stásis* in pre-ontological terms, that is, in terms of a *differantial*[4] turning against the self, which structures the political. This turning against the self of the political can, as Derrida shows, be understood with reference to the destructive drive in Freud, which is likewise preceded by a turning against the self. In placing Schmitt alongside Heidegger, we return to the (unified) concept of war in Schmitt mentioned above, with Heidegger seeking the originary sense of the Greek *pólemos*. This involves a form of originary combat, not between human beings, but between the gathering of Being and its dissimulation. We also return here to *phûsis*, which according to Heidegger is originally another name for Being and we look at Heidegger's invocation of the *phileîn* (love, gift) of Being. Freud and Heidegger can in other words be read as pointing to that which gives rise to the friend-enemy distinction of Schmitt's concept of the political, that is, to a force of self-destruction, or, translated in ethico-political terms, the gift, lovence, that is, a friendship beyond circular return.

3 Derrida's focus is on the 1932 edition.

4 Derrida explores the notion of *différance*, which is at stake here, with reference to the texts of De Saussure, Hegel, Nietzsche, Freud and Heidegger, in *SP* 129–60. The Freudian death drive is central to this notion; see further De Ville (2011a: 28–37); and the discussion below.

Plato[5]

In *The Concept of the Political*, in drawing a distinction between *pólemos* (war between Greeks and barbarians) and *stásis* (internal strife), as well as between *polémios/hostis* (public enemy) and *ekhthrós/inimicus* (private enemy), Schmitt relies in a footnote on Plato's *Republic*.[6] The enemy in the paradigmatic sense (*polémios/hostis*) for Schmitt is associated with *pólemos* (external war) rather than with *stásis*.[7] In his reading, Derrida however shows that Schmitt ignores a certain complexity in Plato's *Republic* insofar as the discussion of war is concerned. As we will see, this has important implications for the structure of the political. Plato, Derrida (*PoF* 90) notes, indeed says that the Greeks view a disagreement (*diaphorá*) between themselves as an internal struggle (*stásis*) and therefore as quasi-familial (*ōs-oikeíous*) and not as war (*pólemos*). It is also correct to say that Plato refers to the barbarians as *natural* enemies whereas the Greeks are *by nature* friends among themselves (*PoF* 90). One should however be careful not to conclude from this that *stásis* or the hostility between Greeks is for Plato an 'unnatural' phenomenon.[8] Plato more specifically refers to civil war as an 'illness', which, as Derrida notes, 'is something else again [*ce qui est encore autre chose*]' (*PoF* 90/*PA* 111).

The two names (*onômata*) which Plato invokes in the *Republic*, as Derrida (*PoF* 91) points out, are supposed to rigorously name, in their legal purity, what belongs to nature.[9] These two names – *pólemos* and *stásis* – pertain to two kinds of disagreement, contestation and discord *(diaphorá)*. *Stásis*, as we saw, refers to the discord (*diaphorá*) between those who share kinship ties or origins – that which is sometimes called civil war. *Pólemos*, on the other hand, that is, war in the strict sense, refers to the discord between strangers or the families of strangers (*PoF* 91). In the case of the Greeks, the naturalness of the bond between them is said to remain intact whether they engage in *pólemos* or *stásis*.[10] The Greeks, Plato

5 References to Plato's texts are, unless otherwise indicated, to Plato 1997. Reference will be made to the Stephanus page numbers.

6 This footnote appears for the first time in the 1932 edition (*BdP* 29), and re-appears with slight modifications in the 1933 edition (Schmitt 1933: 10–11).

7 Meier (1998: 33; 2013: 22–5) contends in this regard that there was a shift in Schmitt's analysis from the 1927 to the 1932 edition. Whereas in the 1927 edition Schmitt regarded only battles with the external enemy (*pólemos*) as war, in the 1932 edition, civil war (*stásis*) was included within the concept of war. This shift corresponds with the changing internal position in Weimar Germany at these particular points in time. Derrida explores a similar 'shift' or tension within the 1932 edition.

8 Schmitt (*CoP* 29 n9) does not expressly say that *stásis* is 'unnatural', but he could be said to imply this by noting that the idea underlying the distinction which Plato draws between *pólemos* and *stásis* is that 'a people cannot wage war against itself [i.e. *stásis* is not really war] and that a so-called "civil war" only means self-destruction [*Selbstzerfleischung*], not however the formation of a new state or even of a new people'.

9 Plato (1997: *Republic* 470b–c) refers here to 'two names' for 'two things'.

10 The barbarians on the other hand are said to be strangers vis-à-vis the Greeks both in respect of kinship ties and origins.

(1955: *Republic* 471b) contends, always end up reconciling with each other, and do not seek to subjugate or destroy each other; they simply attack the 'causes', that is, 'the minority who are responsible for the quarrel'. Even in the case of *stásis*, Plato says, the Greeks remain friends. And then a certain complexity slips in, that is, into the ideal distinctions of the Ideal State, which as Derrida notes are at stake here: Plato indeed refers to *ékhthra* (enmity or hatred) in this context, that is, when invoking the corresponding name *stásis*, but as Derrida (*PoF* 92) points out, this enmity is itself (like *stásis*) according to Plato a form of illness.[11] Derrida summarises Plato's position as follows:

> Sickness is then what emerges, an equally natural sickness, an evil naturally affecting nature. It [i.e. nature] is divided, separated from itself [*Celle-ci s'écarte d'elle-même*]. When such an event occurs [i.e. Greeks fighting amongst themselves], one must speak of a pathology of the community. In question here is a clinic of the city. In this respect the *Republic* develops a nosological discourse; its diagnostic is one of ill health and dissension, a faction inside Greece . . . . *Stásis*, the name that should apply to this hatred or to this enmity (*ékhthra*), is also a category of political nosography.
>
> (*PoF* 92/*PA* 113)

Schmitt is thus, on Derrida's reading, correct to say that Plato draws a distinction between the two forms of disagreement (*diaphorá*), that is, between *pólemos* and *stásis*.[12] A careful reading shows, as Derrida puts it, 'that this difference returns as the same, in the sense that it appears as the same [*qu'une telle différence revient au même, elle appartient au même*]' (*PoF* 113–14/*PA* 133).[13] This is because the

11 See Plato (1997: *Republic* 470c–d). Plato's *Menexenus*, which consists for the most part of a speech by Socrates in the form of a funeral oration, seems to go even further in this diagnosis of *stásis* as an illness (*PoF* 92). Socrates here denies that enmity (*ekhthrós*) or wickedness has any role to play in *stásis* and says that the cause thereof is *dustukhía*, which can be translated as 'a fatal disorder, a stroke of bad luck, misfortune' (*PoF* 92). Derrida's discussion of the *Menexenus* for the most part touches on themes which are not of direct relevance for our present concern, and will thus not be analysed in detail here. Worth mentioning is nonetheless Derrida's reference to Loraux (2006: 252) who refers to *stásis* as an 'absolute evil' and as 'a parasitic evil grafted onto the good nature of the city'. See also *PoF* 273/*PA* 303 where Derrida, within the context of a discussion of the notion of crimes against humanity and with reference to Kant, notes that '[f]ratricide is [considered as] the general form of temptation, the possibility of radical evil, the evil of evil [*Le fratricide est la forme générale de la tentation, la possibilité du mal radical, le mal du mal*]'.

12 Derrida (*PoF* 90) furthermore points out that in the *Republic* Plato does not simply accept this opposition between *stásis* and *pólemos*. He in fact through Socrates calls for its erasure in the form of a law to be laid down. He more specifically admonishes the guardians to treat the barbarians as they now treat the Greeks, i.e. they should not ravage their lands and destroy their houses (Plato 1997: *Republic* 470a–471c).

13 In *PoF* 113–14, this sentence is rendered, correctly, but perhaps a bit simplistically, as 'such a difference amounts to the same thing . . . it belongs to the same'. The word 'revient' (*revenir*: return

two forms of dispute are both 'natural', that is, they both stem from *phûsis*.[14] They also remain natural, even if one of them, civil war (*stásis*), sometimes takes the form of a denaturalization (*PoF* 114).[15] *Stásis* then amounts to a denaturalisation of nature in nature, an evil, an illness, a parasite, a transplant, a foreign body (*un corps étranger*) within the body politic itself, within its own body (*PoF* 114/*PA* 133).[16] *Phûsis* is in other words divided in itself: there is a certain denaturalisation in *phûsis*, an originary difference, or what Derrida would call a *différance* between *phûsis* and its other, as we will also see below in the discussion of Heidegger. A different structure of the political slowly starts to unfold in this reading of Plato.[17]

Schmitt

Pólemos and stásis

Schmitt, as indicated above, appears to follow Plato in suggesting that only external war, that is, a war between Greeks and barbarians (*pólemos*) would be 'real war', as compared to civil unrest, that is, fights between Greeks (*stásis*). This view corresponds with the reign of the *jus publicum Europaeum* (European public law), which lasted from the time of the Peace of Westphalia (1648) until its dissolution between 1890 and 1918 (*NoE* 227–39).[18] The concept of war was in

or come back) however suggests that Derrida is alluding here to Freud's repetition compulsion as well as his later discussion in 'Geschl IV' (which does not appear in the English translation of *PoF*) where at stake is the originary difference or the event of the gift in its relation to *pólemos* in Heidegger's texts ('*Geschl* IV' 171); see further below.

14 In the discussion below, we will see that Heidegger in *Introduction to Metaphysics* (2000: 14–18) insists that the Platonic *phûsis* should be understood in its originary sense, i.e. as Being itself.

15 Derrida (2003d; *PoF* 147), for whom deconstruction can to some extent be equated with denaturalization, is of course not with his analysis supporting a belief in nature; see *PoF* 159. For now, Derrida is simply following Plato's terminology, seeking to establish a certain law.

16 Derrida's analysis here shows a similarity with his analysis elsewhere of Plato, specifically 'Plato's Pharmacy' in *Dissemination* (at 130–5) with its analysis of the rite of the *pharmakos*. In Athens, two *pharmakoi* were sacrificed as scapegoats whenever some calamity befell the city. The *pharmakoi*, as Derrida points out here, were a 'wretched' man and a woman housed on the inside, who represented the evil coming from the outside. The notion of the 'foreign body' (*corps étranger*) also makes its appearance in other texts of Derrida in the context of psychoanalysis, and specifically when he engages with the work of Abraham and Torok; see e.g. *Psy I* 321 and 'Fore' xxx on the crypt incorporated in the self. Derrida partly draws on these analyses in *PoF*. See further Chapter 5, Section B below.

17 It is therefore not possible to agree with Filmer (2007: 14), according to whom Derrida's detour through Plato, to criticise the distinction between *pólemos* and *stásis*, is unnecessary.

18 Schmitt (*NoE* 237/*NdE* 211) interestingly describes the opening of European international law to all states, which led to this dissolution, in the terminology of hospitality: 'a family or housing cooperative of European states and nations', he says, 'suddenly opened its house to the whole world'. In Schmitt's assessment this was 'a fall into the nothing of a spaceless and bottomless generality [*ein Absturz in das Nichts einer raum- und bodenlosen Allgemeinheit*]'.

this era associated with external affairs of sovereignty, and civil war was rendered a purely internal matter of state.[19] The enemy that defines the concept of the political is correspondingly the public enemy (*polémios*), not the private enemy (*ekhthrós*) that one hates (*CoP* 28). A few pages after invoking the Platonic distinction, thereby identifying the *polémios* as defining the political, Schmitt however expresses the seemingly contradictory view that the political can also find expression through domestic conflicts between political parties.[20] He seems to symmetrically align here external war and civil war: 'War is armed combat between organized political entities; civil war is armed combat within a (thereby however becoming problematic) organized unit' (*CoP* 32/*BdP* 33). This move in Schmitt is important for Derrida's reading because, as we will see further below, it will allow him to align Schmitt's understanding of war with Heidegger's analysis of *pólemos*. In view of the privilege accorded to the state in the opening sentence of *The Concept of the Political*,[21] Derrida is of the view that Schmitt ultimately sees civil war as an instance of war in general (*PoF* 121). Civil war would in other words be 'a war between a weakened state and a potential state to be constituted, a war for the seizure or the reconstitution of a state power' (*PoF* 121/*PA* 142). There would thus be in truth, according to Schmitt, only one concept of war, Derrida concludes (*PoF* 121).[22]

19 See Preface to *BdP* 10–11 and *NoE* 141/*NdE* 113, where Schmitt notes that war during the preceding period (the Thirty Years' War, lasting from 1618–1648) had degenerated into civil war (*Entartung des Krieges zum Bürgerkrieg*). Schmitt (*NoE* 142/*NdE* 114) also speaks in this respect of the 'liquidation' (*Liquidierung*) of civil war through the Westphalia treaty. See further Kochi (2006a: 271–2; 2006b: 148).

20 See Schwab (1987: 200–1) on the role of communism in stoking civil war and thereby undermining the epoch of the state.

21 *CoP* 19/*BdP* 20: 'The concept of the state presupposes the concept of the political'. See in this regard Hooker (2009: 17); Schwab in his 'Introduction' to *CoP* 6–8, 12–13; and Hirst (1987: 17). The state thus finds its origin in the political; see also Galli (2015: 11). McCormick (2007: 328) points out in this regard that '[b]efore the modern state, and before Hobbes's theoretization of it, the political was fluid and completely unruly . . . . Hobbes and the modern state make it possible to govern the political more efficiently – not eliminate it . . . but institutionalize it'. In the Foreword to the 1971 Italian edition of *The Concept of the Political*, Schmitt (1988b: 271) further notes that with Machiavelli, Bodin and Hobbes, the state becomes the sole subject of politics; the state and politics were inseparably related to each other. See moreover Chapter 6 below on how, according to Schmitt, this relation became undone.

22 Derrida (*PoF* 121) further notes that Schmitt performs this mediation, which is at the same time a synthetic mediation of the two kinds of enemy, by way of the notion of a 'real possibility' which is present-at-hand (*vorhanden*); see further the discussion below. Derrida is referring here to the following statement of Schmitt, which precedes his aligning of these two forms of warfare: 'The real possibility of battle, which must always be present-at-hand in order to speak of politics, concerns itself in respect of such "primacy of domestic politics" consequently no longer with the war between organised national entities (states or empires), but with *civil war* [*Die reale Möglichkeit des Kampfes, die immer vorhanden sein muß, damit von Politik gesprochen werden kann, bezieht sich bei einem derartigen "Primat der Innenpolitik" konsequenterweise nicht mehr auf den Krieg zwischen organisierten Völkereinheiten (Staaten oder Imperien), sondern auf den* Bürgerkrieg]' (*CoP* 32/*BdP* 32).

Private/public

Derrida's next step is to destabilise the private/public distinction which Schmitt tries to draw. The stakes here are high, because the distinction between *polémios* (public enemy) and *ekhthrós* (private enemy), which as we saw Schmitt seeks to derive from Plato, is relied on by Schmitt to later view (and condemn) the re-invocation of the notion of a 'just war' in the twentieth century (accompanied by a hatred of the enemy), as amounting to a depoliticisation.[23] With the distinction between *polémios* and *ekhthrós*, Schmitt seeks to arrive at a pure concept of the enemy which is stripped of any passion, sentiment or (personal) affect (*PoF* 87). The public enemy should in other words not be hated as this leads to wars of total destruction.[24] In expounding on this distinction, Schmitt refers to Matthew 5:43–4 and Luke 6:27 where Jesus, in response to the common saying 'love your neighbour and hate your enemy' contends that one should instead love one's enemies (*diligite inimicos vestros, agapâte tous ekhthrous umôn*). Schmitt points out that the words used here for 'enemy' in the Latin and Greek manuscripts are respectively *inimicus* and *ekhthrós* and not *hostis*.[25] There was according to Schmitt consequently no obligation on Christian Europe to love the Islamic invader, that is, the public enemy, but only the private enemy.[26] In other words, the command to love one's 'enemy' extends only to the sphere of the private, and does not include the public enemy, even though the latter enemy 'need not be hated personally'.[27]

23 This development in a sense amounts to a return to the period of religious warfare of the sixteenth and seventeenth centuries preceding the *jus publicum Europaeum* where the enemy was associated with personal hatred (i.e. a despised foe); see Schwab 'Introduction' to *CoP* at 8–10.

24 As Derrida (*PoF* 114/*PA* 133–4) points out, the purity of this distinction between *polémios/ekhthrós* and *pólemos/stásis* is an ideal construction (following Plato), which cannot be realised in practice. This inadequation between politics and practice is moreover 'not accidental, since politics is essentially a *praxis*, as Schmitt himself always implies by resorting so insistently to the concept of *possibility* or of *real* and *present eventuality* in his analysis of the formal structure of the political' (*PoF* 114/*PA* 134). This has important implications for the concept of the political itself as we will see further below. In summary, the attempt to establish an ideal essence in this context is an attempt (the typical metaphysical strategy as we saw in Chapter 1) at warding off another, more dangerous spectral enemy. Derrida will seek to re-conceptualise the concept of the political in view of this 'enemy' without the invocation of the ideal.

25 In the English translation at *PoF* 88 the terminology is confused; *cf. PA* 108.

26 See also Kennedy (2004: 105).

27 See further *G&L* 102–7 where Derrida attempts to read this passage in Matthew 5:43–4 as well as in Leviticus 19:15–18 (from which the instruction to love thy neighbour referred to in Matthew comes, and which incidentally does not include any instruction to hate the enemy) as suspending the economy of exchange, and similar therefore to the notion of *aimance*, which we will encounter again below. Derrida particularly points out that the instruction to love one's neighbour in Leviticus is extended to all those belonging to the same nation (*'amith*), which therefore extends this instruction to the sphere of the political in Schmitt's sense. When Matthew speaks of hating the enemy (*inimicus/ekhthrós*), the context thus suggests that this is a reference to the non-neighbour or foreigner (those not belonging to the same nation) and not to the private enemy. This seems to further undermine Schmitt's attempted distinction between the private and the public enemy as well as the attempt to construe a public enemy without private affect.

Driving the point home, Schmitt (*CoP* 29) notes that it only makes sense in the private sphere to love one's enemy.[28] As Derrida (*PoF* 88) points out, this has the consequence that I can also wage war against a friend, provided it is without hatred. I can in other words be hostile towards my friend in public (as a *hostis*),[29] yet love him in private (*PoF 88*). Derrida makes the same point later in *Politics of Friendship*, noting that the political enemy can also be loved 'as friend, lover, neighbour, human being' (*PoF* 125/*PA* 148). The whole concept of the political, with its insistence on the 'public' nature of the enemy,[30] can thus be said to ultimately depend on the fragile, porous and contestable border between the private and the public (*PoF* 88).[31]

In Chapter 6 of *Politics of Friendship*, in analysing Schmitt's 'The Theory of the Partisan' (Section B below), Derrida will refer inter alia to tapping devices,[32] to the police as spy network (which Walter Benjamin refers to as the spectre of the modern state),[33] new forms of cryptography, cybercrime and the institution of psychoanalysis, which all point to the loss of the distinction between the public and the private (*PoF* 144).[34] The importance of psychoanalysis in this respect will be explored below, yet it can be mentioned here that Derrida's analysis of Freud in *Politics of Friendship* points to a 'structure' which undermines any attempt at distinguishing between the private enemy (*ekhthrós/inimicus*) and the public enemy (*polémios/hostis*), as this distinction is itself preceded and made possible by what is most secret/private.[35] The body politic, Derrida (*PoF* 114/*PA* 133) comments, should undoubtedly neatly (*proprement*) identify 'the foreign body of the enemy *outside of itself* [*le corps étranger de l'ennemi* au-dehors]', but it never succeeds in doing so. No pure distinction between the enemy within and the enemy beyond the body politic is thus possible.

28 See further Schwab (1987: 194–5) on the Hebrew Bible, which draws a similar distinction between *soneh* (private enemy) and *ojeb* (public enemy).

29 See further Benveniste (1973: Book 1, Chapter 7) on the link between the Latin *hostis* and hospitality. The word *hostis*, Benveniste notes, first had the meaning of stranger associated with reciprocity, but later '[b]y a development of which we do not know the exact conditions, the word *hostis* assumed a "hostile" flavour and henceforth it is only applied to the "enemy"'.

30 See *CoP* 28/*BdP* 29: 'The enemy is solely the *public* enemy [*Feind ist nur der* öffentliche *Feind*]'.

31 An important question which Schmitt does not seem to provide an answer to in *The Concept of the Political*, and which likewise troubles the border between the private and the public, is raised by Derrida (*G&L* 104): Is the passion or affect with which a community is established, i.e. national or nationalistic affect, private or public (i.e. political) in nature?

32 Specifically to the at-the-time just announced clipper-chip, a now-abandoned method of intercepting private communication.

33 See further *AR* 279–80 on the ubiquity of the police, i.e. their ability and authority to intrude in every sphere.

34 This is also a theme elsewhere in Derrida's texts; see e.g. *OH* 49–65. At stake here for Derrida, as we saw above and as we will see again below, is the question whether it is indeed possible to think hostility without affect, especially after Freud; see *PoF* 124, read with *PoF* 136 n19.

35 See also Derrida and Ferraris (2001: 57); and *ON* 23–7.

It is against the threat of the implosion of this border (between private and public), which is also a border of the self, Derrida (*PoF* 88) comments, that Schmitt attempts to construct his discourse.[36] Schmitt (*CoP* 53–5) himself acknowledges this implosion when he later discusses and condemns so-called 'humanitarian war' for turning the enemy into a figure to be dehumanised and hated.[37] Such wars, as Schmitt points out, amount to the abolition of the idea of a 'just enemy' that one treats with respect and honour, as established by the *jus publicum Europaeum*. After World War I, the latter order comes to an end: the enemy is now criminalised and outlawed: taking action against him amounts to police action (*CoP* 54; *NoE* 124).[38] The waging of war in the name of humanity, Schmitt (*CoP* 54) further contends, is nothing but the ruse of imperialist expansion. The enemy at stake in humanitarian wars, as well as in the Cold War, is no longer the *just* enemy, but the *absolute* enemy who needs to be exterminated in waging a just war against him (*CoP* 36).[39] The Cold War moreover mocks (*spottet*) all classical distinctions: of war and peace and neutrality, of politics and economics, military and civilian and of combatants and non-combatants (*BdP* 18).[40]

36 This comment has to be understood within the broader context of Derrida's analysis of friendship: in the canonical discourses on friendship, fraternal friendship has been regarded as alien to the public sphere – it could thus logically never found a politics. Yet at the same time, in the same discourse, the friend-brother relationship has served as the model for justice and virtue as well as for political and moral reason (*PoF* 277). This contradiction points for Derrida to a certain unconscious logic which is also manifested in the exclusion of friendships between women, and between men and women, from the tradition of friendship, as well as the traditional restriction of women to the private, domestic sphere (*PoF* 277, 279, 281).

37 The re-introduction of the English word 'foe' is significant in this respect, as Schmitt (*BdP* 18–19) notes. Private or personal feelings or affect thus intrude here in the public sphere.

38 This is also the case with the partisan, as Schmitt will point out in 'The Theory of the Partisan'; see Section B below. In the Foreword to the 1971 Italian edition of *The Concept of the Political*, Schmitt (1988b: 272) however remarks that police action is nothing a-political (*nichts Apolitisches*); the world politics, which it forms a part of, results from the will towards pan-interventionism; it is a very intensive form of politics, and not the prettiest either, i.e. world civil-war politics. See further Galli (2015: 104) who aptly notes that this criminalisation of the enemy for Schmitt points to the collapse of the distinction between inside and outside, manifesting itself as a confusion between war and crime.

39 See also Bernstein (2011: 420); and Slomp (2009: 95, 104). In the Foreword to the 1963 publication of *Der Begriff des Politischen*, Schmitt reflected critically on the 1932 text by noting that he had failed to distinguish there between the different forms of the enemy: conventional, real and absolute (*BdP* 17). These distinctions were developed further in 'The Theory of the Partisan', published in the same year (i.e. 1963).

40 As noted above, Schmitt (1988b: 272) refers to the intensification of the political at the time (circa 1971) as 'world civil war politics' (*Weltbürgerkriegspolitik*); see also 'TP' 34, 66, 68/*TdP* 54, 94, 96 where Lenin's revolutionary partisan is associated with international civil war (*internationalen Bürgerkrieges*).

Stásis and political theology

The strict distinctions which Schmitt attempts to maintain in *The Concept of the Political* are thus, by his own account, collapsing in the twentieth century.[41] Derrida's contention is that this does not occur by accident or by way of a 'fall' or 'collapse' of the political, but that it is made possible by the 'structure' or 'law' of the concept of the political itself. The collapse has as a consequence always already begun. Schmitt appears to recognise this 'law', as well as the structure it implies in certain of his texts.[42] Derrida for example points in this respect to Schmitt's discussion of *stásis* in *Political Theology II* (*PoF* 108–9 n13). At stake here is a debate with Peterson (who had argued that there could be no Christian political theology due to the nature of the Trinity)[43] and Blumenberg (who likewise sought to problematise political theology and rejected the idea of modernity as secularisation).[44] In the passages which Derrida refers to, Schmitt (*PT II* 122–3) first notes the importance of the criterion of the friend-enemy distinction for the political and for political theology and then refers to Peterson's invocation of the statement of Gregory of Nazianzus that 'the One – *to Hen* – is always in revolt – *stasiazon* – against itself – *pros heauton*' (*PT II* 122/*PT II* (G) 90).[45] Schmitt (*PT II* 122–3) reminds the reader that this word, that is, *stásis*, as we saw above, was important for Plato in the *Republic*, and adds that this was so for the church fathers as well. *Stásis*, as Schmitt (*PT II* 123) further notes, means state of rest, repose, status; the opposing concept being *kinesis*, movement. *Stásis* however also has the political meaning of unrest, movement, revolt, civil war. 'At the heart of the doctrine of the Trinity', Schmitt contends, 'we encounter a genuine politico-theological *stasiology*' (*PT II* 123/*PT II* (G) 92). He takes this idea from Gnosticism: the two sides of God, that is, God as a God of love/salvation and God as the creator of an evil world, are in a state of open war, or at least in a state of unbridgeable alienation (*PT II* 124).[46] Schmitt (*PT II* 124) refers in addition here to Augustine who's thought Schmitt sees as being in close proximity to Gnosticism.[47] Augustine relocated the difficulty as to the nature of God onto man, who was 'endowed with freedom and created by God' (*PT II* 124/*PT II* (G) 93). Due to this freedom, man

41 This is perhaps even more so today; see 'Auto' 85–136.

42 Schmitt's invocation in *ECS* 26, 56–7, 89–90 of civil war, to make sense of the Heraclitian 'war is the father (and king) of all things', and his invocation of the brother as the enemy, point in the same direction; see further Section C below.

43 Schmitt (*PT II* 75) expresses his disagreement with this.

44 *PT II* 125, see also Hohendahl (2008: 15); Müller (2003: 158–9); and Galli (2015: 54).

45 Galli (2015: 112–13) notes that this figure (of the one at war with itself) can be applied to the conflict at stake in the Cold War, as the two enemies (the United States and the Soviet Union) were simply a reflection of each other, thus amounting to a global civil war.

46 According to Fues (2010: 198–9) the Holy Spirit in Schmitt's reading 'would represent the friend/foe-relation between the preserving and the altering God'.

47 See Hohendahl (2008: 15).

acts in such a way that the world which originally needed no salvation, now does. Augustine furthermore points to the accommodation in the Trinity of the identity of God the creator (father) and God the saviour (son) in their unity – although they are not absolutely identical, 'they are "one"' (*PT II* 124/*PT II* (G) 93). Schmitt (*PT II* 125) concludes that there is inevitably this tension in every religion of salvation and redemption, and this is likewise the case with a world in need of change and renewal. From this he then further concludes that 'the problem of hostility [*Feindschaft*] and of the enemy [*des Feindes*] does not allow itself to be concealed or suppressed [*läßst sich also nicht unterschlagen*]' (*PT II* 123/*PT II* (G) 92). This analysis of Schmitt in *Political Theology II* is linked by Derrida (*PoF* 109) to the opening words of *The Concept of the Political* where Schmitt (*CoP* 19–20/*BdP* 20) refers to the state as 'sheer status [*der Status schlechthin*]', transposing thereby this same structure to the state.[48] Viewed in these terms, *The Concept of the Political* would concern itself with the way in which

> the One divides and opposes itself, opposes itself by posing itself, represses and violates the difference it carries within itself, wages war, *wages war on itself, itself becoming war* [*se fait la guerre*], *frightens itself, itself becoming fear* [*se fait peur*], and *does violence to itself, itself becoming violence* [*se fait violence*], transforms itself into frightened violence in guarding itself from the other, *for it guards itself from, and in, the other* [*il se garde de l'autre*], always Him, the One, the One 'different from itself'.[49]
>
> (*PoF* 109 n13/*PA* 110 n2)

Derrida in the above passage relies on the double meaning of *stásis* as pointed to by Schmitt in *PT II*, in order to explain in a way the 'origin' of this double meaning, as well as of the war of God with himself, and of mankind with itself. At stake in this radical re-conception of (political) theology can be said to be the 'origin' of the distinction between friend and enemy, as well as of the other oppositions which play themselves out in Schmitt. In both Plato and Schmitt we thus find the contention that the two forms of dispute (*pólemos* and *stásis*) are made possible by something else: in Plato this 'origin' is to be found in the other of *phûsis* (the de-naturalisation of nature in nature), and in Schmitt, in what can be referred to as a 'pre-ontological understanding' of *stásis*. The 'basis' for this reading of Plato and

48 See Hirst (1987: 17) on the two conceptions of the state, i.e. static and dynamic, with Schmitt adopting the latter. See also Vardoulakis (2009: 128) who points out that the word *stásis* lies at the root of the state or body politic. See similarly Galli (2015: 6): 'a political order cannot be founded on stability (or staticity) but only on openness to disorder. It is necessary, but never possible, to exit the state of nature'.

49 See also *PoF* 59 where Derrida uses similar terms in discussing the Aristotelian and Nietzschean sayings ('O my friends there are no friends' and 'Foes, there are no foes! Say I, the living fool'). The terminology employed here is a precursor to the autoimmunitary structure that Derrida would later explore in texts such as 'Faith and Knowledge', 'Autoimmunity' and *Rogues*.

Schmitt, showing a *differantial* relation between forces, is inter alia to be found in Derrida's engagement with Freud, to which we now turn.

Freud[50]

In Chapter 5 of *Politics of Friendship*, Freud is invoked by Derrida in an epigraph, thereby clarifying the nature of the 'disorder' in nature which Plato speaks of and the pre-ontological understanding of *stásis* in Schmitt. Here we are also faced with the 'other' of nature (*phûsis*), referred to earlier.[51] The quotation that forms the epigraph of Chapter 5 of *Politics of Friendship* is from *Analysis Terminable and Interminable* (1937), where Freud (2001, XXIII: 246–7) endorses Empedocles's two fundamental principles – *philía* (attractive force, friendship) and *neikos* (repulsive force, strife) – and notes their correspondence in respect of name and function to what Freud views as the two primal instincts: *Eros* and destructiveness. Freud (2001, XXIII: 247/1991, XVI: 93) points here to his own research, which has shown that the instinct of destruction can be traced back to a death drive and he adds the elusive remark that 'no one can foresee in what guise the nucleus of truth contained in the theory of Empedocles will present itself to later understanding [*niemand kann vorhersehen, in welcher Einkleidung der Wahrheitskern in der Lehre des Empedokles sich späterer Einsicht zeigen wird*]'.

Immediately after the quotation of Freud, Derrida refers to the quotation attributed to Aristotle: 'O my friends there are no friends', which serve as a refrain throughout *Politics of Friendship*, as well as to its reversal by Nietzsche: 'foes, there are no foes! Say I, the living fool' (*PoF* 112/*PA* 131). In Derrida's reading, Schmitt can in a sense be said to repeat Nietzsche's aphorism when he laments the disappearance of the enemy in the twentieth century in *The Concept of the Political*. Rather than simply affirming the typical metaphysical oppositions which seem to be at stake here, Derrida at this point speaks of a 'hyperbole that ranges beyond Being' which lies at the root of these oppositions:

> a hyperbole at the origin of good and evil, a hyperbole *common* to both, a hyperbole *qua* the difference between good and evil, the friend and the enemy, peace and war. It is this infinite hyperbole common to the two terms of the opposition, thus making them pass into one another, that makes one's head spin.[52]
>
> (*PoF* 112/*PA* 131)

50 See Bendersky (2000) and Zakin (2011) for (favourable) comparisons between the thinking of Schmitt and Freud on the subject of human nature.

51 See *Dis* 206 where Derrida notes that in the philosophical tradition, *phûsis* has no other, and no outside.

52 See also *Adieu* 86 where Derrida, through Levinas, speaks of peace as no longer being opposed to war, but as in some sense originary.

The shared secret of the dying sage and the living fool, Derrida (*PoF* 113/*PA* 132) suggests, perhaps lies in 'a theory of absolute ambivalence', in the Empedoclean tradition kept alive by Freud, that is to say, a theory that is welcoming or hospitable to a death drive (*accueillante à une pulsion de mort*). We encounter Freud's death drive again when Derrida discusses Schmitt's analysis of combat (*Kampf*). Combat, like the concepts of friend and enemy, is essentially about 'the real possibility of physical killing', Schmitt notes (*CoP* 33/*BdP* 33).[53] As Derrida (*PoF* 122) points out, Schmitt implicitly distinguishes such 'justified' killing in war, from natural death and from murder, as well as explicitly from war crimes, which would consist in a transgression of the laws of war.[54] For Derrida (*PoF* ix/*PA* 13), at stake in this kind of 'justification', that is, in the constitution of the concept of the political through a certain kind of 'repression', is what he refers to as the 'political crime [*crime politique*]'. The latter is to be understood in terms of Freud's death drive: the positing of enemies of whichever kind (who may justifiably be killed), can be traced back to the death drive, which originally is turned against the self.[55] Freud's death drive has the further implication that Schmitt's attempt to construct a pure hostility without affect or at least without private affect cannot succeed (*PoF* 124).[56] This has important implications for the structure of the concept of the political, as appears from the so-called 'three logical tracks [*trois voies logiques*]', which Derrida (*PoF* 122/*PA* 143) notes can follow formally from the co-determination of the friend and enemy concepts:[57]

1. The first is that without this possibility of killing, which on Derrida's reading of Schmitt's account founds a non-natural community (of killing),[58] there

53 Elsewhere Derrida (*PoF* 131/*PA* 154) speaks of the 'obsessive nature of this recurrence [*le caractère obsédant de cette récurrence*]' of the notion of 'real possibility' in Schmitt (see further below), thereby perhaps alluding to Freud's repetition compulsion.

54 See in this respect *AR* 400–1 where Derrida refers to Levinas's view that 'there is no innocent murder, and one is guilty even of murders committed by accident'.

55 See De Ville (2011a: 28–37) on Derrida's transformation in *The Post Card* of Freud's thinking on the death drive in *Beyond the Pleasure Principle*. In brief, this involves the positing of a relation between an absolute astricture and the binding thereof by virtue of the drive for mastery. See also *PoF* 165 where Derrida quotes Schmitt *ECS* 90 to the effect that 'all extermination is but self-extermination'.

56 An etymological analysis underscores the point: As Derrida (*PoF* 136 n19) points out, the words 'enmity' and 'hostility' are not strictly distinguished in everyday language and these words share a common root with words such as *philía*, friendship and love, which all include some element of feeling; see e.g. Benveniste (1973): Book 1 Chapter 7 (hospitality) and Book 3 Chapter 4 (*phílos*). See also *PoF* 124 where Derrida likewise casts doubt on Schmitt's attempt to construct a pure hostility without affect or at least without private affect. Derrida refers in this regard to a footnote added by Schmitt in the 1963 version of *Der Begriff des Politischen*.

57 These logical tracks are related to what Schmitt says about physically killing the enemy; the co-determination of the concepts of friend and enemy at stake here stems from the criterion which Schmitt adopts to characterise the political, i.e. the possibility of distinguishing between friend and enemy.

58 'Non-natural' because at stake here is not what is referred to as 'natural death'; see *PoF* 122/*PA* 143.

would not only be no enemy, but symmetrically also no friend. Friendship in other words presupposes this possibility of killing. This stems from the fact that friendship, Derrida (*PoF* 122/*PA* 143) contends, can only be with a mortal, that is, someone 'exposed to being killed, *possibly by myself*'. At stake is not an accidental killing, but what Derrida (*PoF* 122/*PA* 143) calls an 'essential' (*de façon essentielle*) killing, that is, presumably a killing based on 'human nature' as analysed by Schmitt[59] and by Freud. To love in friendship thus means, Derrida contends, 'that I can kill you, you can kill me, we can kill ourselves – together or each other, the one the other' (*PoF* 122/*PA* 143). This 'real possibility' as Schmitt calls it, means that we are in a sense already dead for each other (*PoF* 122). Derrida refers here to the 1915 essay 'Thoughts for the Times on War and Death',[60] where Freud (2001, XIV: 279) seems to confirm much of what Schmitt says: that the state does not prohibit wrong-doing on the part of the individual because it wishes to abolish it, but because it wants to monopolise it;[61] the interdict against killing the neighbour shows that we 'spring from an endless series of generations of murderers, who had the lust for killing [*Mordlust*] in their blood' (Freud 2001, XIV: 296/1991, X: 350); and that the death of loved ones is always accompanied by ambivalent feelings, because of the inevitable hostility one bears towards them as in some sense strangers (Freud 2001, XIV: 293).

2. The second logical track involves a kind of 'opposition' to the first. This would engage with the commonsensical (and in some sense Schmittian) view that friendship is the exact opposite of hostility and enmity. Yet with reference to Freud, Derrida points out that 'opposition' in such a case actually amounts to repression: what applies to the enemy (I can or must kill you and vice versa) would be excluded through friendship, or at least, repressed, transformed, sublimated. Friendship would thus simultaneously be the (repressed) same and something completely different. Friendship would consist precisely in excluding the structure of possibility which would equate the friend and the enemy (*PoF* 122). This is an allusion to what Derrida calls 'lovence' (*aimance*), or a kind of friendship exceeding all measurement and moderation, all calculation (*PoF* 10),[62] which we will come across again shortly.

59 See *CoP* 58–66, and above. Schmitt (*CoP* 61/*BdP* 61) declares in this respect that 'all genuine political theories presuppose man to be "evil", i.e. views man as by no means unproblematic, but a "dangerous" and dynamic being [*als "gefährliches" und dynamisches Wesen betrachten*]'; see also *DC* 26–30.

60 See similarly Freud (2001, XVIII: 101–2).

61 In Schmitt's language, the state seeks to monopolise the decision as to the friend and the enemy; see McCormick (2007: 328).

62 In Chapter 3 of *Politics of Friendship* where Nietzsche is analysed, this form of love is described inter alia with reference to the gift, disproportion, dissymmetry, 'a certain rupture in reciprocity or equality' (*PoF* 62, 63/*PA* 81, 82), and 'a love more loving than love', i.e. that no longer wants to possess (*PoF* 64–5/*PA* 83–4).

3. In outlining the third logical track, Derrida points out that the concept of the political is what endlessly binds or opposes the friend-enemy/enemy-friend couple in the death drive (seemingly understood here in the sense of a destructive drive) or decision to kill, in the killing or putting to death. Here Derrida explicitly invokes 'lovence' (*aimance*) and, anticipating the analysis of Heidegger to be undertaken below, *phileîn*. These are notions alluding to a kind of hyper-politics, preceding and making possible the political.[63]

Derrida (*PoF* 123/*PA* 145) refers to these logical tracks and the relation between them as an 'undecidable trivality'. A choice between them is in other words not really possible. This is because, as Derrida (2002c: 270–6) puts it in an analysis of Freud, the cruelty drive, which produces war and murder, cannot be eradicated, whilst a certain 'beyond of the possible' without cruelty, must be affirmed.[64]

Heidegger

In gaining a better understanding of the 'structure' of the political which appears from Derrida's analysis, it is necessary to further investigate the link posited by Derrida between Heidegger and Schmitt. This can be done by looking at Schmitt's employment of the notion of 'real possibility' (*reale Möglichkeit*) in *The Concept of the Political* and linking this to Heidegger's notion of death as Dasein's most proper possibility; as well as by enquiring into the relation between Schmitt's concept of combat (*Kampf*) and Heidegger's analysis of *pólemos* as well as of the gift or event of Being (*phûsis*). Apart from 'real possibility', Schmitt also employs a number of other closely related notions, such as eventuality (*Eventualität*), present or present-at-hand (*vorhanden*), real (*real/wirklich/Wirklichkeit*) and possible/possibility (*möglich/Möglichkeit*), either on their own or in other combinations. The notion of 'real possibility' for example plays an important role in Schmitt's analysis of 'combat' (*Kampf*), which, according to him, needs to be distinguished from competition and forms of discursive or symbolic struggle (*CoP* 33/*BdP* 33). For Schmitt, as noted above, both external war and civil war are about armed combat and physical killing (*PoF* 122). This follows from the concept of the political itself, which, according to Schmitt, requires the real possibility of

63 See *PoF* 129; *Rog* 152. We find a similar kind of argument in *Adieu* 88 (and 90) where Levinas's notion of perpetual peace is at stake (as a beyond to the political), which is said to also inhabit war (as well as hostility and murder) as a testimonial trace.

64 See further Meier (1998: 23–5, 50–4) who understands the centrality of the enemy in Schmitt as ultimately a reference to 'the Old Enemy', i.e. to Satan. The question that Derrida would be likely to pose to Meier, in view of our reading here of Freud, is 'what does Satan ultimately represent for Schmitt?' Revealing in this regard is Meier's quotation (at 65 n107) of Kojève in responding to Schmitt's invocation of Theodor Däubler's phrase (the enemy is our own question as figure): 'The "enemy in his ownmost figure" is most likely the Devil, more precisely: the Christian Devil, who shows himself precisely in "animal functions."' See further Section C below and Chapter 3.

combat, which must always be present-at-hand (*Die reale Möglichkeit des Kampfes, die immer vorhanden sein muß*) (*CoP* 32/*BdP* 32). Likewise, the concept of the enemy, Schmitt (*CoP* 32/*BdP* 33) says, implies the eventuality of combat, which is located in the realm of the real (*zum Begriff des Feindes gehört die im Bereich des Realen liegende Eventualität eines Kampfes*). Schmitt specifically mentions in this respect that the essence of the concept of a weapon is that it is 'a means of physically killing human beings' (*CoP* 32–3/*BdP* 33).[65] Schmitt (*CoP* 33) further notes that 'combat' is like 'weapon' to be understood 'in its existential sense', as Schwab's translation has it (*CoP* 33), or rather 'in its ontological originality' (*im Sinne einer seinsmäßigen Ursprünglichkeit*).[66] The whole of human life is a combat (*Kampf*), Schmitt (*CoP* 33/*BdP* 33) adds, and every human being is a combatant (*Kämpfer*), with quotation marks being used in both cases, pointing thereby, on Derrida's reading, to the ontological meaning of these terms (*PoF* 123).[67] As Derrida (*PoF* 123/*PA* 145) further notes, in linking Schmitt and Heidegger, this means at least that ([*c*]*ela signifie au moins que*)[68] Dasein's being-towards-death is not to be distinguished from his being-towards-killing or towards-death-in-combat.[69]

In contrasting the acknowledgement of the political with depoliticisation (*Entpolitisierung*) and neutrality, Schmitt insists that the exceptional case of war has to remain a 'real possibility', otherwise politics will disappear (*CoP* 35/*BdP* 35). Schmitt motivates this statement in various ways, through a discussion of the centrality of the political decision as to the identity of the enemy, the question of

65 See further 'TP' 67/*TdP* 95: 'And the German philosopher Hegel adds: weapons are the essence of the fighter [*die Waffen sind das Wesen der Kämpfer selbst*]'.

66 See Hitschler (2010: 130–46) for a discussion of Schmitt's political existentialism.

67 This is a somewhat bold reading by Derrida of a sentence in Schmitt (*CoP* 33/*BdP* 33), which in full goes as follows: '[Combat] does not mean competition, not the "purely spiritual" combat of discussion, not the symbolic "struggles" in which ultimately every human being is engaged in, because after all the whole of human life is a "combat" and every human being is a "combatant".' Schmitt in this sentence appears to distinguish the ontological understanding of the word combat (*Kampf*) from the everyday meaning and the passage in question on the face of it should be read as expressing the view that to say this (the idea that the whole of human life is a 'combat' and every human being is a 'combatant') would be to adopt a superficial understanding of the words in question; see also Simon (2008: 76). Yet Derrida reads the passage as if Schmitt is stating a general truth, in an ontological sense, with which he (Schmitt) agrees. In support of Derrida's reading, it can be noted that in 'TP' 13/*TdP* 25 Schmitt makes a similar statement in outlining the criteria of the partisan in another context (when he points to concept dissolution – see above) that '[i]n a figurative sense to be a human being means being a combatant [*In einem übertragenen Sinne heißt ja "Mensch sein ein Kämpfer sein"*]'. In '*Geschl* IV' 177/*PA* 361 Derrida likewise notes with reference to Heidegger that '*Kampf* belongs to the very structure of Dasein'.

68 The English translation is problematic here. It reads as follows: 'This does not mean so much that the being-for-death of this human life cannot be separated from a being-for-putting-to-death or for death-in-combat'.

69 See also '*Geschl* IV' 198–9 where Derrida compares Heidegger's notion of a community of struggle with Schmitt's concept of the political.

neutrality, the politics of avoiding war, the frequency and ferocity of war today, the motivations for waging war and the possibility of a (pacifist) war against war. In his analysis of Schmitt's discussion in this respect, Derrida (*PoF* 131) focuses specifically on Schmitt's use of the terms real (*real*), possible (*möglich*), possibility (*Möglichkeit*), reality (*Wirklichkeit*) and present(-at-hand) or presence-at-hand (*vorhanden/vorhandenheit*), which on his reading play an organising role here. Schmitt uses these terms in various forms and contexts, with 'real possibility' (*reale Möglichkeit*) appearing the most frequently.[70] Derrida (*PoF* 125) points in his analysis to the proximity between Schmitt's thinking in this respect and Heidegger's existential analytic in which 'possibility' likewise plays a central role.[71] In 'Heidegger's ear: philopolemology (*Geschlecht* IV)', that is, the second part of *Politique de l'amitié*, Derrida ('*Geschl* IV' 203ff.) goes into this proximity in more detail when he analyses Heidegger's discussion in *Introduction to Metaphysics* (2000: 64–6) of *pólemos* in Heraclitus's saying (*pólemos pantôn men patêr esti pantôn de basileus kai tous men theous edeixe tous de anthrôpous, tous men doulous epoiêse tous de eleutherous*), the first part of which is usually translated as 'war [*pólemos*] is the father (and king) of all things'. Heidegger here analyses and re-translates Heraclitus's saying as follows:

> Auseinandersetzung ist allem (Anwesenden) zwar Erzeuger (der aufgehen läßt), allem aber (auch) waltender Bewahrer. Sie läßt nämlich die einen als Götter erscheinen, die anderen als Menschen, die einen stellt sie her(aus) als Knechte, die anderen aber als Freie.[72]
>
> (Heidegger 1983: 66)

As Derrida ('*Geschl* IV' 204) points out, for Heidegger, *pólemos* in this passage cannot be understood as war in the human sense as it precedes (*waltet vor*) men (and gods) to which it gives birth.[73] Heidegger therefore translates it as *Auseinandersetzung* (debate, argument, discussion, confrontation, dispute, difference, clash, altercation, quarrel, hassle). He furthermore takes issue with

70 A 'commonsensical' understanding of the use of this phrase would perhaps be that Schmitt is simply saying that war, hostility and combat can at any time become a reality; see Simon (2008: 119).

71 For Heidegger, death is the possibility par excellence, as well as Dasein's most proper possibility: 'Death is the possibility of the absolute impossibility of Dasein. Thus death reveals itself as that possibility which is one's ownmost, which is non-relational, and which is not to be outstripped [*die eigenste, unbezügliche, unüberholbare Möglichkeit*]'; see Heidegger (1962: 294/2006: 250–1); as well as Derrida (1993b: 63, 64).

72 Field and Polt (Heidegger 2000: 65) translate the passage as follows: 'Confrontation is indeed for all (that comes to presence) the sire (who lets emerge), but (also) for all the preserver that holds sway. For it lets some appear as gods, others as human beings, some it produces (sets forth) as slaves, but others as the free.'

73 In Derrida's linking of Heidegger and Schmitt, he at times opposes them, and at other times seeks a reading of Schmitt which accords with that of Heidegger; see e.g. '*Geschl* IV' 204 concerning Schmitt's theoanthropolemology and Heidegger's reading of the Heraclitian fragment; see further below.

the (anthropological) translation of *pater* as 'father', and *basileus* as 'king', and translates it instead as *Erzeuger*, the one who produces, generates, makes bloom, rise, come to presence; and the latter as *waltender Bewahrer* – the guardian who rules ('*Geschl* IV' 205). At stake here for Heidegger, and for Derrida, is thus *pólemos* in its originary sense, or what Heidegger (2000: 65/1983: 66) refers to as 'originary combat' (*ursprünglicher Kampf*), and which as Derrida ('*Geschl* IV' 209) points out, gives rise to opposition as well as to joints and couplings.

Derrida ('Geschl IV' 169–71, 179–83, 193–4) further analyses Heidegger's invocation of the voice of the friend in *Being and Time* (1962: 206/2006: 163)[74] as well as in a number of other texts of Heidegger, thereby seeking to bring this voice of the friend into a relation with Heidegger's analysis of *phileîn* (*das Lieben*, *aimance*, in Derrida's terminology, and also associated with the gift) as well as *philía* (friendship, gift). At stake here is the gift of Being, that is, of *phûsis*, to which we return here, in the rising of what is concealed (a double movement of emergence and dissimulation), that is, a giving of that which does not belong to it ('*Geschl* IV' 193–6). How does *pólemos*/*Kampf* relate to this gift? *Pólemos*, in Derrida's reading of Heidegger, refers to the struggle between the gathering of Being and its dissimulation ('*Geschl* IV' 207–9). *Pólemos*, which can be said to be another word for *différance*, can therefore both be equated with Being, that is, with *logos* as gathering *and* with *phileîn* and *philía*, as indeed happens in Heidegger's texts ('*Geschl* IV' 196, 201–2, 207–10).[75]

Through this analysis of Heidegger's texts, Derrida is again pointing to that which gives rise to the friend/enemy opposition, which Schmitt speaks of: a certain friendship as *aimance*, as gift.[76] Schmitt and Heidegger ultimately say something very similar on Derrida's reading, though they approach the notion at stake from different directions, so to speak (*PoF* 249).[77] Schmitt's closeness to Heidegger can for example be detected when the following passage, where Schmitt again invokes the notion of a 'real possibility', is read as alluding to the ontological or perhaps rather the 'hauntological' event:

74 '[H]earing constitutes the primary and authentic way in which Dasein is open for its ownmost potentiality-for-Being – as in hearing the voice of the friend whom every Dasein carries with it [*als Hören der Stimme des Freundes, den jedes Dasein bei sich trägt*].'

75 Hence also the heading/title of this (part of the) text: 'Philopolemology'.

76 The argument in Plato's *Lysis*, which Derrida (*PoF* 153–5) briefly analyses, seems to have a similar structure.

77 See also *PoF* 139/*PA* 160 where Derrida, in introducing the reading of 'The Theory of the Partisan', notes with reference to *The Concept of the Political* that for Schmitt antagonism or opposition is in essence political and the more opposition or antagonism increases in intensity, the more political it is: 'opposition is all the more oppositional – supreme opposition, qua the essence and telos of opposition, negation, and contradiction – when it is political'. Derrida has been (wrongly) accused of overlooking this all-important aspect of 'the intensity of association or disassociation of human beings' (*CoP* 38/*BdP* 38–9, quoted at *PoF* 245) in Schmitt's understanding of the political and thus for reading Schmitt as positing an independent domain of the political; see Meier (2013: 178 n37); Marder (2010: 68). As should be clear from the analysis undertaken in the present chapter, this aspect is in fact central to Derrida's reading of Schmitt.

> The concepts friend, enemy and combat acquire their real meaning precisely because they refer to the real possibility [*reale Möglichkeit*] of physical killing. War follows from enmity, for war is the existential negation of another being. It is the most extreme realisation of hostility [*die äußerste Realisierung der Feindschaft*]. It does not have to be common, normal, something ideal or desirable. But it must nevertheless remain present as a real possibility [*als reale Möglichkeit vorhanden bleiben*] for as long as the concept of the enemy remains valid.
>
> (*CoP* 33/*BdP* 33)

In Derrida's reading, possibility (*Möglichkeit*) is not employed by Schmitt here in the classical Aristotelian sense of the actualisation of a possible.[78] Potentiality and act also do not stand opposed here in the conventionally Aristotelian sense (*PoF* 124). It is instead here about the *radicalisation* of a possible reality or a real possibility (*PoF* 124). With reference to other texts of Derrida (2007b: 445; *Neg* 362) that do not specifically engage with Schmitt, we can say that the *possible* that Schmitt speaks of is thus also not to be understood as opposed to or as distinguished from the impossible. The thought of the possible which is at stake here is that of the possible *as* impossible, or the impossible possible (*Neg* 344). This 'eschatology', as Derrida (*PoF* 124) calls it, opens itself to a certain beyond of the political, in the form of the Nietzschean 'perhaps', as we will see further in the discussion that follows. At issue in for example the most extreme realisation of hostility in war (*CoP* 33) is therefore not an actualisation of war, but instead, as we saw above, yet with the emphasis elsewhere, 'the radicalization of a possible *reality* or a *real* possibility' (*PoF* 124/*PA* 147). The realisation of the possibility at stake in each instance (of war, or of the enemy) would, Derrida notes, be 'but the passage to the limit, the extreme accomplishment, the *éskhaton* of an *already real* and *already present* possibility' (*PoF* 124/*PA* 147). The analogy with Heidegger's discussion of *pólemos* in its originary sense should be clear.[79] The doubling of *pólemos* as *philía*, which as we saw above is also at issue here, perhaps requires greater elaboration insofar as it relates to Schmitt.

In his discussion of Schmitt's notion of war as the exception, Derrida comments that what the thinking of real possibility (*pensée de la possibilité réelle*) perhaps wants us to understand is that the exception is the rule (*PoF* 127/*PA* 151). 'The exception', Derrida continues, 'is the rule of what takes place, the law of the event [*la loi de l'événement*], the real possibility of its real possibility' (*PoF* 127/*PA* 151). This is indeed what Schmitt says, albeit in somewhat different terms (*CoP* 35/*BdP* 35): 'Daß dieser Fall nur ausnahmsweise eintritt, hebt seinen bestimmenden

78 See also *PoF* 17–18.

79 See *PoF* 249/*PA* 279 where Derrida comments that both Schmitt and Heidegger give credit to 'oppositionality itself, ontological adversity, that which holds adversaries together, assembling them in *lógos qua* ontological *pólemos*'.

Charakter nicht auf, sondern begründet ihn erst.'[80] In Derrida's words, 'this exceptionality grounds the eventuality of the event. An event is an event, and a decisive one, only if it is exceptional. An event as such is always exceptional' (*PoF* 127–8/*PA* 151). What precisely is at stake here appears from Derrida's analysis of Schmitt's diagnosis of de-politicisation in the twentieth century.[81] Whilst observing such depoliticisation, Schmitt remarks that the more sporadic wars being waged in the twentieth century are waged with greater intensity, and that, as we saw, they go along with an absolute hostility which seeks to annihilate the enemy as well as to do away with all the classical distinctions mentioned earlier (war/peace, military/civilian, etc.). Derrida (*PoF* 128–30) ties this diagnosis – of a 'withdrawal' of the political,[82] the political to be understood here in terms of an ontological *pólemos* or gathering of adversaries, that is, as Being – to Heidegger's withdrawal of Being,[83] in view of Schmitt's analysis of the exception as unveiling the essence of things (*den Kern der Dinge enthüllende Bedeutung*). What Schmitt diagnoses as depoliticisation, in Derrida's reading, can thus be referred to as a withdrawal of the political (and of Being). This 'withdrawal' at the same time involves a split in as well as a beyond to the political (referred to above as *aimance*), which precedes the friend-enemy couple. The wars being fought less frequently today and therefore more exceptionally, with the real possibility of infinite killing, that is, raising the spectre (or phantasm) of the total self-destruction of humanity, must in other words be understood as revealing the 'true essence' of the political.[84] War today, insofar as it can still be called such,[85] and the real possibility of total destruction tied thereto, thus involve both a 'symptom' (though not in the sense that it can be resolved through analysis) and a phantasm, drive or spectral law making it possible.[86] Derrida therefore ties this 'real possibility',

80 'That this case only arises exceptionally, does not abolish its determining nature, but instead underpins it.'

81 As Derrida (*PoF* 247/*PA* 277) points out, Heidegger would have called this depoliticisation 'nihilistic' – the truth 'of the metaphysical concept of politics carried out to its culmination'. For Heidegger even the world wars are signs of the abandonment, withdrawal, retreat or dissimulation of Being (*PoF* 248). Derrida (1998d), however, does not view the withdrawal of Being as a fall; the withdrawal actually gives rise to metaphysics; see also Chapter 1 above.

82 Derrida (*PoF* 130/*PA* 154) refers to this withdrawal as resulting in a 'dehumanized desert', which alludes to the messianic desert he elaborates on elsewhere; see *SoM* 33, 211.

83 See also Thomson (2005: 174–81).

84 Derrida (*PoF* 129/*PA* 153) notes in this respect, following Schmitt's logic of the exception, that 'rarefaction intensifies the tension and the revealing power' (the 'truth' of the political). See also *Psy I* 387 at 393–4, 396, 404–6 where Derrida brings together the phantasm of the total destruction of nuclear war with Heidegger's gift of Being.

85 See 'Auto' 100–1; and *Rog* 106, 123–4, 156. Some prefer to call today's conflicts 'new wars', which remains a contested term; see inter alia Münkler (2005); Kaldor (2006); and Newman (2004).

86 See Derrida (1999c: 223) where he comments favourably on Jameson's analysis of *Specters of Marx*, specifically the reading that spectrality amounts to 'the most radical politicization' (Jameson 1999: 60).

which as he notes appears to haunt Schmitt, to the Nietzschean perhaps (*PoF* 128–9). The earlier-referred-to disproportionate friendship – or *aimance*, as Derrida calls it – which has no concern for the self, and which precedes the friend-enemy opposition, is thus alluded to by the thought of the real possibility of self-destruction which Schmitt observes in the world of the twentieth century.

The structure of the political

A different structure of the political vis-à-vis what would appear from a traditional reading of Schmitt's *The Concept of the Political* clearly appears from Derrida's reading in *Politics of Friendship*, with the force of self-destruction playing an important role: the age of neutralisation and depoliticisation with its paradoxical intensification of hostility, as exposed by Schmitt, does not in Derrida's reading involve an accidental ruination or perversion of the political, but instead reveals its peculiar 'structure'. At stake in what is happening in the world today is in other words a 'symptom', which at the same time points to its own condition of possibility. It is in the symptom or phenomenon of what Schmitt ('TP' 34/*TdP* 54) would later call an international civil war, that is, the worst form of conflict, and reaching the highest point of intensity of the political, even going beyond it, with the political thereby becoming depoliticised on the one hand, and Schmitt's reaction to this phantasm of self-destruction, that is, the attempt at bracketing or binding the political on the other, that the structure of the political can be glimpsed. Schmitt's friend-enemy distinction, with war as the extreme possibility, can in other words be said to be preceded and made possible by a 'pre-originary' form of friendship characterised by dissymmetry and the perfect gift. The political in this latter 'sense' (in quotation marks because sense or meaning dissolves here) withdraws in its appearance. Derrida's placement of Schmitt alongside Plato, Freud and Heidegger shows a similar structure: in Plato, *phûsis* is with reference to *stásis* shown to divide itself; the destructive drive in Freud is preceded by a turning against the self; and *pólemos* in Heidegger, both conceals and gathers. The concept of the political is in other words haunted by a force of self-destruction or what Derrida would in later texts call 'autoimmunity' as its condition of possibility. From this reading it necessarily follows that every ethico-politico-legal decision is likewise haunted by and exposed to what can be referred to as the law of spectrality, by *philía* (friendship/gift), the originary *pólemos*, *aimance*, the event, the Nietzschean perhaps,[87] and even a 'pre-originary declaration of (perpetual) peace' (*Adieu* 48–50, 80–90; Derrida 2006b: 213). Nonetheless, no decision can be made without violence being done to the perhaps, which inevitably withdraws from the light of day (*PoF* 67).

87 See *PoF* 68–9.

SECTION B PARTISAN

Introduction

Schmitt's 'The Theory of the Partisan'[1] traces the origin and further development of partisanship within the world order, and in doing so enquires anew into the concept of the political. According to Schmitt the partisan appears in the early nineteenth century in 'a new, decisive role, as a novel, hitherto unacknowledged figure of the world-spirit (*Figur des Weltgeistes*)' ('TP' 32/*TdP* 51). The partisan thus starts, already in the nineteenth, yet more surely in the twentieth century, to personify the political. As we saw in Section A above, in *The Concept of the Political* Schmitt defines the political with reference to the drawing of a distinction between friend and enemy. In the latter respect he distinguishes between the private enemy (*ekhthrós*) and the public enemy (*polémios*), and compares the just enemy, treated with respect and honour under the *jus publicum Europaeum*, to the hated, criminalised and dehumanised enemy of the twentieth century. In the Preface to the 1963 (German) re-publication of the 1932 edition of *The Concept of the Political*, Schmitt acknowledges that he failed to distinguish clearly and precisely enough in that text between the different forms of hostility: conventional, real and absolute (*BdP* 17). In addressing this neglected issue, 'The Theory of the Partisan' effectively rethinks the concept of the political through the identification of two forms of partisan: the telluric partisan characterised by real hostility and the revolutionary partisan characterised by absolute hostility, in contrast to the conventional hostility and its degeneration into the hostility towards the 'foe', that is, another form of absolute hostility, at stake in *The Concept of the Political*.[2]

In Chapter 6 of the *Politics of Friendship* Derrida closely analyses Schmitt's 'The Theory of the Partisan', with the aim of establishing the implications thereof for the concept of the political. Derrida's reading of 'The Theory of the Partisan' can arguably be best understood with reference to Derrida's 'transformation' of Freud's thinking on psychoanalysis. As we will see in the analysis that follows, in the background of Derrida's reading of Schmitt's 'The Theory of the Partisan' are a number of Freud's texts, including 'The Interpretation of Dreams' (1900), 'The Uncanny' (1919) and 'Beyond the Pleasure Principle' (1920). Schmitt's criteria for determining the true partisan, his mention of the abyss and the Acheron in the context of exploring the partisan's origins, his recognition of the brother as the enemy ('TP' 61) and his silence about women in the context of partisan warfare are all interpreted by Derrida against the background of Freud's thinking. This reading of Schmitt thus confirms from another perspective the

1 Reliance will be placed here on the Goodson translation (Schmitt 2004a) rather than the Ulmen translation (Schmitt 2007c).

2 For an analysis of the Cold War context within which Schmitt wrote 'The Theory of the Partisan', see Horn (2004).

analysis undertaken in Section A above, namely of a concept of the political that has no identity and is characterised by a force of self-destruction as its condition of possibility.

In the discussion that follows, we will first enquire briefly into Schmitt's four criteria for recognising the true partisan, and the consequent distinction between the two forms of partisan. Of importance for Derrida in this regard is the tension between the criteria of the 'telluric' and of 'mobility' as well as the difficulty in maintaining the distinction between the two forms of partisan. Secondly, we will look at the important role of technology for the figure of the partisan, which Schmitt holds responsible for the collapse of the true partisan into the global revolutionary partisan who is no longer tied to the telluric. Derrida reads Schmitt's positing of the telluric vis-à-vis the global partisan, as a reaction to a generalised delocalisation, which structures existence in general. The third focus point will be Schmitt's attempt to locate the moment of the opening of the 'abyss' (*Abgrund*) of absolute hostility associated with the global revolutionary partisan. This leads to a discussion of the Geneva and Hague Conventions as well as the invocation by Schmitt of the Acheron. On Derrida's reading we find in Schmitt's discussion an acknowledgement of the fragility of the concept of the political as he defined it in *The Concept of the Political* and in 'The Theory of the Partisan', as well as of the distinctions between the different forms of hostility that it relies on. By invoking the 'abyss' and the 'Acheron', Schmitt furthermore appears to be acknowledging the role played by 'unconscious' forces in the coming to the fore of absolute hostility. The latter acknowledgement means that it would be impossible to determine the precise moment when the rigid distinctions of the concept of the political and the bracketing (*Hegung*) of hostility that goes along with it start dissolving. On Derrida's reading this dissolution is always already underway in view of what can be referred to as the 'human structure'. In the next section a discussion takes place of Schmitt's designation of the brother as the enemy, which Derrida reads alongside the figure of the double in Poe's *The Purloined Letter* (1844) and Freud's 1919 essay 'The Uncanny' (Freud 2001, XVII: 217–56). In the latter text Freud relates the double to narcissism, the repetition compulsion and the relation to death. Taking a detour through Derrida's *Dissemination* (1972) with its discussion of Mallarmé's *Mimique* (1886), we will see that on Derrida's reading, the brother as invoked in Schmitt's texts such as *The Concept of the Political* and 'The Theory of the Partisan' points to a mirroring as well as a threat to the self. Schmitt's exclusive focus on the brother and his exclusion of the sister (and woman in general) leads to the fifth point of discussion, namely Derrida's suggestion that woman (*la femme*) may be the absolute partisan, that is, the 'other' or the 'beyond' of the political, which/who also functions as its condition of possibility. With this suggestion, where the figure of 'woman' alludes to an absolute unbinding or what Derrida elsewhere refers to as the 'perfect gift', we arrive, as noted, from another direction at a reconfigured concept of the political. In concluding the chapter we will take a brief look at Derrida's analysis of what is referred to as 'international terrorism' in the twenty-first century in order to establish the implications thereof for the concept of the political as analysed in 'The Theory of the Partisan' and in *Politics of Friendship*.

Criteria

Schmitt ('TP' 3, 9–14) finds the origin of the partisan in the Spanish resistance against Napoleon in the early nineteenth century and proceeds to lay down four criteria which distinguish the 'true' partisan (as ideal-type) from its degenerated historical counterpart.[3] These criteria are: (1) irregularity, (2) intense political engagement, (3) increased mobility and (4) the telluric. The latter characteristic is especially important for Schmitt and he consequently views the autochthonous partisan, associated with *real* hostility (*wirkliche Feindschaft*), and with the ability to make a concrete identification of the enemy in the absence of the ability of the state to do so, as the true partisan ('TP' 41/*TdP* 62). This true partisan stands opposed to the revolutionary (communist) partisan, who is associated with *absolute* hostility (*absolute Feindschaft*) and who fights a global revolutionary war, thereby moving away from his original telluric nature ('TP' 65–6/*TdP* 93). The philosophical recognition of the partisan according to Schmitt takes place in Prussia in 1812–1813 during the time of the French occupation, but quickly disappears again from view ('TP' 28–33). Whereas the telluric partisan remains a marginal figure until World War I, in the hands of Lenin, and later Mao and Stalin, he becomes a central figure of war in the twentieth century. Lenin's revolutionary partisan furthermore explodes the attempt at bracketing war and hostility which, as we saw in Section A above, was imposed by the *jus publicum Europaeum* from the time of the peace of Westphalia (1648) until the end of World War I ('TP' 33–8). Schmitt sees a close association between the telluric partisan, resurrected by Mao, and his own vision of great spaces (*Großräumen*) as set out in *The Nomos of the Earth* ('TP' 41/*TdP* 62).[4] The revolutionary partisan as well as the criminalisation and dehumanisation of the enemy, which characterises the twentieth century with its belief in just wars, would have no place here (Chapter 7 below).

We now need to look in more detail at the four criteria identified by Schmitt. The first criterion – irregularity – appears from Schmitt's discussion of the origin of the phenomenon of the partisan, that is, as noted above, the Spanish people's guerrilla war against Napoleon from 1808–1813, after the defeat in 1808 of the Spanish army ('TP' 3–4).[5] Schmitt notes that although one can say that there have

3 See also Hooker (2009: 163); Müller (2003: 147).

4 Schmitt ('TP' 41) finds support for his idea of a plurality of counterbalanced *Großräumen* in Mao's poem *Kunlun*. In 'GP' 26 Schmitt furthermore points to the link between the telluric requirement for identifying the (true) partisan and of 'earth' as one of the four elements (fire, water, air and earth), which he elaborates on further in *Land and Sea*; see Chapter 7 below.

5 See also Gasché (2004: 13–14) concerning the partisan-like strategies of the Napoleonic army.

always been partisans, in the sense that the laws of war have been breached throughout history and thus by irregular fighting, the (true) partisan, that is, the modern partisan, could come to the fore only after the French Revolution. This is because the first modern, well-organised, regular army was established only at this point in time, and furthermore, because the *irregularity* which defines the partisan can be said to exist only if it can be concretely opposed to a *regularity* which up until then had not existed in this exact sense ('TP' 3). The partisan, as Schmitt points out later, nonetheless cannot divorce himself completely from regularity. He needs the assistance of a regular force or third party, inter alia to attain technologically sophisticated weapons, and so as not to be simply regarded as a criminal. In the long run the partisan furthermore needs to become regularised, either by being recognised as such by an existing regular, that is, by the state that he is waging a battle against, or by taking over the state through his own force ('TP' 52–4).[6]

The second criterion, that is, intense political engagement, likewise distinguishes the partisan from criminal individuals or groups, or from pirates acting simply in their own self-interest ('TP' 10).[7] Schmitt ('TP' 65/*TdP* 92) refers in this respect to Che Guevara for whom the partisan is 'the Jesuit of war', and reads this metaphor as alluding to the absoluteness (*Unbedingtheit*) of political engagement on the side of the partisan. This has the further implication that the bond between members of a partisan group is usually very intense, much more so than between ordinary citizens in the modern state ('TP' 10). The third criterion is that of increased mobility, and Schmitt refers under this heading to 'mobility, speed, and unexpected shifts between attack and withdrawal' ('TP' 11/*TdP* 23). The criterion of 'mobility' should thus be broadly understood as, for example, also related to the 'incalculability of appearance' of the partisan, which is made possible by the absence of a uniform, enabling him to wear the uniform of the opponent, to change uniforms and insignia, as well as to 'go underground' ('GP' 15–16). This 'mobility' is furthermore continuously on the increase, as Schmitt ('TP' 11) points out, because of developments in technology. The fourth criterion also stems from the origin of the modern partisan in Spain: Schmitt ('TP' 4, 50) emphasises the fact that the Spanish guerrillas fought on home soil against a foreign occupier, even though they were ultimately pawns in a global political conflict.[8] The partisan's true meaning for Schmitt ('TP' 13, 65–6) appears here, that is, his fundamentally defensive function. This original and ideal defensive nature is however deformed

6 The telluric partisan, as Hooker (2009: 190) points out, thus inevitably 'folds himself back into a regular system of sovereignty'.

7 See further Schmitt 'Der Begriff der Piraterie' in *FP* 508–17.

8 Nitschke (2011: 144–5) reads Schmitt as saying that the (true) partisan fights for the people that has been dispossessed or oppressed and has to be liberated: 'The partisan is thus the secret [*heimliche*] alter ego of the people: When the people cannot themselves be self-identical [*nicht bei sich selbst sein kann*], then the partisan is required!'

when the partisan through Lenin becomes identified with the absolute aggression of a world revolutionary fighter or with a technological ideology. It is Lenin who, via the thinking of Hegel and Marx, recognises the true potential of the partisan in fighting the communist revolution, and who takes the partisan to its limit. Lenin recognises the enemy as the class enemy, the bourgeois, the Western capitalist and his social order in every country he rules ('TP' 36). Lenin's partisan consequently fights in a revolutionary civil war, both on the national and the international level ('TP' 34). For Schmitt ('TP' 13) this fourth criterion is absolutely essential in recognising the true partisan.[9] It is, as we saw, tied to his essentially defensive nature, which in turn means the limitation of hostility and the 'protection' of the partisan from the absolute claim to abstract justice ('TP' 13). According to Schmitt ('TP' 7–8/*TdP* 18–19), this telluric dimension can for example be seen in the Russian partisans who fought against Napoleon, and in Stalin, who 'seized this myth [*Mythos*] of autochthonous [*bodenständigen*], national partisanship in World War II against Germany'. With Mao Tse-tung, Ho Chi Minh and Fidel Castro there is similarly a link to the soil, that is, with the autochthonous population and the geographical singularity of the land: mountains, forest, jungle or desert ('TP' 13). Yet the partisan, as Schmitt ('TP' 14) points out, runs the risk of being completely dislocated through technological developments. In the Cold War, he notes, he becomes simply a technician in an invisible war, a saboteur and a spy.

The question of technology

As we can see from the above discussion of the four criteria which Schmitt identifies, he seeks in as far as possible to retain the traditional concept of the partisan as it originated in Spain. This can also be seen from his description of the archetype (*Urbild*) of the autochthonous partisan as concerned first and foremost with the defence of home, hearth and homeland from the foreign intruder ('TP' 20/*TdP* 35). In his reading, Derrida will seek to problematise Schmitt's evaluation of the revolutionary partisan as a 'fall' from some essential purity (by virtue of technology) as well as Schmitt's (negative) stance towards what he (Schmitt) refers to as 'conceptual dissolution [*Begriffsauflösung*]' in the twentieth century ('TP' 12–13/*TdP* 24–5).[10] Derrida does so by first of all looking at the question of technology as raised by Schmitt in his discussion of the four criteria. As Derrida (*PoF* 142) notes, Schmitt, specifically in discussing the criterion of *mobility*, but also elsewhere ('TP' 54–7), points to the important role of technology in the transformation of the classical concept of the enemy as well as of the classical concept of the partisan. The question of technology, according to Derrida, is of decisive importance in two respects.

9 See further Chapter 7 below on Schmitt's analysis of man's earth-bound character.

10 See Chapter 1 above on the 'reading strategy' generally employed by Derrida.

First, technology lies at the heart of what Schmitt refers to as 'concept dissolutions [*Begriffsauflösungen*]', and which he (Schmitt) describes as 'notable signs of the times' ('TP' 12–13/*TdP* 25). Derrida here employs an understanding of language as technology, which he has explored elsewhere in more detail (*ET* 36–8). This dissolution even happens in respect of the concept of the partisan itself. Today every loner (*Einzelgänger*) and non-conformist, Schmitt ('TP' 12–13/ *TdP* 25) says, can be called a partisan, irrespective of whether he actually thinks of taking a weapon in hand. Schmitt ('TP' 12–13/*TdP* 25) comments that the employment of the term 'partisan' in this metaphorical sense (*als Metapher*) is not necessarily impermissible, and acknowledges himself having had recourse to it in identifying certain figures and events in the history of ideas.[11] In elaborating on a theory of the partisan, Schmitt notes, specific criteria however need to be kept in mind so that the theme at stake here does not 'dissolve into abstract generalities [*in einer abstrakten Allgemeinheit zergeht*]' ('TP' 13/*TdP* 26). Yet, as Derrida (*PoF* 142/*PA* 163) points out, this threat of concept dissolution is directly related to the criteria which Schmitt himself invokes in recognising the partisan. Although these criteria are indispensable, they are what Derrida (*PoF* 142/*PA* 164) refers to as 'fake criteria, quasi-concepts, criteria of degree of intensity, that is to say, indefinitely extensive'.[12] This can clearly be seen in the criterion of 'intense political engagement' as well as in that of 'increased mobility' in respect of attack and retreat, but can also be said in respect of irregularity, which can exist to a greater or lesser extent ('TP' 3/*TdP* 11). This may sound like critique, but Derrida in a sense endorses these criteria as they testify to the lack of identity of this figure that personifies the political for Schmitt in the twentieth century. Although Schmitt thus constructs the (true) partisan as an ideal, it becomes a spectral figure in his own hands. Schmitt in other words allows for the 'metaphorical' extension of the figure of the partisan, with his own criteria.

The second reason for the decisive importance of technology relates to the growing speed of motorisation, in other words, to what Derrida refers to as 'tele-technological automation', through which a break takes place with autochthony (*PoF* 142).[13] Schmitt ('TP' 14/*TdP* 27) notes that the partisan's mobility is 'so enhanced by motorization that he runs the risk of complete dislocation'. This leads to the cutting off of the telluric roots characteristic of conventional warfare, but also signals a break with the early form of the partisan ('TP' 14). This mutation,

11 Schmitt ('TP' 70 n15/*TdP* 25 n15) mentions that he, in an earlier essay (dating from 1940), called Bruno Bauer and Max Stirner 'partisans of the world spirit [*Partisanen des Weltgeistes*]', and in another essay (dating from 1962) referred to Jean-Jacques Rousseau as such.

12 Something similar can be said concerning Schmitt's definition of the political in *The Concept of the Political*, which is likewise characterised by intensity; see *CoP* 29/*BdP* 30: 'The political opposition [*Gegensatz*] is the most intense and extreme opposition, and every concrete opposition becomes all the more political the closer it comes to the most extreme point, that of the friend-enemy grouping'.

13 See further Briggs (2015) on 'teletechnology' in Derrida's thinking.

as we saw, does not however mean the total abandonment of telluric autochthony in respect of the partisan. Schmitt mentions a number of names here associated with partisan warfare in this sense even after Lenin's transformation of the partisan, including Mao Tse-tung, whose 'revolution is more tellurian based than Lenin's' ('TP' 40/*TdP* 61), Ho Chi Minh (Vietnam) and Fidel Castro (Cuba) ('TP' 13, 40/*TdP* 26, 61).[14] For Derrida, Schmitt's analysis here is significant because it reveals the 'structure' at stake in the figure of the partisan: Schmitt implicitly confirms that 'this territorial drive has always been in contradiction with itself, troubled, displaced, de-localized. *And* [it also means] *that this is the very experience of place*' (*PoF* 142/*PA* 164). Schmitt does not however draw any clear and conceptually rigorous consequences from this, Derrida notes. Schmitt does not seem to fully appreciate, Derrida (*PoF* 142/*PA* 164) contends, that 'telluric autochthonism is already a reactive response to a de-localization and some tele-technology, regardless of its degree of development, power and speed'. This is an important point, which Derrida has also explored elsewhere. As he points out in these other texts, technology dislocates, expropriates, delocalises, deracinates, dis-idiomatises, de-territorialises and dispossesses, thereby giving rise to a 'reaction' or 'response' towards the 'home' ('F&K' 45; *ET* 37, 79). According to Derrida (and this is why 'reaction' and 'response' appear in inverted commas), this takes place in one and the same movement by virtue of what he refers to as 'the law of exappropriation' (*ET* 79–80). There is in other words 'no appropriation without the possibility of expropriation, without the confirmation of this possibility' (*ET* 80). The expropriation at stake here finds its limit in death, which is what technology ultimately points to (*ET* 39). In announcing our own death, technology in turn gives rise to a desire for rootedness, for presence (*ET* 39, 115). Returning to *Politics of Friendship*, Derrida (*PoF* 142–3/*PA* 164) points out that at stake here in Schmitt's analysis is a law (*loi*) which, as he notes, 'regulates historically diverse events, places and contents'. In other words, what Schmitt points to in relation to the modern partisan, that is, that he is losing his telluric character because of technological developments and is in danger of becoming completely displaced, could already be said of the most classical combatant.[15]

Philosophy and the Acheron

> Der Acheron läßt sich nichts vorrechnen und folgt nicht jeder Beschwörung.[16]
> ('TP' 58/*TdP* 85)

14 See above.

15 As Thomson (2005: 174–7) also points out, in line with what was noted in Chapter 1 above regarding the reading of Schmitt undertaken here, technology (here, of warfare, with its deterritorialising effect) does not come second, as the result of an accident, to the originary *pólemos*/political; it inhabits it from the start.

16 'The Acheron does not allow itself to be calculated, and does not respond to every conjuration.'

In his discussion of the four Geneva Conventions of 1949, Schmitt ('TP' 15–18/*TdP* 29–32) is complementary, especially insofar as they give recognition to new forms of enemy fighters while still remaining tied to classical international law and its tradition. The basis of these Conventions 'remains the statist nature of war and the consequent bracketing [*Hegung*] of war with its clear distinctions between war and peace, military and civilian, enemy and criminal, inter-state war and civil war' ('TP' 22/*TdP* 37). Schmitt ('TP' 15–16/*TdP* 29–30) however at the same time mentions that the Conventions failed to take account of further developments in the partisan problematic after the war and that they 'loosened or even challenged these essential distinctions [*Unterscheidungen*]' with the consequence that 'the door is opened for a type of war that consciously destroys these clear divisions (*Trennungen*)' ('TP' 23/*TdP* 37).[17] These Conventions were, like the Hague Convention of 1907, based on a compromise between larger and smaller states, but with Russia this time on the side of the smaller states ('TP' 21). Of particular interest to us here is Schmitt's invocation of the abyss, noting that:

> many of the cautiously stylised compromise-standardisations of the Conventions appear only as the narrow bridge over an abyss [*die dünne Brücke über einem Abgrund*], which conceals a momentous transformation [*folgenreiche Wandlung*] of the concepts of war and enemy and partisan.
>
> ('TP' 23/*TdP* 37)

Schmitt, Derrida (*PoF* 143/*PA* 165) contends, is here effectively acknowledging that the clear distinctions or 'conceptual shores [*les rivages conceptuels*]' he tried to construct so carefully in *The Concept of the Political*, and even here in 'The Theory of the Partisan', are being engulfed by the abyss. This, he notes, also has important implications for the conception of man as political animal (*PoF* 143). Schmitt, Derrida (*PoF* 145) furthermore comments, believes that he can pinpoint with reference to places, events and dates, when this abyss, that is, the destruction of the conventional conception of war and its accompanying limitations and distinctions, opened up. Yet, as Derrida (*PoF* 145) points out, one can always give a counter-example or an earlier example, in an infinite regression. The criticism levelled by Schmitt ('TP' 25/*TdP* 41) against the legal experts of European international law – that they have 'stubbornly repressed from consciousness [*hartnäckig aus ihrem Bewußtsein verdrängt*]' the new reality which has emerged since 1900,[18] can therefore also be raised against Schmitt, Derrida (*PoF* 145)

17 Schmitt appears to be alluding here to what he will later call with reference to Lenin, 'the new theory of absolute war and absolute enmity . . . that would be determinant for the age of revolutionary war and the methods of the modern cold war' ('TP' 35/*TdP* 55).

18 See in this respect Kochi (2006a: 279) who notes with reference to Schmitt that 'the juridical response to the phenomenon of the partisan has been to ignore the facts on the ground, to "criminalise" the partisan and to reaffirm the classical conception of European inter-state war fought by regular armies'.

comments. Schmitt, in other words, locates a mutation in the nature of war and hostility in the twentieth century, but, as Derrida (*PoF* 145/*PA* 167) notes, he is constantly forced to go back, step by step, to acknowledge premises to events in the twentieth century, and the premises of those premises, without (really) acknowledging these. As we will see, Derrida is alluding here to the unconscious, which Freud associated with the mythical Acheron, and which Schmitt himself refers to here in passing. The examples which Derrida gives of this backward movement in Schmitt are, first, the acherontic moment in the Prussian soldier state, that is, the Bismarckian invocation in 1866 of the *Acheronta movere* (stirring the underworld)[19] against the Hapsburg Empire and France,[20] and secondly, the 'acherontic moment' in 1812/13 in Prussia ('TP' 28/*TdP* 45–6).[21] Noteworthy in the latter respect is the Prussian King's edict (of April 1813) calling for partisan warfare against Napoleon. In this document, that is, the Prussian Edict, there is a call by a legitimate king for using every means against the enemy and for 'the unleashing of total disorder [*die Entfesselung der totalen Unordnung*]' ('TP' 29–30/*TdP* 47–8). Schmitt ('TP' 29/*TdP* 47) describes this as 'belonging to the most astounding documents of the whole history of partisanship [*das zu den erstaunlichsten Dokumenten der gesamten Geschichte des Partisanentums gehört*]' and these ten pages as 'definitely belonging to the most unusual pages of all legislative codes in the world [*gehören bestimmt zu den ungewöhnlichsten Seiten aller Gesetzesblätter der Welt*]'. Derrida emphasises what he refers to as the 'fervent tremor' of these remarks and adds that:

> they [i.e. these pages] possess everything to seduce and to fascinate: the paradox of a military legality, political legitimacy, Prussian nationality placed regularly in the service of the irregularity of a revolutionary war, of a partisan war – against a French emperor![22]
>
> (*PoF* 145/*PA* 167)

19 From Virgil (2002: Book VII, line 312): *Flectere si nequeo Superos, Acheronta movebo* [if I cannot sway the gods, I'll stir the Acheron]. The phrase is understood by Freud (1925: 169, para 50) as referring to 'the efforts of the repressed instinctual impulses' or more literally, the 'drive movements' [*das Streben der verdrängten Triebregungen* [mistakenly spelt 'Triebregungsn'], and is employed by Freud (2001, IV) as epigraph on the title page of *Die Traumdeutung* (1900), see also Freud (2001, V: 608). The phrase is in addition mentioned by Freud (1985: 205) in a letter to Fliess on 4 December 1896.

20 Schmitt ('TP' 73 n25/*TdP* 45 n25) adds that the citation *Acheronta movebo* here 'served to paint the devil on the wall', or, as Goodson translates it, 'imagining the worst'.

21 See also 'GP' 21 where Schmitt expresses his agreement with Schickel that in the Prussian documents explosives (*Sprengstoff*) were amassed for the centuries to follow, but adds that they were not ignited (*entzündet*) in Prussia. It was Lenin who realised this potential for the first time.

22 In a further step backward, Schmitt ('TP'64/*TdP* 92) draws a direct link between the French Revolution, with its 'victory of the civilian over the soldier', and the consequent wearing of the soldier's uniform by the civilian in Napoleon's army on the one hand, and partisan warfare, on the other; see also Pan (2013).

Schmitt ('TP 30/*TdP* 48) points out that the Edict was however amended on 17 July 1813 and 'purged of every partisan danger, of every acherontic dynamic [*von jeder acherontischen Dynamik gereinigt*]'. The original Edict, as Schmitt ('TP' 30) further notes, was different from the Spanish guerrilla war against Napoleon, the Tyrolean rebellion of 1809 and the Russian partisan war of 1812, influenced by the philosophical spirit of revolutionary France. Schmitt ('TP' 30–2) refers in this respect specifically to the role of Fichte and Clausewitz in this philosophical discovery of the partisan.[23]

With the events in Prussia as described above, Schmitt contends that a certain alliance is formed between philosophy and the partisan. Yet this alliance did not lead to an insurrectional war against Napoleon in Prussia. Schmitt ('TP' 32/*TdP* 51) explains this with reference to the fact that Clausewitz was a reform-minded vocational officer of his time, and that he was not able to bring to full fruition the seeds (*Keime*) that became visible here. This would only happen much later, and needed 'an active, professional revolutionary [*eines activen Berufsrevolutionärs*]' ('TP' 32/*TdP* 51).[24] Philosophy here remained, as Derrida (*PoF* 147/*PA* 169) notes, following Schmitt ('TP' 5, 33/*TdP* 14, 52), in 'a still-abstract "theoretical form" and, as such, a spark, a flash, a flame, a light awaiting its heir'. 'The Acheron, which man had unleashed', Schmitt observes:

> immediately returned to the channels of state order. After the wars of liberation, the philosophy of Hegel dominated in Prussia. It sought a systematic mediation of revolution and tradition. It could be regarded as conservative, and it was such too. Yet it also preserved the revolutionary sparks and provided through its philosophy of history of continuous revolution, a dangerous ideological weapon, more dangerous than Rousseau's philosophy in the hands of the Jacobins.
>
> ('TP' 33/*TdP* 52)

Following Schmitt, Derrida (*PoF* 147) comments that its early heirs, Marx and Engels, were likewise too philosophical, and thus not philosophical enough, or in the words of Schmitt ('TP' 33/*TdP* 52), they were 'thinkers rather than activists of revolutionary wars'.[25] Lenin was, according to Schmitt, the first authentic heir of the Prussian Magna Carta (i.e. the Prussian Edict), which was in turn inherited by Mao, and further transformed.[26] Schmitt ('TP' 34/*TdP* 53) notes in this respect

23 See further Schmitt 'Clausewitz als politischer Denker' in *FP* 887–918; and Gasché (2004).

24 The central role that Lenin will play here, as heir to Hegel and Marx, is already anticipated in *The Concept of the Political* (63).

25 Schmitt ('TP' 34) notes that Engels still believed that it was possible for the proletariat to attain a democratic majority through general elections, leading to a classless society.

26 Meier (2013: 178 n37) criticises Derrida for regarding Lenin as 'the representative of philosophy [*der Repräsentant der Philosophie*]', yet Derrida is simply following Schmitt here (see 'TP' 36–7/

that the concept of the political takes a subversive turn (*eine umstürzende Wendung*) with the events in Russia in the twentieth century.[27] The classical concept of the political, founded in the eighteenth and nineteenth centuries of European international law based on inter-state war with its bracketings (*Hegungen*), was now replaced by a revolutionary partisan-war (*revolutionären Parteien-Krieg*) ('TP' 34/*TdP* 53).[28] Hostility, Derrida (*PoF* 147) notes following Schmitt, is with Lenin taken to its absolute limit. Schmitt can be said to trace here the origin of absolute enmity from the other, communist side, compared to *The Concept of the Political*, where the focus was on the motivating factors for such enmity on the liberal-capitalist side, that is, the United States. Derrida (*PoF* 148/*PA* 170) then points to the coincidence here between the purest philosophy and 'the most intense concrete determination'.[29] This alliance between philosophy and the partisan moreover releases unexpected forces that, according to Schmitt ('TP' 37/*TdP* 57), led to the explosion (*Sprengung*) of 'the whole Eurocentric world, which Napoleon had hoped to save and the Congress of Vienna had hoped to restore'.[30] Derrida (*PoF* 148/*PA* 170) refers to this event as an 'absolute present', and as 'a parousia of the political'. He however adds that there is inevitably still some play in the merger or identification of the two movements at stake here, that is, of depoliticisation and hyper-politicisation (*la surpolitisation*), which 'gives history its chance' (*PoF* 148/*PA* 170).[31] This further historical development can be seen in the movement away from the thinking of Lenin, who according to Schmitt ('TP' 43/*TdP* 65) was 'somewhat abstract-intellectual in the determination of the enemy'. With Stalin and especially with Mao Tse-tung, partisan warfare is (again) concretised by providing it with a defensive telluric rooting, coupled with

TdP 57–8) who explicitly refers to the alliance established by Lenin between philosophy and the partisan, and the unexpected new explosive forces that it unleashed.

27 The English translation at *PoF* 147 incorrectly attributes this to Mao.

28 Lenin thereby overturns the seemingly Platonic view, relied on by Schmitt in *The Concept of the Political*, that only external war is true war; see Section A above.

29 A few pages earlier, Derrida (*PoF* 146/*PA* 168) had referred to philosophy as the institution which is the actual producer 'of the purely political and thus of pure hostility'. Meier (2013: 178 n37) criticises Derrida for this invocation of pure hostility and pure politics, which he says Schmitt abandoned in 1930. Meier however appears to incorrectly assume that Derrida is speaking here about the (purely) political in contradistinction to the domains of the moral, the economic, etc. At stake here is instead an understanding of politics in its ontological sense, i.e. an understanding of opposition itself, which can be said to have remained a concern for Schmitt, also in 'The Theory of the Partisan'.

30 For a further analysis of the intrinsic relation between philosophy and war, see Section C below.

31 This remark is tied to an earlier comment of Derrida (*PoF* 146/*PA* 168) on the fact that Schmitt speaks in one place of the subversion or dissolution of the concept of the political (*Begriffsauflösung*) ('TP' 12–13/*TdP* 25), and in another of an 'upheaval' in this concept (*eine umstürzende Wendung*) ('TP' 34/*TdP* 53). See further Section A above where this identification was linked by Derrida to Heidegger's notion of the withdrawal of Being, which likewise sets history in motion.

real enmity (*wirkliche Feindschaft*) ('TP' 38–43/*TdP* 58–65). In the words of Schmitt:

> However, with Mao an additional concrete moment is added [*kommt . . . noch ein konkretes Moment hinzu*] in relation to the partisan, whereby he comes closer than Lenin to the heart of the matter, and whereby he attains the possibility of extreme theoretical consummation [*wodurch er die Möglichkeit der äußersten gedanklichen Vollendung erhält*]. In short: Mao's revolution is more tellurian-based than Lenin's.
>
> ('TP' 40/*TdP* 61)

What interests Derrida particularly is the relation posited by Schmitt between, on the one hand, the alliance between philosophy, the partisan and absolute presence, and, on the other, technology, spectrality and the Acheron. He therefore shifts his focus at this point to Schmitt's discrete mention of the brother in the analysis of the movement from Lenin to Mao Tse-tung, that is, in the context of a discussion of absolute and real hostility.

The brother as double

As Derrida (*PoF* 148/*PA* 171) points out, for Schmitt the absolute war, the revolutionary war which drives the theory of the partisan to its most extreme point, the war which violates all the laws of war, 'can be a *fratricidal* war [*cela peut être une guerre* fratricide]'. This theme of a brother enemy, as Derrida further comments, has an immense tradition: both Greek and biblical. This comment takes us back to the question raised earlier about determining precisely when the abyss which Schmitt appeals to, opened up, yet here we move beyond the Freudian unconscious. Derrida's 'thesis' is that there is nothing strange about a brother being the subject-matter (*sujet*) of absolute hostility. There is in fact, he provocatively contends, only absolute hostility for or against a brother (*PoF* 148/*PA* 171). At stake here, as we will see shortly, is more specifically the 'phantasm of the brother', which connects the discussion here with our earlier discussion of technology and the spectrality of the partisan. The equation by Schmitt of the brother and of (absolute) hostility, Derrida (*PoF* 148) contends, accords with the whole history of friendship, which is simply the experience, in this respect, of what appears to be an unspeakable synonymy, a deadly tautology. Derrida notes that Schmitt's mention of the brother happens furtively and is similar to a ghostly apparition. What Derrida (*PoF* 148/*PA* 171) refers to as the 'double passage of a brother [[*d*]*ouble passage d'un frère*]', occurs in the discussion by Schmitt ('TP' 38–9, 41/*TdP* 59, 63) under the heading 'from Lenin to Mao Tse-tung', of the wars in the erstwhile Yugoslavia between 1941–1945, where communist and monarchical partisans fought 'brutal internal battles' against each other (Tito winning with the support of Stalin against Mihailovich who was according to Schmitt supported by the English); and of the 'long, fierce civil war' between Mao

Tse-tung and the Kuomintang (the National People's Party).[32] In the course of this 'war', Derrida (*PoF* 149/*PA* 171) comments, 'absolute hostility directs itself at the brother, and converts the internal war, this time into real war, into an absolute war, and thus into an absolute politics'. At first sight there seems to be a problem with Derrida's reading here, because it seems to confuse the strict distinction Schmitt draws in 'The Theory of the Partisan' between real and absolute hostility.[33] Derrida's contention that the brother in Schmitt becomes the target of absolute hostility, nevertheless finds support in the following passage:

> Various kinds of enmity [*verschiedene Arten der Feindschaft*] are joined in Mao's concrete situation, rising to an absolute enmity [*die sich zu einer absoluten Feindschaft steigern*]. Racial enmity against the white colonial exploiter; class enmity against the capitalist bourgeoisie; national enmity against the Japanese invader of the same race; the enmity against the own national brother [*gegen den eigenen, nationalen Bruder*], expanding in long, embittered civil wars – all this did not paralyze or relativize each other reciprocally, as would be conceivable, but were confirmed and intensified in the concrete situation.
>
> ('TP' 41/*TdP* 63)

What is in other words, according to Schmitt's schema, supposed to involve a restricted form of enmity, that is, complying with the requirement of the telluric, turns out to be the worst form of violence – that between brothers. Derrida (*PoF* 148–9/*PA* 170–1) consequently refers to the hostility at stake here as 'absolute hostility' and to the war as an 'absolute war'.[34] A vertiginous reversal is taking place here in the truth of the political,[35] Derrida (*PoF* 149/*PA* 171) observes, and it happens precisely 'at the moment that one touches the limit, of oneself or one's double [*son double*], the twin, this absolute friend that always comes in the guise of the brother'.

32 There is also a third mention of the brother, which Derrida does not specifically refer to, namely in the discussion by Schmitt ('TP' 61/*TdP* 88) of Salan. Here the brother enemy is said to be a worse, more intensive enemy (*ein für ihn viel schlimmerer, intensiverer Feind*) in comparison to the Algerian front, which Schmitt refers to as Salan's 'absolute enemy'. With reference to the fact that the brother of yesterday reveals himself as the more dangerous enemy, Schmitt notes that there must be some confusion within the concept of the enemy itself (*Im Feindbegriff selbst muß eine Verwirrung liegen*).

33 See the criticism of Meier (2013: 178 n37).

34 Something similar is at stake in the discussion by Derrida (*PoF* 156–7/*PA* 181) of woman as the absolute partisan, as we will see in the discussion below. See also *PoF* 133 and 162 where Derrida casts doubt on the viability of Schmitt's distinction between the annihilation of the enemy (in the case of absolute hostility) and his mere killing (in the case of conventional and real hostility).

35 Derrida appears to be alluding here to *The Concept of the Political* where the friend/brother stood in opposition to the enemy; now the brother becomes the absolute enemy, and where *pólemos* provided the paradigm for war; now *stásis* becomes the paradigm.

The figure of the double[36] makes a number of appearances in the *Politics of Friendship*, inter alia with reference to descriptions of friendship in its ideal sense.[37] In an analysis of Cicero's *On Friendship, or Laelius*, Derrida (*PoF* 4/*PA* 20) for example notes that 'one projects or recognises in the true friend one's exemplar, one's ideal double [*son double idéal*], one's other self, the same as the self, yet better' (*PoF* 4/*PA* 20).[38] The self here, Derrida (*PoF* 4/*PA* 20) furthermore comments, can be likened to 'Narcissus who dreams of immortality [*Narcisse qui rêve d'immortalité*]'. In commenting on Schmitt's insistence on the identification of the friend and the enemy in *The Concept of the Political*, Derrida (*PoF* 116/*PA* 136) somewhat similarly remarks that *philautia* (self-love), or narcissism, the fraternal double, are obscurely at work in this discourse.

Poe's The Purloined Letter

Of interest to us here is specifically the brief discussion by Derrida (*PoF* 151–2) of Poe's *The Purloined Letter* at the point where Dupin has managed to retrieve an incriminating letter which was taken from the Queen by the Minister in an attempt to blackmail her.[39] Although this appears as an aside, the motivating force of Derrida's analysis of 'The Theory of the Partisan' comes to the fore here. In linking *The Purloined Letter* to 'The Theory of the Partisan', Derrida refers to the invocation by Dupin in the last lines of the play of *Atrée et Thyestes* (1707), by the French dramatist Crébillon (1674–1762).[40] At stake in all these texts, as well as in the biblical Cain and Abel, which is also referred to here (*PoF* 151),[41] is a rivalry between brother enemies.[42] At this point in *The Purloined Letter*, Dupin predicts the *self*-destruction of his rival who, as Derrida notes in an analysis of

36 One of the earliest psychoanalytical investigations of the double was undertaken by Rank (1925; 1971) in *Der Doppelgänger*.

37 See *PoF* viii, 4, 116, 149, 152 and 172.

38 See also *PoF* 276/*PA* 307, referring to Montaigne: 'If you press me to say why I loved him, I feel that it can only be expressed by replying: "Because it was him: because it was me."'

39 See *PC* 459–60 and 490–2 where Derrida in the essay 'The Purveyor of Truth', and in an attempt at challenging Lacan's Oedipal reading, refers to the double nature of the narrator (narrating-narrated), the double nature of Dupin himself as well as his doubling of the narrator, and Dupin's identification with all the characters in the 'story' so as to solve the mystery. At stake here, Derrida (*PC* 492/*CP* 521) notes, is a 'labyrinth of doubles without originals'. For further discussion see De Ville (2008).

40 Dupin leaves a note in the Minister's apartment stating the following: 'Un dessein si funeste / S'il n'est digne d'Atrée, est digne de Thyeste' (A plot so deadly, if not worthy of Atreus, is worthy of Thyestes). Like Atreus, Dupin thus acts in revenge in response to an earlier crime – here by the Minister.

41 Schmitt refers to Cain and Abel in *ECS* 89: 'Adam and Eve had two sons, Cain and Abel. Thus begins the history of mankind. Thus appears the father of all things. This is the dialectical tension that keeps world history in motion, and the history of the world is not over yet.' See further below.

42 The story of Cain and Abel can also be read as a story about doubles; see Ng (2008: 1).

Poe's text, resembles him like a brother (Dupin: 'Thus he will inevitably commit himself, at once, to his political destruction'). Also noteworthy is Dupin's equivocal admiration of his rival (i.e. the Minister): 'In the present instance I have no sympathy – at least no pity – for him who descends. He is the monstrum horrendum, an unprincipled man of genius.' For Derrida (*PoF* 152/*PA* 175) this prediction of self-destruction (of the rival) points to 'monstrous truths', which evoke the 'pitiless sympathy' at stake here and elsewhere, that is, in any kind of 'war and death among brothers'. This is a war to death, and takes place 'by virtue of the phantasm of the symbiotic [*selon le fantasme du symbiotique*]', Derrida notes (*PoF* 152/*PA* 175).[43] *The Purloined Letter* with this projection of a dangerous secret of the self onto the figure of the brother (the double thereby both mirroring and threatening the self), thus seems to suggest that the friend as brother, the ideal double as reflection of the self, as constructed in the philosophical tradition, is ultimately so constructed to protect the self against the abyss, against the Acheron, that is, as we will see below, against the doubling of the double.

Mallarmé's Mimique

A detailed discussion cannot be undertaken here of Derrida's analysis of the double in texts such as 'The Double Session' (1970) and *The Post Card* (1980), which enquire into Freud's 'The Uncanny' (2001, XVII: 217–52) and 'Beyond the Pleasure Principle' (Freud 2001, XVIII: 1–64).[44] A few brief comments and a short analysis with the aim of clarifying the appearance of the double in *Politics of Friendship* will have to suffice. At stake in 'The Double Session' (dating from 1969) is the relationship between philosophy and literature to the truth (as *adequatio* or *aletheia*). Derrida contends that both literature and philosophy have in the metaphysical tradition been viewed as a means of conveying the truth.[45] This also applies to the double in general, which has in the metaphysical tradition been understood as the copy of something original, as the imitation of the truth (*Dis* 201). Freud's *Das Unheimliche* (2001, XVII: 249) appears to adopt, but at the same time to question, this approach to the truth insofar as it attributes appearances of the uncanny (including the figure of the double) to childhood experiences (thus a return of the repressed) *and* at the same time suggests with reference to literature that some other mechanism may be at stake here (*Dis* 306 n67; *PC* 342–3, 426–7).[46] Freud's text in other words raises the question whether the

43 In *PoF* 149/*PA* 171 Derrida comments in this regard that there are no brothers in nature and that for there to be a brother, 'a law, and names, symbols, a language, engagements, oaths, speech, family and nation' are required. A brother is therefore always a brother of alliance or by oath; see also *PoF* 159.

44 See also Derrida's analysis of the marionette in Valery's 'Monsieur Teste' in *B&S I* 184.

45 See in this respect the discussions of Gasché (1986: 255–70); and Saghafi (2010: 65–82).

46 Fichte, apart from his role in the philosophical discovery of the partisan (see above), also played an important role in respect of the development of literature on the double in the nineteenth century; see Vardoulakis (2006: 102).

repetition in question involves the repetition of some repressed prior (childhood) event, or instead, of some event that has never been a present past.

Derrida finds especially in Mallarmé's *Mimique* allusions to such a different, non-present understanding of the operation of the double. In *Mimique* the miming is not of any prior thing or reality, but instead follows upon an 'event' of unbinding, or of dying-laughing (*PC* 343, 350; *Dis* 212–13, 220) which, as we will see, never in fact occurs. In the play – *Pierrot Murderer of His Wife* – which Mallarmé comments on in *Mimique* (in a theatre review), Pierrot (performed by Mallarmé's cousin Paul Margueritte) kills his unfaithful wife, Columbine (also performed by Paul Margueritte) on their wedding night by tickling her to death. The Mime character does not copy a pre-existing reality or idea, and follows no prescribed text.[47] Mallarmé speaks in this regard of a 'yet unwritten page' on which the gestures and facial expressions (of the Mime character) are inscribed (*Dis* 208/ *Diss* 240). The Mime character does not act spontaneously either; one can rather say that he 'inaugurates', Derrida (*Dis* 208/ *Diss* 240) notes. What he is required to do is:

> to write himself on the white page he is; he must *himself* inscribe *himself* through gestures and plays of facial expressions. At once page and quill, Pierrot is both passive and active, matter and form, the author, the means, and the dough of his mimodrama. The histrion produces himself here.
>
> (*Dis* 209/*Diss* 244)

The 'event' at stake (the crime, suicide, spasm of laughter/pleasure) is enfolded or doubled in a number of ways: what is staged is Pierrot returning after having buried his wife, and then recalling (by virtue of some force wrenching the secret from him) by way of miming how he had first deliberated on the manner in which he would kill her, by accident came upon the idea and then proceeded to do so – by tying her up while asleep and then tickling her feet until she died in spasms of

47 Mallarmé reports that *Mimique* (of which there are three (different) versions: 1886, 1891 and 1897) was written in response to his having read a pantomime booklet by Paul Margueritte, *Pierrot, Murderer of His Wife*. The booklet contains a prescription which effaces itself insofar as it prescribes to the Mime character not to follow any prescription, i.e. not to imitate anything (no act or word) that pre-exists the play (*Dis* 209). The booklet was furthermore written only after performances of the play had started (in 1881). Mallarmé read the 2nd edition and perhaps also attended the performance; see *Dis* 209, 210–11, and 290 n20. The first edition (1882) contained a preface by Beissier, who reported what he had seen. In the 2nd edition (1886) the preface was replaced by an author's note claiming originality, yet on the title page of the 1882 edition an epigraph appears in the form of a quotation from Théophile Gautier (dating from 1847), referring to the character Pierrot murdering his wife by tickling her (*Dis* 214–15). Derrida (*Dis* 292–3 n22, n23) also mentions other earlier examples of death by foot tickling from the seventeenth and nineteenth centuries, as well as a number of other Pierrot texts where this character finds himself between life and death. These are just some examples of the abyssal complexities of the texts in play here or what Derrida (*Dis* 208/*Diss* 240) refers to as 'a textual labyrinth panelled with mirrors'.

orgasm or as Derrida (*Dis* 213/*Diss* 248) describes it, a kind of 'masturbatory suicide [*suicide masturbatoire*]'. Pierrot himself then shortly afterwards likewise dies after first being overcome by a contagious tickling and then having a hallucination of a portrait of his wife breaking out in laughter and then tickling himself to death.

Commenting on *Mimique*, Derrida (*Dis* 208) notes that the Mime character does not imitate anything; he does not even imitate. Compared to Plato's *Philebus*, here no presence, no speech, and no *logos* precedes or predetermines the 'gestural writing' of the Mime (*Dis* 208/*Diss* 240). Commentators on 'The Double Session' have in general made little of the specific 'crime' committed here. To understand the 'structure' of the double, as well as its role in *Politics of Friendship*, the central role of the 'crime' however needs to be understood. As Derrida points out, the 'crime' is never committed in the present on stage; it is also never observed by anyone; and in the end, no crime is really committed (*Dis* 212). This is because it is the perfect crime, death by *jouissance*, which involves no violence, and leaves no trace, as well as the fact that it is actually an act of love (*Dis* 212, 224). The Mime furthermore plays both Pierrot and Columbine, and as noted earlier, Pierrot himself dies of laughter soon after, and is thereby absolved (*Dis* 224).

Keeping in mind the quotation above of the Mime producing himself, as well as of the specific 'crime' committed, Derrida (*Dis* 217/*Diss* 254) notes the differences between the traditional structure of the double and that of Mallarmé: with the latter, the 'double doubles no simple'; and the double is not anticipated or awaited in advance, at least not by anything that is not already itself double. In the case of Mallarmé's double, reality is death, and inaccessible except through simulacrum. The ghostly Mime character is moreover 'the phantom of no flesh, wandering about without a past, without any death, birth or presence' (*Dis* 217/*Diss* 255). Mallarmé thus positions himself within Plato's structure of the *phantasma* (the simulacrum as the copy of a copy), with the only difference being that there is no model, and therefore, strictly speaking, no copy (*Dis* 217).[48]

The ghostly Mime character (as double) can, reverting to a quasi-Freudian language whilst returning to Schmitt, be said to come to haunt the Pleasure Principle (i.e. narcissism in the form of the friend-brother as ideal self), 'undermining it, persecuting it by seeking an unbound pleasure' (*PC* 352/*CP* 374). We see this in Schmitt's *The Concept of the Political* and in 'The Theory of the Partisan', where the ideal double of the self turns out to itself be double: the brother as friend in *The Concept of the Political*, and in 'The Theory of the Partisan' (and in *Ex Captivitate Salus*) as (absolute) enemy.[49] This (philosophical)

48 See also Hobson (2001: 136); and see further Chapters 4 and 6 below on representation.

49 In the discussion of General Salan and the Algerian War of Independence, Schmitt ('TP' 60–1/*TdP* 87) elusively raises the following questions which could be read to tie in with our discussion of the double: 'Every two-front war poses the question of who the real enemy [*wirkliche Feind*] is. Is it not a sign of inner division [*ein Zeichen innerer Gespaltenheit*] to have more than one single real

construction, or perhaps rather phantasm, of the double as brother, with its structural exclusion of the sister, points to its condition of possibility beyond the political: to woman as the absolute partisan, as we will see below. The self, here transposed into the concept of the political, is in other words an effect of what will be termed below, the 'feminine operation'.

Woman as the absolute partisan

Schmitt, as Derrida (*PoF* 149) points out, never speaks of the sister, at least in the texts that concern themselves with the political. Derrida (*PoF* 155/*PA* 179) refers in this regard to 'a certain desert [*un certain désert*]', which refers back to his analysis in Chapter 5 of *Politics of Friendship* of *The Concept of the Political* at the point where Schmitt speaks of depoliticisation, and which Derrida (*PoF* 130/*PA* 154) likened to a dehumanised desert (*un désert déshumanisé*). The desert at stake here (*PoF* 155) is however one teeming with people, or rather with men. As Derrida (*PoF* 155–6) points out, in Schmitt's 'The Theory of the Partisan' as well as in *The Concept of the Political*), only men are mentioned. All the partisans, generals, politicians, professors, etc. being referred to are men. In Schmitt's account of war and merciless killing, of absolute hostility, Derrida (*PoF* 156/*PA* 180) notes, 'what disappears in becoming indiscernible in the middle of the desert, is woman or the sister'.[50] There is not even a mirage of woman in this desert, Derrida (*PoF* 156/*PA* 180) notes.[51] And there is furthermore no mention by Schmitt of the role women have played throughout history in partisan warfare, in the two world wars (or resistance movements during the war, for example in France) and in wars of national liberation after these wars or, Derrida (*PoF* 156) seems to suggest, of the war for their own liberation from patriarchy.[52] The fact that woman herself does not appear in 'The Theory of the Partisan', that is, in the theory of the absolute enemy, the fact that she never exits from this enforced clandestinity, from such invisibility, Derrida notes, makes one wonder:

> and if woman [*la femme*] were the absolute partisan? If she were the other absolute enemy [*l'autre ennemi absolu*] of this theory of the absolute enemy, the spectre of hostility, conjured for the sake of sworn brothers, or the other

enemy [*einen einzigen wirklichen Feind*]? The enemy is our own question as figure [*Gestalt*]. If we have determined our own figure unambiguously, where does this double enemy come from?'; see further Section C below.

50 As we will see in the analysis that follows, Derrida appears to be alluding here again to the 'withdrawal' of the political, which we encountered in Section A above.

51 Derrida (*PoF* 278–9/*PA* 310) notes that this exclusion of women has taken place throughout the history of friendship, where friendships between women and between men and women are never spoken of. He refers to this as the 'double exclusion of the feminine'.

52 To be fair to Schmitt, in elaborating on the essentially defensive stance in relation to the national soil of the true partisan, he does mention Joan of Arc ('TP' 66/*TdP* 93), although she was not a partisan.

> of the absolute enemy becoming the absolute enemy that one would not recognize in a regular war? She who, following the same logic of the theory of the partisan, becomes an enemy especially formidable who cannot become *an* enemy [une *ennemie*] in his/her blurring and parasiting of the reassuring limits between hostility and hate, but also between enmity and its opposite, the laws of war and lawless violence, the political and its others etc.
>
> (*PoF* 157/*PA* 181)

By raising the question of woman as the absolute partisan, Derrida seeks to further 'reconstitute' the structure of the concept of the political, which he has up to this point shown to be spectral as well as haunted by the brother absolute enemy. By suggesting that woman may be the absolute partisan, Derrida accords a similar 'role' to the figure of woman, as he does in a text such as *Spurs: Nietzsche's Styles*. In the latter text, at stake in the displacement of truth by woman (to be understood here not as female sexuality, but as non-identity, non-figure and as simulacrum, as gift without exchange, is what Derrida (1979: 48–9, 54–5, 56–7, 120–1) refers to as the feminine 'operation'. Read in view of Freud's *Beyond the Pleasure Principle* and Abraham and Torok's *The Shell & the Kernel* (Chapter 5, Section B below), we can in other words detect in 'The Theory of the Partisan' the force of an unbinding, the threat therefore of the (feminine) absolute enemy, always already restricting, that is, concealing herself, dissimulating herself, somewhat analogous to a partisan operation. What tends to happen is that this non-figure or spectre, that is, the one who bears witness to the (return of the) absolute unbinding, is immediately ontologised by the person who conjures it. The spectre is in other words constructed as the double of something real, that is, in the present context, the brother of flesh and blood, whereas he/she actually has another 'nature'. Woman's exclusion by Schmitt from the concept of the political thus reveals the law or the differantial topology that is at stake here.[53] The disappearing figure of woman in 'The Theory of the Partisan' can in other words also be referred to as the gift, that is, the friendship that goes beyond circular exchange. One has to learn, as Derrida (*PoF* 283) notes with reference to Nietzsche (who says that neither men nor women are as yet capable of this), how to give to the enemy.

Today's terror and the structure of the political

The present section can be brought to a close by briefly looking at the issue of the implications of today's terror for the concept of the political. Shortly after

53 Derrida (*SoM* 102–3/*SdM* 137) refers to a topology such as that of Schmitt as an 'ontopology', which he explains as 'an axiomatic linking indissociably the ontological value of present-being (*on*) to its *location*, to the stable and presentable determination of a locality (the *topos* of territory, of soil, of the city, of the body in general)'. As can be seen from the above analysis, Derrida in *Politics of Friendship* looks for traces in Schmitt's text of what one can refer to as a 'differantial topology' or an 'a-topology'.

the events of 11 September 2001, Derrida ('Auto' 102; *Rog* 156) expressed the view that the violence of the early twenty-first century (including that of suicide bombers) is not encompassed by Schmitt's two partisans and that it involves a new form of violence, although it cannot be regarded as completely new. He gave a number of reasons for this 'novelty': the first is that this violence is more clearly suicidal or of an autoimmune nature than previously. Secondly, what is called 'international terrorism'[54] does not only strive for attaining sovereignty over some territory, as was the case with both Schmitt's two forms of partisan (*Rog* 106, 155–6). Nevertheless, this paradigm cannot be said to have completely disappeared (*Rog* 156; 'Auto' 111–12). The third reason is that there is not the same reliance on a third interested party or state, as was the case with the two forms of partisan which Schmitt identifies in 'The Theory of the Partisan' ('Auto' 101).[55] Fourthly, the 'form' which the enemy takes has changed, in the sense that the 'enemy' of sovereign states no longer (or at least 'more seldom') takes the form of an actual or virtual[56] state (*Rog* 155).[57] There is consequently no longer, as was the case during the Cold War, a 'balance of terror' ('Auto' 98). The nuclear, total or absolute threat now comes 'from anonymous forces that are absolutely unforeseeable and incalculable' ('Auto' 98).[58] In the fifth place, the means of waging 'war' and their relation to the telluric has changed, making possible attacks by way of air or surface missiles, attacks on computer systems and informational networks, as well as nuclear, bacteriological, chemical and nanotechnological attacks by non-state actors (*Rog* 155; 'Auto' 101–2).[59] In the sixth place, the integral and co-determining role the media plays in (the impact of) events such as 9/11 (*Rog* xiii, 155; 'Auto' 108–9).[60] Finally, the cause, motivation, aim or message of what is called 'international terrorism' is more difficult to determine than is the case with Schmitt's two forms of partisan ('Auto' 111).[61]

54 Derrida ('Auto' 103) takes issue with the tendency to restrict the act of terrorism to non-state actors. States can and often do perpetrate terror; see also Chomsky (2016). Furthermore, as Derrida ('Auto' 108) points out, terror can be perpetrated 'simply' through relations of force, i.e. without any identifiable subject or actor being conscious of or feeling responsible for it.

55 See also Münkler (2005: 112–13).

56 See 'Auto' 105 where Derrida refers to Palestine as an example of a 'virtual state'.

57 See also De Benoist (2013: 61) who points out that Al Qaeda forms a scattered international network rather than a hierarchical organisation (the Islamic State however appears to be more hierarchically organised; see Glenn (2015)); and see Münkler (2005: 113) who points out that the enemy of 'terrorist groups' are no longer necessarily states as such, but rather 'whole civilizations'.

58 De Benoist (2013: 63–6) points out that the war against terrorism is likewise a total (police) war. However, according to him there is an asymmetry at stake here in respect of actors, objectives, means and, most important, psychology. The latter form of asymmetry relates to the difference in perspective as to the value of life and death (at 68–70).

59 Münkler (2005: 108) refers in this respect to the use of the enemy's own civilian infrastructure to wage attacks.

60 See also Münkler (2005: 110–12).

61 See also Münkler (2005: 110–16).

Derrida thus sees in the suicidal or autoimmunitary violence of today (which includes both the actions of the suicide bomber[62] and of the United States (and its allies)[63] as dominant world power, tied to the unlimited proliferation of nuclear capability) a modification, which points much more clearly to what is at stake in the structure of the political ('Auto' 94–102; *Rog* 156).[64] In suicide bombings (and the autoimmunitary actions of the United States and its allies) this structure comes very clearly to the fore.[65] Whereas the terminology which Derrida employs in this analysis slightly changes after 2001, the structure of the political identified through his reading of *The Concept of the Political* and 'The Theory of the Partisan' stays the same.[66] Derrida's 'thesis', already in *Politics of Friendship*, is that violence, in whatever form, is derived from the same 'source'. This 'source' is the Freudian death drive, which is alluded to by Derrida in the interview in *Philosophy in a Time of Terror* as well as in *Rogues* by the notion of autoimmune actions. Translated into the language of *Politics of Friendship*, such actions can be said to at the same time point towards an asymmetrical friendship with no return to the self, beyond the friend-enemy couple.[67]

62 See Bargu (2010: 8) who, tying in with our discussion above, views suicide bombers or what she refers to as 'human weapons' as 'carriers of the acherontic movement in today's world'.

63 De Benoist (2013: 61–2) points out in this respect that as a consequence of the imposition of the United States' new world order, associated with 'the global opening of markets, guaranteed access to energy resources, the suppression of regulations and borders, the control of communications, and so on . . . it is no longer the logic of territory that characterises the action of the partisan but the "maritime" logic of deterritorialisation/globalisation which favours the emergence of a new form of terrorism, as it opens up new means of action to it'; see further Chapter 7 below.

64 We see this structure, or rather 'stricture' of unbinding vis-à-vis binding already in Derrida's reading of *The Concept of the Political* (Chapters 4 and 5 of *Politics of Friendship*), specifically with reference to *stâsis*; see Section A above. It also appears from the reading of 'The Theory of the Partisan' as discussed above.

65 See also Chomsky (2016: 42, 249–55).

66 Schmitt ('TP' 68/*TdP* 96, also at 'TP' 56/*TdP* 81) incidentally predicted new forms of hostility in future as well as unexpected manifestations of new partisanship, or what he called elsewhere the further development of the 'immeasurable partisan problematic' ('GP' 10).

67 In Heideggerian language, it can be said that at stake here is the gift of Being which in a kind of Hegelian twist to Heidegger increasingly 'reveals' itself today.

SECTION C SELF

Introduction

In *The Concept of the Political* Schmitt points to the centrality of the question of human nature (Section A above). Schmitt (*CoP* 61/*BdP* 61) finds support for his definition of the concept of the political specifically in the reflections of political thinkers who view man as 'evil, i.e. as in no way unproblematic, but as a dangerous and dynamic being [*als "gefährliches" und dynamisches Wesen*]'. In 'The Theory of the Partisan' the question of human nature again comes to the fore insofar as Schmitt defines the partisan with reference to the telluric.[1] In the present chapter, we move back in time to the text 'Weisheit der Zelle'/'Wisdom of the Prison Cell' (*ECS* 79–91), dated April 1947 (hereafter 'Weisheit', to trace what appears to be an a-chronological development as well as a further a-temporality in Schmitt's thinking regarding the concept of the political. In this semi-autobiographical text, Schmitt uses both his own situation and that of humanity in general, to reflect on the concept of the political, with the question of human nature taking centre stage. Before we start with the analysis of 'Weisheit', let us first look briefly at the context within which this text was written.

After World War II, Schmitt was interned briefly by the Russians in April 1945 and thereafter again on two occasions (from September 1945 to October 1946 and from March 1947 to May 1947) by the Americans. During his second detention he was interrogated by Robert Kempner at Nuremberg to determine whether he should be charged for participating, directly or indirectly, in the planning of wars of aggression, war crimes and crimes against humanity.[2] During his time in Nuremberg, Schmitt wrote a number of smaller texts, inter alia 'Weisheit', which was published in 1950 under the title *Ex Captivitate Salus*. In 'Weisheit' Schmitt again takes up the issue of the enemy. The enemy figure is here not however, or at least not in the first place, explored with reference to external or civil war as in *The Concept of the Political*, or to partisan warfare as in 'The Theory of the Partisan', but to the self, or the brother. As he does in his other texts, Schmitt here suggests, perhaps more explicitly, that the self, and by implication, the concept of the political, is haunted by a force of self-destruction. The concept of the political, with reference to which law is ultimately to be understood, in 'Weisheit' implodes on itself. In this section, the implications of this implosion will be enquired into primarily through an analysis of 'Weisheit', and of Derrida's *Politics of Friendship* (1997a: 159–67), where he discusses this text of Schmitt.

1 See also *L&S* 1, and Chapter 7 below.
2 See Bendersky (1987; 2007); Schmitt (1987; 2007b).

Defining man: nakedness

Schmitt (*ECS* 79) starts off his reflections by asking himself which of the definitions of man in circulation appears self-evident (*dir unmittelbar einleuchtet*). For him this is the fact that the human being (*der Mensch*) is naked.[3] The most naked is the human being who, without clothes, appears before another who is clothed; someone who has been disarmed, appearing before someone who is armed; someone who is powerless, appearing before someone powerful. This is an experience that Adam and Eve already had when they were driven from paradise, Schmitt (*ECS* 79) notes. This of course raises the further question whether the definition of man is to be attached to the first or the second category of person in every instance, and, in addition, which of these is closer to paradise. In the versions of paradise promoted in the present age,[4] Schmitt (*ECS* 79) comments, human beings instead go around clothed. In contrast, Schmitt (*ECS* 79) sees himself as clearly naked and proceeds to quote Daübler's *Perseus*: 'Now you stand naked, naked as at birth [*geburthaft nackt*], in desert expanses [*in wüsten Weiten*]'.[5] Schmitt's comparison of himself in his small prison cell, where he was kept in solitary confinement, with the desert expanses in Daübler's poem, most likely has the aim of pointing to a feeling of solitude and vulnerability common to both. The pieces of clothing that were left for him, he says, only confirm his nakedness in an objective sense. Even more so, the clothing underlines his nakedness in a highly ironic, as well as unpleasantly accentuated manner. One experiences oneself being thrown back onto one's last reserves, Schmitt (*ECS* 80) notes. Further emphasising his own vulnerability, he notes that his remaining physical powers can very easily be extinguished. Yet, at least for the moment, he adds, he still has some strength. Then, continuing his reflections on the definition of man, he recalls the sentence in Wagner's 1876 *Twilight of the Gods* (*Götterdämmerung*): '*Einzig erbt ich den eigenen Leib, lebend zehr ich ihn auf* [Singularly do I inherit my own body, living, I feed on it]'.[6] This passage is sung by Siegfried in what Schmitt (*ECS* 80) refers to as 'a wonderful collapsing and crashing interval [*einem wunderbar auf- und abstürzenden Intervall*]'. It captures in unparalleled fashion an exuberant physical feeling of happiness, Schmitt says, which still rides upon the waves which led to the 1848 revolution in Germany. Schmitt however notes that the passage is originally to be found in Max Stirner[7]

3 The answer to the question posed here has a direct relation to the concept of the political. As Schmitt points out in *GL* 306, the reason for people's nakedness in paradise is the absence there of enemies.

4 The (false) earthly paradise at stake here seems to allude to the reign of the Antichrist; see Hooker (2009: 49).

5 The lack of precise references in the text is due to Schmitt's imprisonment at the time, and the confiscation of his library by the Americans.

6 *Zehren*: live off, feed on, wear out, sap, ruin, weaken, gnaw at, undermine.

7 The reference here is most likely to Stirner (2006: 135/1845: 167) where he says: 'this, that I consume myself, means only that I am [*dass Ich Mich verzehre, heisst nur, dass Ich bin*]' and where

and that with Stirner we approach the idea of paradisiacal nakedness in contrast to modern versions of paradise where, as we saw, man is clothed. At stake here appears to be Stirner's radical individualism, which to some extent also finds expression in Wagner's Siegfried, and which Schmitt, as appears from a passage in the *Glossarium* on Stirner, clearly finds problematic:

> Thus at any rate: glorious solidarity: Millions of us can call out in a speaking choir 'nothing is beyond me, and I am I'. You can perhaps say that of yourself, and the millions in your speaking choir who shout with you can do so too. I can unfortunately only say of myself that I don't know whether I am I/ego [*ob ich Ich bin*] and whether nothing is beyond me [*ob mir nichts über mich geht*]. I do not know how things stand with this I/ego/self of mine [*wie es sich mit diesem meinem Ich verhält*], whether it is a fixed star or a marsh light, or both. Are you singular [*ein Einziger*] or are you a thousand and countless selves in your I/ego/self [*bist Du tausend und zahllose Ich in Deinem Ich*]? All of this I do not know. I do not know who I am. If you know who you are, all the better. Let your knowledge serve you.
>
> (*GL* 48, entry of 22 Nov 1947)

Stirner and his ego

Schmitt (*ECS* 80–1) notes that he has known Stirner since high school (*Unterprima*) and that this knowledge prepared him for many things, which would otherwise have surprised him. Stirner's *The Ego and Its Own* was published in 1844 and Schmitt (*ECS* 81) notes that the depths of the European thought process from 1830–1848 prepare one also for present world events. What Schmitt (*ECS* 81) refers to as 'the debris field [*das Trümmerfeld*]' of the 'self-decomposition [*der Selbstzersetzung*]' of German theology and idealist philosophy, had since 1848 developed itself into a force field of theogonic and cosmogonic approaches. What is exploding in the present, Schmitt notes, was already prepared before 1848.[8] The fire that is burning in the present was then built. There are, he continues, with clear reference to the recent-at-the-time developed atom bomb, certain uranium mines of intellectual history (*Uran-Bergwerke der Geistesgeschichte*). These include the pre-Socratics, some church fathers and also certain writings of the time before 1848. The poor Max (Stirner), Schmitt (*ECS* 81) notes, also falls within this category (of atomic thinkers). This categorisation of Stirner should not be read as unqualified praise: 'On the whole', Schmitt (*ECS* 81) says, Stirner is 'hideous, boorish, pretentious, boastful, a tormentor [*ein Pennalist*], a depraved student [*ein verkommener Studiker*], oafish [*ein Knote*], an egomaniac [*ein Ich-Verrückter*],

Stirner (2006: 324/1845: 412) refers to the mortal creator of the self 'who consumes himself [*der sich selbst verzehrt*]'.

8 See also Schmitt (2002b: 102/*DC* 84–6).

obviously a severe psychopath [*ein schwerer Psychopath*]'. Stirner, Schmitt (*ECS* 81) continues his mocking, crows with a loud, unpleasant voice: 'I am I. I feel no authority over me', and his word-sophisms are unbearable. This vehement denunciation of Stirner can partly be ascribed to the latter's view in relation to self-identity, which is for Schmitt the issue at stake here. As we saw above, Schmitt (*CoP* 61) agrees with those thinkers who regard man as a dangerous and dynamic being. In *The Nomos of the Earth* (1950), in a discussion of Hobbes's *homo homini lupus*, Schmitt mentions Stirner as one of those who had (wrongly) denied the truth of this maxim. Schmitt's polemic in Section 7 of *The Concept of the Political* against anarchism and liberalism, which both believe in man's goodness, and either opposes or mistrusts the state, in the latter instance seeking to limit its powers by making it the servant of civil society, can thus be read as directed also at Stirner.[9] 'Every consistent individualism', Schmitt (*CoP* 70/*BdP* 69) says, amounts to a 'negation of the political'.

Schmitt does however give Stirner credit for something. Apart from the back-handed compliment that Stirner counts among the atomic thinkers of the nineteenth century, Schmitt (*ECS* 81) also credits Stirner for realising that the 'I' (*das Ich*) is not an object of thought (*Denkobjekt*).[10] This is likely to be at least partially a reference to Stirner's statement that the 'I' (as spirit/ghost) 'is to be found at the back of or behind things, so I must later find myself also behind thoughts, that is, as their creator and owner [*Wie Ich Mich hinter den Dingen finde, und zwar als Geist, so muss Ich Mich später auch hinter den Gedanken finden, nämlich als ihr Schöpfer und Eigner*]' (Stirner 2006: 17/1845: 14).[11] How is this ambivalence towards Stirner to be understood? Perhaps by taking account of the fact that the same Stirner, also in the reading of Schmitt,[12] did battle with ghosts, which he showed to continuously haunt the 'I'.[13] Schmitt appears to adopt a reading in

9 See especially *CoP* 60–1/*BdP* 60–1, and see further Meier (1998: 7–9) on Schmitt and the anarchist Bakunin. At some point Schmitt nevertheless implicitly relies on Stirner to criticise liberalism, see e.g. *CoP* 71 where Schmitt points to the contradiction in liberal thought between the belief in individual freedom and the duty that is placed on this same individual to sacrifice his life for the collective when the occasion arises.

10 In *GL* 100, Schmitt, after having quoted a passage from Stirner's *The Ego and Its Own*, likewise comments: 'I am I/Ego; I am no object of thought, but me/Ego; no idea and no concept [*Ich bin Ich; Ich bin kein Denkobjekt, sondern Ich; keine Idee und kein Begriff*].'

11 See also Stirner (2006: 311/1845: 396): 'The truth, or "truth in general", people are bound not to give up, but to seek for . . . . And yet the truth is only a – *thought*; but it is not merely "a" thought, but the thought that is above all thoughts, the irrefragable thought; it is *the* thought itself, which gives the first hallowing to all others; it is the consecration of thoughts, the "absolute", the "sacred" thought.' Stirner (2006: 312) then continues by pointing out that the self is much more than the truth and that truth only exists insofar as it has been made a property of the self.

12 *GL* 48: 'The remarkable thing about Max Stirner is . . . the desperation of his struggle with the fraud [*Schwindel*] and ghosts [*Gespenstern*] of his time.'

13 See e.g. Stirner (2006: 41/1845: 44) where he conjures the 'ghosts' constructed by Christianity: 'But through Christ the truth of the matter had at the same time come to light, that the veritable

'Weisheit' of Stirner (similar to that of Derrida in *Specters of Marx*) in terms of which Ego equals ghost. Derrida spells out this equation as follows:

> Stirner has often been read, in fact, as a Fichtean thinker. But this Ego, this *living individual* would itself be inhabited and invaded by its *own specter*. It would be constituted by specters of which it becomes the host and which it assembles in the haunted community of a single body. Ego=ghost [*Moi=fantôme*]. Therefore 'I am' would mean 'I am haunted' . . . . Wherever there is Ego, *es spukt*, 'it spooks.'[14]
>
> (*SoM* 166/*SdM* 212)

In further support of this reading, we see that Schmitt (*ECS* 81–2), after expressing his admiration for the title of Stirner's *Der Einzige und sein Eigentum* – declaring it to be the most beautiful, or in any event, the most German (*deutschesten*) book title in the whole of German literature – notes that 'in this moment Max is the only one/the Ego (*der Einzige*)' who visits him in his prison cell. This visit, Schmitt (*ECS* 82) says with perhaps a tint of irony, touches him deeply (*rührt mich tief*) in view of Stirner's rabid egoism. This Ego/ghost haunting Schmitt in his prison cell, as we will see further below, can be said to stand at the 'origin' of thought, which would explain why Schmitt (*ECS* 81) contends that it cannot be the object of the latter. The ghost thus appears to tell Schmitt something about the definition of man that he is searching for.[15]

The ultimate drive (*letzten Antrieb*) or true longing (*wahre Sensucht*) of the 'I'-lunatic (*Ich-Verrückten*) Stirner is, according to Schmitt (*ECS* 82), to be found expressed in a letter written by Stirner.[16] With this we return to the Stirnerian

spirit or ghost is – man. The *corporeal* or embodied spirit is just man; he himself is the ghostly being and at the same time the being's appearance and existence. Henceforth man no longer, in typical cases, shudders at ghosts *outside* him, but at himself; he is terrified at himself. In the depth of his breast dwells the *spirit of sin*; even the faintest thought (and this is itself a spirit, you know) may be a *devil*, etc. – The ghost has put on a body, God has become man, but now man is himself the gruesome spook which he seeks to get behind, to exorcise, to fathom, to bring to reality and to speech; man is – *spirit* .. . . Man has become to himself a ghost, an uncanny spook, to which there is even assigned a distinct seat in the body (dispute over the seat of the soul, whether in the head, etc.).'

14 See likewise Saghafi (2011: 34): 'I hunt you down. I chase you. I pursue you, because I am pursued. I am pursued – by myself. I am afraid – of myself. I scare myself. I am haunted (by myself), so I obsessively chase you. I chase you away, I exclude you, I banish you – because I am haunted. It's as if I am after my own ghost.'

15 The ghost of Stirner visiting Schmitt in his prison cell can, in view of Schmitt's critique in 'Weisheit' of the modern versions of paradise and his view of Stirner as one of the 'fathers' of the modern era, in addition be read as a reference to the unholy alliance between liberalism and technology; see also *CoP* 80–96 for Schmitt's 1929 essay 'The Age of Neutralizations and Depoliticizations'.

16 It has not been possible to trace the date or addressee of the letter Schmitt is referring to here.

paradise mentioned in the discussion above. In this letter Stirner declares that the new paradise will consist of an overcoming of self-estrangement and self-alienation in a perfect bodily presence. Man would then again become like the animals of the forest and the flowers in the fields. Schmitt (*ECS* 82) compares Stirner's paradise to Hieronymus Bosch's *The Garden of Earthly Delights* (1500) and Rossini's *The Thieving Magpie* (1817). In this paradise there will be a pure identity of man with himself – he will experience a feeling of happiness of 'a blissfully accelerated blood circulation [*Glücksgefühl eines selig beschleunigten Blutkreislaufs*]'. Schmitt (*ECS* 82) as a result refers to Stirner as one of the first 'Panists' of German literature.[17]

Modern technology

This modern Pan, Schmitt (*ECS* 82) however notes, was overtaken by modern natural science. The happiness that Stirner speaks of is today even more of an illusion than when he lived. Schmitt (*ECS* 82–3) compares this Stirnerian bliss (of an ego reconciled to itself) with the feeling experienced by city-people who visit the countryside on holiday, the fleeting awakening of cheerful feelings in a child on the beach and the bliss of a poet laureate. The pleasure at stake here is thus no longer one of eternity as it is for Stirner and for Christianity. There is now a resignation to the fact that although more is desired, the holiday cannot last forever. Today this 'poor I' (*arme Ich*) can only wed his own echo and in this infertile, self-indulgent marriage, the 'I' is no longer forlorn (*vereinsamt*) as in Stirner's paradise, but for a long time already organisationally monopolised (*organisatorisch vereinnahmt*). Schmitt (*ECS* 83) plays here with the German words *Pan* and *Plan*, nature and technology. Planning (*die Planung*) has for a long time already monopolised the 'I': the plan appears and Pan stops smiling. Pan founders and planning appears on the agenda (*Der Pan versinkt, der Plan tritt auf den Plan*).

Today new versions of paradise again wink on the horizon, Schmitt (*ECS* 83) notes. He refers here to the paradise of a thoroughly planned world, with all the splendours brought about by an unlimited productive power and an infinitely increasing consumer power, accompanied by a generously extended leisure time and corresponding recreational activities. This is the paradise of a technicised earth (*technisierten Erde*) and a highly organised humanity (*ECS* 83). Social limitations now replace the natural limitations which have been overcome. These social limitations do not only capture us (*erfaßt uns nicht nur*); they change us. It is now no longer about understanding the world and humanity, but about their transformation.[18]

17 See also *ECS* 48 on the mythological Pan, who plays an important role in Däubler's *Nordlicht*; see further Schmitt (2009b).

18 The issue here is again the political, which technology seeks to neutralise, see *CoP* 95; *DC* 38–9; Meier (1998: 3–6); McCormick (1999: 253); and Lievens (2013: 125).

Failures in the artificial paradise of technology can however lead to experiences of hell, as Schmitt (*ECS* 84) points out with reference to the destruction of the sewage system in Berlin in 1946/7, thereby bringing to light the backside (*Kehrseite*), so to speak, of this paradise. These failures nonetheless are avoidable and affect only the vanquished, Schmitt (*ECS* 84) points out. Different from the optimism of earlier generations, the benefits of technology are not for everyone, but favour the elite, that is, the gods of the new paradise.[19] After remarking (somewhat sceptically, one can assume) that technology may perhaps be able to free us from all hardship in 50 or 100 years, Schmitt (*ECS* 85) returns to the opening sentences of 'Weisheit' and asks the question whether man in this new paradise is naked or clothed. This again raises the question of the political. Perhaps the new productive powers of technology, he says, can ensure that we (Schmitt *ECS* 85 emphasises the 'we') can afford to wear fantastic new costumes every day, or perhaps even better: there may no longer be clothing. Technology would improve to such an extent that we (or at least the new elite) would gird ourselves with light and heat covers. Or even better, the substance of our own bodies, Schmitt (*ECS* 85–6) speculates, could be transformed into radiation (*Strahlung*) resulting in the technically transfigured body, analogous to the way in which those who can fly today are technically perfected angels. The new elite would then be neither naked nor clothed (*ECS* 86), and in this way, it can be added, have transcended the political. The latter distinction would lose its meaning in a new level of human existence (*einer neuen Daseinsstufe*). This new superhuman elite would no longer be human. This new man would be the wholly other (*das ganz Andere*).[20] Some theologians, Schmitt (*ECS* 86) notes, say that God is the wholly other, yet, he adds, the wholly other is completely incalculable (*ganz unberechenbar*). Why would the new man then not be the wholly other, he asks rhetorically.[21] Man, as is well-known, is something that has to be overcome (*überwunden*), Schmitt (*ECS* 86) notes.[22] Why should he not in this way be overcome? He would then no longer be begotten, no longer conceived and no longer born (*ECS* 86). Even Huxley's *Brave New World* (1932) with its logical,

19 In *CoP* 90–1/*BdP* 89–90 Schmitt unmasks the claim of technology's neutrality and points out that it is always an instrument and a weapon and therefore simply a new terrain of struggle (*Kampfgebiet*). It cannot in other words free mankind from the political.

20 Schmitt's analysis here corresponds with Schmitt (2002b: 114/*DC* 110–12) about Donoso Cortés's recognition of man's tendency to terrorise and destroy all others who do not submit to him, as well as the rise of the superman (*Übermensch*), with his murderous counter-concept, the subhuman (*Untermensch*), which opens the terrible abyss of enmity. The subhuman, with which Schmitt clearly associates himself here, 'deserves' only extermination and destruction in the eyes of the superman.

21 See Meier (2013: 55–6) on man making himself into a god.

22 This statement is presumably to be read with Schmitt's comments in *CoP* 64 about anthropological optimism, i.e. that man is good and educable in the sense that he can be taught to overcome the friend-enemy relation of the political; see further Zakin (2011: 98–101).

highly scientific family planning would then be old-fashioned. Schmitt's own question as to the definition of the human, he points out, would become old-fashioned too (*ECS* 86). Everything would then simply be radiation (*Alles ist dann nur noch Strahlung*).[23] Although Schmitt's irony appears palpable on some level, it is clear that this new man as described by him (as totally other, incalculable and as neither naked nor clothed, but radiating) also tells us something about human nature in general.[24] At stake, as suggested above, is a transcendence of the political.

Being-placed-in-question

Schmitt (*ECS* 86) next raises the question whether he has been placed on earth to ensure through his labour that technology can transform us into radiation (*Strahlung*). If this is indeed the case, the question arises as to whose command he should subject himself to, in order to undertake his labour. He raises this question, he notes, because he has for a long time already not been alone and lonely (*für mich allein und einsam*), but organisationally monopolised (*organisatorisch vereinnahmt*) (*ECS* 86).[25] Schmitt however cuts himself short. These questions may actually no longer be asked in the new world. In fact, questions may no longer be asked at all. One must instead answer the questions posed to oneself. Questionnaires are now prepared by others, which place one in question together with one's questions (*die dich mitsamt deinen Fragen in Frage stellen*) (*ECS* 87).[26]

23 Radiation is of course associated with an exceeding of boundaries, which ties in closely with the reading of Schmitt adopted here.

24 Schmitt (*ECS* 49–51) also speaks of *Strahlung* in the 1946 essay 'Zwei Gräber' (*ECS* 55–78) when he sets out how he understands Däubler's *Das Nordlicht*. Whereas he at first gave it a Christian meaning, he says that he now knows that the Northern Lights convey knowledge of mankind. It is the meteorological sign of a self-saving humanity, an autochthonous radiation (*Strahlung*), which is sent from the earthly followers of Prometheus into the cosmos. Schmitt notes that he came to this new insight through Proudhon who contends that it is the destiny of the earth to gradually cool down and die like the moon. Mankind will then have to die with his planets if he does not succeed in sublimating himself to spirit (*sich zum Geist zu sublimieren*), that is, to spirituality, consciousness, freedom. Schmitt (*ECS* 49) concludes that for Däubler, the polar light is the telluric witness and guarantor specifically of this salvation of mankind through the spirit, ghost or spectre and in the spirit, ghost or spectre (*durch den Geist und im Geist*).

25 As we will see below, Schmitt appears to suggest here that one is always already confronted by the evil genius of Descartes, represented here by modern technology.

26 See in this respect the opening pages of *ECS* 9–10 where Schmitt reports that he was asked towards the end of 1945 to fill in a questionnaire (in 14 points about his Nazi sympathies and anti-Semitism) by Eduard Spranger (1882–1963), at the time Rector of the Friedrich Wilhelms University and member of an executive committee tied to the Berlin local authority with the function of investigating political affiliations to national socialism. Spranger told Schmitt that what he (Schmitt) had thought and said may be interesting and clear but that it was never clear who he was as a person. Schmitt refused to complete the questionnaire. He however referred to himself on this occasion as a Christian Epimetheus, which Meier (1998) makes much of in his analysis of Schmitt as a political theologian. We will explore the implications of Schmitt's statement further below with reference to what it tells us about the (philosophical) question.

Schmitt makes a call to the reader (and to himself perhaps) to finally grasp what this means (*Begreife endlich, was das bedeutet*). Schmitt is clearly using his own position to say something about the definition of man which he is searching for. In the opening essay of *Ex Captivitate Salus* ('Gespräch mit Eduard Spranger') we see something similar when Schmitt (*ECS* 11) notes that he finds the prosecutorial function (to which he is being subjected) even more uncanny (*unheimlicher*) than the inquisitorial function. He ascribes this to his own theological roots, because, as he points out, *Diabolos* means prosecutor (*Ankläger*) (*ECS* 11). His experience of his own prosecution, Schmitt suggests, places him in a similar position to Descartes who was confronted by the *spiritus malignus*.[27]

Following Derrida, we can say, also with reference to what happens later in 'Weisheit', that a movement takes place from the question, that is, 'Who is then my enemy?' (*ECS* 89); 'Who can I ultimately recognise as my enemy?' (*ECS* 89); and 'Who can really place me in question?' (*ECS* 89), towards an inscription of the question into a preceding self-questioning, that is, a being-placed-in-question (*PoF* 162–3). This self-questioning no longer qualifies as a theoretical question, a question of knowledge or recognition (*PoF* 162). The question is posed by someone, who first of all puts the question to himself, as an attack, a wound, a complaint, the calling into question of the one who questions (*PoF* 162–3). The enemy and the question are therefore inseparable, as expressed in Däubler's *Hymne an Italien* (1916), which Schmitt (*ECS* 90) quotes on the second-last page of 'Weisheit': 'The enemy is our own question as figure'.[28] Yet one poses the question of the enemy (as Schmitt does) only because one is first of all being placed in question by it (*PoF* 150).[29]

The 'question' which is at stake here is clearly not simply any question, but the philosophical question itself, which as Heidegger has shown, is closely connected to the nature of man.[30] Derrida (*PoF* 150) is indeed alluding here to Heidegger,

27 See further below.

28 Däubler (1919: 65): 'Der Feind ist unsre eigne Frage als Gestalt. Und er wird uns, wir ihn zum selben Ende hetzen [And he will hound us, and we him, to the same end/for the same purpose]'. References to this passage in Däubler can also be found in *GL* 213, 217 and 'TP' 61/*TdP* 87. In the latter text, Schmitt ('TP' 61/*TdP* 87), after having invoked this phrase from Däubler, notes the following: 'The enemy is not something to be eliminated for a particular reason, something to be annihilated as worthless. The enemy stands on my own level. For this reason I must contend with him in battle, in order to assure my own standard [*Maß*], my own limits, my own figure.' For an interpretation of this citation in Schmitt, see e.g. Meier (1998: 44–8); Groh (1998: 64–73); and Thiele (2011).

29 See similarly *OH* 3–5 on the question of the foreigner, who places me in question.

30 See Heidegger (2005: 32/1982: 44): 'This understanding of Being (*Seinsverständnis*) which comes to expression in philosophy [i.e. of the Being of beings] cannot be invented or thought up by philosophy itself. Rather, since *philosophizing is awakened as a primal activity of man* (*das* Philosophieren als Urhandlung des Menschen in diesem selbst erwacht), arising thus from man's nature prior to any explicit philosophical thinking, and since an understanding of Being is already implicit in the pre-philosophical existence of man (for otherwise he could not relate to beings at all) philosophy's understanding of Being expresses what man is in his pre-philosophical existence.

and one could explore the issue at stake here also through a reflection on the essence of language, as Derrida does in more detail elsewhere.[31] In *Politics of Friendship* Derrida notes that the whole history of the (philosophical) question, starting with the question of Being, as well as the whole of history which has been governed by the latter question (i.e. philosophy, epistemology, history, research, investigation, inquisition, etc.), has been accompanied by polemical violence, strategy and arms techniques.[32] Without suggesting that the question itself should be renounced, Derrida (*PoF* 150/*PA* 173) notes that at stake in 'Weisheit' can be said to be a movement beyond and before the question, before and beyond all war which enables the deployment of the question; in other words, a movement towards 'the perhaps', towards that 'space' and 'time' that 'precedes' the friend and enemy passing into each other in the form of the brother.[33] One would, Derrida (*PoF* 150/*PA* 173) suggests, have to hear an exclamation mark before the question mark. The Aristotelian 'O my friends, there is no friend!' and the Nietzschean reversal: 'O enemies, there is no enemy!', point for Derrida (*PoF* 150) towards this movement. This double outcry would be addressed both to the friend and to the enemy who is no longer or not yet (*PoF* 150). In other words at stake is a friendship – exceeding all measurement, moderation and calculation, and involving no concern for the self, thereby characterising the perfect gift – before the friend-enemy distinction of the political as well as before the Schmittian and Däublerian notion of the enemy as our own question as figure, in this way leading to a re-positioning of the political (*PoF* 244, 249).[34] Schmitt appears to also allude to this in 'Weisheit' when, after having quoted Däubler to the effect that the enemy is our own question as figure, he (implicitly) refers to the sayings of Aristotle and Nietzsche, whilst insisting (as in *The Concept of the Political*) on the necessity of making this distinction:

> Woe to him who has no *friend*, as his enemy will judge him.
>
> Woe to him who has no *enemy*, as *I* will become his enemy on the day of judgment.
>
> (*ECS* 89–90; *PoF* 165/*PA* 190)

Self-deception

Again underlining his own/man's vulnerability in the new world, Schmitt (*ECS* 87), having invoked the issue of being placed in question by questionnaires, notes

This awakening of the understanding of Being, this self-discovery of the understanding of Being, is the birth of philosophy from the Dasein in man.'

31 See Derrida (1989: 129–36).

32 See also '*Geschl* IV' 201–2/*PA* 397–8 where Derrida engages with Heidegger's Rectorate address.

33 See *Glas* 191a/*Glas* (F) 215a: 'The question is already strict-uring, is already girded being [*La question est déjà stricturante, l'être ceint*].'

34 See further Derrida ('*Geschl* IV' 175/*PA* 359) on the friend as the figureless (*le sans-figure*).

that it would show a lack of taste to delude oneself (like Stirner, perhaps) due to the luxury of one's solitary confinement into thinking that one is simply forlorn (*vereinsamt*) in the cell and not already for a long time monopolised (*vereinnahmt*). He concludes the section by asking himself/the reader whether he wants to succumb anew to deception (*Willst du von neuem dem Betrug erliegen?* (*ECS* 87)). This question can of course be understood as an admission of having been misled by national socialism, but read in the context of Schmitt's reflections on his own/man's non-autonomy, being placed in question and being prosecuted, at stake here (in addition) seems to be the question of 'human nature' or the structure of the human, particularly the relation to self-deception.

Self-deception, Schmitt (*ECS* 87) notes, belongs to isolation. Someone who is isolated thinks by himself and speaks to himself, and in soliloquy we of course speak to a dangerous sycophant (*einem gefährlichen Schmeichler*) (*ECS* 87).[35] The moralists, Schmitt (*ECS* 87) says, are correct in regarding an autobiography as a sign of vanity.[36] Yet, he notes that vanity would be the most harmless and amiable of the motives that come into play here, that is, in his semi-autobiography.[37] The holy, Schmitt notes further in a quasi-confession of guilt, do not write autobiographies. In the deepest core of the prison cell, he says, lies soliloquy and self-deception (*ECS* 87). Schmitt (*ECS* 87) compares this to the excruciating dread of Descartes who philosophises in his solitary room by the fireplace, and who thinks only of escaping the evil, deceptive spirit (*dem bösen, betrügerischen Geist*), that is, the *spiritus malignus* from whose treachery we are never safe, the least when we think ourselves secure. In the fear of deception, Descartes becomes a masked man, *l'homme au masque*. Similar to the new man, whom Schmitt spoke of earlier, the masked man is no longer naked and also no longer clothed. '*Larvatus prodeo* [I proceed wearing a mask]', he says (about himself), quoting Descartes (*ECS* 88). The dread, Schmitt (*ECS* 88) says, is so much more excruciating, as one

35 As noted in Section B above, Schmitt also alludes to this division within the self in 'TP' 60–1/*TdP* 87 with reference to General Salan who fought against both the French and the Algerian Front: 'Is it not a sign of inner division [*innerer Gespaltenheit*] to have more than one single real enemy? The enemy is our own question as figure [*Gestalt*]. If we have determined our own *Gestalt* unambiguously, where then does this double enemy come from?'

36 Balakrishnan (2000: 256) contends, with reference to the opening sentence of *ECS* 9 ('Wer bist du? *Tu quis es?*', i.e. Who are you?), that in *Ex Captivitate Salus* Schmitt answers the question 'Who was Carl Schmitt?', which would make of 'Weisheit' a kind of autobiography.

37 In seeking to understand what Schmitt is alluding to here, reference can be made to *B&S II* 86–7/*SB&S II* 136 where, in an analysis of Defoe's *Robinson Crusoe*, Derrida points out that 'every autobiography . . . presents itself through this linguistic and prosthetic apparatus – a book – or a piece of writing or a trace in general . . . which speaks of him without him, according to a trick that constructs and leaves in the world an artefact that speaks all alone [*tout seul*] and all alone calls the author by his name, renames him in his renown [*le renomme en sa renommée*] without the author himself needing to do anything else, not even be alive'. The fantasy (of being buried alive) which provokes such writing as well as technology (see also *B&S II* at 130), we will come across again in the discussion below.

comes closer to the source (*zur Quelle*), where there are ever more deceptions. Someone who thinks only of evading deception (*dem Betrug zu entgehen*) walks straight into it. The deceptions at stake here, Schmitt (*ECS* 88) comments, casting the net as wide as possible, are those of feeling and of mind, of flesh and spirit, of vice and virtue, of man and of woman. Schmitt notes, again in a quasi-confession, that he always again succumbs to deception. Yet, he says, he has always again evaded it (*bin ich ihm entgangen*) (*ECS* 88), presumably, in view of what Schmitt had just said, after having first faced up to its inescapability.[38] Also with the 'final jump [*der letzte Sprung*]', Schmitt (*ECS* 88) says, he will succeed in doing so. He ends the paragraph with a call: 'Come, dear death [*Komm, geliebter Tod*]'.

After having made this call to death, perhaps expressing thereby his deepest desire,[39] Schmitt (*ECS* 88) nonetheless acknowledges that death too can deceive us. He mentions two (mis-)understandings of death here: as a jump into the sphere of freedom,[40] and as the sweet heathen/heaths dying.[41] Schmitt's mention of death in the same breath as deception, suggests that he sees death as the ultimate deceiver.[42] All deception, Schmitt (*ECS* 88) further notes in support of this reading, is and remains self-deception. The self-shielding (*Selbstverpanzerung*) of Max Stirner, that is, seeking to exorcise the ghosts troubling man, Schmitt (*ECS* 88) notes, is self-deception of the highest order.[43] Stirner's combination of harmlessness and cunning, honest provocation and deceitful swindle, Schmitt (*ECS* 88) describes as 'unsightly' or 'hideous' (*häßlich*). Like every person obsessed with the 'I' (*jeder Ich-Verrückte*), he sees in the non-I the enemy.[44] In this way, the whole world becomes his enemy and he imagines that they must believe it when he, non-committedly (*freibleibend*), offers them a brotherly kiss (*ECS* 88).[45] In this way Stirner conceals himself from the dialectical splitting force

38 See also *PoF* 160.

39 See the discussion below.

40 An allusion to Engels (1894: 318): 'It is only from this point that men, with full consciousness, will fashion their own history; it is only from this point that the social causes set in movement by men will have, predominantly and in constantly increasing measure, the effects willed by men. It is humanity's leap from the realm of necessity into the realm of freedom [*Es ist der Sprung der Menschheit aus dem Reiche der Notwendigkeit in das Reich der Freiheit*].'

41 An allusion to Däubler's 'Grünes Elysium' (1916): 'Die Pflanzen lehren uns der Heiden sanftes Sterben [plants teach us the sweet heathen/heaths dying]'.

42 Death and Descartes' evil genius (see further below) would in other words be equated in the formless form of a death drive; see Derrida 'To Do Justice to Freud' in *Res* 70–118, and for analysis De Ville (2011a: 107–11).

43 See also *PoF* 161.

44 Schmitt (*GL* 220) charges Germans with at first seeing in every non-I the enemy, and then, in coming to their senses, treating the whole world as friend.

45 This appears to be an allusion to, on the one hand, all the 'enemies' to ownness, which Stirner detects in the family, community, society, state, nation, mankind, religion, fixed ideas, etc. and, on the other, to Stirner's epoch of egoism where there will be a union of egoists [*Verein von Egoisten*], but where one will nonetheless continue to live egoistically (Stirner 2006: 161/1845: 196).

of the 'I' (*der dialektischen Aufspaltungskraft des Ich*) and seeks to escape the enemy by deceiving him (*ECS* 88–9). However, the enemy is an objective power. He, that is, Stirner and probably also humanity in general, will not escape from him and the real enemy (*echte Feind*) does not allow himself to be deceived (*ECS* 89).

Descartes and the self as enemy

In the last two pages of 'Weisheit', which we will explore further below with reference to their Hegelian heritage, Schmitt reflects further on the enemy, asking who one can ultimately recognise as one's enemy, and concludes that this can only be someone who can put me in question. When I recognise someone as enemy, he continues, I accept that he can place me in question. But who can really place me in question? He then asks, and answers: 'Only I myself. Or my brother. That is it. The other is my brother. [*Nur ich mich selbst. Oder mein Bruder. Das ist es. Der Andere ist mein Bruder*].'[46] In his analysis of this passage, Derrida (*PoF* 163/*PA* 188) notes that the '*oder*/or' in this sentence fulfils the function of both an alternative and of equivalence, that is, 'myself as my brother: myself or, if it is not me, my brother'.[47] With the notion of being one's own enemy, Derrida (*PoF* 163) further comments, Schmitt both confirms and contradicts everything he (Schmitt) had said about the enemy up to this point. We in other words find in 'Weisheit' the same insistence on correctly identifying the enemy, as in *The Concept of the Political* and in 'The Theory of the Partisan'. Yet whereas Schmitt's concern in these latter two texts is in the first place to guard the borders of the self, that is, of the proper, in 'Weisheit' the enemy is said to be lodged within the proper, the familial, the own home, at the heart of resemblance and affinity, within the *oikeiotes*, where actually, in terms of the logic of *The Concept of the Political* and 'The Theory of the Partisan', only the friend should have been lodged (*PoF* 163, 172).[48] The enemy as the most improper, as Derrida (*PoF* 163) points out, is here identified with the proper, with the self. The most proper is in other words the most foreign, the most *unheimlich*. The enemy did not appear only after the friend, to oppose or negate him, but was always already there (*PoF* 172).

46 See likewise *GL* 217: 'History in a nutshell. Friend and enemy. The friend is the one who affirms and confirms me. The enemy is the one who places me in question (Nürnberg 1947). Who can then place me in question? In essence after all only me myself [*nur ich mich selbst*]. The friend is our own question as figure [*Gestalt*]. Concretely this means: only my brother can place me in question and only my brother can be my friend.'

47 This should be read with *PoF* 273/*PA* 303 where Derrida refers to the crime against humanity (which Schmitt was accused of) as 'the crime of crimes' and contends that this crime should be understood in terms of fratricide as 'the general form of temptation, the possibility of radical evil, the evil of evil'. See in this regard also Section B above.

48 We nevertheless saw in Sections A and B above that the attempts by Schmitt in *The Concept of the Political* and 'The Theory of the Partisan' to guard the borders of the self ultimately fail.

Schmitt arrives at this point, as we saw, by seeking a definition of man with reference to his own situation as well as of humanity in general in the new era. Descartes' evil genius, through which he (Descartes) places in question the metaphysical foundations of knowledge, plays an important role here as well. Descartes asks in this respect what the position would be if the God he believes in and has always trusted were to be an evil genius who is deceiving him so that all his certainties are actually deceptions. To understand what is at stake here, it will be useful to briefly look at Derrida's 'Cogito and the History of Madness'.[49] The evil genius invoked by Descartes can, Derrida (*WD* 52–3/*É&D* 81) contends, be likened to a 'total madness [*folie totale*]' which exceeds metaphysics, that is, 'a total derangement over which I could have no control because it is inflicted upon me – hypothetically – leaving me no responsibility for it'. After this invocation, Descartes however quickly seeks to reassure himself that he is not mad. He does so by way of language, which is, as Derrida (*WD* 54–5) points out, necessarily tied to reason, and therefore in itself entails a break with madness. Madness in this 'sense' continues to haunt philosophy, as we can also see from the reflections of Stirner and Schmitt on the Ego/ghost. The typical reaction of philosophy, when daring to go to the limit, is to immediately seek reassurance, as Descartes for example does by relying on God and reason to support the *cogito*. Philosophy, Derrida (*WD* 61) contends, can in fact only exist insofar as it suppresses madness, that is, the mad man within us. Schmitt, as we saw above, realises that one cannot simply escape the deception of the evil genius – then one walks straight into it. Schmitt's invocation of Descartes in this context, as Derrida points out in his analysis of 'Weisheit', necessarily has important implications for the enemy, which as we know is central to Schmitt's concept of the political, and therefore at the same time for his definition of man:

> Without an enemy, I go mad, I can no longer think, I become powerless to think myself, to pronounce '*cogito, ergo sum*'. For that I must have an evil genius, a *spiritus malignus*, a deceitful spirit. Did not Schmitt allude to this in his cell? Without this absolute hostility, the 'I' loses reason, and the possibility of being posed, of posing or of opposing the object in front of it; 'I' loses objectivity, reference, the ultimate stability of that which resists; it loses existence and presence, being, *logos*, order, necessity, and law. 'I' loses the thing itself. For in mourning the enemy,[50] I have not deprived myself of this or that, this adversary or that rival, this determined force of opposition constitutive of myself: I lose nothing more, nothing less, than the world.
>
> (*PoF* 175–6/*PA* 200)

49 For a more detailed discussion see De Ville (2011a: 95–112).

50 That is, if one loses the enemy, as Schmitt in *The Concept of the Political* complains is happening in the twentieth century.

Hegel and the enemy

Hegel's analysis of the struggle for recognition between self and other in the development of self-consciousness, as outlined in the *Phenomenology of Spirit* (1807), is alluded to in the following paragraphs of 'Weisheit' which need to be quoted here in full:[51]

> Who is then my enemy? Is he who feeds me in this cell my enemy? He even clothes and houses me. The cell is the garment that he donates to me. I thus ask myself: who can then ultimately be my enemy? And indeed in such a way that I recognise him as enemy, and must even recognise that he recognises me as enemy. In this reciprocal recognition of recognition lies the greatness of the concept. This is hardly suitable for an age of the masses with its pseudo-theological enemy-myths. The theologians tend to define the enemy as something [*etwas*] that has to be destroyed. I am however a legal scholar and not a theologian.
>
> Who can I ultimately recognise as my enemy? Obviously only he who can place me in question. Insofar as I recognise him as enemy, I recognise that he can place me in question. And who can really place me in question? Only I myself. Or my brother. That is it. The other is my brother. The other proves himself [*erweist sich*] to be my brother, and the brother proves himself to be my enemy. Adam and Eve had two sons, Cain and Abel. Thus begins the history of humanity. Thus appears the father of all things. This is the dialectical tension which keeps world history in motion, and world history is not as yet at an end.
>
> Thus be careful, and do not speak recklessly of enemies. Man assesses himself by means of his enemy. Man appraises himself through that which he recognises as hostility [*Feindschaft*]. Evil [*Schlimm*] indeed is the destroyer, who justifies himself thereby that the destroyer must be destroyed. However all destruction is simply self-destruction. The enemy on the other hand is the other. Remind yourself of the great statement of the philosopher: the relation to oneself, through the other, that is the truly infinite. The negation of negation, says the philosopher, does not amount to neutralisation, but the truly infinite depends on it. The truly infinite however is the foundational concept of his philosophy.
>
> (*ECS* 89)

51 See Hegel (1977: 111/1986: 145): 'Self-consciousness exists *in* and *for itself* when, and by the fact that, it so exists for another; that is, it exists only in being acknowledged. [*Das Selbstbewußtsein ist* an *und* für sich, *indem und dadurch daß es für ein Anderes an und für sich ist; d.h. es ist nur als ein Anerkanntes*.]' See Ottmann (1993/94) for the important role that Hegel plays in Schmitt's thinking as a whole, and in particular in respect of the political.

The master in Hegel's *Phenomenology of Spirit* is prepared to look death in the face, and in this way succeeds in subjecting the bondsman who fears death; yet the bondsman ultimately attains mastery through his labour. From the above-quoted passages as well as *The Concept of the Political*, it is clear that Schmitt reworks the terms of this struggle between master and bondsman, thereby providing in a certain sense a 'correction' to Hegel.[52] Schmitt's implicit objection to Hegel's account in *The Concept of the Political* is that he does not take the antithesis, that is, hostility, seriously enough: the antithesis in Hegel is always already viewed in terms of its imminent sublation in the synthesis.[53] As noted above, for Schmitt (*CoP* 58–68), the friend-enemy distinction is tied to human nature and remains a real possibility even in an era of seeming depoliticisation.[54] No synthesis takes place.[55] 'Weisheit' appears to amount to a further 'reworking' of Hegel's struggle for recognition.[56] To gain an understanding of the nature of this reworking, as well as of Derrida's reading of Schmitt in this respect, it will be helpful to look again at what Freud says about negation (*Verneinung*):

> To negate something in a judgment is, at bottom, to say: 'This is something which I would prefer to repress.' A negative judgment is the intellectual substitute for repression; its 'no' is the hall-mark of repression, a certificate of origin – like, let us say, 'Made in Germany'.[57]
>
> (Freud 2001, XIX: 236/1991, XIV: 12)

> Affirmation – as a substitute for uniting – belongs to Eros; negation – the successor to expulsion – belongs to the instinct of destruction.[58]
>
> (Freud 2001, XIX: 239/1991, XIV: 15)

52 See Balakrishnan (2000: 112); Kennedy (2004: 101–2).

53 See Rissing and Rissing (2009: 68); Meier (1998: 15, 54, 65); Müller (2003: 95–6). See also *CoP* 74/*BdP* 73 where Schmitt, after referring to Hegel's dialectic, notes that 'the triple structure weakens the polemical punch of the double-structured antithesis [[*d*]*er Dreigliedrigkeit fehlt . . . die polemische Schlagkraft der zweigliedrigen Antithese*]'.

54 See also Strauss (2007: 111).

55 See Simon (2008: 88).

56 Derrida (*PoF* 164–5), with reference to Schmitt's remark in the quotation above that all destruction amounts to self-destruction, points out that at stake here is the Hegelian notion that the infinite passes through the annihilation of self. Schmitt himself in the same passages points to the biblical and Greek origins of enmity of brothers and posits the Hegelian infinite between these two heritages.

57 'Etwas im Urteil verneinen, heißt im Grunde: "Das ist etwas, was ich am liebsten verdrängen möchte." Die Verurteilung ist der intellektuelle Ersatz der Verdrängung, ihr "Nein" ein Merkzeichen derselben, ein Ursprungszertifikat etwa wie das "*made in Germany*".'

58 'Die Bejahung – als Ersatz der Vereinigung – gehört dem Eros an, die Verneinung – Nachfolge der Ausstoßung – dem Destruktionstrieb.'

Schmitt, as Derrida (*PoF* 152) points out, was criticised by Otto Brunner for giving primacy to the enemy in his analysis of the concept of the political. Schmitt responded to this objection in the 'Foreword' to the 1963 German edition of *The Concept of the Political* by pointing out that the focus placed on negation in his analysis is not to be confused with giving it 'primacy' or viewing the enemy in a positive light. This critique, Schmitt says, 'ignores the fact that every development of a legal concept [in legal theory] emerges with dialectical necessity from the negation' (*BdP* 14). Likewise, the legal process shifts into gear only once a right has been negated. Criminal law for this reason posits a crime or misdeed (*eine Untat*) at its origin. This does not mean that a positive view is attached to the crime or that primacy is given thereto. In analysing the logic employed here, Derrida points out that for Schmitt 'starting with the enemy' does not stand in opposition to 'starting with the friend', but means that one takes one's point of departure in the antithesis (*du contraire*) without which there is neither friend nor enemy. Schmitt's insistence on the role of negation, Derrida concludes, takes us to the ultimate limit of the political, and thus to a kind of origin. He transcribes Schmitt's reasoning in respect of method as follows:

> If I were to take my point of departure in the friend, as you invite me to do, I would have to give a preliminary definition thereof. But this would be possible only with reference to an opposing term: the enemy. One must therefore take one's point of departure in this oppositional negativity, i.e. in hostility, in order to access the political. 'Starting with the enemy' is not the opposite of 'starting with the friend'. It is, on the contrary, to start from the *antithesis* without which there is neither friend nor enemy. In short, hostility is required by method and *by definition* – the very definition of definition. By the dialecticity or the diacriticity, by the necessity of the *subject* [*topique*] as well, which cannot function without the possibility of war. There is no space, there is no place – either in general or for a thought, for a definition or for a distinction – without the real possibility of war.[59]
>
> (*PoF* 152–3/*PA* 175–6)

The negativity at stake in the above quotation is what Derrida (*PoF* 139/*PA* 160) refers to earlier, with reference to Schmitt's alignment of the political and of Hegelian oppositional negation (defining the latter with reference to the political), as 'oppositional negativity in general', and as 'supreme opposition, *qua* the essence and telos of opposition, negation and contradiction'. Derrida however suggests that Schmitt goes beyond this oppositional negativity in 'Weisheit' when he (Schmitt, *ECS* 89) declares that the enemy is ultimately the self, or the

59 At stake here for Schmitt, as Derrida (*PoF* 153) points out with reference to what Schmitt says about the genesis of legal concepts, is also the pre-legal origin of the legal.

brother,[60] and that all destruction is simply self-destruction.[61] We find an allusion here to the 'origin' of hostility/destruction in what Derrida (*PoF* 155) refers to in his analysis of Plato's *Lysis*, which follows immediately after the discussion of the negative in Schmitt, as an 'aneconomic friendship'. Although Derrida does not analyse the Schmitt-Hegel connection in detail here, we can gain some insight into what is at stake in this regard when we look at Derrida's reading of Hegel with reference to Bataille in the essay 'From Restricted to General Economy: A Hegelianism without Reserve' (*WD* 251–77). In this text, Derrida analyses Bataille's reading of Hegel, with a somewhat similar focus on the negative in Hegel's dialectic. In Bataille's reading, what Hegel calls 'abstract negativity', that is, an 'absolute renunciation of meaning', and an 'absolute risking of death' comes into play (*WD* 256/*É&D* 376).[62] Here the master does not look death in the face in order to become the master of the slave and thus to attain recognition and freedom, but rushes headlong towards death (*WD* 254–5). This negativity, as Derrida (*WD* 256/*É&D* 376) puts it, 'never takes place . . . never presents itself, because in doing so it would start to work again'.[63] This 'negativity without measure', this renunciation of recognition, which is also at stake in 'Weisheit', exposes Hegelian self-consciousness as servile and vulgar consciousness (*WD* 259, 265–6, 276).

Echo

Schmitt (*ECS* 90) ends his reflections in 'Weisheit' by invoking wordplay: his own imprisonment is again the focal point:

60 The relevance of the brother here appears from Schmitt's own designation of civil war as a savage war between brothers; see 'TP' 38–9, 41/*TdP* 59, 63 as discussed in Section B above; and *ECS* 56–7. See further Schmitt's reading of Heraclitus's saying that 'war is the father of all things' as a reference to civil war (*ECS* 26); and the reference to the killing of Abel by Cain in the quotation from 'Weisheit' above, which Schmitt (*ECS* 89) refers to as lying at the origin of history.

61 Such a reading of Schmitt would be in line with a certain reading of the passage in Freud on 'Negation' quoted above as well as Derrida's reading of Freud on Empedocles's two fundamental principles (attraction and repulsion) as outlined in Section A above.

62 See in this regard Hyppolite's reading of negation/death in Hegel (Hyppolite (1974: 18); read with Hegel's Preface to the *Phenomenology of Spirit* (1977: 19)): 'Whereas in nature death is an external negation, spirit carries death within itself and gives it positive meaning. The whole *Phenomenology* is a meditation on this death which is carried by consciousness and which, far from being exclusively negative, an end point in an abstract nothingness, is, on the contrary, an *Aufhebung*, an ascent'; see also Derrida (*B&S II* 152–3).

63 See Meier (1998: 23–5, 50–4) who understands this centrality of the enemy as ultimately a reference to 'the Old Enemy', i.e. Satan. The question that Derrida would be likely to pose to Meier, even whilst accepting the coherence of this reading, is what Satan ultimately represents for Schmitt, beyond consciousness and the unconscious.

> This is the wisdom of the prison cell. I lose my time and gain my space (*Raum*).[64] Suddenly I am overcome by the quiet/silence/peace/rest (*Ruhe*)[65] which shelters the meaning of words.

Schmitt (*ECS* 90) then points to the association between *Raum* (space) and *Rom* (Rome), declaring them to be the same word.[66] Schmitt (*ECS* 90) proceeds by pointing to the wonders of the German language, specifically its spatial and germinal powers (*Raumkraft und Keimkraft*). The German language, he notes, makes possible the rhyming of 'word' (*Wort*) and 'place' (*Ort*). Even the word 'rhyme' (*Reim*) has retained or conserved (*bewahrt*) its spatial sense and allows poets to utilise the dark play (*das dunkle Spiel*) of 'rhyme' (*Reim*) and 'home (country)' (*Heimat*) (*ECS* 90–1).

In rhyme, Schmitt (*ECS* 91) contends, a word searches for the sibling sonority of its meaning (*den geschwisterlichen Klang seines Sinnes*). German rhyming, Schmitt (*ECS* 91) notes, is not the kind of bonfire (*Leuchtfeuer*) rhyme of Victor Hugo. German rhyme is in the nature of Echo, clothing and decoration or finery (*Echo, Kleid und Schmuck*) and at the same time a divining rod (*Wünschelrute*) to localise meaning (91). The words of the prophetic poets (*sibyllinischer Dichter*) Theodor Daübler and Konrad Weiβ, Schmitt (*ECS* 91) comments, now take hold of him (*ergreift mich*). The dark play of their rhyme, he notes, becomes sense and appeal or meaning and entreaty (*wird Sinn und Bitte*). I listen to their words, Schmitt (*ECS* 91) says. I hear and suffer and acknowledge, that I am not naked, but clothed and on my way to a house/home (*zu einem Haus*) (*ECS* 91). Schmitt (*ECS* 91) concludes 'Weisheit' by first paraphrasing a section of Weiβ's poem '1933' ('I see the defenceless rich fruit of the years [*die wehrlos reiche Frucht der Jahre*], the defenceless rich fruit, upon which the law of meaning [*dem Recht der Sinn*] grows') and then quoting from it:

Echo wächst vor jedem Worte;	Echo grows before every word
wie ein Sturm vom offnen Orte	like a storm from open places
hämmert es durch unsre Pforte	it hammers through our gates
	(*ECS* 91)

Echo stands here for rhyme, which Schmitt suggests is there from the first word, and which has a certain containing power.[67] With this emphasis on meaning, home and place, we appear to have moved far away from Descartes' *spiritus malignus*, Stirner's ghostly Ego and being placed in question, that is, from

64 See likewise *GL* 60.

65 *Ruhe* also has the meaning of 'resting place' or 'death': *die ewige Ruhe/die letzte Ruhe finden.*

66 See likewise Schmitt 'Raum und Rom – Zur Phonetik des Wortes Raum' in *SGN* 491–5.

67 See Connors (2011: 148).

delocalisation, meaninglessness, madness, *Unheimlichkeit*.[68] If we continue to follow Derrida's reading, then Schmitt's invocation of meaning, home and place at this point, however, amounts to a response to the deterritorialising effect of modern technology (which we also encountered in Section B above), that is, the expression of a drive for rootedness, for presence, in view of that which technology announces: our own death (*ET* 38–9). Technology, as Derrida (*B&S II* 77, 82, 117) shows in a reading of Defoe's *Robinson Crusoe*, is in the first place a response to our foundational phantasm (fear and desire) of being dead while alive, more specifically the image of being buried or swallowed alive. Technology mimics the functioning of this phantasm or self-destructive power, which itself functions in a mechanical fashion, thereby disobeying the (own) interest of reason and the law (*B&S II* 84–5).[69] Ovid's *Metamorphoses* (8 AD) can be read as testifying to the same phantasm. Echo does not simply repeat the words of Narcissus which she hears, as Schmitt seems to suggest. In repeating his (narcissistic) words ('Is anyone here?', 'Come!', 'Why do you run from me?', and 'Here let us meet') she gives them a new meaning which speaks of her overflowing love for him. When speaking in this inaugural fashion, she still keeps literally to, yet at the same time disobeys the law, that is, the limitation placed upon her by the goddess Hera (*PoF* 24, 160, 165–7; *Rog* xi–xii). When she attempts to embrace Narcissus upon his invitation to the voice he hears, he flees from her when he sees her, with the words 'Hands off! Embrace me not! May I die before I give you power o'er me!'; she repeats 'I give you power o'er me!' Here we again touch on delocalisation, meaninglessness, madness and *Unheimlichkeit*.[70] The Echo which storms through the portals invoked by Weiβ and Schmitt, now in fact appears to be a threatening and self-destructive force, which disrupts meaning and home.

The concept of the political

We saw in the above analysis that in 'Weisheit', Schmitt does not reject his earlier view of human nature or of the political, but that a certain development nevertheless takes place. He refers to his own vulnerability, his nakedness, his being placed in question, his persecution, his being haunted by a ghost, his wearing of a mask and his subjection to deception by Descartes' evil genius. In seeming contrast, the new man, to be transformed by modern technology, is portrayed as the totally other, as the incalculable and as radiating. Yet the relation between the superman (man becoming technology and thus becoming spectral) and the subhuman, with which Schmitt associates himself, is not one of simple opposition, but rather what was

68 See also Connors (2011: 146–7).

69 This interlinkage between life and death again returns us to the question of spectrality; see *B&S II* 117.

70 See likewise *SQ* 97–107 on Paul Celan's poetry, more specifically the impossibility of appropriating language, as well as its spectrality.

referred to above as a 'stricture' or a binding. This appears also from Schmitt's invocation of Stirner's 'atomic' thinking and his idea of the self consuming itself. He mocks Stirner's belief in self-identity, and speaks of the enemy as ultimately the self, or the brother. The above speaks of a division in the self, that is, of a self being haunted by a force of self-destruction; or rather, of the 'self' becoming a self only through a binding of this force of self-destruction (*PC* 402/*CP* 429). Schmitt no doubt stands sceptical towards the modern era and the 'overcoming' of man that is taking place, yet it appears from his analysis that this overcoming is a 'symptom' and that its appearance today is only possible because it is 'written' in man from the beginning. The implications of Schmitt's analysis in 'Weisheit' of what can be termed the 'differantial stricture [*stricture différantielle*]' of the living being (*PC* 351/*CP* 373) for the concept of the political with its friend/enemy distinction, are undeniable. Schmitt's text shows the latter concept to be haunted, similar to every (human) being, by a force of self-destruction. Freud (2001, XVIII: 7–64) identified this force in 'Beyond the Pleasure Principle' as the death drive. At stake in this 'force' would be a kind of friendship, that is, an act of loving, which Derrida (*PoF* 7/*PA* 23) refers to as 'lovence' (*aimance*), which is disproportionate, without calculation, with no concern for the self, with no expectation of any return.

Chapter 3

Constituent power

Introduction

The theory of constituent power found its first exposition in the writings of Abbé Emmanuel Joseph Sieyès (2003: 136–40) during the French Revolution, but its beginnings are sometimes traced back to ancient Greece (Zweig 1909: 5–9), the Roman Republic (Spang 2014: 15), the Middle Ages (Lindahl 2015: 164), or the modern era, specifically with reference to Machiavelli, Spinoza and Marx (Negri 2009: 29). Schmitt gave the theory of constituent power a vigorous reinterpretation in *Dictatorship* (1921) and in *Constitutional Theory* (1928) by merging Sieyès's thinking on constituent power with his own analyses of sovereignty and the concept of the political. In *Constitutional Theory* Schmitt furthermore explores the implications of constituent power for the modern liberal-democratic constitutional state. Constituent power is for him tied to the essence of the constitution, or what Schmitt (*CT* 75–88/*VL* 20–36) refers to as the positive concept of the constitution (*der positive Verfassungsbegriff*).[1] The constitution in this sense involves a decision about the nature and form of political existence. This decision is a conscious one, 'which the political unity, through the bearer of constituent power, reaches *for itself* and *gives to itself* [für sich selber *trifft und* sich selber gibt]' (*CT* 75–6/*VL* 21).

In recent reflections on constituent power, Schmitt's thinking in this regard has often come in for critique. The detail of these reflections need not be entered into at this point, suffice to say that the issues of identity and representation,[2] unity and plurality, as well as the so-called secularisation thesis, sovereignty and ontology, which are at the heart of Schmitt's thinking in this respect, feature prominently. The critical sentiment towards Schmitt can of course be appreciated, yet such critical readings risk bypassing some of Schmitt's central insights in respect of the concept of constituent power. The present chapter seeks to approach Schmitt differently by providing a close reading of the above-mentioned texts, and thereby

1 See further Chapter 5, Sections A and B below.
2 See Chapter 4 below.

bringing to the fore a certain hyper-political dimension to be found there. The main focus of the present chapter will be the notion of the people that appears from Schmitt's texts. It will furthermore be shown how Schmitt's analysis in this respect finds an echo in Derrida's conception of democracy and sovereignty. In exploring the notion of the people, Schmitt's analysis of political unity as a precondition for the exercise of constituent power will be closely followed, as well as his exposure of the secularised theology at stake in the notion of the people as the bearer of constituent power. This analogy between God and the people reveals the nature of the unformed and un-constitutable nature of the people, as well as its sovereignty, decisions and expressions of will. It shows the 'subject' of constituent power to be secondary, preceded by a self-destructive force, a *demos* without *kratos* and which does not simply return to itself.

Political unity

As we saw in the introduction above, Schmitt adopts and defends the positive concept of the constitution as opposed to the absolute, relative and ideal concepts. In terms of Schmitt's positive concept, the constitution as such refers to the decision by the bearer of constituent power as to the form and nature of the political unity. The positive concept thus requires that a distinction be drawn between the formation of the state or the political unity on the one hand, and its precise form and nature, which can change over time, on the other. This change can be far-reaching, for example by establishing a new state ethos, a completely new principle of state integration and a new understanding of the friend-enemy relation (*CT* 200–1/*VL* 161–2).[3] Schmitt (*CT* 126–7) acknowledges that in certain instances, for example with the revolutionary events in the United States, the formation of the state (or of states) and the act of constituent power coincide.[4] This is not however always the case, and the events in the US do not illustrate the principle at stake here. This principle is instead to be found in the French Revolution. Here the formation of the state, which established the political unity

3 This change in the nature of the political unity can also take place through the actions of constituted powers; see Schmitt (2002c: 297/*SGN* 47) where he points out that the task of parliament is to integrate the heterogeneous population and to constantly re-build political unity. The analyses of Lindahl (2007) and Botha (2010), who both point to the continuous re-founding of a political community, thus find a certain degree of support in Schmitt.

4 In 'Declarations of Independence' Derrida (*Neg* 46–54) explores the origins of the US Declaration and points to the fact that 'the people' who declares itself independent – by way of its representatives, and by invoking God – cannot be said to exist before the Declaration, but to only come into being through such Declaration. Following Schmitt's logic, Derrida's analysis cannot be extended to the adoption of a constitution, as it would as a rule be preceded by the political unity of the people, i.e. the state. As we will see in what follows, the people according to Schmitt nevertheless remains formless, even after the establishment of a state, making for a certain correspondence between the analyses of Schmitt and Derrida; see further De Ville (2011a: 43–73).

of the people or the nation, preceded the (revolutionary) act of constituent power and was not affected thereby (*CT* 126–7).[5] With political unity already a reality in the form of the state, the constituent act concerns itself only with the form and nature of such political unity. In every act of constituent power, Schmitt (*CT* 103/ *VL* 51) contends, political unity is presupposed: 'Every constitution is based on this preceding political unity'.[6]

The state in Schmitt's conception thereof does not act only through its constituted organs as normativism would have it. As he points out, such an approach would imply that the state is not itself the bearer of anything, that is, not even of the political unity, but that it is instead borne by these organs (*D* 122/*DD* 138). Like Sieyès, Schmitt (*D* 125/*DD* 141) views the nation as the substance of the state (*die staatliche Substanz*) which 'can manifest itself at any time, in the immediacy of its plenitude of force or power [*in der Unmittelbarkeit ihrer Machtfülle*]' as compared to constituted powers or state organs, which are of a mere commissary nature. Schmitt speaks in this respect of the people or the nation as 'the primordial force of all stately being [*Urkraft alles staatlichen Wesens*]' (*D* 123/*DD* 139), as 'the primordial ground of all political events, the source of all power [*Urgrund alles politischen Geschehens, die Quelle aller Kraft*]' (*CT* 128/*VL* 79), and as 'the primordial ground of all political life [*Urgrund alles politischen Lebens*]' (*CT* 129/*VL* 81).

In his analysis of what can for now be referred to as the 'collective subject' of constituent power,[7] in a chapter on the genesis (*Entstehung*) of the constitution, Schmitt again relies on the French Revolution as paradigmatic example. Here he draws a distinction between *das Volk* (the people) and *die Nation* (the nation), though not much turns on this distinction. The latter notion describes for Schmitt (*CT* 101/*VL* 50) in a concise manner the idea of a people (*Volk*) awakened to political consciousness of its own capacity to act.[8] In distinguishing his own

5 In *The Nomos of the Earth*, Schmitt appears to in a sense take a step further backwards, i.e. to the act of appropriation that preceded the formation of the state or the political unity of the people. Here he points to the three meanings of *nomos* – appropriation, division and production – which lie at the foundation of legal orders, both domestic and international. As in *Constitutional Theory*, he notes that jurists tend to focus on the constituted order, rather than the constituent processes which preceded such order, specifically appropriation (*NoE* 82). This step back is significant insofar as it reveals a law (*nomos*) as well as a lawless law (a-*nomos*) that precedes both the political unity and constituent power (see Chapter 7 below). This (lawless) law is similarly at stake in the present chapter.

6 See also Isensee (1995: 10–12; 2004: 4); Preuss (1999: 168–9); and Böckenförde (1997: 10). Galli (2015: 6–7, 9, 11) nevertheless points to the inherent instability and openness to the void of disorder of such political unity, which can e.g. be seen in Schmitt's analysis of the exception, the decision and the political.

7 Neumann (2015: 106) points to the difference between Hobbes and Schmitt in respect of constituent power as respectively constructed by the individual wills of the people and by the homogeneous collective subject, i.e. the people.

8 Schmitt here (*CT* 101/*VL* 50) and elsewhere (see e.g. *CT* 76, 77, 127/*VL* 21–2, 23, 78, 79) repeatedly mentions the 'conscious [*bewußtn*]' nature of the constituent act.

'existential' position from the abstract and ideal conceptions of the constitution (including the normativism of Kelsen) Schmitt notes the following:

> A Constitution is not based on a norm, the correctness or rightness (*Richtigkeit*) of which would provide the basis for its validity. It is based on a political decision, emerging from political *being* [*aus politischem* Sein *hervorgegangenen*] concerning the nature and norm of its own being [*Art und Norm*[9] *des eigenen Seins*]. The word 'will' [*Wille*, i.e. in the definition of constituent power in the preceding paragraph, as 'the political will, the force and authority of which is capable of taking the concrete total decision concerning the nature and form of one's own political existence'] denotes – in contrast to any dependence on a normative or abstract correctness [*Richtigkeit*] – the essentially *existential nature* [*das wesentlich* Existentielle] of this ground of validity.
>
> (*CT* 125/*VL* 76)

Schmitt (*CT* 64, 125/*VL* 9, 76) further contends that the word 'will' in the context as outlined above 'in contrast to mere norms, denotes an ontological figure [*seinsmäßige Größe*]' as the origin of an 'ought [*eines Sollens*]' and that such will entails 'concrete political being [*konkretes politisches Sein*]'. The will at stake in the exercise of constituent power is clearly tied to existence, and more specifically to the continued preservation of such existence.[10] Schmitt thus insists on the existential and concrete nature of the political will or decision expressed by way of constituent power, as well as its continued existence after the enactment of a constitution (*CT* 125–6).[11] This stands opposed to the (liberal) ideal concept of the constitution, which would make the validity of a constitution dependent on some standard of normative or abstract correctness (*einer normativen oder abstrakten Richtigkeit*) (*CT* 125/*VL* 76). Schmitt (*CT* 126) furthermore insists on the unity and indivisibility, in other words the sovereignty, of constituent power.[12] As indicated above, it is not simply another power in addition to the legislature,

9 It is tempting to give a Freudian reading to this 'slip of the pen'. Instead of the consistent references elsewhere to the constituent decision as one about the nature/type and form ('die Art und Form') of political unity, Schmitt refers here to 'die Art und Norm' (type and norm, nonetheless translated by Seitzer as 'type and form'). It however seems that this 'slip' appeared for the first time in the 8th edition (published in 1993), after Schmitt's death; see 'Vorbemerkung des Verlages zur 8. Auflage'. In the first edition, which I had access to (and seemingly until the 7th ed.) the passage appears as 'die Art und Form'.

10 See in this regard *CT* 76/*VL* 22. The drive to self-preservation is not originary in nature; see Nietzsche (1989: 21 (par 13)) and Freud (2001, XVIII: 39); see further below.

11 See also *CT* 64, 65, 271.

12 Schmitt (*CT* 102) notes that with the transfer of sovereignty from the monarch to the people, unity and indivisibility intensify because the people now politically identifies with itself in its (own) state.

executive and judiciary: 'It is the comprehensive foundation [*umfassende Grundlage*] of all other "powers" and "separation of powers"' (*CT* 126/*VL* 77).[13]

Political theology

In view of the above, it is perhaps not surprising that Schmitt's notion of (the political unity of) 'the people' has been called 'substantialist'[14] or a 'celebration of an ontology of substances'.[15] These readings are further supported by the link which Schmitt (*CT* 126/*VL* 77), in his elaboration of the 'subject' of constituent power, appears to draw between the medieval understanding of God and the secularisation of the concept of constituent power. Schmitt seems to suggest here that 'the people', existing as a being prior to the Constitution and as the bearer of the legal order, takes the place of the transcendent God.[16] There is nonetheless a certain complexity to be found in Schmitt's texts in this respect which needs to be taken account of.

Under the heading of 'The subject of constituent power', in analysing its founding nature, Schmitt (*CT* 128) refers to Sieyès's notion of the nation as always existing in the state of nature,[17] from where it expresses itself in constantly new formations. This is followed by a remark concerning the origin of Sieyès's thinking about the relation between constituent and constituted power in Spinoza's idea of the *natura naturans* (nature naturing, or God as generating power) and *natura naturata* (nature natured, or the creation). *Natura naturans* here would be the inexhaustible source or basis of all forms, though not graspable in any form itself (*CT* 128/*VL* 80).[18] Out of itself, it produces ever new forms, though itself without form (*CT* 128). Although Schmitt points to the fact that there are differences between what he calls here the 'positive theory or doctrine (*die positive Lehre*) of constituent power' and Spinoza's pantheistic metaphysic,[19] it is clear from his

13 See further Preuss (1999: 164) who reads Schmitt as arguing against the idea of a constitution terminating the revolution in favour of the idea of the institutionalisation of a permanent revolution, i.e. political decision-making needs to stay true to the revolutionary spirit of the founding generation.

14 See e.g. Wall (2012a: 78); and Loughlin (2010: 226).

15 See Lindahl (2008a: 16).

16 See Lindahl (2008a: 16–17; 2015: 165).

17 In *D* 124/*DD* 140 Schmitt notes that at stake here is not the nation in relation to other states in terms of international law, but the nation in its relation to its own constitutional formations and functionaries. In its state of nature, the nation has only rights, no duties, whereas constituted powers have no rights, only duties.

18 One hears a certain echo of this notion of formlessness when Derrida (*Rog* 25–7, 36–7) in reading Plato, notes that democracy has no single form, model or paradigm, i.e. no essence, and the concept of democracy thus 'suffers' from a certain indeterminacy or freedom of play. This also appears from Derrida's reading of Rousseau for whom there is no 'true' democracy, no proper form, no *eidos*, making democracy as such unpresentable; see *Rog* 74.

19 Phemister (2006: 81) notes in this respect that 'Spinoza's conception of God is the conception of a necessary being immanent within the created world of nature (*natura naturata*) that comprises the

description of constituent power in *Constitutional Theory* and in *Dictatorship*, that the people as the bearer of constituent power is indeed to be perceived of as unformed or un-constitutable, similar to the *natura naturans* (*D* 123–5/*DD* 139–41).[20] In *Dictatorship*, Schmitt gives a dramatic portrayal of Sieyès's theory of constituent power as giving expression to the unorganisable organising (*unorganisierbar Organisierende*),[21] and of its force or powers as abyssal in nature: 'From the infinite, ungraspable abyss of its force (*dem unendlichen, unfaßbaren Abgrund ihrer Macht*), new forms emerge incessantly, which it can shatter (*zerbrechen*) at any time, and through which its own force (*Macht*) is never categorically limited' (*D* 123/*DD* 139). The people as constituent power is undoubtedly sovereign in Schmitt's account. As we saw earlier, he describes it as a unity and as indivisible (*CT* 126/*VL* 77).[22] Schmitt therefore recognises a certain strength (*Stärke*), but importantly also a weakness (*Schwäche*) in its unorganised nature: it has to decide on the basic nature of its political form and organisation, without itself being formed or organised (*CT* 131/*VL* 83).[23] Its expressions of will (*Willensäußerungen*) are for this reason/hence (*deshalb*), Schmitt (*CT* 131/*VL* 83) says, easily misjudged, misconstrued or falsified. It is not however immediately clear what the link is between the unformed and unorganised nature of the people and the misjudgement, misconstruction and falsification of its expressions of will, which Schmitt refers to here. Schmitt (*CT* 131–2) after all indicates that the people can always express itself through a simple 'yes' or 'no', especially when it comes

modes that follow from God's eternal essence (*natura naturans*)'. Schmitt's conception of God is transcendent, though for him in a democracy, this transcendence is transformed into the immanence of the people. There can consequently be no appeal to a transcendent source of power such as God in a democratic state. Such an appeal (unless the will of God is equated with the will of the people) would re-instate the distinction between high and low, superior and inferior and would entail a denial of immanence; see *CT* 266–7.

20 See also *CT* 128, 129, 271 and 279 on the formlessness of the people. On a certain reading, notions such as the 'multitude' and the 'crowd' can be understood as an attempt to portray this formlessness vis-à-vis the notion of 'the people', understood as an expression of unity; see Hardt and Negri (2004: xiv, 99); Virno (2004: 22–3, 25); Wall (2012a: 77).

21 Kalyvas (2009: 123–4) detects a 'disquieting', 'blatant' and 'fatal' 'contradiction' or 'tension' in Schmitt between this notion and the idea of a 'popular sovereign . . . capable of lucid and self-conscious political action', and ascribes this contradiction to Schmitt's 'sometimes peculiar and rigid understanding of democracy' (at 124). In the present chapter, a different reading is contended for.

22 Schmitt speaks in similar terms of the state and its authority (*CT* 101), the nation (*CT* 103) and the political unity (of France) (*CT* 104).

23 Schmitt (*CT* 268–79) distinguishes between the people as unformed and unorganised insofar as it is the bearer of constituent power as well as of public opinion and of acclamation on the one hand, and as constitutionally organised insofar as the constitution provides for a certain procedure for the exercise of its will through elections/voting on the other; see also Schmitt (2014b: 49). Schmitt (*CT* 271, 279) insists that the latter procedures do not mean that the people are in every respect formed and organised. For an analysis of acclamation and public opinion in their relation to glory and sovereignty (including the role of the media in this regard), see Agamben (2011).

to the fundamental decision concerning its own total existence.[24] It might be that the difficulty lies in the translation by a national assembly or convention of this 'yes' or 'no' into something more concrete, that is, the specific nature and form of political existence, or the related possibility that some political party, or a racial, ethnic or other minority group, may falsely claim to act in the name of the people.[25] Yet these may not be the difficulties, or at least not the only difficulties, that Schmitt is alluding to. In view of the analysis undertaken in Chapter 2, Sections A–C, and Schmitt's own pronouncements in the *Glossarium* on free will,[26] the misjudgement, misconstruction and falsification of the will of the people go beyond what it consciously desires. The latter, as we saw earlier, concerns as a rule its own self-preservation. Misjudgement, misconstrual and falsification are inevitabilities, it appears, because the conscious expression of will always already involves a translation of non-conscious forces, that is, of a certain desire, which as we will see below, Schmitt associates with God as well as with democracy in its perverted sense.[27]

Schmitt points out further that the people, because of its unorganised nature, cannot itself draft a constitution, that is, *exercise* constituent power.[28] For this purpose it needs representatives (Chapter 4 below), in the form of a national assembly or convention (*CT* 132–3). Schmitt (*D* 127) refers to such an assembly as exercising a sovereign dictatorship. The delegates, that is, the extraordinary representatives in such an assembly, have extremely broad powers and are not

24 Schmitt (*CT* 271–9) recognises two forms through which this 'yes' or 'no' can be expressed: acclamation or protest and public opinion; see further Neumann (2015: 156–62).

25 See *CPD* 27; and Isensee (1995: 45).

26 Schmitt (*GL* 314) responds as follows to Alfred Andersch's insistence on mankind's free will: 'It [i.e. free will] means something completely different than determinism or indeterminism. It means something which every decent person does, which you and I have always done, when we fell in love, when we became politically inspired, when we worked hard [*als wir uns ins Zeug warfen*]. That was in truth not freedom of will; it was blind pre-command [*Vorgebot*]. That is the word and thereby also the matter and the situation: blind pre-command [*das blinde Vorgebot].*' Two interpretations appear possible here: (1) an attempt by Schmitt to escape responsibility for his political choices by ascribing such choice to a blind pre-command; see Linder (2015: 11); and (2) a reference to a certain law of law (*das blinde Vorgebot*) that precedes such choices. This law, which Derrida (1997b: 14) speaks of in terms of identity, i.e. as 'a self-differentiating identity, an identity different from itself, having an opening or gap within itself. . .this impossibility of being one with oneself', as Schmitt himself points out, goes beyond both determinism and indeterminism. See further Chapter 4 below.

27 Such a reading would resonate with the analysis of Derrida (*Rog* 28–41) of a certain inherent weakness of democracy – its openness to perversion, abolition or suicide, or what Derrida refers to as autoimmunity; see also *CPD* 28; and see Chapter 2, Sections A–C above for a discussion of the concept of the political, which, as noted there, is inextricably linked to sovereignty and to constituent power in Schmitt's thinking.

28 Schmitt (*D* 125/*DD* 141) in this respect draws a distinction between the 'substance' of constituent power and its 'exercise'. See likewise Pasquino (1988: 375, 379).

bound by any imperative mandate.[29] As Sieyès (2003: 139) also contended, they do not convey an already existing will, but partake in the formation of such will (*D* 125). The delegates nevertheless remain unconditionally dependent on the will of the people, even though this will may be unclear. The people in other words remains sovereign, with the power to at any time revoke its delegation of power to the constituent assembly.[30] The question of clarity of will brings us back to the unformed nature of the people discussed above, as well as the difficulty in the translation of unconscious desires, which, as we saw, Schmitt seems to allude to. Schmitt (*D* 125) comments that the will of the people *should* in fact be unclear, as that is part and parcel of the unconstitutability of constituent power. Should it be clear or precise, that is, shaped in some or other way, it would no longer be a constituent, but a constituted will. This construction of constituent power by Sieyès, Schmitt (*D* 124/*DD* 140) furthermore notes, points ahead to the philosophy of the nineteenth century[31] in terms of which God, the centre of the world, is viewed as an 'objective obscure' (*objektiv Unklares*).[32]

In order to gain an understanding of what is at stake here, Schmitt's description in *Dictatorship* and *Constitutional Theory* of the nature of constituent power on the analogy of God as 'objective obscure' as well as 'natura naturans' needs to be read with the Gnostic understanding of God analysed by Schmitt in *Political Theology* II.[33] Schmitt (*PT II*: 122) refers to the conception of God of Gregory of Nazianzus (329–390AD) ('The One – *to Hen* – is always in mutiny – *stasiazon* – against itself – *pros heauton*'), which Schmitt (*PT II* 122–5) in turn ties to the

29 Preuss (2015a: 6) contends that this Assembly, despite its name, is a constituted power.

30 In a democracy, the Assembly that drafts the constitution can clearly take many forms and attempts can be made to limit and control its powers, as for example in Arato's multi-stage model of constitution-making (see e.g. Arato 2010), yet it cannot, despite claims to the contrary, escape the link to sovereignty which Schmitt spells out here; see also Kalyvas (2000: 1537–8).

31 Schmitt appears to be alluding here to counter-revolutionary thinkers like Donoso Cortes who, together with de Maistre and Bonald find a regular recurrence in his texts. Cortes is at times the primary focus; see *DC*. Cortes (1879: 30–1) for example speaks of God in the following terms: 'God himself, who is the author and governor of political [*sic*], is the author and governor of domestic, society. In the most hidden, in the highest, in the most serene and luminous point, of the heavens, there exists a tabernacle, inaccessible even to the choirs of the angels; in that inaccessible tabernacle is perpetually verified the prodigy of prodigies, the mystery of mysteries. There is the Catholic God, one and triple; one in essence, triple in persons.'

32 See also Isensee (1995: 21) on the analogy in the theory of constituent power between God and his decrees and the people and their will. The people, he points out, take on a similarly mysterious form with the attributes of 'primum principium, immotum movens, norma normans, genitum, non factum, creation ex nihilo [first principle, immovable mover, norming norm, engendered, not made, creation out of nothing]'. According to Isensee, the will of the people is likewise mysterious, unfathomable, in no need of justification and impossible to explain.

33 See also Schmitt (2005c: 166 (10 July 1914)), which suggests that he regarded himself as a Gnostic; see further Groh (2014); Linder (2015: 16–20); Vatter (2015: 14–19).

concept of the political.[34] In his analysis of this passage, Schmitt expresses his agreement with an understanding of God in such dualistic terms:

> Gnostic dualism juxtaposes the God of love, a God external to this world, viewed as God of salvation, to the just God, the Lord and creator of this evil world. The two gods are in a state of open war, or at least in a relationship of unbridgeable alienation similar to a kind of dangerous Cold War, in which the enmity can be more intense than any enmity found in the simplicity of a fight on traditional battlefields. The reason for the persuasiveness and contradictory difficulties of Gnostic dualism is not so much the prevalence of the old mythical and metaphorical symbols of light and darkness; rather, they stem from an almighty, all-knowing and all-benevolent creator God who cannot be the same as a God of salvation for the world he created.[35]
>
> (*PT II* 124/*PT II* (G) 93)

Schmitt further comments as follows about the nature of the relationship between Gods of such a kind:

> The lord of a world in need of change, that is, a failed [*verfehlten*] world (to which is attributed this need for change because he does not support the change, but rather resists it) and the liberator, the inducer of a changed, new world cannot be good friends. They are, so to speak, enemies *per se* [von selbst].[36]
>
> (*PT II* 125/*PT II* (G) 94)

It thus appears that the people as the bearer of constituent power, by analogy, needs to be understood as at war with itself or characterised by a force of self-destruction. Schmitt, as we saw, refers to this force with the notions of *natura naturans* and the formless and unorganised nature of the people. It is exactly this force that is most difficult to translate.

Fear and the Leviathan

Schmitt's reflections on the state in *The Leviathan in the State Theory of Thomas Hobbes* (1938) provides further support for the above reading of the *natura*

34 It appears that Schmitt (*PT II* 123) agrees with Hans Blumenberg's assessment that the Christian Middle Ages entailed an unsuccessful attempt at mastery or overcoming of Gnosticism, and specifically of its friend-enemy conception of God; see further Chapter 4 below.

35 Groh (2014: 88) reads these passages as referring to a Christological dualism in terms of which the second person of the trinity is split. As God-man, Christ contains in himself the evil world of man as well as the role of saviour. See further Chapter 2, Section A above.

36 See further Herrero (2015: 157–77), who indirectly responds to those who seek to discredit Schmitt's so-called secularisation thesis.

naturans, the unformed and unorganised nature of the people, as well as the analogy to God as the 'objective obscure' and as at war with himself. Here Schmitt (*TL* 31) follows Hobbes in the contention that what ultimately drives the multitude/people to form the state is fear of the state of nature.[37] This is because, according to Hobbes, man is in the state of nature a wolf to man (*homo homini lupus*). Schmitt dramatises the situation as follows:

> The terror [*Schrecken*] of the state of nature drives anguished individuals [*angsterfüllten Individuen*] to come together; their fear [*Angst*] rises to an extreme [*steigert sich aufs äußerste*]; a spark [*Lichtfunke*] of *Reason* [Ratio] flashes – and suddenly there stands in front of them a new god.
>
> (*TL* 31/*DL* 48)

Derrida's analysis of Hobbes's reflections on the origins of the state in *The Beast & the Sovereign I* ties in closely with the reading of Schmitt undertaken here.[38] Worthy of note in view of our earlier discussion is, in the first place, Derrida's description of Hobbes's Leviathan as appearing 'in the formless form of animal monstrosity, in the figure without figure of a mythological, fabulous, and non-natural monstrosity, an artificial monstrosity of the animal' (*B&S I* 25/*SB&S I* 49, read with the following page). Schmitt (*TL* 21/*DL* 34) clearly had a great affinity for this image of the state as having to secure peace, which as he points out stands in a close relation to the other elementary force (*elementarer Gewalt*), the Behemoth, who represents the 'revolutionary, anarchistic force of the state of nature', or civil war.[39] The (extreme) fear which Schmitt points to in the passage above likewise forms an important part of Derrida's analysis in *The Beast & the Sovereign I*.[40] Derrida shows here how Hobbes's Leviathan, and thus sovereignty itself, is constructed and maintained through an uncanny fear, a fear not in the first place of one's fellow man, but of the wolf (or beast) within the self, that is, the Freudian drive to self-destruction and Heideggerian *Unheimlichkeit*.[41] Schmitt

37 Also see Schmitt (*PT* 51/*PT* (G) 54), quoting Engels with approval: 'the essence of the state, as that of religion, is mankind's fear of itself'.

38 See further De Ville (2012).

39 As we will see in Chapter 6 below, according to Schmitt, Hobbes had however underestimated the mythological forces at stake in invoking the image of the Leviathan.

40 In Virno (2004: 21–35), the fear/anguish at stake here is instead of the multitude, associated by Hobbes with the state of nature (for Virno the multitude is united in their feeling of not-at-homeness in the world), as distinguished from the people, who is closely associated with the sovereign state, and which has now become obsolete. See similarly Douzinas (2013: 130–3) on the fear of the crowd.

41 Derrida's analysis in *The Beast & the Sovereign II* concludes (at 278–90) with an analysis of the notion of *Walten* in Heidegger's *Introduction to Metaphysics*, where Heidegger (2000: 156–76) analyses Sophocles' *Antigone*, specifically the section where man is characterised as essentially *deinon* and which Heidegger translates as uncanny (*unheimlich*). Here we again find the tension between the un-homely and being-at-home (see Chapter 2, Section B above). Heidegger

(*TL* 21/*DL* 34) puts it in similar terms, with reference to Vaugn for whom 'the Leviathan is "the only corrective" to the Behemoth. The absolutism of the state is, accordingly, the oppressor of the irrepressible chaos inherent in man [*eines im Kern, nämlich in den Individuen, ununterdrückbaren Chaos*]' (*TL* 21–2/*DL* 34). It is the repression of this uncanny love of fear, that is, of the wolf or the beast, Derrida (*B&S I* 210/*SB&S I* 281–2) suggests, which furthermore leads to the contradictory logic (in Hobbes) of excluding the possibility of concluding a covenant with brute beasts or with God (God is thus like the beasts), while at the same time maintaining God as the model of sovereignty (the sovereign as son of God). God, in other words, 'is' nothing but the beast repressed; or, one could say, the beast is God, without being (God) (*B&S I* 50/*SB&S II* 82).[42] This conception of God, which shows certain similarities with Schmitt's conception of God's dualism,[43] would open the way for a move beyond political theology. It calls for a re-conception of the structure of sovereignty as well as of the people as the bearer of constituent power. Derrida's analysis shows that the self, and ultimately sovereignty, is never purely present to itself. It instead arrives at itself by way of a certain 'binding' of forces, as we saw above. Sovereignty in this way, whether the bearer thereof is the monarch[44] or the people, ultimately shows itself to be

(2000: 167/1983: 166) points out that man as subject takes possession of these 'violent forces' (*Gewalten*), allowing him to believe that he is the author, master, inventor and possessor of 'language and understanding, building and poetry'. In doing so, man however, in Derrida's words, 'ignores the fact that he is first of all gripped, seized, that he must take them [i.e. these powers] on, and then he becomes basically a foreigner . . . to his own *Unheimlichkeit*' (*B&S II* 288/*SB&S II* 394). Man furthermore remains exposed to the violence of *Walten* even though he can exercise this force himself, which makes of him, in Heidegger's assessment, the uncanniest of beings (*B&S II* 287). The creators of the polis (i.e. the foundation and place (*Grund und Ort*) of the being of man), seeing that they are without constitution (*Satzung*) and limit (*Grenze*), are specifically mentioned as un-homely in this sense (Heidegger 2000: 163/1983: 162). Like building, such state-founding, Heidegger (2000: 167/1983: 166) notes, 'is not an application of the faculties that the human being has, but is a disciplining and disposing/taming and joining of the forces that come to grip man and by virtue of which beings disclose themselves as such [*ist nicht eine Betätigung von Vermögen, die der Mensch hat, sondern ist ein Bändigen und Fügen der Gewalten, kraft deren das Seiende sich als ein solches erschließt, indem der Mensch in dieses einrückt*]'.

42 This conception, if one can call it such, of God is in line with the movement towards a God without sovereignty, explored by Derrida (*Rog* 114), with reference to Heidegger.

43 See above, and see *PoF* 109 n13 where Derrida reads Schmitt's *Political Theology II* in similar quasi-psychological terms; see further Chapter 2, Section A above.

44 See Böckenförde (1994: 61–3) who points out that the monarch can only be regarded as the bearer of constituent power in a world order legitimated by God, and where the monarch acts as the representative of God's omnipotent will. This world order came to an end with the French Revolution, so that thereafter only the people can be regarded as the legitimate bearer of constituent power. It however appears that for Schmitt (*CT* 136–9) the French Revolution did not announce a clean break from the principle of monarchic legitimacy in respect of being the bearer of constituent power, but an alternative source of legitimacy, which only in the twentieth century became generally established.

a drive for mastery, which is necessarily divisible, that is, located within a field of force.

Demos without sovereignty

The conception of sovereignty explored above has important implications both for the subject of constituent power and for the decision at stake in constituent power, as Derrida spells out in *Politics of Friendship* and in *Rogues*.[45] In his analysis of democracy in *Rogues*, Derrida seeks to think this concept in a way that goes beyond the question of who has the proper authority, that is, of who has the right to give or to take some right, to give him or herself some right, questions that are central to Schmitt's analysis as well as to some of those who have recently written in opposition to Schmitt. The subject of decision[46] can no longer be the classical subject, that is, free and self-willed, but one that is 'originally affected' by the decision (*PoF* 68/*PA* 87). A 'decision' by such a 'subject' must necessarily involve a certain passivity, an exposure which surprises the very subjectivity of the subject (*PoF* 68/*PA* 87).[47] This requires 'a certain unconditional renunciation of sovereignty . . . a priori. Even before the act of decision' (*Rog* xiv). A certain hospitality can be said to be at stake here, towards the impossible itself, in view of what Derrida (*PoF* 68/*PA* 87) refers to as 'an old forgotten invitation'.[48] This hospitable and passive decision entails a decision of

The notion of legitimacy is incidentally central to Schmitt's theory of constituent power (see *CT* 136–9) and stands opposed to the liberal and legal positivist insistence on the mere legality of a constitution. For Schmitt, as Galli (2015: 17) points out, legitimacy precedes legality. In Derrida's thinking, incalculable justice (or the law of law) would in turn precede (Schmitt's conception of) legitimacy; see *AR* 250; and see further Chapter 7 below.

45 These reflections go beyond the question that some constitutional theorists tie to the concept of constituent power, i.e. 'who are we?', a question that retains the notion of essence. The conception of sovereignty as analysed here ties in more closely with the Levinasian move of Diamantides (2015: 115) to displace the question 'who are we?' with the question 'is it righteous to be we?'.

46 The relation between Schmitt's seeming privileging of 'decisionism' in *Political Theology* and of concrete order thinking *On the Three Types of Juristic Thought* remains the subject of debate; see e.g. Brännström (2016) and Ojakangas (2007: 213–14).

47 This is one of Derrida's main arguments in 'Declarations of Independence' (*Neg* 46–54), which is often overlooked. The undecidability between constative and performative speech acts at stake there is only one step in the process of going beyond this traditional opposition and beyond the notion of performative mastery towards a notion of the perverformative or performative powerlessness, i.e. of a 'subject' of speech acts always already dispossessed of the ownership of the text that it seemingly produces (for itself); see further De Ville (2011a: 54–6). See likewise Derrida (1998c: 39/1996: 69) where he notes that the experience of law as language 'would be ostensibly *autonomous*, because I have to speak this law and appropriate it in order to understand it *as if* I was giving it to myself, but it remains necessarily *heteronomous*, for such is, at bottom, the essence of any law. The madness of the law places its possibility lastingly [*à demeure*] inside the dwelling of this auto-heteronomy.'

48 Despite the similarities on the face of it between Derrida's notion of the democracy to come and the multitude in Negri (2009) (as not representable, as without sovereignty, as inventive, as

> the other in me that decides and rends [*l'autre en moi qui décide et déchire*] . . . a rending decision as decision of the other. Of the absolutely other in me, of the other as the absolute that decides of me in me [*une décision déchirante comme décision de l'autre. De l'autre absolu en moi, de l'autre comme l'absolu qui décide de moi en moi*].
>
> (*PoF* 68/*PA* 87)

Who exactly 'is' this displaced subject of constituent power? We saw above that although Schmitt insists on the political unity of the people as precondition for the exercise of constituent power, the people nevertheless remains formless.[49] There is yet another dimension to this formlessness in *Constitutional Theory*. In discussing the 'place' occupied by the people in relation to an existing constitution, Schmitt (*CT* 271–2/*VL* 242–3) points out that the people cannot be viewed as an official or a state organ, and then refers also to other negative determinations of who the people are. In political theory, he notes, this 'peculiar negativity' (*eigenartige Negativität*) is likewise recognised, or rather, 'there is no failure to appreciate it'.[50] '[I]n a special sense of the word [*in einer besonderen Bedeutung dieses Wortes*]', Schmitt points out, the people are all 'who are *not* honoured and distinguished, all who are *not* privileged, all who are *not* prominent due to property, social position, or education' (*CT* 271/*VL* 242–3).[51] He refers here to Schopenhauer who stated that those who do not understand Latin belong to the people. Exactly who is so excluded can furthermore change in the course of time, as the examples of the French (bourgeois) and Russian (proletariat) Revolutions show. Schmitt (*CT* 272/*VL* 243) relies here on the notion of a 'negation that wanders further' (*wanderte die Negation weiter*), which ties in closely with the role and importance he attaches to negation in the 1963 Preface to *The Concept of the Political* (*BdP* 14; Chapter 2, Section C above). There as here he insists on an 'originary' role for the antithesis in Hegel,[52] and substitutes Hegel's tripartism for

desirous), there are certain marked differences, as can be seen here in the notion of the impossible. With the latter notion we appear to go beyond Negri's conception of constituent power in terms of *potentia*/*potenza* (strength, i.e. a constituent subject 'capable of producing absolute events' (27)), which he contrasts with *potestas*/*potere* (power) or sovereignty (22). There appears to be a greater similarity between Derrida's notion of the impossible and Agamben's invocation of potentiality (if understood as powerlessness, impotence (*impotenza*)) in this context; see Agamben (1998: 45) where he seeks to go beyond Negri. See also Lindahl (2013: 186) who reads Schmitt's notion of the 'formless forming' as referring to an 'unordered domain of superabundant possibilities'.

49 A distinction needs to be drawn between the pre-ontological formlessness at stake here and the notion of plurality which some have opposed to Schmitt's notion of political unity; see e.g. Van der Walt (2010a 15–16; 2010b 111–16); Botha (2010: 74–6).

50 Schmitt's language here (*VL* 242) is torturous, and the English translation (*CT* 270) struggles to portray the succession of negatives employed here.

51 There are clearly resonances here with Ranciere's understanding of the *demos* as the part which has no part (1999: 9).

52 See also *PoF* 152–3.

a bipartite antithesis because of the latter's polemical striking power (*polemische Schlagkraft*) (*CoP* 74/*BdP* 73). The bearer of this negation (*Träger dieser Negativität*), Schmitt (*CT* 271–2/*VL* 242–3) notes, appears in ever new forms and in each case sets itself up in opposition to those who *do* possess honour, privilege, education, property, social position, etc.

In view of the link which Schmitt (*CT* 271–2/*VL* 242–3) posits between, on the one hand, the peculiar and 'originary' negativity at stake here and the notion of the people as essentially without organisation and form on the other (*als nichtorganisierte und nichtformierte Größe*), we can raise the same question here as Derrida does in relation to Hegel:

> What might be a 'negative' that could not be *relevé*? And which, in sum, as negative, but without appearing as such, without presenting itself, that is, without working in the service of meaning, would work? but would work, then, as pure loss?
>
> (Derrida 1982: 107/1972a: 126)

The *demos* understood in terms of negativity thus conceived would be without limit as well as without *kratos*, that is, without power or sovereignty (*Rog* 100; 'Auto' 120). This inevitably means a break in the link insisted on by Schmitt between the state, that is, the political unity of the people, and constituent power.[53] The *demos* would be in principle without limit in the sense that it would not be subject to any exclusion in respect of the whole world of singularities, that is, living and non-living[54] beings, whether human or non-human (*Rog* 54; Chapter 6 below). Democracy in this unconditional sense, or what Derrida (*Rog* 8–9) refers to as the 'democracy to come' makes of democracy a concept that we do not as yet know the meaning of. It resists the idea that there are any democracies worthy of the name in existence today. This is because democracy as conceived in the tradition, also in Schmitt, has always entailed a return to the self of those included,[55] and it has consequently always been exclusionary, both in a political and in a socio-economic sense. Yet as Derrida shows in *Rogues* (with reference to Plato and Aristotle in Chapter 2, but also elsewhere) the tradition at the same time portrays democracy as a concept without essence, which Schmitt also seems to allude to with his notion of a peculiar negativity, in speaking of the people as *natura naturans*, as formless, as unorganised, and in criticising, as we will see further in the discussion below, the 'boundless extension' (*grenzenlose*

53 See above.

54 Non-living beings would be included specifically insofar as the memory of these beings is concerned; see *Rog* 54.

55 See Loughlin (2014: 219–20); Spang (2014: 18); Lindahl (2008b: 335). This movement towards the self, as Derrida (*Rog* 15/*Voy* 36) points out, takes place by virtue of desire and pleasure: 'circle of a self-enjoyment [*cercle d'une jouissance de soi*]', i.e. through autoaffection.

Ausdehnung) of the concept of democracy (*CT* 257/*VL* 225). This 'without essence' refers to the plasticity of democracy, that is, its tendency to continuously and forcefully change its form, with the constant risk of civil war (*Rog* 74). Democracy understood thus, finds itself unceasingly appropriated and conditioned within space and time both by theorists of democracy and by those calling themselves the (representatives of the) people. In Schmitt specifically, as we will see further in Chapter 4 below, this appropriation and conditioning comes to the fore in the emphasis placed on the representation of sovereignty, so that democracy can effectively protect itself from itself.[56]

The democracy to come can be said to issue an urgent call for what Derrida (*Rog* 73/*Voy* 107) refers to as 'the impossible' to be made possible. What would this entail? A political revolution as traditionally conceived, that is, as a seizure of power, would not by itself be capable of bringing about the democracy to come (*FWT* 83). What is required and what the democracy to come calls for is a revolution within the revolution, a poetic revolution, beyond all sovereignty (*B&S I* 269–73; *Rog* 29).[57] The poetic revolution is to be understood in close association with the concept of decision explored earlier in this section.[58] This call applies not only to decisions within the nation state, but also in the field of international law, with the sovereign state at its foundation.[59] Derrida's notion of the New International, the primary aim of which would be to transform or re-invent international law, including its concepts and the field of permissible intervention (*SoM* 105–6), can be understood as closely aligned to such a poetic revolution. The New International is determined by what can be called Schmitt's 'peculiar negative', that is, it is an alliance 'without status, without title, and without name, barely public even if it is not clandestine, without contract, "out of joint," without

56 Schmitt's analyses of sovereignty and commissarial dictatorship (to ensure a return to order under a state of exception) can be read as an acknowledgement of another structural 'characteristic' of democracy (closely aligned to its indeterminacy – see above), which Derrida highlights in *Rog* 35–6/*Voy* 60: its own deferral, that is, the dictation 'that democracy be *sent off* [renvoyer] elsewhere, that it be excluded or rejected or expelled under the pretext of protecting it on the inside by expelling, rejecting or sending off to the outside the domestic enemies of democracy'. In Schmitt's reading of the Weimar Constitution, the president had almost unlimited powers to 'save the constitution' (including the temporary suspension of most of the provisions of the Constitution and thereby of (certain) democratic rights and freedoms as well as democratic institutions) from the possibility of a political party (a domestic enemy of democracy) seizing power and then abolishing democracy. At stake in commissarial dictatorship is thus ultimately the safeguarding or preservation of the nature and form of political existence decided upon in the constitution through the exercise of constituent power.

57 This should be understood in view of the analysis of the political in Chapter 2, Sections A–C above. For Schmitt (*PT II* 125/*PT II* (G) 94), revolution, 'in contrast to reformation, reform, revision and evolution', is tied to the concept of the political: 'Revolution', Schmitt notes here, 'ist eine feindliche Auseinandersetzung'.

58 See also Thomson (2005: 171–3).

59 See Chapter 7 below on the coming *nomos* of the earth; and see further Kreuder-Sonnen (2013) on the extension to the transnational and international levels of the state of exception.

coordination, without party, without country, without national community ... without co-citizenship, without common belonging to a class' (*SoM* 107/*SdM* 141–2). It is in other words an alliance of those seeking to 'realise' or at least 'negotiate' with the impossible, that is, the 'democracy to come', in its alignment with absolute hospitality or justice beyond law.[60]

Conclusion

The above analysis has sought to show that Schmitt's texts stand open to a reading in respect of constituent power where the *demos* is viewed as formless and as a groundless force. The political unity which Schmitt speaks of is thus always a fictional unity, a fiction with its source not in the imagination, but in *khōra* (Chapter 5, Section A below). Schmitt's conception of the *demos* is such that it does not provide for a presence, a substance, an identity or ontology, but rather for a certain hauntology on the model of a dualist conception of God. The God at stake here consists of a loving God of salvation and a just creator-God, in a state of permanent war with each other.[61] The fiction of the sovereignty of God can only appear as the result of a certain repression of weakness, of what was referred to above as a force of self-destruction. Constituent power returns to itself, yet it contains within itself, thereby exceeding itself, a force, the weakest force, that is, a certain powerlessness.[62] For Schmitt, constituent power is in other words split in itself, before the distinction between friend and enemy comes into play.[63] As we have seen in recent years, protest, resistance and rebellion against the existing order can take multiple forms, can be organised by many different means and can have different aims on the local, national and/or global level. The conception of constituent power explored above undoubtedly gives the *demos*, both nationally and globally, the right, no, *the obligation* to call to account and even to re-constitute constituted powers when the latter stray too far from the obligation of absolute hospitality.

60 See Derrida (2005c: 125–6; *SoM* 81–2; *Rog* 87–8). There are clear resonances in respect of hospitality between Derrida's New International and Hardt and Negri's notion of the multitude; see e.g. Hardt and Negri (2000: 103): 'The multitude is a multiplicity, a plane of singularities, an open set of relations, which is not homogeneous or identical with itself and bears an indistinct, inclusive relation to those outside of it'.

61 See also Chapter 2, Section A above.

62 The approach adopted here shows a certain correspondence with those that seek to 'escape' from sovereignty by dislocating constituent power from constituted power, i.e. by construing constituent power as not having its *telos* in the constituted, as suggested e.g. by Wall (2012b: 57–65), following Benjamin, Negri and Agamben.

63 Agamben (2000: 30) likewise sees a split in the people, but then understood in terms of biopolitics as 'on the one hand, the *People* as a whole and as an integral body politic and, on the other hand, the *people* as a subset and a fragmentary multiplicity of needy and excluded bodies'. See also Minca and Rowan (2016: 137–52, 174–82) who find support for such a reading in Schmitt's *State, Movement, People*. *Cf. B&S I* 326–7 and 330 for a somewhat sceptical assessment of the potential of biopolitics to reinvigorate politics.

Chapter 4

Identity and representation

Introduction

Political representation, a consequence of the modern state, is today said to be in crisis, specifically the representation offered by mainstream political parties. Representative state institutions in general are likewise under scrutiny. This 'crisis' can be detected inter alia in the low turnout for many elections, the declining membership of political parties, the general distrust in politicians and the declining interest in mainstream politics (Tormey 2015: 15–36). Those who participate in recently formed movements and parties no longer want to be 'represented', but rather to directly act themselves (Tormey 2015: 2; Douzinas 2013: 166–7, 194). The calls for an end to representation have been explained with reference to the perception of a by-and-large decadent and self-serving political class, the accompanying resistance to being represented by this class, as well as the effects of neo-liberalism (Tormey 2015: 60–7). The latter has led to gross inequality and concentrations of wealth, and is characterised by a suspiciously close relationship between political representation and capitalist interests (Tormey 2015: 129–30; 2012; Hardt and Negri 2011). Because of 'globalisation', structural changes are furthermore taking place in the nature of modern society, specifically a movement away from fixed collective identities towards a more complex mix of (non-)identities as well as towards individualisation (Tormey 2015: 68–82).

Schmitt's reflections on representation and identity in texts such as *Constitutional Theory* and *Roman Catholicism and Political Form*, although written in a different context and with different concerns in mind, can be read as offering at least a partial response, more specifically a conceptual response, which lays claim to a certain universality, to the present 'crisis' of political representation. We saw in Chapter 3 above that Schmitt describes the people not only as a political unity and as the subject of constituent power, but also as *natura naturans*, as formless and as unorganised. 'The people' in these latter senses, as noted, radically disrupts any sense of the identity of a people, in line with Derrida's thinking on identity.[1] At

1 See e.g. *TOH* 11; Derrida (1997b: 14) where he speaks of the 'impossibility of being one with oneself'.

stake here, it was contended in view also of the discussion in Chapter 2, Sections A–C above, is a certain alterity within the self, that is, a force of self-destruction, or autoimmunity.[2] We will see in the present chapter that the identity of a people is, according to Schmitt, furthermore dependent on representation so that there is no real possibility of escaping from representation. Different from what is sometimes contended, Schmitt fully appreciates the lack of purity and inevitable interrelatedness of these two principles as manifested in every state form. The present chapter will moreover show a reconceptualisation as well as a certain radicalisation by Schmitt of the notion of representation. Representation for Schmitt does not simply reproduce, but enhances, and does not draw its strength in this regard from the represented, but from the un-representable, that is, from the force of self-destruction analysed in Chapters 2 and 3 above. This has certain important implications for constituent power as well as for constituted powers.

The formation of identity

We saw in Chapter 3 above that Schmitt at first sight seems to require the presence or existence of a people as a political unity as precondition for the act of constituent power. In *Constitutional Theory* we for example read the following:

> The people must as political unity be present-at-hand, and be presupposed, if it is to be the subject of a constituent power [*Das Volk muß als politische Einheit vorhanden sein und vorausgesetzt werden, wenn es Subjekt einer verfassunggebenden Gewalt sein soll*].[3]
>
> (*CT* 112/*VL* 61)

Support for the idea of the people as a presence and as self-identical, also appears on the face of it from the following passage:

> The thought/concept/idea [*Gedanke*] of representation contradicts the democratic principle of the self-identity of the people present as a political unity [*Der Gedanke der Repräsentation widerspricht dem demokratischen Prinzip der Identität des anwesenden Volkes mit sich selbst als politischer Einheit*].[4]
>
> (*CT* 289/*VL* 262)

2 See e.g. 'F&K' 51/*F&S* 79: 'no community [is possible] that would not cultivate its own auto-immunity, a principle of sacrificial self-destruction ruining the principle of self-protection', and 'F&K' 64/*F&S* 98: 'A certain interruptive unravelling is the condition of the "social bond", the very respiration of all "community"'.

3 See also *CT* 271/*VL* 242: 'Alongside/next to all normativisations, the people remain present-at-hand as a directly *present*, real entity [*Neben allen . . . Normierungen bleibt das Volk als unmittelbar* anwesende *. . . wirkliche Größe vorhanden*]'.

4 See in this respect Lindahl (2008a: 13) who contends that according to Schmitt 'whereas constituted powers represent the people, the latter, when exercising constituent power, is immediately present

Let us however look at the latter passage more closely. Schmitt in this section (entitled 'The political component of the modern constitution') is enquiring into the political concept of democracy and its implications. He starts off the section by defining democracy as 'a *state form* that corresponds to the principle of identity [*Prinzip der Identität*] (in particular, of the concretely present people with itself as political unity)' (*CT* 255/*VL* 223, emphasis added).[5] He ties this understanding of democracy to the notion of the people as the bearer of constituent power which gives itself its own constitution (*CT* 255; Chapter 3 above). In addition, he notes that democracy can point to a method for the exercise of specific state activities (*CT* 255), which is how liberal constitutionalism as a rule views democracy. Democracy would then designate a *governmental* or *legislative form*, and in the system of separation of powers, one or more of these powers, for example the legislature or executive, would be organised according to democratic principles with the widest possible participation of state citizens.[6] After discussing a number of other conceptions of democracy, Schmitt (*CT* 257/*VL* 225) bemoans the lack of clarity which has come about insofar as the meaning of democracy is concerned as a result of the 'boundless extension [(*grenzenlose Ausdehnung*]' of this concept into 'a completely general *ideal concept* [*zu einem ganz allgemeinen* Idealbegriff]'. Its ambiguity is now such that it preserves a place for various ideals and 'for everything that is ideal, beautiful and pleasant [*ideal, schön und sympathisch*]'.[7]

A few pages earlier, in Chapter 16, in discussing the rule-of-law component of the modern constitution, Schmitt (*CT* 235) had pointed to the three state forms traditionally recognised: monarchy, aristocracy and democracy. In the modern liberal constitution, because of its emphasis on freedom and the consequent need to limit state power, these state forms however become mere governmental or legislative forms (*CT* 235). An absolute monarchy thus becomes a constitutional

to itself'. Lindahl (2003; 2008a: 13; 2008b: 337; 2015) has, in opposition to Schmitt's thinking in this regard, advocated the idea of the paradox of constituent power. In terms of the latter approach, constituent power not only entails the institution of a new legal order by a collective self, but also the constitution of the collective self by such legal order.

5 See *CPD* 26/*GLP* 35 on the other forms of identity that are of importance in a democracy: of governing and governed, ruler and ruled, of the subject and object of state authority, identity of the people with its parliamentary representatives, identity of the state and the current voting population, identity of state and law, identity of the quantitative (the numerical majority or unanimity) with the qualitative (correctness (*Richtigkeit*) of laws). Schmitt emphasises that at stake here is not some actual or palpable identity, but the recognition thereof.

6 See further Schmitt (2002c: 296/*SGN* 45–6) where he points out that democracy for liberalism is not about the form of state, but that it (democracy) instead determines the organisation of the legislature and the executive. In this way all the consequences of democracy in the political sense are avoided.

7 See also *CPD* 24–5; *GLP* 32–4. An echo of this (perverted) sense of democracy as beautiful is to be found in *Rog* 26 where Derrida analyses Plato's description of the multi-coloured beauty and attraction of democracy, linking this to a certain seduction and provocation; see also the discussion in Chapter 3 above on the lack of essence of democracy; and see Chapter 1 above on the metaphysical strategy employed here by Schmitt.

monarchy and a pure democracy becomes a constitutional democracy (*CT* 235). The rule-of-law principle consequently prevents the principle of political form from being rigorously implemented, thereby moderating and limiting monarchy and democracy for the sake of liberal freedom. The liberal constitution can be said to be a mixed constitution as it combines and mixes different elements and principles of political form (democracy, aristocracy and monarchy, as well as identity and representation) (*CT* 236–7). Schmitt (*CT* 238) points out that because of this mixture of forms, liberal constitutionalism is not able to engage with the issue of political unity and constituent power. These matters are therefore simply ignored or obscured through the invocation of notions such as the sovereignty of the constitution. The question as to the bearer of constituent power is however unavoidable, Schmitt (*CT* 238–9) argues, because this ultimately determines the state form. It is in this context that Schmitt (*CT* 239–42) discusses at some length the two principles of state form: identity and representation, which are at stake in the quotation above. The way in which a political unity realises these two opposing principles, he notes, ultimately determines its concrete form (*CT* 239).

In analysing these two principles, Schmitt (*CT* 239) first reminds the reader of the relation between the state and the people (Chapter 3 above). The state, he says, is a specific status of a people, and more specifically the status of political unity. The people are furthermore the subject of every conceptual determination of the state. State, he notes, is a condition/state (*Zustand*), and indeed the condition of a people (*CT* 239/*VL* 205). The people can furthermore attain and retain their political unity in one of two ways:

> It can already be factually and directly capable of political action by virtue of a strong and conscious similarity, as a result of firm natural boundaries, or due to some other reason. Then it is as omnipresent entity [*realgegenwärtige Größe*] in its immediate *identity* with itself a political unity. This principle of the identity of the always-present people [*des jeweils vorhandenen Volkes*] with itself as political unity, is based on the idea that there is no state without people and a people must therefore always actually be present [*immer wirklich anwesend*] as an existing entity [*vorhandene Größe*]. The opposing principle proceeds from the idea that the political unity of the people can never be present as such in its real identity [*niemals in realer Identität anwesend sein kann*] and must therefore always be personally *represented* by people.
>
> (*CT* 239/*VL* 205)

At stake here are clearly the principles of identity and representation in their ideal sense.[8] They cannot however find application in this pure sense in any state, as we will again see in what follows. Schmitt (*CT* 239) then proceeds to point out that

8 See also *CT* 248.

all possible state forms, that is, monarchy, aristocracy and democracy, can be traced back to these two opposing principles. The question of the bearer of constituent power, Schmitt (*CT* 239) points out, is likewise dependent on such bearer's position in respect of these two opposing principles. Where the people are the bearer of constituent power, the political form of the state is determined by the principle of identity. The nation, Schmitt (*CT* 239/*VL* 205) says, invoking Rousseau, '*is* there [ist *da*]; it does not require representation and also cannot be represented'.[9] Absolute monarchy, on the other hand, is based solely on the principle of representation. Political unity in terms of this state form is only brought about through representation (*CT* 239).[10] At the same time, Schmitt (*CT* 239–40) points out that in no state is it possible to do away with all elements of these two principles. The latter are in other words opposing points of orientation [*entgegengesetzte Orientierungspunkte*] for the concrete design of a political unity (*CT* 240/*VL* 206). There is thus no state without representation (*CT* 240). Schmitt (*CT* 240/*VL* 206) notes that not even in a direct democracy where all active citizens assemble in one place can one speak of an immediate presence and identity [*umittelbaren Anwesenheit und Identität*] of the people. Even in the extreme case, it will only be all the adult members assembled in this way, and also only for the time-period that they participate in such assembly.[11] Furthermore, the active citizens assembled together do not as such constitute the political unity as a sum total of individuals, but only *represent* such unity. This unity transcends an assembly in a determined time and space (*CT* 240). The individual state citizen is furthermore present (*anwesend*) not in his individual capacity, but as state citizen, and thus in a representative capacity (*CT* 240/*VL* 206). Schmitt concludes the paragraph as follows:

> A complete, absolute self-identity of the then-present people as political unity is at no place and in no moment present [*vorhanden*]. Every attempt to realise a pure or direct democracy must respect this limit of democratic identity. Otherwise direct democracy would mean nothing but the dissolution of the political unity.[12]
>
> (*CT* 241/*VL* 207)

It should thus be clear that Schmitt does not espouse the idea of a people being immediately *present* to itself when exercising constituent power. No

9 See also *CT* 272.

10 See also *CT* 308.

11 See also Tormey (2012: 134) on the inescapability of representation, even in respect of today's so-called post-representative movements.

12 See further *CT* 248/*VL* 214–15 where Schmitt notes that the rigorous realisation of the principle of identity would mean minimal government with the consequence that 'a people regresses from the condition of political existence into one that is subpolitical, thereby leading a merely cultural, economic, or vegetative form of existence and serving a foreign, politically active people'; see further Neumann (2015: 153).

anti-representation bias is moreover to be found in Schmitt.[13] There is, as Schmitt clearly spells out, no state without both the principles of identity and of re-presentation. Representation is required because the state form that one finds in every state essentially means the representation of the political unity (*CT* 241). Without representation it would not be possible to bring about and maintain political unity. The principle of representation can likewise not be realised completely by ignoring the people who is always present in some or other way [*immer irgendwie vorhandenen und anwesenden Volkes*] (*CT* 241/*VL* 208). But there is much more to Schmitt's conception of representation and its relation to presence, as we will see in the discussion that follows.

Representation reconceived

Although there are signs of the traditional conception of representation in Schmitt, that is, of representation being understood as a reproductive re-presentation, a weakened double of the thing itself,[14] he can as noted in the introduction above also be said to radically rethink the classical concept of representation.[15] He more specifically seeks to think its being not starting from ontology, that is, from an originary presence, but from what can, with reference to Derrida (*WM* 147), be called a certain 'force'. In his analysis of the concept of representation in *Constitutional Theory*, Schmitt relies on his earlier exposition of this concept in *Roman Catholicism and Political Form* (1923) (*RC* 18–33) and in *The Crisis of Parliamentary Democracy* (1923) (*CPD* 97–8 n5). Schmitt (*RC* 7) praises the *complexio oppositorum* to be found in the Catholic Church, noting that there appears to be no antithesis which it does not embrace. He further notes that the formal peculiarity (*formale Eigenart*) of Roman Catholicism 'is based on a strict realization of the principle of representation' (*RC* 8/*RK* 14). The pope is not a prophet, but instead the representative (*Stellvertreter*) of Christ (*RC* 14/*RK* 23–4). 'Such a ceremonial function', Schmitt (*RC* 14/*RK* 24) notes, in a passage to which we will return, 'precludes all the fanatical excesses [*fanatische Wildheid*] of an unbridled [*zügellosen*] prophetism'. The office of the priest, who likewise represents Christ (Schneider 1957: 75) is similarly independent of charisma and his position is thus separate from his concrete personality. Yet compared to the modern official, the position of the priest 'is not impersonal, because his office is part of an unbroken

13 Such a bias against representation in favour of presence (i.e. the living present) is incidentally associated by Derrida with the prejudice against writing, which ultimately involves a repression of the relation to death; see De Ville (2011a: 58–60).

14 See e.g. Böckenförde (1997: 18) who points to a certain tension in this respect in *Constitutional Theory*, i.e. between the representation of something real, and the representation of something which is only thereby brought into existence. In respect of the first-mentioned, Böckenförde says that representation here 'appears like a picture of something already present'.

15 The analysis that follows proceeds along similar lines as Derrida's analysis of Marin's work on representation and the image in *WM* 142–64.

chain linked with the personal assignment and concrete person of Christ' (*RC* 14/*RK* 24). Schmitt (*RC* 14/*RK* 24) regards what can be referred to as the 'structure of mourning (of Christ)' at stake here, as 'truly the most astounding complexio oppositorum'. In such distinctions, he comments, 'lie the rational creativity and humanity of Catholicism. The church thus remains within and gives direction to the human spirit, without exhibiting the dark irrationalism [*das irrationale Dunkel*] of the human soul' (*RC* 14/*RK* 24). One should keep this exposition in mind when reading Schmitt's definition of representation which follows only a few pages later:

> To represent in an eminent sense can only be done by a person, that is, not simply by a 'deputy' but an authoritative person or an idea which, if represented, also become personified. God or 'the people' in democratic ideology, or abstract ideas like freedom and equality can all conceivably constitute a representation .... Representation invests the representative person with a special dignity, because the representative of a noble value cannot be without value.
>
> (*RC* 21/*RK* 36)

In *Roman Catholicism and Political Form* Schmitt (*RC* 19/*RK* 32) furthermore bemoans the contemporary disappearance of the representative capacity in society in general, which he then attempts to reinvigorate with reference to the Church. In *Constitutional Theory*, Schmitt (*CT* 243–5/*VL* 209–11) likewise insists that representation belongs to the political sphere and that it is something existential (*etwas Existentielles*). Representation is moreover essentially to be understood as rendering a being that is invisible (*ein unsichtbares Sein*), visible and present or brought to mind/envisioned (*vergegenwärtigen*) by way of a publicly present being (*ein öffentlich anwesendes Sein*) (*CT* 243/*VL* 209). As we saw in *Roman Catholicism and Political Form* above, this dialectic of the concept of representation – in terms of which the invisible is presumed as absent (*als abwesend vorausgesetzt*) and yet at the same time is rendered present (*anwesend*) – cannot be applied to simply any being (*CT* 243/*VL* 209–10). An elevated sense of being is required, which is capable of elevation into public being (*das öffentliche Sein*), that is, into an existence (*einer Existenz*) (*CT* 243/*VL* 210). In a similar way in which the Church represents the person of Christ (*RC* 19, 30), a people finds representation in the state:

> In representation . . . a higher type of being (*höhere Art des Seins*) comes into concrete appearance [*zur konkreten Erscheinung*]. The idea of representation rests on a people existing as a political unity, having a higher, further enhanced, and more intense type of being [*Art Sein*] as compared to the natural existence [*natürlichen Dasein*] of some human group living together. If the significance of this distinctiveness of political existence erodes and people give priority to other forms of their existence [*Daseins*], the appreciation for a concept like representation also falls away.
>
> (*CT* 243/*VL* 210)

Contrariwise, according to Schmitt,

> [s]omething dead, something inferior or valueless, something lowly cannot be represented. It lacks the enhanced type of being that is capable of an existence, of rising into public being.[16]
>
> (*CT* 243/*VL* 210)

Representation, Schmitt (*CT* 245) further points out, concerns the political unity or the people as a whole. Not simply any organ can therefore fulfil this function; only someone who rules can represent. Only the government (*die Regierung*) (as opposed to the administration or a commercial agency (*Geschäftsbesorgung*)) is thus capable of representing and realising the spiritual (*geistige*) principle of political existence (*CT* 245/*VL* 212). By means of this spiritual existence (*geistiger Existenz*) the government distinguishes itself from both a commissioned employee and a violent oppressor. The difference between a real government and a pirate thus does not lie in ideas such as justice or social utility, but in the fact that every real government (*echte Regierung*) represents the political unity of a people, not the people in its natural presence or existence (*Vorhandensein*) (*CT* 245/*VL* 212).

For Schmitt, representation in the political domain can thus only be personal. A decision, when it is really required, would otherwise be impossible. Representation conceived as such applies in Schmitt's view primarily to the (head of the) executive, who exercises a commissarial dictatorship in a state of exception,[17] but also to a constituent assembly, which as we saw (Chapter 3 above), has unlimited powers or, as Schmitt (*D* 124–5/*DD* 140–1) puts it, 'any arbitrary power or force [*jede beliebige Vollmacht*]' in adopting a constitution, that is, a so-called sovereign dictatorship. Yet, depending on 'the strict realisation of the principle of re-presentation [*der strengen Durchführung des Prinzips der Repräsentation*]' (*RC* 8/*RK* 14), Schmitt (*RC* 25–6, 30–1/*RK* 43, 51–2) leaves open the possibility that

16 'Etwas Totes, etwas Minderwertiges oder Wertloses, etwas Niedriges kann nicht repräsentiert werden. Ihm fehlt die gesteigerte Art Sein, die einer Heraushebung in das öffentliche Sein, einer *Existenz*, fähig ist.'

17 The invocation by Agamben (1998: 9; 2005: 1–31, 57–9) of Walter Benjamin to the effect that the exception has become the rule in Western democracies finds support in Derrida's thinking, yet it takes on an a-phenomenological 'meaning': it does not simply mean that there is a coincidence between the rule and the exception; the exception is understood as the event (*Ereignis*) that gives Being and which necessarily returns in the enforcement or conservation of the rule; see Chapter 2, Section A above and see further below. Agamben's analysis in *Potentialities* (at 160–74) of the 'real state of exception', again with reference to Benjamin, however seems closer to that of Derrida. See somewhat similarly Žižek (2000: 114) who reads Schmitt's notion of the exception in Lacanian terms: 'it stands simultaneously for the intrusion of the Real (of the pure contingency that perturbs the universe of symbolic *automaton*) *and* for the gesture of the Sovereign who (violently, without foundation in the symbolic norm) imposes a symbolic normative order: in Lacanese, it stands for *objet petit a* as well as for S_1, the Master-Signifier.'

a legislature[18] and even a court[19] with sufficient independence, a kind of super-state (*Über-Staat*) and super-sovereign (*Über-Souverän*), which directly and personally represents a certain idea of justice (which Schmitt in turn distinguishes from justice in the political sense, that is, retaining the status quo), can fulfil this function.[20]

It needs to be noted here that Schmitt's objections elsewhere to a court acting as the guardian of the constitution[21] are inter alia tied to the technological motivation behind granting such constitutional jurisdiction to the courts in liberal constitutionalism, that is, to neutralise and de-politicise, by legalising or juridifying politics.[22] Echoing the argument in *The Concept of the Political*, Schmitt (*HdV* 111) however points out that the political cannot be bypassed, as every sphere of human activity becomes political when it comes into contact with deciding conflicts and questions. The political, he continues, can connect itself to any (subject) matter (*Materie*), and simply gives it a new turn (*eine 'neue Wendung'*) (*HdV* 111). Schmitt ends the section by implicitly alluding to his own earlier argument in *The Concept of the Political* about depoliticisation, which in view of the analysis in Chapter 2, Section A above, we can read as pointing to a certain beyond of the political, which would inevitably 'return' in the event of a sovereign decision being taken:

> Everything that is somehow in the public interest is somehow political, and nothing which substantially concerns the state, can in earnest be de-politicised. The flight from politics is [at the same time] a flight from the state. Where this flight ends, and the one who flees will end up, no one can foresee; it is in any

18 In *CT* 250–1 Schmitt leaves open this possibility for parliament, however not as conceived under liberalism, that is, where members of parliament represent party interests. Instead, parliament should act as representative of the people, conceived as a unity; see also *CT* 242; *RC* 25–6; and *CPD* 5, 97–8 n5.

19 See Schmitt's remarks concerning an International Court of Justice in *RC* 30–31; and see Voigt (2015a: 231). See further *CT* 82 where Schmitt comments on the fact that a constitution sometimes contains a number of compromises so that no decision is actually taken regarding certain matters. It is then left to the legislature, and to precedent to take the required decision.

20 Schmitt (*RC* 29/*RK* 49) further remarks that secular jurisprudence or legal science (*weltliche Jurisprudenz*) shows a similar kind of complexio of opposing principles and tendencies: 'As in Catholicism, within it lies a peculiar mixture of the faculty of traditional conservatism and revolutionary resistance in a natural law sense.'

21 See e.g. *HdV* 19, 32–3 where Schmitt notes that a judiciary presupposes norms whereas a guardian of the constitution needs to act beyond norms; a court furthermore acts *post eventum* and is thus always politically too late; for a critical discussion of Schmitt's position, see Neumann (2015: 220–36), and specifically on this point, 229–30.

22 Schneider (1957: 191) in his analysis of Schmitt on this point puts it as follows: 'The attempts to save the state through neutralisation in the sense of "depoliticisation" by experts, by neutral judges and officials . . . arise from a belief, which is at least connected to the belief in technology, a belief that it will someday be possible to construct a self-regulating, perfectly functioning state machinery, which makes all human decision-making superfluous.'

> event certain that the consequence will be either political demise or a different kind of politics.[23]
>
> (*HdV* 111)

It thus appears that all three of the branches that traditionally belong to the *trias politica* can potentially be 'sovereign' or take 'sovereign decisions', in accordance with the analysis in Chapter 3 above of these concepts.[24] What then are the implications of the concept of representation thus conceived for constituted powers were they to be true to the concept? We need to return here to Schmitt's analysis of representation in *Constitutional Theory* and in *Roman Catholicism and Political Form*. We saw above that Schmitt (*CT* 245/*VL* 212) expresses the view that only the government is capable of representing and realising the spiritual (*geistige*) principle of political existence. Schmitt (*RC* 14/*RK* 24), as we saw, draws a distinction between representation in this 'spiritual' sense, and prophetism, which he associates with fanatical wildness or savagery (*fanatische Wildheid*). Schmitt (*RC* 14/*RK* 24), as further noted, expresses his amazement in relation to this 'most astounding [*erstaunlichste*] complexio oppositorum'. As we likewise saw above, the representation at stake here illustrates for Schmitt (*RC* 14/*RK* 24) 'the rational creative power as well as humanity of Catholicism'. In this way, Schmitt (*RC* 14/*RK* 24) continues, the Church 'remains within the human-spiritual [*Menschlich-Geistigen*]; without dragging into the light the irrational obscurity/darkness [*das irrationale Dunkel*] of the human soul, it gives it direction'.

It is noteworthy that the drawing of the distinction between representation and prophetism is preceded in the same paragraph by a discussion of the peculiar rationalism of the Catholic Church which 'morally seizes [*erfaßt*] the psychological and sociological nature of human beings' (*RC* 13/*RK* 23). Schmitt (*RC* 13–14/*RK* 23) refers here to the Catholic Church's association with reason and common sense, its opposition to sectarian fanaticism, its suppression of superstition and sorcery during the Middle Ages and also to Max Weber's remark that the Church had 'knowingly and magnificently succeeded in overcoming Dionysian cults', as well as 'ecstasy and destruction in contemplation [*Ekstase und Untergehn in der Kontemplation*]'. This rationalism of the Church, Schmitt (*RC* 14/*RK* 23) continues, lies in its institutional nature and is in essence juridical. Its great achievement lies in the specific way in which it makes the priesthood into an office, as discussed above. In psychoanalytical terms, Schmitt's exposition of the

23 'Alles, was irgendwie von öffentlichem Interesse ist, ist irgendwie politisch, und nichts, was wesentlich den Staat angeht, kann im Ernst entpolitisiert werden. Die Flucht aus der Politik ist die Flucht aus dem Staat. Wo diese Flucht endet, und wo der Flüchtende landet, kann niemand voraussehen; jedenfalls ist sicher, daβ das Ergebnis entweder der politische Untergang oder aber eine andere Art von Politik sein wird.'

24 In terms of the dominant constitutional model in the world today, it is Constitutional Courts or their equivalents that are most likely to be regarded as such, despite Schmitt's objections.

complexio oppositorum speaks of introjection, a successful work of mourning, which as we will see in more detail in Chapter 5, Section B below, cannot however completely succeed, that is, it cannot evade incorporation.[25] At stake in the *complexio oppositorum*, as appears from Schmitt's use of words in this paragraph such as 'grasp' (*erfaßt*), 'victory' (*victoire*), 'battles' (*Kampfe*), 'repressed' (*unterdrückte*), overcome (*überwinden*), and 'kept at a distance' (*fern gehalten*) in relation to human nature (*RC* 13–14/*RK* 23–4), is therefore nothing less than the 'origin' of the Church which finds itself incorporated, subjected, disciplined and enslaved in being surpassed (Chapter 5, Section B below).[26] This 'origin', similar to the beyond of the political referred to above, necessarily makes a haunting return in the event of every sovereign decision. The purity of the concept of representation within the Church, which as we saw Schmitt expresses his admiration for and wishes to extend to the state as well, therefore is not attained without a certain *pólemos*. 'Fanatical' and 'unrestrained' prophetism, which Schmitt (*RC* 14/*RK* 24) associates with the 'irrational obscurity of the human soul', has to be battled against, incorporated and overcome for 'pure' representation to arise. Representation understood thus does not involve only a reversal of the traditional relationship between presence and representation, but a certain beyond to this opposition.[27] Returning to Derrida (1976a: 163), we can speak here of the abyssal structure of representation in its relation without relation to prophetism. The latter can, in view of Schmitt's analysis, also be referred to as the un-representable (Derrida 2007a: 128),[28] as absolute hospitality, or the gift without return to the self (Chapter 5, Section B below).[29] The un-representable, even though it inevitably needs to be limited or constrained (Derrida 1976a: 179–92), also calls for affirmation.

25 See also *WM* 159–61.

26 Note in this respect the apt remark of Patočka (1996: 101): '[S]exuality illustrates how inevitably the orgiastic realm is brought into a relation to the sphere of responsibility. This bringing into relation to responsibility, that is, to the domain of human authenticity and truth, is probably the kernel of the history of all religions. Religion is not the sacred, nor does it arise directly from the experience of sacral orgies and rites; rather, it is where the sacred qua demonic is being explicitly overcome. Sacral experiences pass over [into] religious as soon as there is an attempt to introduce responsibility into the sacred or to regulate the sacred thereby.' For commentary, see Derrida (2008a: 3–35).

27 See also Chapter 2, Section B above on the double, and Chapter 6 below on representation in cinema.

28 This would also be applicable if representation is understood in a linguistic sense, i.e. of language as a system of representation; see De Ville (2011a: 57–60). The Constitution here would in a sense 'represent' the people, as Lindahl (2008a), for example, explores by way of speech act theory.

29 See also Lindahl (2013: 253–60) who argues that because of the lack of foundation of a legal order, a certain 'respons*a*bility' arises in the event of claims that fall within the category of the 'a-legal', i.e. to respond by acknowledging such lack of foundation. This 'respons*a*bility' can be said to seek to avoid a simple return of the collective to itself, and to entail at least a form of conditional hospitality.

Conclusion

The analysis above has sought to show the inextricable relationship between identity and representation in Schmitt's thinking. We saw that according to Schmitt these principles cannot find application in their pure sense in any state, due to their interlinking nature. Insofar as the structure of representation is concerned, we saw that it establishes itself by overcoming what Schmitt refers to as 'fanatical' and 'unrestrained' prophetism, and which he associates with an 'irrational obscurity or darkness of the human soul'. It was contended above that this 'overcoming' should be understood in a quasi-psychoanalytical sense as also involving an 'incorporation', the 'object' of which returns in every sovereign act of self-preservation. This structure of representation has important implications for both constituent and constituted powers if they are to be 'true' to the 'democracy to come' (Chapter 3) as well as to a certain unconditional equality and freedom (Chapter 6). Insofar as the sovereign dictatorship of a constituent assembly is concerned, it should no longer be thought of primarily in terms of sovereignty, that is, as the strongest force, but, to paraphrase Schmitt (*CT* 243), in terms of something inferior or valueless, something lowly that cannot be represented, that is, the weakest force. Insofar as constituted powers are concerned, this structure of representation has important implications for the principle of separation of powers, which according to the liberal model is to be understood primarily with reference to unlimited individual freedom, and thus as requiring limitation. All constituted powers falling within the *trias politica*, that is, the legislature, executive and judiciary, as well as the powers of the future that will replace them, whether or not representative in the traditional sense, must represent this weakest 'force' in their role as guardians of the constitution.[30]

30 See further Derrida and Roudinesco (2004: 83) on a different understanding of revolution; and the essay 'Force of Law: The "Mystical Foundation of Authority"' in *AR* 230–98 on the role of specifically the judiciary in this regard.

Chapter 5

The concept of the constitution

The modern idea of a written constitution dates from the end of the eighteenth century.[1] This development has brought with it the almost inevitable question: what is a constitution? The posing of this question amounts to a search for the essence of a constitution in general, or for the essence of a particular constitution. The importance of the 'what is' question lies in the fact that the essence so found has a number of important implications, inter alia in relation to the question as to the continued existence of constituent power after its exercise (Chapter 3), the relation of the constitution to the state, that is, whether transnational constitutions or an international constitution is possible (Chapter 7), constitutional interpretation, the question of sovereignty (Chapter 3) and the limits or restrictions imposed in relation to constitutional amendments (*CT* 140–66). In constitutional theory one would usually speak in this respect of the 'concept of the constitution', and various such 'concepts' have been explored.

Schmitt (*CT* 59–93) distinguishes between four concepts of the constitution, although he adopts and defends (only) the positive concept as opposed to the absolute, relative and ideal concepts of the constitution.[2] Schmitt (*CT* 59–66) divides the absolute concept into two variants: (1) the existential or what can be called the 'ancient' concept of the constitution where every state in a certain sense 'has' a constitution and where each state can be equated with its constitution;[3] and (2) the normative, where the constitution is viewed as fundamental legal regulation or as 'a unified, closed *system* of higher and ultimate *norms*' (*CT* 62/*VL* 7). The relative concept identifies a constitution by way of formalistic criteria such as its written nature or whether it has been adopted according to the correct procedure (*CT* 67–74). In accordance with the ideal concept, a constitution only qualifies as

1 See *CT* 97–111; Stern (1984: 61–3); Grimm (2012a: 100–5); and Schuppert (2003: 743–4) on the historical developments which led to the era of the modern, written constitution.

2 See also Neumann (2015: 101); *cf.* Loughlin (2010: 212–13); Van der Walt (2009: 279–80; 2014: 305–7); Wall (2012a: 78); Lindahl (2008a: 13).

3 This 'Constitution' is usually regarded as 'descriptive' in nature in comparison with the modern constitution which has a prescriptive nature; see Grimm (2012a: 103, 106).

such if its content satisfies certain criteria, for example in liberal constitutionalism where a constitution must protect individual freedom and private property through the rule of law and separation of powers to qualify as such (*CT* 89–93).

Schmitt's positive concept requires the drawing of a distinction between the constitution and constitutional law(s) (*CT* 76). The constitution as such refers to the decision on the form and nature of the political unity, which is often to be found in its preamble. This would for example be the decision by the people to establish a constitutional democracy of the federal type over a certain territory (*CT* 77–8). Constitutional law(s) on the other hand, would refer to all additional secondary norms of a constitutional type, including those in the constitutional document itself (*CT* 78).[4] The positive concept furthermore requires that a distinction be drawn between the formation of the state or political unity, on the one hand, and its precise form and nature, on the other (Chapter 3).

In the two sections that follow, a certain intersection in Schmitt's thinking on the concept of the constitution and that of Derrida on *khōra* and the crypt will be explored. In Section A Schmitt's reflections in *Constitutional Theory* on the constitution as something that is 'given' to a concrete political unity will be read alongside Derrida's analysis of Plato's *Timaeus* (c. 360 BC) and the notion of *khōra* that is explored there. *Khōra*, as we will see, in a certain sense 'gives place', which is arguably also the primary function of a constitution. In Section B Schmitt's analysis of the relation between liberal constitutionalism and the concept of the political will be juxtaposed to Freud's case study of the Wolf Man, more specifically the subsequent reading thereof by Abraham and Torok, as well as by Derrida. According to Schmitt (*CT* 93/*VL* 41) liberal constitutionalism seeks to 'repress' or 'force back' the political component of the constitution, whereas it actually lies at the 'origin' of the constitution, and continues to have an effect on such constitution. Somewhat similarly the crypt is understood by Abraham and Torok as a 'false unconscious' from which issues a law demanding the impossible that radically displaces the self.

4 See further Preuss (2015b: 149) who points out that the distinction in Schmitt between the constitution (i.e. the decision by the constituent power about the form and nature of the political unity) and constitutional laws provides a challenge to modern constitutionalism which recognises no legitimate political power beyond the constitution. This is because the constitution in the real sense according to Schmitt points to a political power which does not attain its legitimacy from the normativity of the constitutional text, but in itself – the people – as constituent power; see further Chapter 3 above.

SECTION A *KHŌRA*

Introduction

In Chapter 3 and in the introduction above we encountered Schmitt's so-called 'positive concept of the constitution [*der positive Verfassungsbegriff*]', which as we saw involves a conscious decision about the nature and form of political existence, 'which the political unity reaches for itself and gives to itself [*sich selber gibt*] through the bearer of constituent power' (*CT* 75–6/*VL* 21).[1] Schmitt's positive concept, as we further saw, requires the drawing of a distinction between the constitution and constitutional law(s). The constitution as such refers to the decision on the form and nature of the political unity, for example a constitutional democracy in the form of a federal state, which is often to be found in the preamble to the constitution. Constitutional law(s) on the other hand refers to all other constitutional law provisions, whether or not contained in the constitutional text itself. The modern idea of a constitution as a conscious, political decision by the people that returns to itself in its own identity can clearly be seen here,[2] as well as the repetition of the Platonic legacy, which appears from the attempt to arrive at the essence of the constitution (Chapter 1). The notion of the constitution as gift[3] is implicit in this modern conception, and is brought to the fore more explicitly in Schmitt's text.[4] In elaborating on the notion of a constitution as something that is given, Schmitt (*CT* 76/*VL* 22) insists that a constitution cannot come into being by itself, as is supposed by the absolute conception of the constitution proposed by normativism. A constitution also does not attain its validity from the fact that it is normatively correct, as is supposed, for example, by the liberal ideal concept of the constitution, or because of its systematic closure (*ihrer systematischen Geschlossenheit*) (*CT* 76/*VL* 22). Schmitt (*CT* 76/*VL* 22) spells out the nature of this gift as follows: 'It [i.e. the constitution] does not give itself (to itself), but is given to a concrete political unity [*Sie gibt sich nicht selbst, sondern wird für eine konkrete politische Einheit gegeben*]'. A few lines down, Schmitt (*CT* 76/*VL* 22) explains that a constitution attains its validity by virtue of the existing political will of those who give it (*des existierenden politischen Willens desjenigen, der sie gibt*), that is, the constituent power. Yet it is difficult to deny that the sentence quoted above can also be read as alluding to something else, that is, to a gift in the

1 See also *CT* 102, 127/*VL* 50, 79.

2 See Derrida (1992a: 10–12); *Rog* 12–14 where this idea of a gift and of democracy, understood as a circular return to the self, is placed in question.

3 See also Van der Walt (2012a; 2012b) for a reflection on the European Constitution as gift.

4 See in this respect also the Weimar Constitution ('Das deutsche Volk hat sich diese Verfassung gegeben'), the German *Grundgesetz* ('Im Bewußtsein seiner Verantwortung vor Gott und den Menschen. . .hat sich das Deutsche Volk kraft seiner verfassungsgebenden Gewalt dieses Grundgesetz gegeben') and the constitution of Switzerland ('Das Schweizervolk und die Kantone . . . geben sich folgende Verfassung').

absence of any subject, *to* a political unity, and thus also *to* the constituent power acting by virtue of this political unity (Chapter 3 above), a reading which Schmitt subsequently seeks to close down.

Schmitt's reflections in *Constitutional Theory* on the constitution as gift resonate with Derrida's *Khôra* (1993d), which involves a detailed reading of certain sections of Plato's *Timaeus*, which concerns itself with the origins of the universe. In the latter texts a gift is likewise at stake, one which appears to move beyond the notion of a circular return. Of central importance in the *Timaeus* is the notion of *khōra*, which falls neither within the intelligible nor the sensible realm. *Khōra* can be described as a kind of placeless place which gives place (*Rog* xiv). The *Timaeus* thus appears to stand in tension with what is traditionally regarded as Plato's philosophical schema, and therefore also with the whole Western philosophical tradition. This chapter seeks to enquire into the implications for the concept of a constitution of the notion of *khōra*. It will proceed by closely following Derrida's analysis in *Khōra* as well as other texts where this notion is at stake so as to determine the 'nature' and 'place' of *khōra* within and beyond the Platonic philosophical schema. This will be followed by an analysis of the relation between *khōra* and the political, focusing specifically on the abyssal narrative at stake in the *Timaeus* and its implications for the *Republic*'s giving of place, as well as the role Socrates plays in the elaboration of *khōra*. Finally, the question will be raised whether the function of a constitution is not ultimately, like *khōra*, to give place.[5] This gift is not however to be understood as a giving of place to itself by the constituent power, but as a gift with no subject and no return to the self.

Derrida's reading of the *Timaeus*

In the *Timaeus* (Plato 1997: 1224–91)[6] we find an account of the classical Platonic schema in terms of which there is: (1) an intelligible, ideal world (that which always is, unchanging), which can be grasped by reason and understanding; and (2) the visible world which becomes, but never is, that is, the representation or image or copy of the eternal world. The demiurge (craftsman) uses the ideal forms as model and inspiration to make the visible world (Plato 1997: *Timaeus* 28a–b; *Psy II* 171). Yet in the *Timaeus* mention is also made of a third element (*triton genos*), referred to as *khōra*, that is, the 'place' in which the sensible copies are inscribed, and which Plato notes we perceive as in a dream (Plato 1997: *Timaeus* 52b–c). As Sallis points out, this third element is needed to allow us to speak about the things in the sensible world (fire, air, water and earth), which continually take different forms. These things, because of their changing form, cannot be said to be simply copies of an unchanging Ideal world (Sallis 1999: 104–6). *Khōra* is

5 See further Chapter 6 below.

6 References to Plato's texts are, unless otherwise indicated, to Plato (1997). Reference will be made to the Stephanus page numbers.

furthermore needed because without it, things/images would have remained mere phantoms. *Khōra* as a formless wax or plastic material on which and by means of which sensible things are made according to the forms of the intelligible realm makes this possible (Sallis 1999: 108–9). The demiurge, looking at the ideas, copies them and inscribes those copies/images into *khōra*, thus making the world. This means, as Derrida points out, that *khōra* 'must already have been there, as the "there" itself, outside of time or in any case outside of becoming, in an outside-time without common measure with the eternity of ideas and the becoming of sensible things' (*Psy II* 171). It thus seems to be eternal; like the Ideal forms it is always already there, but it is not a stable presence unaffected by time (*CW* 10). It is also not temporal in the way in which the sensible world is such (*CW* 10). *Khōra* 'is' 'the anachrony of Being. It/she anachronises Being [*Elle anachronise l'être*]' (*ON* 94/*Khôra* 25; *CW* 17). *Khōra* furthermore does not have the meaning of past, that is, a present that is past (*CW* 29).[7]

The *Timaeus* allows for at least two understandings of *khōra*. The traditional and dominant interpretation makes *khōra* fit into the Platonic schema (*Psy II* 171–2). Understood thus, in terms of what Derrida (*ON* 89/*Khôra* 16) calls 'the logic of participation', *khōra* would be both intelligible and sensible. The other reading, proposed by Derrida (*Psy II* 172–5), following what he calls 'a logic of exclusion' (*ON* 89/*Khôra* 16), would make of *khōra* something heterogeneous to metaphysics, that is, its pre-origin. *Khōra* would on this latter reading thus not fit into the Platonic system, and therefore also not within Western philosophy, the inheritance of Plato, yet would make the latter possible.[8] *Khōra* would thus be neither sensible nor intelligible. It cannot in other words be conceived of intellectually or through the senses (*CW* 108).

The *Timaeus* refers to *khōra* as inter alia the mother, the matrix and the nurse/midwife (*CW* 10). The father, it is said, can be compared to the Ideas, and the child, to the sensible world; the mother would then be like *khōra* (Plato 1997: *Timaeus* 50d).[9] Yet Derrida points out that if the logic of exclusion applies (as he contends it should), *khōra* cannot really be described by way of metaphor, as Plato appears to be doing here. The 'mother' and other similar metaphors are borrowed from the sensible world and are thus inadequate in describing something of a third genus which is neither sensible nor intelligible.[10] Metaphor also traditionally

7 In the essay 'Ousia and Grammē' Derrida (1982: 55–7) explores the Aristotelian notion of *hama* as the common origin of both space and time and as the condition for all appearing of Being.

8 See Wolfreys (1998: 41). Naas (2003: 27) similarly describes *khōra* as not involving 'a simple modification or refinement of Plato's project or program but something that would actually lodge and shelter it, keeping it from being its own source and origin, keeping it from founding itself'.

9 See Grosz (1994: 23) on how this analysis fits into 'Greek collective fantasies: in procreation the father contributes specific characteristics to the nameless, formless incubation provided by the mother'.

10 Plato also speaks in this respect of *khōra* as a sieve which 'separates things into the world of the sensible and the intelligible' (*CW* 92). In his collaboration with Peter Eisenman on a garden for

stands opposed to the literal or the proper, an opposition which is derived from the Platonic schema (*CW* 70; *ON* 92).[11] As a third genus, *khōra* goes beyond metaphysical polarity, preceding these oppositions and therefore also goes beyond sense (*ON* 92–3). *Khōra* is thus not really the mother, the nurse, the matrix (*CW* 10). It/She does not engender the sensible forms that are inscribed in it/her, and cannot be considered an origin in the traditional sense (*CW* 29; *ON* 124). It/She does not 'couple' with the father, that is, with the ideal order (*ON* 124).[12] One cannot therefore situate this 'third order' within a triangle or a trinity or group or family (*Psy II* 175).[13] The notion of *khōra* involves another kind of origin, a pre-origin or archi-origin, which as Derrida (2004b: 54) points out, 'is both more and less than an origin'.

In view of what was said above about the 'nature' of *khōra*, translating Plato's *Timaeus* is necessarily a very problematic exercise, risking retrospective projection (*ON* 93). As Derrida (*ON* 93) points out, it almost inevitably happens that metaphysics guides this interpretation, that is, both of the word *khōra* and of Plato's descriptions thereof. Yet Derrida (*ON* 93–4) regards this as inevitable, due to the very structure of *khōra*. Interpretations of *khōra* attempt to give it a form by determining it (*ON* 94). *Khōra*, however, can only offer or promise itself by withdrawing itself from determination, from all the marks or impressions to which it is exposed (*ON* 94). These interpretations, as Derrida (*ON* 95/*Khôra* 27–8) puts it, 'would come to give form to *khōra* by leaving on it the schematic mark of their imprint and by depositing on it the sediment of their contribution'. Yet *khōra*, like the law in Kafka's *Before the Law*, does not allow itself to be touched or reached in this way (being inaccessible, impassive, amorphous and still 'virgin'),[14] and also cannot be reduced to these determinations (*ON* 95). *Khōra* nevertheless gives place or acts as receptacle to these interpretations and appropriations. Everything is inscribed on it, but at the same time it remains virgin (*CW* 70).[15]

It appears that the best way to describe *khōra*, though this still remains inadequate, is by way of negation, somewhat similar to the procedure followed by

the Parc de la Villette, Derrida drew a sieve in the shape of a harp, to be incorporated in some way into the garden (*CW* 92). The garden was however never built; see Tschumi (2005: 117).

11 Yet, as Derrida (*CW* 70) points out, we cannot avoid metaphors in speaking about *khōra*, even though we know that they are inadequate.

12 As we saw above, Plato (1997: *Timaeus* 50d) refers to the ideal order as the father and the sensible order as the child.

13 See also Chapter 2, Section B above on Derrida's reading of Poe's *The Purloined Letter*.

14 'Virgin' is not to be understood anthropologically (*ON* 95). As Derrida (*ON* 126/*Khôra* 95) further points out, the 'necessity' at stake here '(*khōra* is its sur-name) seems so virginal that it does not even have the figure of a virgin any longer'.

15 These metaphors are likewise inadequate; no essence is thereby designated, seeing that *khōra* as we saw above does not belong to the *eidos* or to the copies/images thereof (*ON* 95).

negative theology.[16] One can say that *khōra* is not a word or a concept; it/she is not a proper noun or a common noun. *Khōra* is not a ground; it/she is nothing; it/she is not intelligible, not sensible, not something (identical to it/herself), not a being, not a person, not a thing; it/she does not exist (*CW* 70, 109).[17] One can also not ask about the essence of *khōra*, as essence has no meaning in respect to it/her (*CW* 17; *ON* 94). It/She has nothing of/as its/her own – and it/she remains without form, formless (*CW* 18; *ON* 97).[18] This is another reason why it/she cannot really be described like an existent (mother, nurse or receptacle). These are as noted (inadequate) figures from the sensible world and not properties that *khōra* can receive (*CW* 18, 30). *Khōra* may possess these as properties, but not as its/her own (*CW* 19). *Khōra* does not have an identity (*CW* 19; *ON* 99). As noted, it/she remains unformed, formless (*ON* 97). *Khōra* merely lets itself/herself be lent these properties, which it/she receives. *Khōra* is furthermore not to be equated with empty space or the void (*CW* 10; *Psy II* 110; Sallis 1999: 114). It/She is in other words not 'nothing' in the sense of the void (*CW* 109).[19] One can speak here of an abyss or a chasm, but then of a specific kind (*ON* 103): not between the sensible and the intelligible, between Being and nothingness, between Being and the lesser being, between Being and beings, between *logos* and *mythos*, but 'between all these couples and another which would not even be *their* other [*entre tous ces couples et un autre qui ne serait même plus* leur *autre*]' (*ON* 104/*Khôra* 46).[20]

Khōra 'is' a third 'something' which does not belong to Being (*CW* 70). One can still say that there is *khōra* (*il y a khōra*) (*ON* 96/*Khôra* 30; *CW* 18), although Derrida remains wary of this expression along with the Heideggerian *es gibt* as it 'still announces or recalls too much the dispensation of God, of man, or even that of Being of which certain of Heidegger's texts speak (*es gibt Sein*)' (*Psy II* 173/*Psy II* (F) 175; *ON* 96). At stake here, as noted, is a pre-origin, that is, 'the spacing which is the condition for everything to take place, for everything to be inscribed' (*CW* 10, 30).[21] *Khōra* appears to give everything, to give place to everything, yet

16 Derrida (*CW* 12) notes in this respect that *khōra* cannot be represented, except negatively. The differences between deconstruction and negative theology should nonetheless not be overlooked; see *Psy II* 143–95; and De Ville (2011a: 154–5 n39). See further Chapter 2, Section C on the negative in Schmitt.

17 *Khōra* thus has no reference to anything real; see *CW* 11, and see also Naas (2003: 35), noting that *khōra* 'is a reference that can have no present referent'.

18 See in this respect Chapter 3 above on the constituent power as formless.

19 See also *ON* 105–6: as the void it would simply be non-being; see also Chapter 7 below on the void in Schmitt's texts.

20 For Heidegger, as Derrida (*ON* 103–4; *Psy II* 187) points out, *khōra* names the place, locus or site (*Ort*) of the difference between Being and beings.

21 The notion of 'spacing' can be understood with reference to the philosophical privileging of speech vis-à-vis writing, which Derrida deconstructs in his early texts; see Wigley (1995: 67–74). Derrida shows there that the prejudice against writing is tied to what it represents, i.e. space, exteriority, death and absence vis-à-vis the voice, which is viewed as without space, as interior, as tied to life,

as we saw, the *Timaeus* says it is a virgin place, that is, it is totally foreign, totally exterior to anything that it receives (*CW* 10). It is thus absolutely blank, everything printed on it is absolutely effaced (*CW* 10). Therefore in a way, it does not receive anything; it does not receive what it receives and does not give what it gives.[22] What becomes inscribed in it effaces itself immediately, while remaining there. It cannot really be said to be a place, because it has no depth (*CW* 10). To think *khōra* it is necessary to go back to a beginning that is older than the beginning, in the same way in which the origin of Athens, as we will see below, must be recalled from beyond the Athenians' own memory (*CW* 30). *Khōra* can in this respect be referred to as a fiction, but without story, similar for example to Kafka's *Before the Law* and certain texts of Blanchot (*CW* 11).[23]

There is moreover a certain (absolute) singularity or uniqueness about *khōra*, which is tied to the impossibility of speaking of it in the language of metaphysics and of giving it a proper name (*Psy II* 173–4).[24] It is therefore not strictly speaking accurate to refer to it as a 'third kind' (*triton genos*) (*ON* 124/*Khôra* 91–2). Yet this impossibility does not reduce one to silence. It imposes an obligation in spite of, or even *because of* this impossibility (*Psy II* 173). There is in other words only one *khōra*, although it entails a pure multiplicity of places (*Psy II* 173) and even though it is divisible (*ON* 97). It is necessary, Plato (1997: *Timaeus* 50b) says, to always refer to *khōra* in the same way or manner in order to respect its singularity (*ON* 98; *Psy II* 173). This is, Derrida (*Psy II* 173; *ON* 98) contends, not a question of giving it the same (proper) name, but of calling it, addressing oneself to it in the same way. Derrida (*Psy II* 174) calls this an injunction without order which has always already taken place: 'one must think that which – standing beyond all given philosophemes – will have nevertheless left a trace in language'. This trace is to be found in all languages, and the obligation (which is also the obligation which drives deconstruction) is to rediscover this trace in different bodies of

and as immediate presence. Metaphysics can thus be said to involve the attempt at mastery of space by keeping it (i.e. space) on the outside; see Wigley (1995: 69). Derrida proceeds to show that speech necessarily involves a certain writing and a spatiality, which leads him to posit what he calls 'arche-writing' as pre-origin of the speech-writing opposition; see De Ville (2011a: 53). In view of what was said above about the association between space and writing, arche-writing can also be referred to as 'spacing' (*l'espacement*). Spacing, like *khōra* in the *Timaeus*, thus refers to the 'repressed' origin of metaphysics. Derrida spells out the implications of spacing for the notion of identity, which is also at stake in his texts on *khōra*, in *Positions* (1981: 94/1972c: 130): 'spacing [*l'espacement*] is the impossibility for an identity to be closed on itself, on the inside of its proper interiority, or on its coincidence with itself'.

22 See also *ON* xv where Derrida notes that *khōra* does not give anything, i.e. neither the ideal paradigms of things nor the copies that the demiurge inscribes in it. Derrida's reticence here regarding the terminology of the gift must be understood in view of the fact that giving and receiving are anthropomorphic schemas (*CW* 17). *Khōra* is in other words not a subject who would be able to receive or conceive (*CW* 17; *ON* 99). This does not however mean that there is no relation between *khōra* and the gift, as we will see below.

23 See further below.

24 Here we again appear to be close to negative theology; see above.

language. *Khōra* thus clearly has ethical implications. At stake in *khōra*, Derrida ('F&K' 21/*F&S* 35, par 24) contends, is 'an utterly faceless other [*un tout autre sans visage*]' and without *khōra*, which also goes under the name of 'the desert in the desert' in Derrida's texts,[25] there would be no relation to the singularity of the other ('F&K' 19, par 22).[26]

In Derrida's analysis of *khōra*, psychoanalysis is hinted at a few times, for example the fact that *khōra* can only be perceived as in a dream and the invocation of a recollection beyond memory.[27] Is *khōra* therefore a different name for the unconscious? Derrida in 'How to Avoid Speaking: Denials' (*Psy II* 143–95) distinguishes *khōra* from the unconscious or the *id*: '*Khōra*' he says, 'is not even the *ça*, the *es* of the giving before all subjectivity' (*Psy II* 173) [Khora *n'est même pas* ça, *le* es *du donner avant toute subjectivité*]' (*Psy II* 173/*Psy II* (F) 175]. In the same breath, Derrida (*Psy II* 173/*Psy II* (F) 176) notes that *khōra* 'is radically ahistorical, because nothing happens through it and nothing happens to it'. *Khōra* is in other words not the result of the repression of historical (childhood) events as the unconscious is to some extent for Freud. The unconscious as perceived by Freud furthermore still participates in a circular economy, whereas *khōra*, as we saw, exceeds this economy. *Khōra*'s psychoanalytic parallel therefore appears to be not the unconscious, but instead the 'crypt' within the divided self, that is, a kind of false or artificial unconscious, which Derrida ('Fore' xiii, xix) explores with reference to the texts of Nicolas Abraham and Maria Torok.[28] Derrida's adoption, yet also transformation and generalisation of the crypt,[29] makes it almost indistinguishable from *khōra*. This similarity with *khōra* can for example be seen from the following characterisations of the crypt as described by Derrida: at stake in the crypt is 'something' which is in a radical sense unpresentable and unknowable ('Fore' xiv/*Fors* 12); this 'something' does not relate to the memory of a past traumatic event, but to a memory 'of what has never been' ('Fore' xxxiii/*Fors* 46); the crypt furthermore has no essence and is spoken of as a 'singular "beyond-place" or "no-place" [*non-lieu*] . . . a no-place or non-place within space,

25 See further below. The desert in the desert points to an abyss, i.e. '*there where one neither can nor should see coming what ought or could* – perhaps – *be yet to come. What is still* left to come'; see 'F&K' 7/*F&S* 16, par 9.

26 See in this respect also Derrida's analysis in a text such as *Speech and Phenomena and Other Essays on Husserl's Theory of Signs* where he points out through Husserl's texts how a certain non-presence lodged within presence makes it possible for the self to relate to the self and to others. This non-presence refers to (our relation to) death; see further De Ville (2011a: 14–19).

27 See also Kristeva (1984: 25–30) for a psychoanalytical reading of *khōra*. She understands the so-called 'semiotic *chora*' as a space or phase characterised by the operation of the instinctual drives, which precedes the (Lacanian) mirror stage as well as symbolic order and which is also pre-Oedipal. The semiotic *chora*, though repressed, furthermore remains in operation even after entry into the (Lacanian) symbolic order.

28 See also *Psy I* 142, and see further Section B below.

29 See also Marder (2008: 189).

a place as no-place' ('Fore' xxi/*Fors* 25); it is finally only because of this 'place', that we are able to speak of place in general ('Fore' xxxii/*Fors* 45–6).

Khōra and the political

The abyss at stake in *khōra*, the discussion of which appears right in the middle of the *Timaeus*, is, as Derrida (*ON* 104) notes, also reflected in the structure of the *Timaeus* itself, and specifically in the opening scene on political places or a politics of place. The scheme coming to the fore in this 'preamble' to the *Timaeus* is in other words analogous to the later discourse on *khōra* (*ON* 110). The narrative told in the preamble is more specifically placed in an abyss. At stake here is a narrative which is about the founding of Athens (much earlier than the collective Greek memory stretched), its laws (which corresponded in fact with that set up in Plato's *Republic* as ideal) and its bravery in war (it is said to have defeated a great Atlantic power). It had however lost its written archives through a great earthquake and since then had to rely on oral accounts based on memory (Derrida and Caputo 1997: 88–9). Critias was told this narrative by his great-grandfather (also called Critias), who was told this by Solon (responsible for the Athenian Constitution in the sixth century BC), who was told this by an Egyptian priest, who in turn read about it in the sacred texts preserved in Egypt (*ON* 114–15).[30] Critias had already recounted this story the evening before to his friends, recollected it during the night and repeated it again to his friends first thing that morning (Plato 1997: *Timaeus* 26b), and is repeating it here for the sake of Socrates. Relying on the language used to describe *khōra*, one can say that each story is the receptacle of another, and that *khōra* gives place to all these (fabulous, fictive, legendary or mythic) stories.[31] *Khōra* it/herself, Derrida (*ON* 117/*Khôra* 76) notes, 'does not however become the object of any *story* [*récit*], whether true or fabled'. This is because it lacks any reference as well as organisation with a beginning and an end (*CW* 11).

In the *Timaeus*, Socrates himself furthermore takes the place of *khōra*, playing the role of *khōra* (*CW* 13). As we will see again below, he also pretends for a moment to resemble the poets/sophists (men of the image/simulacra), as *khōra* does in respect of the 'metaphors' used to describe it/her, and he addresses and effaces himself before the philosophers/politicians. He acts here as *receptive*

30 As Sallis (1999: 43) points out, at stake here is an erased memory which not even the Socratic recollection of the *eidos* can recall. It is furthermore not fortuitous that it is expressed in writing; see further *ON* 122; and *Dis* 158 (on the importance of the grammatical 'metaphor'); see also above.

31 At stake in *Khōra* is not however myth, but something beyond the *mythos/logos* opposition, which precedes and exceeds this opposition. It can be called a myth within the myth or an open abyss in myth, but it also appears as heterogeneous to myth, as neither true nor probable (*ON* 90, 113). In the account of the priest, writing (of the other, i.e. the Egyptians (*ON* 114)) is e.g. explicitly contrasted with myth; see similarly Chapter 6 below on the Leviathan myth in Hobbes.

addressee, let us say, as a *receptacle of all* that will henceforth be inscribed (*ON* 110/*Khôra* 61): 'Your speeches are your hospitality gifts, and so here I am, all dressed up for the occasion. No one could be more prepared to receive your gifts than I' (Plato 1997: *Timaeus* 20c).[32] Socrates should of course not be equated with *khōra*, as Derrida (*ON* 111) notes, but he puts himself in its/her place, that is, in place itself, the placeless place. Socrates receives from this place the words of those who address him; yet they themselves receive the words from him (i.e. Socrates) because it is he who makes them talk, and us too (*ON* 111). Derrida elaborates on the 'place' of Socrates in relation to *khōra* in the insert to the text, by commenting that *khōra*

> announces, without promising, a thought, or rather, a putting to test of the political. And when Socrates makes a show of addressing himself to the others and of speaking of *politeia* in passing (and as the passerby he is, in a life that is too short), there he begins to resemble it, to resemble her, *khōra*, to play her in a fiction that will always have gone unnoticed, to figure her, she who is the intangible, the ungraspable, the improbable, totally near and infinitely far away, she who receives everything beyond exchange and beyond the gift. She as what *is necessary* [il faut] still, *Necessity*, without debt.[33]
>
> (*ON* xvi; *Khôra* non-paginated insert)

In the opening scene to the *Timaeus*, the discussion in the *Republic* is recalled where a proper place, position or occupation (*khorān*) was assigned to everyone, that is, to the rulers, the guardians and the craftsmen in constituting the city in the best way possible (Derrida and Caputo 1997: 86; Plato 1997: *Timaeus* 17c). The children have a potential place, whereas the poets and the sophists (as well as the slaves, though they are not at stake here) have no place. In the discussion of Plato's *Republic*, a description is specifically given of the possessions of the guardians, of the education of the children of the city and of marriage, which show a remarkable likeness to the description of *khōra* given above. Insofar as the guardians of the city are concerned, which can include both men and women, they would not have anything that belongs to them, that is, nothing that is properly their own, neither gold nor silver. They will receive a salary from those they protect only in accordance with their limited needs (Plato 1997: *Republic* 416a–417b, 464a–e).[34]

32 Derrida (*ON* 110–11/*Khôra* 60) notes that in this 'preamble' where Socrates declares himself ready to receive discourses in exchange for those offered by him the previous day, it is still a matter of gift and counter-gift, thus of a circular economy. Later on in the *Timaeus*, in the discussion of *khōra*, there however appears to be a movement beyond debt. The question of receptivity is also raised here by Derrida in its relation to sense/sensibility. At stake here is the receptivity (of *khōra*) or the gift of hospitality in an 'originary' sense, i.e. preceding sensibility.

33 See in respect of Necessity (*Anankē*), Plato (1997: *Timaeus* 48a-b); *EO* 115–16; Derrida (1995b: 1, 78–9) which together with the 'Straying Cause' can be read as alluding to the Freudian death drive.

34 See further Plato (1997: *Timaeus* 18b); *ON* 104–5; Sallis (1999: 18).

The likeness with *khōra* – to have nothing that is one's own – is unmistakable, as Derrida (*ON* 105) points out. This is likewise the case with regard to the education of children: property or ownership and legitimacy should have no role to play here, neither in respect of the father nor the mother (Plato 1997: *Republic* 457d–e, 460b–d).[35] Parents should not even know who their actual offspring are. We saw above that *khōra* is compared to a nurse, does not generate and nothing belongs to it/her. Of interest here is also the mention of the sieve-like function of *khōra* and the word *khōra* itself (*khōran*), which appears in the context of the place allocated to children through a sifting process (Plato 1997: *Republic* 459e–460b).[36] In the site at stake here, Derrida (*ON* 105) notes, the law of the proper no longer has any meaning. Marriages are furthermore to be (secretly) arranged by the drawing of lots (the use of a sieve, alluding thereby to *khōra*) to ensure that the children from such marriage have the best possible nature (Plato 1997: *Republic* 460a–d; *ON* 105–6).[37]

Another important aspect of the *Timaeus* relates to what Socrates says about the ideal political order sketched in the *Republic*, and which brings us back to the question of fiction. Derrida (*ON* 121) notes in this respect that the *Timaeus* is itself a (written) fiction (F1), where what is at stake (in the introductory session) is a fictive account of a discussion the previous day (the *Republic*, F2) with as its content the fictive model of an ideal city.[38] The *Timaeus* thus acts, like *khōra*, as receptacle to the account in the *Republic* (*ON* 117). While busy recounting the features of the ideal model (F3), Socrates makes a statement which Derrida (*ON* 117/*Khôra* 77) reads as an interruption of 'this mythopoetic string of events', but by means of which he launches it even more forcefully.[39] According to Socrates this fictive account of the ideal city is a dead representation and he desires for it to come into motion through a second graphic fiction (*CW* 27; *ON* 118). This can be done by

> a speech depicting our city in a contest with other cities, competing for those prizes that cities typically compete for. I'd love to see our city distinguish itself in the way it goes to war and in the way it pursues the war: that it deals with the other cities, one after another, in ways that reflect positively on its own education and training, both in word and deed – that is, both in how it behaves towards them and how it negotiates with them.
>
> (Plato 1997: *Timaeus* 19c–d)

35 See further *CW* 21; *ON* 105; Plato (1997: *Timaeus* 18d).

36 See further Plato (1997: *Timaeus* 19a); *ON* 107; Sallis (1999: 19).

37 The notion of chance invoked here can be explored further with reference to Derrida's essay 'My Chances/*Mes Chances*: A Rendezvous with some Epicurean Stereophonies' in *Psy I* 344–76.

38 See Sallis (1999: 21–3) for certain problems in relation to the positing of such a connection between the *Timaeus* and the *Republic*.

39 As later appears and as Derrida (*ON* 122–3/*Khôra* 88) points out, this 'interruption', a seeming attempt to move from the (fictive) ideal city to the city in action/reality, and which Socrates declares himself incompetent to do, is taken up by yet further fictive accounts; see further below.

The first description in the *Republic*, Derrida (*ON* 118) notes, is of 'the city in itself, internal to itself, at peace with its own interiority, in its domestic economy'. At stake in this call for another graphic description or image is the state's movement outside of itself, which Derrida (*ON* 118/*Khôra* 78) refers to as a '*decisive exposition* of the city . . . [in] all the senses of the word' [*À tous les sens de ce mot, c'est une* exposition décisive *de la cité*].[40] Socrates interestingly notes that he is incapable of giving fitting praise to the city in this respect.[41] He thus withdraws and keeps silent not only about *khōra*, but also about this analogous 'exposure' of the city in war. He likens himself in this respect to the poets as well as the sophists who cannot understand those who have a place, that is, those who 'act by means of gesture and speech, in the city or at war' (*ON* 107/*Khôra* 55). Insofar as the poets are concerned, Socrates notes that he has nothing against this race/tribe (*poiētikon genos*), yet owing to their place, conditions of birth and education, they will have difficulty describing what happens in the city in actions and words (*ergois, logois*) (*ON* 107). This is so in respect of the ancient as well as contemporary poets (Plato 1997: *Timaeus* 19d–e). Socrates notes that they can only imitate what they have been trained to imitate and war lies outside of their training (Plato 1997: *Timaeus* 19d–e).[42] The sophists, even though Socrates 'praises' them for their ability to make long speeches and doing many other fine things, seem according to him to be incapable of giving such an account 'because they wander from one city to the next and never settle down in homes of their own' (Plato 1997: *Timaeus* 19e). The sophists are consequently 'bound to misrepresent whatever these leaders accomplish on the battlefield when they engage any of their enemies, whether in actual warfare or in negotiations' (Plato 1997: *Timaeus* 19e). Unlike the philosophers and politicians – a *genos* who have a place and which includes Socrates' interlocutors (Critias, Timaeus and Hermocrates) – the *genos* or tribe of the sophists can thus be said to have no fixed domicile, no proper place (*CW* 22;

40 This should presumably be understood with Derrida's analysis of Schmitt's *The Concept of the Political* in *Politics of Friendship*, where as we saw, war was central to the analysis; see Chapter 2, Section A above. See in this respect also 'F&K' 17–18 where Derrida ties the messianic, which stands in a close relation to *khōra*, to an exposure of the self; and see Derrida and Thévenin (1998: 132) on the passive exposure of the subjectile, which Derrida likens to *khōra* (135).

41 Derrida (*ON* 149 n8) points to a similar movement in Rousseau's *Social Contract*. He points out that for Rousseau war returns us to a specific form of savageness. It involves the social contract going outside of itself. It thus entails a certain suspension of the social contract, showing the limits thereof, similar thus to Schmitt's state of exception; see Chapter 3 above. In the last chapter of the *Social Contract*, Rousseau specifically refers to that which he cannot deal with in his book: the external relations of the state, including international law, commerce, the laws of war, negotiation, leagues and treaties. Derrida notes that Rousseau here opens his eyes to 'perceive the outside of the fable or of the ideal genesis', but closes the book; see for similar comments, Derrida (2014: 16).

42 Sallis (1999: 31) remarks in this respect that the vision of the poets is restricted 'to what lies within the range of the city', which makes them incapable of describing 'the relation of the city to the outside, to another city'. The ambit of the sophists on the other hand 'is too external to the city for them to be capable of depicting the city at war'.

Plato 1997: *Timaeus* 19e). There is no room for the poets and the sophists in the political place (the *agora*) where affairs are spoken of and dealt with (*ON* 108–9). They are also excluded from the 'meaning' of *khōra* in the general or political sense, that is, 'place occupied by someone, country, inhabited place, marked place, rank, post, assigned position, territory or region' (*CW* 23; *ON* 109). For those who have place, the truth is that the poets and sophists have no place.

We noted above that Socrates places himself in the position of *khōra*, a third *myth*, and we just saw that he refers to the poets and sophists as a '*genos*'. On Derrida's reading, Socrates withdraws (like *khōra*) through simulation (pretending to be like the poets and the sophists, that is, those who feign) so as to give a place to those who have a place. Although Socrates pretends to be like the poets and sophists, that is, as having no place, this does not mean that he assimilates himself to them. He operates from a kind of non-place (*CW* 22–3; *ON* 107). He is of a third genus (neither that of the sophists, poets and other imitators, nor that of the philosopher politicians, the men of action and of their word), and 'in the neutral space of a place without place, a place where everything is marked but which would be "in itself" unmarked' (*CW* 23; *ON* 109). The question of capacity in the case of Socrates, that is, in describing the actions of the city, is to be understood with reference to his own non-place – that of *khōra* – and the consequent effacing of himself. Socrates thus gives the philosopher politicians the word by pretending to belong to the *genos* of the simulators. He can in this respect be said to 'induce and to programme the discourse of his addressees' (*ON* 121/ *Khôra* 86). This is followed by still further fictive accounts as we saw above, even though these are presented as real events. The ideal order of the *Republic* can thus be said to be inscribed in an abyssal narrative account with no fixed origin.[43] We also see something similar in the fictional account given of Solon (F6),[44] who is supposed to speak of the real (political) event. He is referred to as a poet of genius who would have been more famous (as a poet) than Hesiod and Homer if it was not for his political involvement (Plato 1997: *Timaeus* 21d). Derrida (*ON* 123) points to the irony of this statement, in view of what Socrates had said earlier (Plato 1997: *Timaeus* 19d–e) about poets, and the 'realist' turn which the text pretends to take here, that is, the invitation by Socrates to speak about the political, about the city engaging in war. A dynamic tension seems to be at stake here, Derrida (*ON* 123–4) notes, between Solon as statesman (political philosopher) and the identifiable and transmissible meanings associated with politics and philosophy (the ideal state and its accomplishments), on the one hand, and a textual

43 By describing Plato's *Timaeus* in terms of an abyssal fiction, Derrida (*ON* 106, 113) appears to be alluding to what he elsewhere refers to as a kind of phantasm involving self-destruction (*B&S II* 77), which functions as the condition of possibility of fiction in general.

44 F4 is the account of Critias which he had told the night before, F5 is the account of the conversation which the older Critias would have had with Solon and F7 is the account of the Priest of what he had read in the scriptures (*ON* 122).

drift taking the form of a myth or a 'saying' here, on the other. This 'mythical' account has no subject at its origin, no legitimate father, as the *Phaedrus* requires for the philosophical logos (*ON* 124).[45]

Constitutions as giving place

The question was anticipated above whether a constitution's function, similar to *khōra*, is not perhaps ultimately to give place. This is indeed what can be said to be at stake in the opening scene of the *Timaeus* as well as in the *Republic*, which as Derrida (*ON* 104/*Khôra* 47) notes, entails 'a discourse on *places* [places], notably political places, a politics of place entirely commanded by the consideration of sites [*lieux*] (positions in society, the region, territory, country)'. Schmitt, as we saw, effectively criticises liberal constitutional theory for thinking of the constitution in terms of the father (the ideal order) giving birth to the son (the constitution). Schmitt seeks another father, a real, concretely existing father, the subject of constituent power, to give birth to the son.[46] In doing so, he renews, but also repeats the Platonic legacy, which as Heidegger tells us, constantly finds new ways of contemplating Being as presence and in terms of beings.[47] Heidegger therefore at first calls for a contemplation of Being itself, and later of the giving of Being (and of time).[48] The *Timaeus* likewise goes beyond metaphysics by contemplating this other of Being in the 'form' of *khōra*. How is the constitution's giving of place then to be understood if the role of *khōra* is recognised in this 'birth'? We saw above that *khōra* is associated with expropriation, uprootedness, homelessness, dislocation, dissolution of identity, that is, a total exposure and giving of the self. *Khōra* and the analogous 'abyssal desert' and 'desert in the desert' are also associated by Derrida with the gift, with justice beyond law, with absolute hospitality,[49] with the democracy to come, and with autoimmunity.[50] This 'non-place', which is unpresentable, unknowable, undiscoverable and has no

45 See Naas (2003: 22–36) on Derrida's exploration of the relation between myth and philosophy with reference to Hegel. Derrida seeks an understanding of myth here (*ON* 100–2), which is not subject to the mastery of philosophy; see also above.

46 See Chapter 3 above, and see analogously *ON* 126 on the position in philosophy.

47 See De Ville (2011a: 114–18).

48 See further De Ville (2011a: 125–8).

49 In Derrida's texts on hospitality, 'place' likewise plays an important role, including 'places' of absolute hospitality such as Jerusalem and Sinai (*Adieu* 105–6, 119), Oedipus's secret tomb in a foreign land (*OH* 75–117), the laws of hospitality behind glass and above a bed in Klossowski's *Roberte ce Soir* (*OH* 121–31 and Derrida (2006b: 216–19, 224)), and cities of refuge (Derrida 2001c: 3–24) that inevitably remind one of *khōra*.

50 See *SoM* 33, 210–12; 'F&K' 18, par 22; *Rog* xiv–xv, 82–3; Derrida (2007c: 21); and see further Saddad (2013: 61–2) on the connection between democracy to come and *khōra*; and De Vries (1999: 108–12) on the connection between *khōra* and hospitality. Ashe (2003) has, like De Vries, raised the possibility of a new thinking of tolerance with reference to Derrida's 'Faith and Knowledge'.

essence, does not participate in a circular economy like the unconscious still does, but exceeds such economy. It can be referred to as the pre-origin of place, insofar as it makes it possible for us to speak about place in general. As is pointed out in the *Timaeus*, a command issues from it, to speak of it, but it 'is' a law which does not exist.

Derrida (*ON* xvi/*Khôra* insert) explicitly links *khōra* to the gift, referring to *Khōra* as 'she who receives everything beyond exchange and beyond the gift [*elle qui reçoit tout par-delà l'échange et par-delà le don*]'. In a discussion with Kearney and Marion 'On the Gift', Derrida further notes that

> without the indifferent, non-giving structure of the space of the *khora*, of what makes place for taking place, without this totally indifferent space which does not give place to what takes place, there would not be this extraordinary movement or desire for giving, for receiving, for appropriating, for *Ereignis* as event and appropriation.
>
> (Derrida 1999a: 67)

The traditional conception of the gift involves the giving of some thing by some one (a subject) to an other (subject) (*GT* 10–11). In *Given Time* (1991) Derrida shows that this traditional conception of the gift actually cancels the gift as it involves an economy of exchange. A gift can only qualify as such if it involves no circular return to the self whether in consciousness or in the unconscious (*GT* 12, 15). The relation between the gift, economy and law is likewise specifically addressed in *Given Time*: 'Among its irreducible predicates or semantic values', Derrida (*GT* 6/*DT* 17) notes, 'economy no doubt includes the values of law (*nomos*) and of home (*oikos*, home, property, family, the hearth, the fire indoors)'. Furthermore, '[*n*]*omos* does not only signify the law in general, but also the law of distribution (*nemein*), the law of sharing or partition [*partage*], the law as partition (*moira*), the given or assigned part, participation' (*GT* 6/*DT* 17). In our analysis of *khōra* and the political above, we saw that *khōra* as un-placeable place 'precedes' such sharing, and giving (taking place).[51] *Khōra* does not determine the way in which such appropriation, sharing and giving should take place. *Khōra* in other words does not function as foundation, and although no politics, ethics or law can thus be deduced from it, this does not mean that it leaves no trace in these fields in relation to what has to be done (*Rog* xv).

Schmitt's *Constitutional Theory*, as we saw, speaks of the constitution in terms of a gift, that is, a giving of place, by the constituent power to itself. All modern constitutions do this, whether explicitly or implicitly. This is indeed how it appears and this is also what the metaphysical tradition, starting with Plato, has taught us

51 See further Chapter 7 below on *nomos*, with Schmitt, as we will see, seeking to extend its meaning to include 'appropriation', as well as a certain a-*nomos*, which 'precedes' *nomos*.

about origins, about the ideal and the image. Yet, if we take Plato seriously, that is, the text of Plato and not the dominant interpretation of Plato, we see that a founding document is not anchored in whoever claims to set itself up as constituent power. As Derrida's *Khōra* shows, and as he spells out in 'Declarations of Independence' and 'Force of Law', founding documents are ultimately without author and origin, basing themselves on the fiction of a fabulous retroactivity.[52] Constitutions do not thereby simply become fictitious, as this fictional strategy, as we saw, finds its 'source' elsewhere. The constituent power is in a similar position to Socrates, who appears as the author of the ideal state in the *Republic* (as a philosopher-politician, that is, one who has a place), *and* in the *Timaeus* effaces himself, that is, acts as receptacle by putting himself in the place of *khōra* (a place without place).

It thus appears that constitutions have another 'origin', or rather a pre-origin: *khōra*. From here issues a call for justice as gift without exchange, of absolute hospitality, that is, a justice irreducible to law (*Rog* xv). Constitutions (whether national, transnational or international) are in other words derived from *khōra*, that is, the non-place of the event. According to Derrida,

> [t]here is gift, if there is any, only in what interrupts the system as well as the symbol, in a partition without return and without division, without being-with-self of the gift-counter-gift [*dans une partition sans retour et sans répartition, sans l'être-avec-soi du don-contre-don*].
>
> (*GT* 13/*DT* 25–6)

This ties in closely with Derrida's reference to *khōra* in 'On the Gift' as the absolute universal place, a place of resistance, and the condition for a universal politics (Derrida 1999a: 76). *Khōra*, as we saw, precedes the work of the architect-Demiurge, and thus also the performative speech acts of constituent power. This is to say that the constituent power necessarily adopts a constitution 'in view of' the law (of law) or a-*nomos* (Chapter 7 below) at stake in *khōra*. Following Derrida's reading of Blanchot, one can say that at stake in the drafting and adoption of a constitution is not strictly speaking the 'narrating voice', but the 'narratorial voice'. The narrating voice (*La voix narratrice*)

> is the voice of a subject recounting something, remembering an event or a historical sequence, knowing who he is, where he is, and what he is talking about. It responds to some 'police,' a force of order or law .... Now, the

52 Derrida points out in 'Declarations of Independence' (*Neg* 46–54) that the people who declare themselves independent, paradoxically only come into being through the performative act of the declaration, and therefore cannot really be said to be the 'author' of this document; see further De Ville (2011a: 43–73). In 'Force of Law' Derrida (*AR* 269–70) similarly argues that such founding always takes place in a sphere which is neither fully legal nor illegal.

> narrative voice [*la voix narrative*] . . . has no fixed place [*n'a pas de lieu arrêté*] . . . . It takes place place*lessly*, being both *a-topical*, mad, extravagant, and *hypertopical* [*Elle a lieu* sans *lieu, elle est à la fois* a-topique, *folle, extravagante et* hypertopique] . . . . The neuter *il*, 'it,' of the narrative voice is not an 'I,' not an ego . . . .
>
> (Derrida 2011b: 130–1/1986c: 150)

What was said earlier about Socrates taking the place of *khōra* testifies to a certain *Unheimlichkeit* (uncanniness), a pre-originary 'not-at-home-ness', a strangeness, which structures man and all living beings in general.[53] As Derrida (2013: 38) puts it, 'I belong to that which does not belong to me, to my own, to a language, a site, to a 'my home,' that do not belong to me and which I will never possess'. This uncanniness or homelessness is necessarily reflected in texts, including a constitutional text, in what can be called 'cryptonyms' (Section B below).[54] A demand issues from the non-place which precedes and conditions place in general, including the making-place of a constitution, to speak of that which the cryptonyms hide. At stake here is a concept of the constitution with nothing proper to it, a concept that has become 'hospitable to its other, to an other than itself that is no longer *its* other' (*AR* 362). This re-conception of the Constitution would call for a radical rethinking of the 'giving of place' on the national, transnational and international levels. The most obvious denial of place lies in 'killing', yet this notion would in accordance with the law of hospitality at stake here have to be extended beyond conscious killing and beyond the human to all living beings.[55]

Killing starts when there is an indifference to those who do not have food and water (Derrida 2013: 38–9; *G&L* 85–6). The recognition of this law beyond law would necessarily call for urgent action to be taken on a national, transnational and international level in relation to shortages of food and water, illness, shelter and lack of sanitation facilities. It would likewise call for a rethinking of the concept of citizenship and thus of obligations (national and international) towards refugees, both political and economic (*ET* 17, 57; Derrida 2007c: 21). Beyond this basic minimum, 'giving place' also calls for an extension of democracy, both on the level of the state and beyond the state (Derrida 2007c: 21; *Rog*

53 See Heidegger (2000: 159–63) who links this uncanniness specifically to the foundation of states (163), and see *B&S I* 264–6; see further *AR* 402–5, and *Adieu* 56 on man's being a stranger on earth, a guest, a hostage, an exile; and see *B&S II* 95–7, 101 where Derrida comments on Heidegger's notion of philosophy as nostalgia, i.e. a drive to be at home everywhere; yet this is because those who philosophise are not at home everywhere; this drive is furthermore a drive that pushes us towards the world; 'our being is this being-pushed' (101). A similar tension between the de-localisation brought about by technology and the drive towards the being-at-home is to be found in 'F&K' 45 and *ET* 79; see further Chapter 2, Sections A and B and Chapters 6 and 7 on technology.

54 See e.g. 'F&K' 40 on the crypts dispersed in Derrida's own text.

55 See also Chapter 6 below on the demands of equality.

53, 87; *ET* 65), as well as for a radicalisation of equality and freedom (Chapter 6 below). At stake is an unconditional giving, which can within a legal system only find expression in conditional forms, but which would in each instance have to come as close as possible to the demand of the unconditional. This unconditional demand of giving extends moreover to the whole field of national, transnational and international law.

SECTION B CRYPT

How indeed could one put the unnameable into words?

(Abraham and Torok 1994: 158)

Introduction

As we saw in earlier chapters, Schmitt's focus in *Constitutional Theory* is the Weimar Constitution, which was adopted after the end of World War I. The Weimar Constitution confirmed the abolition of the monarchy, and established a liberal constitutional democracy for the German Reich. Schmitt seeks to analyse the Weimar Constitution as a typical example of the modern liberal constitution based on the rule of law. This 'type', also referred to by Schmitt (*CT* 90–3/*VL* 37–41) as the 'ideal concept of the constitution', was and still is today the 'normal' or most prevalent form of constitution. In his discussion of the ideal concept, Schmitt (*CT* 93/*VL* 40–1) notes that the peculiarity thereof lies in the fact that it undertakes an organisation of the state from a perspective which is critically and negatively disposed towards state power (*Staatsgewalt*). It namely seeks to protect the citizen from the abuse (*Mißbrauch*) of such power. Liberal constitutionalism is not that concerned with organising the state itself, but rather with the organisation of the means and methods of its control (*Mittel und Methoden seiner Kontrolle*). It therefore seeks to create guarantees against state abuse (*Übergriffe*) and to bring about restraints (*Hemmungen*) in the exercise of state power. Schmitt (*CT* 93/*VL* 41) however points out that a constitution which only includes such liberal rule-of-law (*bürgerlich-rechtsstaatlichen*) safeguards would be unthinkable, as the state itself or the political unity, in other words, that which requires control (*das zu Kontrollierende*), must be present-at-hand (*vorhanden*) or must be organised at the same time. The endeavour or desire (*Bestreben*) of the liberal constitutional state, Schmitt (*CT* 93/*VL* 41) notes, consists in repressing or forcing back the political (*das Politische zurückzudrängen*), limiting all expressions of state life in a series of normative frameworks (*Normierungen*), and transforming all state activity into competences, that is, precisely circumscribed, in principle limited jurisdictions (*prinzipiell begrenzte Zuständigkeiten*). From this it follows that the liberal rule-of-law component (*das Bürgerlich-Rechtsstaatliche*) can be only one part of the total state constitution, whereas the positive decision concerning the form of political existence makes up the other component (*CT* 93/*VL* 41). Constitutions of contemporary liberal states consequently always consist of a combination of two components. On the one hand the rule-of-law principles aimed at protecting liberal freedoms against the state, and on the other hand the political component from which the actual state form (monarchy, aristocracy, democracy or a 'status mixtus') is to be derived. In the combination of these two components lies the peculiarity of the contemporary liberal rule-of-law constitution (*CT* 93/*VL* 41).

The language which Schmitt uses in the passages analysed above so as to uncover the hidden 'political' dimension of the modern liberal constitution clearly resonates with Freudian notions such as repression, symptom-formation, binding, resistance, censorship, as well as in general with Freud's description of the operation of the conscious and unconscious mental processes.[1] It is as if Schmitt is signalling here that *Constitutional Theory* is essentially engaged in an analysis in the psychoanalytical sense of the modern liberal constitution. In terms of this 'analysis', the political component of the constitution would thus represent the unruly unconscious (the *id, das Es*), whereas the rule-of-law component would, like the conscious system (the *ego, das Ich*),[2] seek to ensure 'normality' by censoring and repressing the political component. Yet, as the analysis in Chapter 2, Sections A–C above sought to show, the political cannot simply be equated with Freud's *id*. Something more complex appears to be at stake here, which comes to the fore in Freud's case study of the Wolf Man, yet perhaps more clearly in the subsequent analyses of the case study by Nicolas Abraham and Maria Torok, as well as by Derrida. Freud (2001, XVII: 10) attached great importance to his analysis of the 'constitution' of the Wolf Man,[3] which, as he noted, allowed him to descend 'into the deepest and most primitive strata of mental development'.[4] Of interest to us here is specifically the notion of the 'crypt' as analysed by Abraham and Torok in *The Wolf Man's Magic Word* (1976), as well as in the 'Foreword' to this text, written by Derrida. As will appear from the analysis that follows, the crypt can be described as a 'false unconscious', and the forces at stake in its formation and operation do not involve repression.

Should the passage in Schmitt's *Constitutional Theory* referred to above be read in view of the above texts, it would suggest a choice in favour of 'to force back' rather than 'to repress' as translation for *zurückzudrängen*. We saw in Chapter 2, Sections A–C above that the political, similar to the crypt, harbours a force of self-destruction. The present chapter will seek to show that this force of self-destruction, which precedes and infuses both the rule-of-law and the political components of the constitution, is incorporated in every constitution. A certain incorporation, similar to what we will see in respect of the Wolf Man, thus also takes place in a constitution, and Schmitt's *Constitutional Theory* stands open to such an understanding of the concept of the constitution. The force at stake here has a similarly 'subversive' role in relation to the controlling, restraining and limiting functions of the modern constitution as the crypt has in relation to the constitution of the self. The present chapter will proceed by first looking briefly at the respective

1 See in general Laplanche and Pontalis (1973).

2 This is admittedly somewhat of an oversimplification, because, as we will see below, the ego itself is for Freud (2001, XIX: 18) partly unconscious.

3 The use of the word 'constitution' in this context is intentional, *cf.* Schmitt (*CT* 59/*VL* 3) contending that '[T]he word "constitution" should be restricted to the constitution of the state, i.e. of the political of the people, if an understanding is to be possible'.

4 See further the 'Editor's Note' in Freud (2001, XVII: 3); and Johnson (2011: 7–10) on the importance of this case for psychoanalysis in general. The Wolf Man is moreover referred to explicitly or implicitly in many of Freud's other texts.

readings of Freud, Abraham and Torok as well as Derrida; thereafter an enquiry in more detail will follow of the analysis of Abraham and Torok as well as Derrida's reading thereof. The chapter will end with a discussion of the link which Derrida himself posits between the events preceding the founding of a state or the adoption of a new constitution[5] on the one hand and the crypt on the other.

The Wolf Man

Freud's 'From the History of an Infantile Neurosis'

Sergei Konstantinovich Pankeiev (1886–1979), a Russian aristocrat, became Freud's patient at the age of 23 in February 1910 and his therapy with Freud lasted until July 1914. Freud's case study was written in 1914, but only published in 1918, under the title 'From the History of an Infantile Neurosis' (Freud 2001, XVII: 1–122). Pankeiev went to Vienna again in 1919 and was treated by Freud from November 1919 until February 1920. Thereafter relapses occurred and on Freud's advice he was treated by Ruth Mack Brunswick. He was in therapy with Mack Brunswick from October 1926 to February 1927, as well as intermittently thereafter, until 1938. In later years he was also treated by other analysts.[6]

Some traumatic incident seems to have occurred when Sergei was around four years old, with sudden and drastic changes in his behaviour. At first he was a quiet and well-behaved child. Upon his parents' return from a summer holiday he however 'had become discontented, irritable and violent, took offence on every possible occasion, and then flew into a rage and screamed like a savage' (Freud 2001, XVII: 15/1991, XII: 38). He furthermore suffered from an animal phobia: his sister (Anna) would show him pictures of a wolf, which made him scream with fear every time and say that the wolf would eat him (Freud 2001, XVII: 15–16). The phobia extended to other animals as well such as horses, and was accompanied by cruelty to beetles and caterpillars, as well as, in his imagination, to horses (Freud 2001, XVII: 16). There was also evidence of an obsessional neurosis with religious characteristics, which probably occurred at a later time than the animal phobia and cruelty (Freud 2001, XVII: 8, 16–17). The obsessional neurosis involved repeating the same religious rituals, such as making the cross and kissing pictures of saints (Freud 2001, XVII: 61–71). It was accompanied by blasphemous thoughts such as associating God with excrement and with 'swine' (Freud 2001, XVII: 66/1991, XII: 97).[7] The symptoms recounted above lasted until Sergei was eight or ten years old (Freud 2001, XVII: 8 n1, and 17).

5 Derrida does not draw the same clear distinction between the two, as does Schmitt; see Chapter 3 above.

6 See Johnson (2011: 2).

7 At the time of the obsessional neurosis, Pankeiev takes on the role of Christ and his father becomes God; see Freud (2001, XVII: 64–6).

His relationship with his father changed towards the end of his childhood from one of affection to one of estrangement and fear, following inter alia from his father's depression and the father's apparent preference for Sergei's sister (Freud 2001, XVII: 17). The main focus of Freud's case study is the infantile neurosis, though at the time he came to see Freud, neurotic symptoms were again on display (Freud 2001, XVII: 8, 17–18). He lacked independence, couldn't deal with life and suffered from disturbances of his intestinal function which required the regular administration of enemas (Freud 2001, XVII: 73, 74–5).[8] He furthermore showed neurotic symptoms in relation to money (represented for him by faeces), with him inter alia accusing his mother of having stolen his inheritance.[9]

The question is what caused this change in Sergei's character, as well as the phobias, perversities and the obsessive piety (Freud 2001, XVII: 17). From the analysis it appeared that his older sister (by two years) had 'seduced' him when he was 3¼ years old by touching his genitals (Freud 2001, XVII: 20–4). This was not however according to Freud the primary source of his neurosis. His pseudonym comes from the well-known dream he had just before turning four, of five, six or seven white wolves on a walnut (or Christmas) tree outside his bedroom window, which suddenly opened by itself. The wolves had big tails and their ears were pricked; they looked at him; he screamed from fear of being eaten by them and woke up. It took a long time to convince him that this had simply been a dream. Freud's interpretation of the dream, which at the same time was meant to explain the neurosis, was that he had as a 1½-year-old child, upon waking up, witnessed his parents engaging in *coitus a tergo* and that the manifest dream content consists of a transformation or distortion of this 'primal scene [*Urszene*]' (Freud 2001, XVII: 37, 39/1991, XII: 64, 65).[10] In exploring the latent dream thoughts, Freud (2001, XVII: 29–31) refers to the picture of the wolf which his sister liked to tease him with and which Freud connects with the fairy tales of 'Little Red Riding-Hood' and especially 'The Wolf and the Seven Little Goats' (both of which Sergei

8 Freud (2001, XVII: 100) points out that the enemas had for a reason to be administered by a man and that Pankeiev in subjecting himself to this procedure took the place of his mother in the so-called 'primal scene' (see below). The excrement represented a baby – as fruit of the copulation. After an enema, Pankeiev felt as if he had been reborn. Freud explains the phantasy of rebirth as a euphemism for the fantasy of incestuous intercourse with the mother. Pankeiev combined both fantasies (sexual intercourse with the mother and the father) into one (XVII: 102).

9 See Mack Brunswick (1928: 441). With the Russian Revolution, the family lost all their money and property.

10 Freud (2001, XVII: 56–7) ascribes Sergei's sister's actions to herself having witnessed a similar scene when she was young. He however also mentions an alternative possibility, namely that Sergei had witnessed animals copulating and then transferred this to his parents (XVII: 57–8). Freud later mentions (as is the case in *Totem and Taboo* with the primal horde (XIII: 159–60)) that it does not really matter whether the primal scene was a real experience or a phantasy, as the unconscious does not draw such a distinction. To be noted is that Freud (XVII: 97, 119–20) attributes scenes of observing parental intercourse, being seduced as a child and threats of castration to a phylogenetic heritage, linked to the Oedipus complex.

was familiar with); white flocks of sheep on the estate, many of which had died because of an epidemic; and a story his grandfather used to tell about a wolf that had entered the window of a tailor, who pulled off its tail and who was later chased up a tree by a pack of wolves (including the wolf in question). The wolves in the latter tale tried to reach the tailor by climbing on top of each other, first on the wolf that had lost its tail. Freud (2001, XVII: 32, 64) understood the wolves in the dream and in the earlier-referred-to phobia as representing Sergei's father who possibly at some point playfully 'threatened' that he would eat him.[11] The strong sense of the 'reality' of the dream (*Wirklichkeitsgefühl*) according to Freud (2001, XVII: 33/1991, XII: 59) meant that it had to be related to an occurrence that really took place. The wolves looking at him had to be understood in the obverse sense of him looking at something (Freud 2001, XVII: 34). The immobility of the wolves likewise stood for its obverse – the most violent activity, that is, the primal scene (Freud 2001, XVII: 35). The sudden opening of the window should be understood as him suddenly waking up.

We cannot go into more detail here of Freud's analysis, save to mention that the Oedipus complex and its inversion plays an important role (Freud 2001, XVII: 119) with the father being viewed as the castrator. The case history also illustrates well Freud's theory of *Nachträglichkeit* (deferred or delayed action) with the primal scene constantly seeking a return. The trauma here is in other words tied to the Oedipus complex.[12]

Abraham and Torok's Cryptonymy

The analysis of the Wolf Man by Abraham and Torok (1986) is based on all extant documentation, including the analysis of the Wolf Man by Mack Brunswick (1928),[13] the account of his later life by Gardiner (1964), and his memoirs (Gardiner 1991).[14] They stand critical towards Freud's theory of the Oedipus complex and consequently also of the 'primal scene' as constructed by Freud.

11 Deleuze and Guattari (2004: 29–43) criticise Freud for reducing the wolves to one wolf and his understanding of it as a reference to the father. They argue for an interpretation in line with the notion of multiplicity.

12 See also Rashkin (1992: 14).

13 At the time that Pankeiev saw Mack Brunswick, he had developed a hypochondriac obsession about a scar on his nose as well as about his teeth. This was coupled with paranoia in the form of delusions of persecution concerning the doctors treating him. It further appeared from the analysis that Pankeiev had in 1922 received valuable family jewels from an acquaintance who had travelled from Russia to Vienna, which he had refrained from telling Freud about despite the fact that Freud had supported him financially for six years since 1919 through donations by fellow analysts. Mack Brunswick concluded that these symptoms were the result of an identification with both his mother and his (castrated) father. Abraham and Torok (1986: 9) however take the view that the nose obsession involved Pankeiev taking on the identity of his sister before her suicide, who had at this point complained of pimples on her face.

14 This text was first published in 1971 under the title *The Wolf Man and Sigmund Freud.*

They contend that the cause of Sergei's dreams and symptoms instead lie in his witnessing of a scene of seduction by his father of his older sister (by two years), who, as we saw, later in turn seduced Sergei. The witnessing of this scene was not however according to them what brought about the neurosis, but rather the silence imposed on Sergei by his mother after the revelation of the event from fear of the scandal that might ensue should it become known. He was namely prohibited from speaking certain words, which led to the construction of a crypt in his ego where these words were kept.[15] The dream of the wolves is consequently read as giving expression to the words spoken by the mother to the English governess about the truthfulness of the account given by the young Sergei, the governess's response, as well as the mother's explanation to the children as to why the governess had left their employ (Abraham and Torok 1986: 29–40). The mother namely tells the governess that the boy was dreaming or lying about witnessing a crime, that is, seeing his sister with his father's fly wide open. Later, the mother tells the children that the governess had left because she had been acting like a fox and a police dog as well as her 'big tales' (Abraham and Torok 1986: 37).[16] The event as constructed by Abraham and Torok would thus also explain Sergei's mother's abdominal disorders (Freud 2001, XVII: 77–8), as well as the suicides of his sister and father.[17] Compared to Freud's analysis of Pankeiev, a different 'place' as well as 'force' is central to the analysis of Abraham and Torok (1986: lxxi/1976: 79): 'The Place was not the Unconscious, the Force was not repression [*Le Lieu n'était pas l'Inconscient, la Force n'était pas le refoulement*]' ('Fore' lxxi/*Fors* 79). According to them the place where the trauma was registered was instead the crypt, 'A false unconscious [[*u*]*n faux Inconscient*]'; and the force of repetition at stake here involved a 'false "return of the repressed" [*un faux "retour du refoulé"*]' (Abraham and Torok 1986: lxxi/1976: 80).

Derrida and Freud's Wolf Man

Derrida's most important text on the Wolf Man is his 'Foreword' to Abraham and Torok's *The Wolf Man's Magic Word: A Cryptonomy*, dating from 1976. The Wolf Man also makes his appearance, whether implicitly or explicitly, in other texts of Derrida, and it is notable how in every one of these, Freud's *Beyond the Pleasure Principle* plays a significant role in rethinking many of the 'themes', concepts or

15 The notion of the crypt within the self involves a further development of Freud's 1938 essay 'Splitting of the Ego in the Process of Defence' (Freud 2001, XXIII: 275–8); see Abraham and Torok (1994: 152–3).

16 The different elements of the wolf dream are in accordance with the procedure to be described below, transcribed as follows: dreaming – the son as witness; window – eye; walnut tree(s) – sin or misdeed; lying (in bed) – telling a lie; six (wolves) – sister; wolves – fly; white – wide (open fly); cry out – divulge, dishonour.

17 Pankeiev's sister committed suicide by mercury poisoning in 1906, aged 21, and his father committed suicide in 1907. His mother died in 1953, aged 89; see Gardiner (1964: 86).

matters that came to the fore in Freud's analysis of the Wolf Man. These include memory (traces), repression, the archive, trauma, repetition, pleasure, resistance to analysis and dreams. Derrida's reading in each instance leads to the 'transformation' of these themes, concepts or matters so as to include the operation of the death drive in accordance with Derrida's reading of Freud's *Beyond the Pleasure Principle* (XVIII: 3–64) in *The Post Card* (1987: 257–409). Freud's texts can be said to already open themselves to such a reading. The trace for example becomes 'the erasure of selfhood, of one's own presence' which 'makes possible . . . something that can be called repression in general' (*WD* 230/*É&D* 339).[18] The role of the archive in preserving the traces of the past is acknowledged, but is itself made possible by a drive to completely destroy the archive.[19] An interview with Derrida in *Philosophy in a Time of Terror* shows clearly how Derrida ('Auto' 96–8) understands trauma.[20] These comments on trauma find their place within a broader discussion of a certain autoimmune logic or death drive at stake in the events of 11 September 2001.[21] According to Derrida ('Auto' 96), trauma and event are inextricably related: 'any event worthy of this name, even if it is a "happy" event, has within it something that is traumatizing'.[22] Derrida ('Auto' 96) seeks here to go beyond the idea that the traumatic event

> is linked to presence or to the past, to the taking place of what has happened, once and for all, in an undeniable fashion, so that the repetition compulsion that might follow would but reproduce what has already happened or been produced.[23]

Derrida does not reject this construction of trauma, but wants to add a further dimension to it by rethinking its chronology. The event at stake here, Derrida ('Auto' 97) notes, is not appropriable and this is because of the dimension of the future. A traumatic event in the present or past 'bears on its body the terrible sign of what might or perhaps will take place, which will be *worse than anything that*

18 See further Wood (2009: 115); and see *Points* 208–9/*PdS* 222 where Derrida notes that: '"cinder" renders better what I meant to say with the name of trace, namely, something that remains without remaining, which is neither present nor absent, which destroys itself, which is totally consumed, which is a remainder without remainder . . . . Cinders is the destruction of memory itself; it is an absolutely radical forgetting.' See furthermore *SP* 152 where the trace is said to involve a past that has never been and that will never be present; and *GT* 16–24 on a radical or absolute forgetting that exceeds repression and that ties in closely with Heidegger's forgetting of Being.

19 See Derrida (1995b: 19, 29; 2002d: 42, 44).

20 See also *Points* 372–95 ('Passages – from Traumatism to Promise').

21 It is noteworthy in this context that in 'Mourning and Melancholia', Freud (2001, XIV: 243/1991, X: 428–9) points out that mourning does not take place only in relation to the loss of a loved person, but also 'the loss of some abstraction which has taken the place of one, such as one's country, liberty, an ideal, and so on'.

22 See also *Points* 381.

23 See in this vein, e.g. Caruth (1996).

has ever taken place' ('Auto' 97). The temporality of the traumatic event at stake here in other words does not proceed from 'the now that is present' or 'from the present that is past but from an im-presentable to come (*à venir*)' ('Auto' 97). He describes this 'trauma' as more terrifying than a weapon that wounds because it comes from the future, a future radically to-come ('Auto' 97). A traumatic event that is experienced is thus terrifying because it is inscribed within this more terrifying trauma. 'Traumatism', Derrida ('Auto' 97) notes, 'is produced by the *future*, by the *to come*, by the threat of the worst *to come*, rather than by an aggression that is "over and done with"'.[24] Repetition as well as deferred action (*Nachträglichkeit*) is similar to trauma not to be understood as simply secondary, derivative, repeating something original that precedes it, in this way collaborating with the pleasure principle (PP), but also as 'original' insofar as it is 'older' than the PP, 'undermining it, threatening it, persecuting it by seeking an unbound pleasure' (*PC* 351–2/*CP* 373–4).[25] Pleasure, which is, similar to unpleasure, thus essentially without measure, needs to restrict itself to ensure the mastery of the pleasure principle (*PC* 400).[26] The strongest form of resistance, that is, absolute resistance, is said to be posed by the repetition compulsion, which exceeds the analytical concept of 'resistance to analysis'.[27] To conclude, in the case of dreams, Derrida (*WD* 209) emphasises their originary, inventive and, to some extent, illegible nature.[28]

The Wolf Man's crypt

Introjection and incorporation

According to Abraham and Torok, following Ferenzci, introjection is the process of 'normal' functioning where the ego or the self (*le Moi*) takes libidinally charged objects inside itself thereby enlarging the self.[29] Obstacles to introjection would

24 Hacking's argument (1995: 183–97; 2004: 17–20) that trauma is historical and contingent, i.e. dating from the last quarter of the nineteenth century, when the notion of physical trauma was extended to speak of psychical hurt or a wound to the soul, is in a way surmounted here. In other words, assuming that Hacking is correct (yet one can raise questions about the possibility of drawing a rigorous distinction between physical and psychic trauma, and thus also about the attempt at precisely 'dating' psychic trauma), the '(traumatic) event' which Derrida invokes here goes beyond any historically contingent notion of trauma, including 'national' or collective trauma'; on which, see e.g. Shamai (2016) and, more critically, Plotkin-Amrami and Brunner (2015). For a similar kind of argument about madness in relation to Foucault's *History of Madness*, see Derrida's 'Cogito and the History of Madness' (*WD* 31–63).

25 See also Chapter 2, Section B above.

26 See also Derrida 'Me–psychoanalysis' (*Psy I* 134–5).

27 See *Res* 23.

28 See also *Res* 10–16; and Wood (2009: 110).

29 Torok in Abraham and Torok (1994: 112/1987: 235) quotes Ferenzci in this regard as follows: 'I have described introjection as a mechanism allowing the extension to the external world of the

include incorporation, the illness of mourning, the crypt and the phantom.[30] In the case of a traumatic event[31] there is insufficient time for introjection, and incorporation occurs. Abraham and Torok set out the procedure at stake here as follows:

> Inexpressible mourning erects a secret tomb inside the subject. Reconstituted from the memories of words, scenes, and affects, the objectal correlative of the loss is buried alive in the crypt as a full-fledged person, complete with his own topography.[32] The crypt also includes the actual or supposed traumas that made introjection impracticable. A whole world of unconscious fantasy is created, one that leads its own separate and concealed existence.[33]
>
> (Abraham and Torok 1994: 130/1987: 266)

In the case of Pankeiev, the construction of the crypt (incorporating thereby his sister and his father, as well as others such as his mother, the nursery maid (Nanya), his German tutor,[34] the doctor[35] and his therapists made it possible for him to love and at the same time to annihilate these love objects (Abraham and Torok 1986:

primitive autoerotic interests, by including these objects of the exterior world in the self/ego . . . . To take things to the foundation, the love of man can be borne, precisely, only for himself. In as far as he loves an object he adopts it as part of his self/ego.' See further 'Fore' xvi; Rashkin (1992: 170 n15).

30 See Rand's 'Introduction' to Abraham and Torok (1994: 16). The transgenerational phantom according to Abraham in Abraham and Torok (1994: 165–205) involves the 'inheritance' of an unspeakable secret of an other, i.e. a love object. This secret can either be kept knowingly by a parent, or it can be lodged in the crypt of the parent and then inherited as a foreign body within the unconscious of a child; this would cause the inheritor to act as if he/she was 'driven by some stranger within' (1994: 188/1987: 448), similar to what happens in the case of a crypt within the self; see also Rashkin (1992: 21–32). The phantom does not play a role in Abraham and Torok's analysis of the Wolf Man.

31 The 'event' which leads to incorporation is not restricted to the loss of a love-object through death. In the case of the Wolf Man, in the analysis of Abraham and Torok, this already happened in relation to his sister-father when he was a boy, and they were still alive. See likewise Freud (2001, XIX: 28–9/1991, XIII: 257) who points out that what he calls the replacement or substitution of an object-cathexis by an identification (or 'the setting up of the object inside the ego [*Aufrichtung des Objekts im Ich*]') is a common occurrence, especially in the early stages of development.

32 Abraham and Torok (1994: 131) further point out that incorporation will only take place if the love-object is the cause of a shameful secret and when the love-object functions as an ego ideal. It is in other words the secret of the love-object that has to be kept, his/her shame that needs to be covered up; see further below.

33 See also Freud 'Mourning and Melancholia' (2001, XIV: 248–9) where he describes what happens to the libido in the case of the loss of a love-object. The libido is not directed at a new love-object, but is withdrawn into the ego where an identification takes place of the ego with the abandoned object. The ego is now judged as if it were the lost object.

34 See in this respect Freud (2001, XVII: 69).

35 This is presumably a reference to Professor X, the 'leading Viennese dermatologist' who treated Pankeiev's nose; see Mack Brunswick (1928: 443).

4–5; Derrida 'Fore' xii).[36] Whereas Abraham and Torok appear to strictly distinguish introjection from incorporation, Derrida points to passages in their texts which instead indicate that these processes are to be viewed as interrelated. In Derrida's reading it is impossible, except as theoretical ideal, to draw a rigorous distinction between incorporation and introjection as there are necessarily compromises and negotiations between these processes ('Fore' xviii; *Points* 321). Derrida can furthermore be said to overturn the privilege accorded by Abraham and Torok to introjection,[37] and to 'affirm' incorporation as understood by him. This affirmation of incorporation, together with the fact that incorporation, like introjection, does not wait for the death of the other,[38] opens the door to a 'translation' of incorporation into what can be called a hyper politico-legal-ethical demand, similar to what is at stake in Schmitt's concept of the political.[39]

The crypt

Derrida takes on board the notion of the crypt as constructed by Abraham and Torok, and specifically emphasises its location as well as the radical dislocation of the self which it brings about. As we will see, the crypt's 'place' in the topography is a non-place, it is a 'foreign body' both/neither inside and/nor outside of the self, which is marked by absolute pleasure. As Derrida ('Fore' xiv/*Fors* 12) notes, the crypt within the self, as identified by Abraham and Torok, is similar to a crypt in a temple or cemetery, 'isolated from general space by partitions, an enclosure, an enclave', with pillars, beams, studs and retaining walls.[40] The self can thus be said to become a cemetery guard (Abraham and Torok 1994: 159), although as Derrida ('Fore' xxxv) points out, the self is not the owner of what it is guarding. The crypt is furthermore not simply on the inside of the ego, but at the same time an outcast in respect of the general domain of introjection ('Fore' xvi). The (love-) object is kept like a stranger, and the self thus no longer deals with it; dealing as it always does, only with itself ('Fore' xvii). At stake here is furthermore a certain clandestinity: the crypt is a hidden place and erases 'the traces of the act of concealment [*effaçant les traces de la dissimulation*]' ('Fore' xvii/*Fors* 18; Abraham and Torok 1994: 159). The crypt could in Derrida's reading be said to mark 'the place of an intense pleasure [*jouissance*], of a *real* intense pleasure

36 See also Freud (2001, XIV: 256) where he points to the struggles over the object in the case of melancholia, with love and hate contending with each other.

37 See Kirkby (2006: 466).

38 See *B&S II* 168/*SB&S II* 242: '[M]ourning does not wait for death, it is the very essence of the experience of the other as other [*il est l'essence même de l'expérience de l'autre comme autre*] . . . . One is always in mourning for the other.' See further *Points* 321; 'Editor's Introduction' to *WM* 12; and De Ville (2011a: 136–7).

39 See Chapter 2, Sections A–C above.

40 See also 'Fore' xv and *EO* 57.

[*d'une jouissance* réelle][41] though walled up, buried alive in its own prohibition' ('Fore' xxxiv/*Fors* 50).[42] As compared to the 'normal' process of introjection, the object is, as we saw, 'magically' incorporated and not digested or assimilated (*EO* 57; 'Fore' xvii). Abraham and Torok (1986: 21/1976: 121) refer to these love-objects as '*incorporated* guests [[*l*]*es Hôtes* incorporés]'. The object so incorporated, according to Derrida (*EO* 58), can also be spoken of as a 'living dead', as it is not 'killed off' as in the case of 'normal' mourning, but continues to 'speak' from its place in the crypt. Although the crypt is sealed off, because of the contradictory desires enclosed in it (loving and annihilating),[43] it cannot completely retain these forces ('Fore' xv, xxii).[44]

The crypt and the word-thing

According to Abraham and Torok (1994: 127–8), introjection takes place essentially by way of language. In the case of incorporation, the expressive or representational function of language however falls into disarray. Meaning dissolves.[45] This is because unspeakable words are buried alive in the crypt, words which have been withdrawn from circulation as a result of the incorporation of a love-object that was abruptly lost (Abraham and Torok 1994: 159–60; 'Fore' xxxv–xxxvi). The memory buried in the crypt can be said to be of an idyll or romance (*d'une idylle*), experienced with a valued object, yet for some reason unspeakable (Abraham and Torok 1994: 140–1/1987: 297). The reason for this we

41 The notion of the 'real' should be understood here with reference to Abraham and Torok's anasemic (see below) re-conception of reality as 'what is rejected, masked, denied precisely as "reality"; it is that which *is*, all the more so since it must not be known; in short, Reality is defined as a *secret*. The metapsychological concept of Reality refers to the place, in the psychic apparatus, where the secret is buried' (1994: 157/1987: 253; see also 'Fore' xviii). Pleasure, as Derrida (*Psy I* 134) points out, is in turn to be understood beyond its everyday sense, i.e. 'translated into a code where it no longer has any sense, where, by making it possible, for example, what one feels or understands as pleasure, pleasure itself no longer signifies "what one feels" (Freud speaks, in *Beyond the Pleasure Principle*, of a pleasure experienced as pain . . .)'; see also 'Fore' xxi; and Ellmann (2000: 229–30). Anasemia can be said to refer to the way in which psychoanalysis has changed the meaning of inherited concepts, in line with a theory of counter-sense (*contresens*); see 'Fore' xxxi–xxxiv/*Fors* 44. The terms so transformed 'attempt the impossible: to grasp through language the very source from which language emanates [*saisir par le langage la source même dont le langage émane*]' ('Fore' xxxii/*Fors* 46).

42 Derrida ('Fore' xxxv/*Fors* 51) points with reference to Torok to the intensity of the libidinal outpouring that can sometimes occur, reaching the point of orgasm, and he speaks in this regard of the 'corpse of an exquisite pleasure, disguised by repression as an exquisite pain [*le cadavre d'un plaisir exquis, déguisé par le refoulement en douleur exquise*]'; see further Lock (1982: 883), and see below.

43 The desire at stake here, as Derrida ('Fore' xxiii) further notes, no longer belongs to him, i.e. to the Wolf Man.

44 See similarly Derrida's 'Freud and the Scene of Writing' (*WD* 196–231).

45 See 'Editor's Note' in Abraham and Torok (1994: 105).

find in Torok's essay 'The Illness of Mourning and the Fantasy of the Exquisite Corpse':

> *The illness of mourning does not result, as might appear, from the affliction caused by the objectal loss itself, but rather from the feeling of an irreparable crime or a sin beyond redemption [d'un péché irréparable]: the crime or sin of having been overcome with or invaded by desire [péché d'avoir été envahi de désir], of having been surprised by an overflow of libido [d'avoir été surpris par un débordement de la libido] at the least appropriate moment when it would behove us to be grieved in despair.*[46]
>
> (Abraham and Torok 1994: 110/1987: 232; italics in the original)

In *The Wolf Man's Magic Word* Abraham and Torok (1986: 81/1976: 232) express the manoeuvre at stake here by reversing Freud's famous expression 'Wo Es war, soll Ich werden' into 'wo Ich war, soll Es werden' (where there was Ego, there should be *id*). The Ego, as they point out, 'cannot quit the place where it had once been; it can only withdraw into seclusion and construct a barrier separating it from the other half of the Ego' (Abraham and Torok 1986: 81/1976: 232). The sole purpose of the manoeuvre, they further comment, '*is to preserve this non-place in the place where the intense pleasure* [*la jouissance*] *should no longer take place, but thanks to which it can take place elsewhere*' (Abraham and Torok 1986: 81/1976: 232–3).[47] The unspeakable words thus mark, as Derrida ('Fore' xxxvi/ *Fors* 52) puts it, 'the fact that the desire was in a certain way satisfied, that the intense pleasure [*la jouissance*] *did take place*'.

In the analysis of Abraham and Torok, the word that may not be uttered by Pankeiev is the Russian word *tieret* (rub, grind, crunch, wound, polish, that is, masturbate) (Abraham and Torok 1986: 18, 46).[48] This is the word that remains hidden in the Wolf Dream,[49] and of the skyscraper/*Wolkenkratzer* (erection, scraping)[50] as well as in the memory of the nursery maid scrubbing the floor

46 See also Freud (2001, XIV: 246–8) where he points to the delusion of moral inferiority in the case of melancholia.

47 Italics in the original; see also 'Fore' xx.

48 The word *natieret*, sharing the same root, similarly means to rub down, rub, scrub, wax, scrape or wound oneself; see Abraham and Torok (1986: 18). His other secret words were *goulfik* (fly) and *vidietz* (witness); see Abraham and Torok (1986: 40). The authors also describe the Wolf Man as the 'secret lover' of his magic word (Abraham and Torok 1986: 22/1976: 122).

49 In the analysis with Mack Brunswick, a number of other wolf dreams of Pankeiev were recounted; see Mack Brunswick (1928: 453, 460–1, 462–3).

50 These dreams were conveyed by Pankeiev to Mack Brunswick: 'I am lying at your feet. I am with you in a skyscraper where the only way out is a window. A ladder from this window extends down to uncanny depths. To get out I must go through the window'; see Abraham and Torok (1986: 70/1976: 211); see also Abraham and Torok (1986: 13).

(Abraham and Torok 1986: 46).[51] The (magic) word *tieret*, in the view of Abraham and Torok (1986: 46), 'operates only from the unconscious, that is, as a *word-thing*'.[52] What is the role of the unconscious here? In the *id*, Abraham and Torok (1986: 81) contend, something similar takes place as in the Ego.[53] They note that the crypt is lodged in an enclave between the ego of introjection and the dynamic unconscious (1986: lxxii; 1994: 159). The 'ultimate "referent"' or the 'Thing' can be said to be encrypted, 'not *within* the crypt . . . but *by* the crypt and *in* the Unconscious' ('Fore' xxvi/*Fors* 33). The Thing, one could thus say, is a crypt effect ('Fore' xiii). The 'Thing' as ultimate referent however never presents itself as such ('Fore' xxvi).[54] Following Abraham and Torok (1986: 81), Derrida ('Fore' xlii/*Fors* 63) calls *tieret* the 'pleasure word [*le mot-plaisir*]' which is chased (from the crypt) toward the (cryptic) unconscious 'where it functions like a thing'. The 'word-thing' in the unconscious crypt however functions in a different way from unconscious memory. This operation must be understood with reference to Abraham's earlier work on the symbol.

In general, as Abraham and Torok point out, psychoanalysis searches for the repressed cosymbol in the unconscious:

> Psychoanalytic listening consists of a particular way of treating language. Whereas usually one receives meanings, the analyst receives symbols, that is, data that lack a part and that are at the same time, in principle, determinable and yet unknown. To recover the complement of the symbol, the retrieval of the indeterminacy, that is the single target of this listening. From the beginning of psychoanalysis and until this day, theoretical efforts concern research that permits finding the unknown complement which lacks a symbol, which 'symbolizes with' or that – we might say brutally – 'co-symbolizes'.
>
> (Abraham and Torok 1986: 79/1976: 229–30)

51 See further below.

52 See in this respect Laplanche and Pontalis (1973: 447–9) who point out that in the unconscious system only thing-representations are to be found; the conscious system is characterised by the fact that thing-representations therein are bound to the corresponding word-representations. As we will see below, for Derrida *tieret* is ultimately neither a word nor a thing.

53 See also 'Fore' xx.

54 Derrida also explores the 'Thing' in a number of other texts such as *Signsponge* and *Parages*. In *Signsponge* Derrida (1984: 12–16, 50) notes with reference to Francis Ponge that the Thing is first of all the entirely other which dictates the law to which I ought to subject myself; it furthermore demands the impossible from me in my singularity, a demand which is in each case singular. The thing is furthermore not an object and cannot become one; it is not a subject either; it remains beyond exchange and priceless, and it is impossible to reappropriate. In *Parages* Derrida (2011b) refers with reference to Blanchot to the Thing as remembering us (61), as death (135, 139), as that which does not happen or does not come about (155–6), as that which takes place without taking place (158, which Derrida compares with the French judgment of *non-lieu*). Elsewhere (165) the *récit* (a narrative without story) is referred to as the coming of the Thing, and the Thing is described as a *récit*-effect which takes place placelessly.

The crypt complicates and radicalises the theory of the symbol by adding a further structure which needs to be passed through. At stake is thus not simply a co-symbolic operation, but one that is intra-symbolic (Abraham and Torok 1986: 80). Derrida ('Fore' xx/*Fors* 22–3) notes in this respect that the cryptic fortress 'fractures the symbol into angular pieces, arranges internal (intra-symbolic) partitions, cavities, corridors, niches, zigzag labyrinths, and craggy fortifications'. A split in other words takes place in respect of the symbol within the self as well as the unconscious, so that a certain dissemination, fragmentation, disjoining or unbinding occurs. Words, as Derrida ('Fore' xlii/*Fors* 63) puts it, take 'allosemic pathways in this strange relay race, passing the baton to non-semantic associations, to purely phonetic contaminations'. As mentioned above, the magic, silent, taboo pleasure word and co-symbol *tieret* (to rub, grind, wound, polish) is in this way transformed into 'scrubbing floors' (Abraham and Torok 1986: 46, 83; 'Fore' xlii).[55] In the latter respect *tieret*, as a thing of the cryptic unconscious, crosses the border of the unconscious and finds expression as a tableau; but it can also, as a word, and by crossing the walls of the crypt without going through the unconscious, find expression as a word, that is, a cryptonym ('Fore' xlii–xliii). Furthermore, the forms of disguise employed include rhyming, homophones, synonyms, paronyms and antonyms. All the languages Pankeiev could speak – Russian (his mother tongue), German (the language he spoke with Freud) and English (the English governess mentioned earlier) – are moreover of relevance in this respect (Abraham and Torok 1986: 31).[56]

Whereas for Abraham and Torok, based on a psychoanalytical reading, the splintered symbol can be said to ultimately signify 'something (a drama, scene, or simply a lexical or phonetic element) that must for some reason be kept hidden or out of circulation' (Rashkin 1992: 39), in Derrida's reading it points to an event which never took place in a present past and which lacks meaning. The symbol is thus ultimately indecipherable.[57] The nature of this indecipherability inter alia appears when Derrida ('Fore' xlvii), towards the end of his commentary, points

55 This example is of a memory of Pankeiev of himself as a boy of 2½ seeing the nursery maid scrubbing floors, which sexually excited him. Freud (2001, XVII: 91–6) notes that his later love objects were invariably peasant girls.

56 There are thus two modes of return of the word-thing *tieret*, thereby showing its double destiny: (1) by crossing the partition created in the unconscious disguised as an alloseme (variant meaning) and transformed into an image or symptom; (2) without passing through the unconscious and disguised as a cryptonym ('Fore' xlii–xliii; Abraham and Torok 1986: 81). This is to be compared with the traditional Freudian model where the only boundary that needs to be crossed by repressed desires is that of the unconscious ('Fore' xx).

57 See in this respect also Abraham and Torok (1994: 153) where they, with reference to another case history, point out that the genuine symbol or magic word 'originates in a different world, a world that cannot be symbolized'. They also speak in this respect of '*the symbol of what cannot be symbolized*' (at 153). This should be read with 'Fore' xxxii–xxxiii/*Fors* 46, where Derrida, with reference to Abraham's 'Introduction to Hermann' refers in this respect to a 'transphenomenal *complement* [complément *transphénoménal*]'.

with reference to Abraham and Torok (1986: 26, 31) to the importance of the root 'tr' in the vocabulary of the Wolf Man: truth; Turkey (a dream he had that involved the Turkish flag); the river Tierek which he visited upon the death of his sister where he was served trout; Theresa (his wife);[58] the silent word *tieret*; *rtout* (mercury, which his sister poisoned herself with); as well as the mention by the Wolf Man in a letter to Muriel Gardiner of the Germanic root of certain Russian words, for example *Trud*, meaning force. Of interest to Derrida here is specifically the link between truth (as expressed by Pankeiev in his dreams recounted to Freud and Mack Brunswick about lying (in bed), standing (at the prow of a ship; and looking out of his window at a meadow) and its 'rhymes' as collected in 'The Wolf Man's Verbarium', for example tooth, two (teeth extracted) (Abraham and Torok 1986: 43–76, Appendix), ending in *Trud*, which Derrida links to an 'entire history of Being' ('Fore' xlvii/*Fors* 71).[59] This last remark takes us back to the notion of 'absolute forgetting' or amnesia (*amnésie*)[60] which plays an important role in Derrida's texts, specifically in relation to the gift (of Being) (Section A above). We can also link the remark about truth/force with what was said earlier about 'the Thing', so that the 'event' at stake here can be referred to as 'the Thing' from which a law issues which demands the impossible, again in line with a certain reading of Schmitt's concept of the political (Chapter 2, Sections A–C above).

The crypt beyond metaphysics

In Derrida's reading of Abraham and Torok, the structure or law of the crypt is transformed and generalised, taking it beyond its therapeutic context.[61] Derrida shows that their text speaks of the crypt as an inaccessible 'non-place', located neither inside nor outside of the self, which escapes in a certain sense from the circular economy of metaphysics. Both a psychoanalytical reading of *The Wolf Man's Magic Word* and one that takes the text beyond psychoanalysis as well as beyond metaphysics are possible. The psychoanalytical reading would oppose incorporation to the healthier introjection and would see the crypt as a matter of contingency and as an obstacle to health. Derrida's reading places incorporation and introjection in a differantial relationship (*Points* 321) and makes of the crypt a universal structure, which is not formed only (pathologically) in response to a

58 Theresa committed suicide in 1938; see Abraham and Torok (1986: 6).

59 See also the discussion under the heading 'Derrida and Freud's Wolf Man' on repression and forgetting.

60 See *PoF* 100/*PA* 123.

61 Derrida ('Fore' xi) starts off his commentary by noting that he will be writing on *this* crypt, i.e. the first fragment of the first word of the title: *Cryptonymie: Le Verbier de l'Homme aux Loups*. He thereby indicates that he will be writing on a broken symbol (see above) and perhaps also that his focus will be on the crypt in the text or analysis of Abraham and Torok of the Wolf Man, showing how it is itself marked by a foreign body/absolute pleasure; see 'Fore' xlvii–xlviii.

past or past present traumatic event.[62] The 'mytho-dramatico-poetic' genesis of the words, images and symptoms of the Wolf Man constructed by Abraham and Torok is an attempt, albeit ultimately impossible, to narrate the 'event', 'pleasure' or 'Thing' at stake here ('Fore' xxvi/*Fors* 33).[63] The event that is 'narrated' by Abraham and Torok, Derrida ('Fore' xxvi/*Fors* 33) further comments, never appears. With reference to Abraham's *Introduction to Hermann*, Derrida ('Fore' xxxiii/*Fors* 46) remarks that

> [t]here is a memory left of what has never been, and to this strange recollection [*anamnèse*] only a mythical narrative [*un récit mythique*] is suitable, a poetic narrative [*un récit poétique*], but a narrative [*récit*] belonging to the age of psychoanalysis, arch-psychoanalysis and anasemia.[64]

This attempt to go back beyond the origin, to the source of all meaning, is another way of speaking about the stricture of *différance*.[65]

The Wolf Man's analysis thus cannot be 'saved', though Abraham and Torok, based on a psychoanalytical reading, still try to do so.[66] In other words, a dictionary cannot contain the dissemination at stake here ('Fore' xxxvii). The Wolf Man's analysis, as Abraham and Torok (1986: 49) themselves acknowledge, is interminable.[67] The Wolf Man's dreams, one could alternatively say, inevitably have a 'navel', which as Freud (2001, IV: 111 n1/1991, II/III: 116 n1) notes, is indecipherable, and which 'reaches down into the unknown'.[68] At stake in the crypt is likewise 'something' which is in a radical sense unpresentable and unknowable ('Fore' xiv).[69] As we saw earlier, Derrida furthermore speaks of it as a 'singular beyond-place or no-place . . . a no-place within places [*les lieux*], a

62 See also Marder (2008: 189).

63 The attempts by Freud as well as Abraham and Torok to construct the primal scene can on one reading be said to be an attempt at positing a simple and present origin, yet, as we will see now, Derrida believes that Abraham and Torok take a step further, beyond the origin.

64 See also Section A above on the distinction between the narrative and the narrating voice.

65 See Leavey (1986: 97–103).

66 See Abraham and Torok (1986: 16).

67 See 'Fore' xx/*Fors* 22 where Derrida, quoting Abraham and Torok, notes that what comes to the fore here is 'a subject particularly resistant to analysis, a subject carrying within him a "puzzle of shards about which we would know nothing: neither how to put it together nor how to recognize most of the pieces"'. See also *Res* 1–38.

68 'Jeder Traum hat mindestens eine Stelle, an welcher er unergründlich ist, gleichsam einen Nabel, durch den er mit dem Unerkannten zusammenhängt'; see also *Res* 10–16.

69 The 'Thing' or 'word-thing' (*tieret*) buried in the cryptic unconscious, Derrida ('Fore' xxi) contends, is likewise neither a thing nor a word. It is instead 'a mark or a code, a morsel of code, which can only be translated in a long interminable sentence or in the scene of a picture with several subjects, several objects, several entrances or exits. Trace without the vigil of a presence, Thing without origin, Origin to be de-signified according to anasemia' ('Fore' xliv/*Fors* 66).

place as no-place' ('Fore' xxi/*Fors* 24).[70] It is moreover only because of this 'place' that we are, according to Abraham and Derrida, able to speak of place in general ('Fore' xxxii).

The notion of the crypt implies a fundamental restructuring of the self, of the subject, as inhabited by a foreign body. Something similar can be said about institutions in general (see below) as well as the language of metaphysics. Derrida can be said to show in his texts that the language of metaphysics contains certain cryptonyms. Like the Wolf Man, metaphysical language is haunted by an encrypted absolute (un)pleasure, that is, pleasure experienced as pain. This can for example be seen in its hierarchical and oppositional terms (e.g. speech versus writing), which believes itself to be rooted in a 'present origin', but which actually hides its own relation to death.[71] It can be detected as well in certain concepts such as justice, the gift and hospitality. These concepts are to be found across cultures, and partake in a circular economy, yet at the same time exceed such economy. Like *tieret* they are pleasure words, which remain in hiding even though they show themselves. In other words they secretly speak of an absolute (un)pleasure, but they can appear only in their restricted, bounded form.

Constitution, memory and trauma

In conclusion let us return to the concept of the Constitution and its relation to the crypt. Geoffrey Bennington (2011: 25) speaks with reference to Derrida's 'Force of Law' and 'Mochlos, or The Conflict of the Faculties' of the 'traumatic memory' of the 'non-legal foundation' of institutions, including the state. Bennington (2011: 27) notes in this respect that the origin of the state is necessarily violent and marked by illegitimacy.[72] He proceeds to tie this founding violence to the crypt or a secret enclave within the state itself (Bennington 2011: 28). In support of Bennington's reading, it can be added that Derrida in 'Force of Law' (*AR* 241–3) explicitly invokes the language of the crypt in speaking about the founding and instituting of law,[73] which would cover both the founding of a new state and the adoption of a new constitution (*AR* 252). He says in this respect that 'there is a silence walled up in the violent structure of the founding act [*Il y a là un silence muré dans la structure violente de l'acte fondateur*]' (*AR* 242/*FdL* 33). This will of course be different in respect of every state or constitution depending on the specific trauma or traumatic event that preceded its formation or adoption whether in the form of war, revolution, genocide or colonialism and those who

70 Derrida ('Fore' xix) relies in this respect inter alia on Abraham and Torok's contention that the crypt lies 'between "the dynamic unconscious" and the "Self of introjection"'.

71 See further De Ville (2011a: 49–53).

72 Abraham and Torok interestingly point to 'illegitimacy' in the family context as a secret which can lead to the construction of a crypt.

73 See similarly Wigley (1995: 156).

suffered such trauma would, to a greater or lesser extent, be conscious thereof. Yet something universal and trans-phenomenal, a 'trauma' that remains secret, similar to that explored above in respect of the Wolf Man, is also at stake here. Bennington (2011: 28) refers to this as something secret or unspeakable in the founding of institutions. From Derrida's 'Force of Law' and 'Declarations of Independence' we know that the founding act is neither legal nor illegal, becoming legal only retrospectively (*AR* 242, 269–71/*Neg* 46–54). Its repetition by way of conserving violence is likewise both legal and illegal, because it takes place within the institution that was violently and pre-legally founded (Bennington 2011: 25; *AR* 271–2). Further support for Bennington's suggestion of linking the crypt, illegitimacy and illegality is to be found in an earlier mentioned passage in the 'Foreword' to *The Wolf Man's Magic Word* where Derrida ('Fore' xxxiv/*Fors* 49–50) notes that:

> the violated sepulchre *itself* was never 'legal.' It is the very tombstone of the illicit, and marks the spot of an intense pleasure [*jouissance*], of a *real* intense pleasure [*d'une jouissance* réelle] though walled up, buried alive in its own prohibition.

The above passage furthermore shows how the 'illegality' which Bennington refers to, but does not elaborate on further, should be understood. Derrida ('Fore' xv, xxxix/*Fors* 14, 57) refers to the pleasure, mentioned above in the same breath as 'the illicit', as a 'deadly pleasure [*plaisir mortifère*]' and a 'thanato-poetic pleasure [*plaisir thanatopoétique*]'. It is thus not simply the legal/non-legal foundation which is secreted in a constitution, but also trauma, absolute (un)pleasure, the desire for death or self-destruction, which Derrida in 'Force of Law' translates into justice and elsewhere into absolute hospitality (welcoming the stranger) and the perfect gift, that is, giving without expecting a return. Despite this universality, it remains a singular crypt which disguises and hides itself ('Fore' xiv). Each singular crypt, we can also say, is marked by the death drive, or what was referred to above by a number of other names. At stake here is the (forgotten) memory of self-destruction which *nachträglich* comes back to haunt in every act of constitutional self-preservation (*AR* 271–3). What Derrida says about philosophical discourse in *Points* therefore needs to be extended to constitutional discourse, that is, to what Schmitt, as we saw in the Introduction to the present section, says in *Constitutional Theory* about the relation between the political and the rule-of-law components of the constitution:

> It has to 'deal,' so to speak, with the traumatism. At the same time discourse repeats it – when one repeats a traumatism, Freud teaches us, one is trying to get control of it – it repeats it as such, without letting itself be annihilated by the traumatism, while keeping speech 'alive,' without forgetting the traumatism totally and without letting itself be totally annihilated by it. It is between these two perils that the philosophical experience advances.
>
> (*Points* 382/*PdS* 395)

Chapter 6

Human rights

Introduction

Carl Schmitt was, at least on the face of it, not a supporter of what he called, with reference to the Weimar Constitution, basic/fundamental rights (*Grundrechte*) or liberal rights (*Freiheitsrechte*). He saw these rights as weakening the state in favour of divisive private interests and thus as a-political. The a-political nature of human rights is in similar fashion being criticised today, with these rights being said to have been appropriated by an emerging empire in its collaboration with states, transnational bodies and global corporations, for its own disciplinary and bio-political ends.[1] Human rights nonetheless remain in the spotlight today, because of mass migration, indefinite emergency rule, oppression and terrorism in its many guises and the unequal distribution of wealth. These issues, as well as the brutal violence perpetrated against animals, continue to raise questions as to the scope of entitlement, content and future of human rights.

A reflection on the foundations of human rights has been undertaken in many different ways. Schmitt's analysis of fundamental rights in the modern liberal constitution does not at first sight appear to involve an enquiry into their foundations, but rather to be restricted to an analysis of how they find expression specifically in the Weimar Constitution. A closer look however reveals that Schmitt is indeed concerned here with the foundations of human rights, and he explores such foundations with reference to the two components of the modern liberal constitution, which he identifies in *Constitutional Theory*: (1) the rule-of-law component, which protects the freedom of the individual by way of the system of separation of powers; and (2) the political component where equality stands central. Freedom and equality are said to be different in respect of their presuppositions, their content and their operation (*CT* 256/*VL* 224).

The present chapter will proceed by first enquiring into the nature of freedom as it appears in Schmitt's texts, specifically his analyses of freedom of expression and freedom of religion, both of which he regards as being originary in nature.

1 See e.g. Douzinas (2007); Grear (2006); Sokhi-Bulley (2011); Cheah (2014).

In respect of freedom of opinion, its non-political and political dimensions are explored as well as what can be referred to as its 'spectral' dimension, the latter arising from Schmitt's analysis of cinema in *Constitutional Theory*. The originary nature of religious rights comes to the fore in *The Leviathan in the State Theory of Thomas Hobbes* (1938), where Schmitt explores the Leviathan myth as a force of self-destruction incorporated within the concept of the state itself by Hobbes. At stake here is the right to freely choose a private religion, which, according to Schmitt, was subsequently exploited by Jewish authors to undermine the state. Through an exploration of Schmitt's anti-Semitic remarks, we arrive at a different structure of freedom than the typical liberal conception thereof, in line with Derrida's exploration of freedom in *Rogues* (2003) and *For What Tomorrow* (2001). In analysing equality, Schmitt insists on its political nature as well as the closely related need to first of all understand equality as presupposing an inequality, which makes possible the formation of the political unity and thus the possibility of distinguishing between friend and enemy. A structure similar to that of freedom appears when Schmitt carefully distinguishes his own 'substantial' conception of equality from the equality of everything that bears a human face, which he associates with meaninglessness, folly, evil and self-destruction. A certain 'radicalisation' of freedom and equality thus appears from Schmitt's analysis, which no longer opposes equality and freedom in traditional fashion, but instead points to a certain unconditionality in both. Furthermore, although it mimics traditional approaches (such as natural law, theology and deontology) and more recent approaches (such as psychoanalysis) to the foundations of human rights, Schmitt's 'enquiry' into these foundations cannot easily be categorised as falling strictly within the scope of any of these approaches.

Freedom

The *telos* of the modern liberal constitution according to Schmitt is the protection of the sphere of freedom of the individual, which is believed to precede the state and to be in principle unlimited. Such freedom finds expression in the form of fundamental rights or liberal rights. State authority, on the other hand, is in principle limited in accordance with the principle of separation of powers, specifically insofar as interference with fundamental rights is concerned. The notion of unlimited freedom and the corresponding limitation of state powers find expression in what Schmitt refers to as the principle of distribution or allocation (*Verteilungsprinzip*) and as we saw above it gives expression to the un-political or rule-of-law component of the constitution.[2] The state in this account is secondary,

2 Böckenförde (1997: 11–12) notes in this regard that '[t]hose elements of a constitution . . . which affect the state unity in a hindering, balancing, liberating, and perhaps pluralizing way – i.e., basic rights, separation of powers, and the accommodation of an autonomous realm of economic and commercial activities – cannot be called political in the Schmittian sense, because they relativize and limit the political unity of the state on behalf of unpolitical and liberty-serving goals of the individual'.

and its authority and tasks are derived from and determined by individual freedom (Schneider 1957: 104). Any limitation of such freedom would have to be authorised by legislation, thus by parliament (*CT* 213/*VL* 175–6). The motivating idea behind the protection of freedom in the modern constitution comes to the fore in *The Concept of the Political* where Schmitt refers to Hegel's polemic-political definition of the liberal (*des Bourgeois*):

> as a person [*eines Menschen*] who does not want to leave the apolitical riskless private sphere, who in the possession and in the justice of private ownership sets himself up as individual [*einzelner*] against the totality, who finds the substitute for his political nullity in the fruits of freedom and acquisition and above all 'in the total *security* [Sicherheit] of the enjoyment thereof', who consequently wants to be spared bravery and be exempted from the danger of a violent death.
>
> (*CoP* 62/*BdP* 62)

In *The Concept of the Political*, Schmitt seeks to show that this liberal worldview is illusory.[3] He does something similar in *Constitutional Theory* through his analysis of freedom rights or fundamental rights, to which we now turn.

Freedom rights and the political

Freedom's double nature

Not all rights contained in the modern liberal constitution qualify as fundamental rights, only the so-called pre- and super-state rights, that is, those rights that are not granted by statute, but which are recognised and protected as preceding the state (*CT* 202). The state can interfere with these rights only to an extent that is in principle measureable and only in accordance with a regulated procedure. These fundamental rights do not pertain to legal objects, but to spheres of freedom, from which defensive rights are derived. This includes freedom of religion, personal freedom, property and the right to free expression (*CT* 202). In protecting these rights, the state finds the justification for its own existence (*Existenzberechtigung*) (*CT* 202/*VL* 164). Fundamental rights are thus only those that belong to the individual person according to the liberal idea (*CT* 203). Schmitt (*CT* 203) points out that because these rights precede the state they apply in respect of all human beings, irrespective of state citizenship. That is because these are individual rights, that is, rights of the isolated, individual human being (*CT* 203).

Schmitt (*CT* 203–4) nonetheless points out that the fundamental rights, or at least some of them, potentially contain a political component. These are rights of

3 See also Meier (2013: 45–6).

the individual that are held and exercised in collaboration with other individuals such as freedom of opinion, as well as freedom of speech and of the press, freedom of religion, freedom of assembly and freedom of association. They remain fundamental rights as long as 'the individual does not leave the non-political condition of the mere social and only the individual's [right to] free competition and discussion are recognised' (*CT* 203/*VL* 165). They can quickly lose their non-political character and thus their character as individual freedom rights, along with the absoluteness of protection they are entitled to (*CT* 203–4/*VL* 165).[4] Their status depends both on the actions of individuals and the way in which these rights find expression in a constitution. As soon as, for example, freedom of association leads to coalitions or associations which engage in battle against each other and oppose each other with specific social means of power such as labour strikes and exclusions from the workplace, the limit of the political has been reached and an individualistic fundamental or freedom right is no longer present (*CT* 204). Although derived from the right to freedom of association (*Vereinigungsfreiheit*), the right to form coalitions (*Koalitionsrecht*), the right to strike (*Streikrecht*) and work stoppage (*Stillegungsrecht*) are, according to Schmitt (*CT* 204/*VL* 165), not freedom rights in the sense of the liberal constitutional state. When a social group gains such possibilities for battle (*Kampfmöglichkeiten*), whether by means of constitutional provisions or toleration in practice, the basic presupposition of the liberal constitutional state has fallen away (*ist entfallen*) and 'freedom' then no longer means the in principle unlimited possibilities of action of the individual, but the unhindered exploitation of social power through social organisations (*CT* 204/*VL* 165–6).[5] Although in essence freedom seeks to depoliticise, it at the same time heightens the risk of the dissolution of the state, either by way of civil war or the capture of the state by an undemocratic party seeking to abolish democracy.[6]

Freedom, in Schmitt's analysis, can consequently be said to have a potential or perhaps even inherently political character. He nevertheless explicitly denies the principle of freedom any role in determining the state form. It cannot be the basis of democracy in the sense of self-rule because there is no necessary relation between the liberal insistence on freedom and democracy. Freedom can easily co-exist with monarchical rule (*CT* 256/*VL* 224–5). Yet Schmitt is very clear that what he says about freedom, that is, that it is a-political, only applies to freedom as it is understood in liberal thinking, not to freedom as such.[7] This distinction

4 Schmitt seems to be alluding here to the contrast which he later draws between the right to assembly granted by the modern liberal constitution, on the one hand, and 'genuine popular assemblies and acclamations' of the people in their capacity as sovereign, on the other (*CT* 272–3/*VL* 244).

5 See similarly *SMP* 26–7.

6 See also Römer (1990: 382) who raises the question whether it is not precisely in the autonomous societal sphere, in respect of property, private autonomy and freedom of contract, that a class war is being waged between the owners of property and of the means of production, on the one hand, and those who have only their labour to sell, on the other.

7 See e.g. *CT* 256/*VL* 224–5 where Schmitt notes that the meaning of freedom is not restricted to the meaning attributed to it in liberal constitutionalism.

within the concept of freedom itself is confirmed by Schmitt in the essay 'Was bedeutet der Streit um den "Rechtsstaat" (1935)?' where he notes that freedom cannot be captured by liberalism in every respect (and in this way de-politicised):

> Words such as 'right' or 'law' [*Recht*] and freedom [*Freiheit*] have thousands of times been misused and desecrated [Schmitt is thinking here specifically of their understanding in the modern liberal state] and nonetheless remain pure and virginal [*rein und jungfräulich*], when a brave people seriously reflects on them.[8]
>
> (Schmitt 1935a: 200)

Freedom of opinion and the political

Schmitt (*CT* 204) further points out that fundamental rights are all absolute rights. They are, in other words, in principle unlimited and any interference in respect of these rights by the state is viewed as an exception. The Weimar Constitution consequently distinguishes between rights which are absolute in principle (fundamental rights) and those which are relative from the start. The distinction between absolute and relative, and thus also between fundamental and other rights, however becomes difficult to draw, partly because of the manner of drafting of constitutional clauses and because of developments in technology (*CT* 204–7). Schmitt (*CT* 205/*VL* 166) draws his example here from what he refers to as 'the most important societal freedom right [*dem wichtichsten gesellschaftlichen Freiheitsrecht*]', the origin or source (*Ursprung*) of all other societal freedom rights, and the presupposition of the liberal idea of free discussion: the right to the free expression of opinion with its 'consequences' of freedom of speech and press freedom. Schmitt (*CT* 205) points out in this respect that the right to the free expression of opinion in Article 118 of the Weimar Constitution is seemingly not protected in an absolute sense, as it should actually be in line with the liberal ideal. Article 118 at the time provided as follows:

> Every German has the right, within the limits of the general laws, to freely express his opinion through word, writing, print, image, or in other manner. No work or professional relationship may hinder him in this right, and no one may disadvantage him if he makes use of this right.
>
> Censorship is not permitted. However, exceptions may be established by statute for film or cinema [*Lichtspiele*]. Also, statutory measures are permitted for preventing the display and sale of defamatory and pornographic literature as well as for the protection of youth.

8 See further Schmitt (1935b) where he seeks to appropriate the concept of freedom for the newly established Nazi regime's 'constitution' as against (liberal) constitutional freedom, which had become 'a weapon [*Waffe*] and slogan [*Parole*] of all the enemies and parasites of Germany', which led to foreign rule [*Fremdherrschaft*], and turned the German people into slaves.

Schmitt (*CT* 206) notes that the exception in respect of cinema is of particular interest for the development of the liberal fundamental rights themselves, and gives three reasons for this:

1. It shows how the individual is increasingly drawn into society and thus no longer the isolated individual of liberalism, as well as how, through changes in technology, the liberal principle of distribution (unlimited freedom and limited state powers) is coming to an end.
2. Cinema is exceptional insofar as it is not a true instance of the expression of ideas as is for example the printed media. Except where it simply contains images of words, it is 'only image and mimetic representation [*nur Bild und mimische Darstellung*], thus not language and not mediated thinking by way of the spoken or written human word. It is not the bearer of any real discussion' (*CT* 206/*VL* 168). Cinema is in other words not the conveyor of truth, as representation is understood to function according to the traditional philosophical understanding. Its force comes from elsewhere.[9] Schmitt here appears to already allude to a different understanding of representation, which Derrida (*Dis* 187–315) would spell out in more detail, that is, that any form of representation, including cinema (and television), is not a copy of something original (the imitated or the truth preceding the imitation), but mimetic in an originary sense: the imitation precedes the imitated. At stake in re-presentation is thus not the repetition of some prior event, but instead an 'event' that has never been a present past. Schmitt's remarks on the so-called spirit of technicity (*Geist der Technizität*) in 'The Age of Neutralization' (1929) confirm this understanding of the operation of technology.[10] Schmitt points out there that although the spirit of technicity appears to be simply lack of spirit (*Geistlosigkeit*), it remains spirit:

    > perhaps an evil and diabolical spirit [*vielleicht böser und teuflischer Geist*], but not to be dismissed as mechanistic and not attributable to technology. It is perhaps something horrendous [*Grauenhaftes*], but not itself technical and mechanical. It is the belief in an activistic metaphysics – the belief in an unlimited power and domination of man

9 See also the discussion of the double in Chapter 2, Section B above, and of representation, in Chapter 4 above.

10 Schmitt *CoP* 95/*BdP* 94 also speaks of the 'religion of technicity' and links it explicitly with depoliticisation. He notes that this religion is adopted by great masses of industrialised people because they seek radical results and unconsciously (*unbewußt*) believe that absolute depoliticisation is to be found here, i.e. that which man has sought for centuries, which leads to the end of war and the start of universal peace. 'Yet', Schmitt notes, 'technology can do nothing but intensify either peace or war; it is equally available to both, and the name and invocation/conjuration [*Beschwörung*] of peace, changes nothing. Today we see through the fog of names and the words with which the psycho-technical machinery of mass suggestion operates.'

> over nature, even over human nature [*die menschliche Physis*]; in the unlimited 'receding of natural limits', in unlimited possibilities for change and happiness in respect of the natural this-worldly existence of humanity. One can call this fantastic and satanic [*Das kann man phantastisch und satanisch nennen*], but not simply dead, spiritless or mechanised soullessness [*nicht einfach tot, geistlos oder mechanisierte Seelenlosigkeit*].[11]
>
> (*CoP* 94/*BdP* 93)

Technology, including cinema, should, in spite of appearances, thus be not simply associated with death, but viewed in terms of whence it originates, that is, with reference to the fantastic and the satanic, or what with reference to Freud (2001, XVIII: 1–64) and Derrida (*B&S II* 83–8) can be referred to as an uncanny self-destructive compulsion.[12]

3. It shows how the need for liberal discussion, from which truth is supposed to arise,[13] is receding in importance. Schmitt does not elaborate on this point, but it can be read as tied both to point 2 above as well as the ensuing matter he raises here, namely that of the potential use of cinema for purposes of mass persuasion, that is, indoctrination or propaganda, which denies any notion of individual autonomy. The function of the state is in other words shifting from the protection of freedom, here specifically allowing the free discussion of ideas in the service of the truth, towards the control or censorship by decision of forces of destruction which, as was suggested above and as we will see again below, find their origin in a 'freedom' which precedes the liberal notion of freedom.[14] Schmitt (*CT* 206) notes in this respect that the influence over the masses by means of cinema (in 1933 he adds radio) is of such significance that no state can leave this powerful psycho-technical apparatus (*mächtigen psycho-technischen Apparat*) without control.[15] It consequently has to be withdrawn from politics. But then Schmitt corrects himself: as the political is unavoidable,[16] cinema should be placed 'in the service of the existing order',

11 See further *CoP* 95–6/*BdP* 95 where Schmitt expresses the view that no simple antithesis is at stake here. Spirit does not fight with spiritlessness, nor life with death, but spirit with spirit and life with life.

12 See further the analysis of technology in Chapter 2, Section C above and in Chapter 7 below.

13 See *CPD* 33–9, 48–50.

14 See also *LL* 6 where Schmitt points out that whereas a hundred years ago there was a movement towards freedom; at that point in time (1932), there was a movement towards the total (administrative) state.

15 See also *VRA* 360.

16 See also *HdV* 111, and see Strauss in *CoP* 104 (par 9), noting that the political is 'not a "relatively independent domain" alongside others' and that the political is fundamental, authoritative and inescapable. Meier (2013: 30–5), as noted in Chapter 2, Section A above, persuasively argues that there was a shift in Schmitt's thinking in respect of the political between especially the first (1927)

even if the state 'does not have the courage to use it openly as a means of integrating a social-psychological homogeneity' (*CT* 207/*VL* 168). In 1933 ('Further Development of the Total State in Germany') before the Nazi takeover, Schmitt would actively encourage such use. A state which employs modern mass media in this way, which Italy at the time exemplified, Schmitt notes, would be able to prevent its own dissolution:

> No state can afford to relinquish to others the new technical media for the transmission of news, the influencing of the masses, mass persuasion, the creation of a 'public', more exactly, a collective opinion. Thus, behind the formula of the total state, a correct awareness stands firm, namely that the present-day state has got new means of power and possibilities of monstrous intensity [*ungeheurer Intensität*], the range and consequences of which we hardly suspect, because our vocabulary and our imagination are still deeply rooted in the nineteenth century.
>
> In this sense, the total state is at the same time a particularly strong state.[17] It is total in the sense of quality and energy, in the way the fascist state calls itself a 'stato totalitario', by which it wants to say first of all that the new means of power belong exclusively to the state and serves its increasing power. Such a state does not allow the development within itself [*in seinem Innern*] of any forces which are hostile, obstructive or divisionary in respect of the state. It does not think of handing over the new means of power to its own enemies and destroyers, and to let its power be buried under any watchwords, liberalism, *Rechtsstaat*, or whatever one wishes to call it. Such a state can distinguish between friend and enemy.[18]
>
> (*FA* 21–2/ *VRA* 360–1)

and second (1932) editions of *The Concept of the Political*. Whereas Schmitt in 1927 attempted to show that the political has its own domain alongside others and remains restricted to foreign policy or external warfare (Meier 2013: 25–30), in 1932 the political is said to be reachable from every domain (see e.g. *CoP* 78) and civil war stands on an equal footing with external war. Furthermore, in Meier's reading, the 'conception of domains is replaced by a model of intensity', with the brother now becoming a potential enemy (Meier 2013: 30–1). Everything now becomes potentially political (Meier 2013: 35). See also Taubes (2013: 45–6), and see Chapter 2, Sections A–C above.

17 Schmitt (*FA* 39) distinguishes in this regard between the (weak) quantitative total state where private interests dominate and the (strong) qualitative total state which is able to distinguish between friend and enemy. Whereas the quantitative total state seeks to cater for all interests, the qualitative total state itself determines a substantive vision, which the rest of society must adhere to. Although he contrasts these two forms of state, he nevertheless holds the view that all states are potentially total in the strong sense, and this is especially so in the event of the state of exception. Here the 'particular centre of the state' (*HdV* 76) or what can be referred to as the 'seat of sovereignty' of the specific state comes to the fore; see also Schwab (1989: 77–9).

18 In later years, Schmitt would change his view somewhat in respect of the existence of the total state; see 'GP' 23–4 where Schmitt points out that the notion of a 'total state' is actually a misnomer.

Freedom, specifically freedom of speech, thus poses the threat of state dissolution and to avoid this Schmitt believed that the state had to have a monopoly over the modern mass media.[19] With his endorsement of the qualitative total state as a response to this threat, the distinction between the rule-of-law component and the political component of the Constitution is effectively dissolved in favour of the latter component.[20]

Freedom rights and the beyond to the political

Religious freedom as originary right

The rise of the modern state, as Schmitt (*CT* 198) points out, was accompanied by the establishment of national churches. Religion was consequently not regarded as a private matter (*CT* 198). The Baptists and Puritans however believed in the absolute privatisation of religion whereby the state and public life were rendered relative and devalued whereas religion came to be regarded as the most important value (*CT* 198). Religion was now a matter for the individual, whereas the church and the state only became a means to arrive at this absolute value (*CT* 198). Schmitt (*CT* 197–8) thus accepts that there is historical evidence to support Jellinek's analysis which posits religious freedom as the first of all fundamental rights and the right from which all fundamental rights have been derived, even though the issue cannot be regarded as settled. For Schmitt (*CT* 197–8) the originary nature of religious freedom is rather a structural or systematic matter. As we saw above, the principle of distribution or allocation is hereby established: the individual as such is the bearer of an absolute value and remains with this value in the private sphere; his private freedom is consequently something which is in principle unlimited; the state is only a means and thus relative, derivative; it is limited in all its powers as well as controllable by the private sphere (*CT* 197–8). These ideas, as Schmitt (*CT* 197) points out, first found expression in the US states' Bills of Rights of the eighteenth century. The essential rights incorporated were freedom, private property, security, the right to resistance, freedom of

The state with its bureaucratic machinery can never be total, only a (political) party (i.e. a part/*ein Teil*) that rejects the existing unity and wishes to establish a new unity with itself representing such new unity can be such; see further Chapter 2, Section B above.

19 See further 'Auto' 109 on the relation between the media and terror since World War I. Today 'control' of the media is, at least in established democracies, more subtle than at the time Schmitt was writing. In the United States, for example, such control is not exercised directly by the state, but rather through corporate and elite interests; see Chomsky (2011: 68–9, 163–7, 233–41).

20 According to Agamben (2005: 2–3), with the Nazi takeover in Germany, the exception effectively became the rule, lasting for 12 years. Such a state of exception, according to Agamben (2005: 1–31), characterises all Western (liberal) democracies today. For criticism of this analysis, specifically as to its alleged Schmittian pedigree, see Kistner (2009; 2011); see further Chapter 3 above.

conscience and religious freedom (*CT* 197). The purpose of the state was to secure these rights (*CT* 197).

Hobbes's Leviathan *and the private sphere*

Schmitt (*TL* 53–64) further elaborates on this analysis of the origin of the fundamental rights.[21] Here the issue is the philosophical origin of the liberal idea of the private sphere. In Hobbes's *Leviathan* the basis is according to Schmitt laid for liberal constitutionalism, which was then developed further by Spinoza, Mendelssohn and Stahl-Jolson.[22] It is in the context of a discussion about the belief in miracles that Hobbes introduces the distinction between outer confession and inner faith, which, according to Schmitt (*TL* 53–6), was ultimately the reason for the collapse of the Leviathan. Hobbes describes the sea monster Leviathan, a combination of god and man, animal and machine, as the bringer of peace and security (*TL* 53). This mortal god requires absolute obedience and there is no right of resistance against him (*TL* 53). The state is the highest and final power within the territory and has the final say in respect of questions of justice, as to right and wrong, as well as in respect of religion, what counts as truth and error, including whether a specific event is to be regarded as a miracle (*TL* 53). Schmitt (*TL* 54) reminds the reader that the importance of miracles at the time Hobbes wrote was related to the monarch's reputed powers of healing illnesses as well as the battle with the Roman Catholic Church. In other words miracles had a political meaning (*TL* 54). Although Hobbes was a sceptic as to the existence of miracles, this was in terms of his state model ultimately a matter of authority: 'A miracle is what the sovereign state authority commands its subjects to believe to be a miracle' (*TL* 55/

21 As Hooker (2009: 41, 50) points out, Hobbes is central to Schmitt's thinking insofar as it was Hobbes who laid the foundation for the modern state, and which, as we saw, Schmitt closely associates with the concept of the political and with the era of the *jus publicum Europaeum* (see Chapter 2 above and Chapter 7 below). This era was nevertheless then (in the early twentieth century) coming to an end with the seemingly inevitable movement towards universalism, and Schmitt's *The Leviathan in the State Theory of Thomas Hobbes* seeks the seeds of this dissolution or destruction within the concept of the state itself as constructed by Hobbes.

22 The reference here is to Friedrich Julius Stahl (1802–1861), whose Jewish origins Schmitt sought to emphasise after the Nazi takeover by referring to his Jewish surname (Jolson) before his conversion to Lutheranism; see also *SMP* 33 where Schmitt notes that 'his real name is Joll Jolson'. In the 1920s Schmitt relied inter alia on Stahl to point to the contradictions in liberalism; see *DC* 32–3; *CoP* 64, 65, 70. In *CT* 169, 313–5, 33 Stahl's views on constitutional monarchy are furthermore discussed and cited at length. In the two 1935 essays – 'Der Rechtsstaat' (1935) and 'Was Bedeutet der Streit um den "Rechtsstaat"?' (*SGN* 112 and 123–4) – Stahl (here also referred to as Jolson) is however accused of falsifying the notion of the *Rechtsstaat* through neutralisation and mechanisation (*Technisierung*) into a merely formal concept, thereby placing this notion in the service of normativism and liberalism. In 1936 Stahl's total existence is said to be characterised by an 'atrocious and uncanny changing of masks' (*DJ* 32); see further Neumann (2015: 379–83), and below.

DL 82). Hobbes's example is that of the sacrament of Holy Communion. Should an ordinary person declare that the bread turns into the body of Christ, it would be of no consequence, yet if this is declared by state authority, a miracle is indeed at stake and everyone has to remain true to the command by way of confession (*TL* 55). The outward actions of ordinary persons thus need to comply with the commands of the sovereign, yet they need not believe in the truth of the command (Dyzenhaus 1994: 9).

Yet it is exactly at this point of sovereignty, where the sovereign acts as lieutenant of God, and where political power and religion are united that a schism appears (*TL* 55–6). This is because of the distinction Hobbes draws here between public and private reason (*TL* 56). It is by virtue of public reason that the state declares whether something counts as a miracle (*TL* 56). Hobbes nevertheless leaves room for the individual to decide by private reason what to believe inwardly, on the basis of the general freedom of thought, and to keep this judgement in his heart (*TL* 56). In the event of the external confession of faith, as we saw, private judgement however comes to an end and the sovereign decides what is true and false (*TL* 56). According to Schmitt (*TL* 56), the distinction drawn here between public and private, faith and confession, in the centuries that followed was determinant of the development of the liberal constitutional state. The neutral state found its origins here, characterised by individual freedom of thought and conscience and finding expression in the freedom rights of the individual (*TL* 56–7). Such freedom, as we saw above, threatens the state's monopoly of the political and thus poses the risk of dissolution. The state as constructed by Hobbes thereby contained within itself the seeds of its own destruction at the hands of illiberal forces (*TL* 74/*DL* 118). The distinction between inner and outer, in the words of Schmitt (*TL* 57/*DL* 86), 'contained the seed of death that destroyed the mighty Leviathan from within and brought down the mortal god [*Er wurde zum Todeskeim, der den mächtigen Leviathan von innen her zerstört und den sterblichen Gott zur Strecke gebracht hat*]'.[23]

Spinoza's inversion

It was the 'Liberal Jew' Spinoza who according to Schmitt (*TL* 57/*DL* 86) noted the barely visible schism introduced by Hobbes and proceeded to invert the relation posited by Hobbes between external/internal and public/private in the *Tractatus Theologico-Politicus* (1677).[24] For Hobbes, as we saw above, sovereign power and the attainment of peace stood at the forefront, with individual freedom of thought only being recognised as a background proviso (*hintergründiger Vorbehalt*) (*TL* 58/*DL* 88). For Spinoza however '[i]ndividual freedom of

23 See also *SMP* 37 where Schmitt likewise emphasises the importance of political unity and the danger of uncertainties and splits, which inevitably lead to disintegration.

24 For criticism of this analysis, see Galli (2015: 89).

thought is the form-giving principle, the necessities of public peace as well as the right of the sovereign power having been transformed into mere provisos [*bloße Vorbehalte*]' (*TL* 58/*DL* 88). This inversion, which would determine the ultimate fate of the Leviathan, is derived from what Schmitt (*TL* 58/*DL* 89) calls 'Jewish existence [*jüdischen Existenz*]': 'A small intellectual switch emanating from Jewish existence accomplished, with the most simple logic and in the span of a few years, the decisive turn in the fate of the Leviathan' (*TL* 58/*DL* 88–9). After mentioning a few other advocates of the notion of freedom of thought, including, as noted, Mendelssohn and Stahl-Jolson, whose Jewish origins are again emphasised, Schmitt (*TL* 61/*DL* 94) notes that if public power is restricted to the external realm 'it is hollow and already soulless from within [*hohl und von innen her bereits entseelt*]'.

It is important to note that this threat to the Leviathan, allegedly exploited by Jewish forces, does not in Schmitt's reading appear for the first time after its construction by Hobbes. The 'Jewish exploitation' thus already involves a 'return'.[25] The threat at stake here is in other words already a haunting presence prior to the Hobbesian construction.[26] The name 'Leviathan' moreover appears to have been deliberately chosen by Hobbes to (secretly) incorporate, in the hope of at the same time overcoming this threat.[27] This is because of the associations which the name carried and Schmitt (*TL* 5–15) refers here to Jewish,[28]

25 See also Dyzenhaus (1997: 91) who aptly puts it as follows: 'The seeds of the idea of civil society as the realm of the inner are also the seeds of Leviathan's death. In this way the mythical forces which Hobbes's Leviathan were meant to combat are in fact unleashed by it and strike back'.

26 See Dyzenhaus (1997: 93–4), who refers here to religious civil war; and see *GL* 19.

27 See Balakrishnan (2000: 210); and see *TL* 26/*DL* 43–4: 'Because of Hobbes' psychological peculiarity, it is possible that behind the image of the Leviathan a deeper, secretive meaning [*eine tiefere, geheimnisvolle Bedeutung*] lies hidden. Like all the great thinkers of his times, Hobbes had a taste for esoteric disguises [*Verhüllungen*]. He said about himself that now and then he made "overtures", but that he unveils only half of his real thoughts, and that he acts like people who open a window for a moment, and then close it again quickly out of fear of a storm.' See also Schmitt's essay 'Die vollendete Reformation' in *DL* 151: 'A curtain at the bottom centre [of the frontispiece of Hobbes's *Leviathan*] indicates that not only is much said here, but also that some things are concealed [*deutet an, daß hier nicht nur viel gesagt, sondern außerdem auch einiges verborgen ist*]'. See further Kistner (2009: 245) who points to the analogy between Freud's account of the totemic feast and mythical accounts of the Leviathan; Schmitt's reference to Jewish-cabbalistic interpretations of the Leviathan myth (*TL* 8–9); and Chapter 4 and Chapter 5, Section B above on incorporation.

28 See *TL* 8–9/*DL* 16–18 where Schmitt elaborates on Jewish interpretations of the Leviathan and Behemoth myths during the Middle Ages, which according to him shows 'the unique, totally abnormal condition and attitude of the Jewish people toward all other peoples [*die ganz singuläre, mit keinem andern Volk vergleichbare, völlig abnorme Lage und Haltung des jüdischen Volkes gegenüber allen andern Völkern*]' (*TL* 8/*DL* 16). According to Schmitt (*TL* 9/*DL* 18), the Leviathan and Behemoth are for the Jews 'images of heathenish vitality [*Lebenskraft*] and fertility [*Fruchtbarkeit*], the "great Pan"', which Jewish hatred and Jewish feelings of superiority have each turned into a beast or monster [*Untier*]'.

Medieval-Christian and early modern interpretations[29] of the Leviathan, which presumably informed Hobbes's mythical construction of the state as a satanic sea monster.[30] In Schmitt's view, Hobbes had however in doing so underestimated the demonic force associated with the Leviathan (*TL* 81–2/*DL* 123–4), which would inevitably make a return.[31]

The Jewish spirit and the 'origin' of fundamental rights

Schmitt's collaboration with the Nazis and his anti-Semitic views are no secret. As noted in Chapter 1 above, the argument that this can be attributed to opportunism for a short period of time has been discredited[32] with the publication of his 1912–1915 *Diaries*[33] and his *Glossarium*, containing notes from 1947–1951.[34] As can be seen from the above discussion, Schmitt's anti-Semitism is also clearly evident from *The Leviathan in the State Theory of Thomas Hobbes*. Some have argued that this book and its anti-Semitic rhetoric provide further evidence of the nature of Schmitt's political theology.[35] Such a reading, although convincing in many respects, remains restricted to Schmitt's conscious intention with these utterances.[36] The question that requires an answer to is what Judaism, beyond consciousness and even beyond the unconscious, represents for Schmitt.[37] The question is raised with the expectation that an answer could lead us to the 'origin' of fundamental rights.

29 In these interpretations the Leviathan is depicted as the devil in his battle with God over the soul of mankind; see *TL* 7–8, 22–4.

30 See *DL* 144; and see Chapter 7 below on the association of the sea with not only the unconscious, but a force beyond the unconscious, as well as Meier (1998: 102, 107), associating the Leviathan with the evil enemy as such, the Devil or Satan. The contradictions that come to the fore in Hobbes's image are incidentally typical of mythology, see De Ville (2010; 2011b).

31 See also Salter (2012: 144) who points out that the myth as invoked had the 'capacity to be repeatedly mobilised as a political weapon in unpredictable ways', also by those who wanted to destroy the state.

32 See Dyzenhaus (1997: 98); Neumann (2000: 281–2; 2015: 374–91); Bendersky (2005); Hooker (2009: 54–9); Gross (2015).

33 See e.g. Schmitt (2005c: 140, 197, 245).

34 See e.g. *GL* 17 (entry of 25 Sept. 1947) where Schmitt cites Peter F. Drucker with approval, as saying that Jews, more so than communists, qualify as 'demonic enemies'. Schmitt (*GL* 18) then proceeds to comment that this is because the communist can improve and change himself whereas the Jew cannot. 'The Jew', he says, 'always stays a Jew'. It is furthermore specifically the assimilated Jew who is said to be 'the true enemy [*wahre Feind*]'. See also Schmitt (1940: 22) where Jews are accused of disturbing and poisoning relations between the French and the Germans.

35 See e.g. Meier (1998: 101–21, 123–32); Strong 'Foreword' in *TL* xxv–xxvi; and Hooker (2009: 55–7).

36 For criticism of this political-theological reading of Schmitt, see Bendersky (2005; 2015: 4, 8).

37 The analysis undertaken here follows Derrida's approach, e.g. in *Glas* 30–56 where he undertakes a similar reading in respect of Hegel. Judaism is here associated with homelessness (*Glas* 41), death (*Glas* 44), a lack of essence (*Glas* 50) and radical or absolute expropriation (*Glas* 51–2).

The opening and closing remarks of Schmitt at the conference which he organised in 1936 with the theme *Das Judentum in der Rechtswissenschaft*[38] provides some clues in this regard.[39] The two speeches presented by Schmitt at the conference speak of the identity of the German nation and the need to expunge therefrom that which is alien (Jewish being, *jüdisches Wesen*), but to which there is nevertheless a susceptibility or predisposition (*Anfälligkeit*) (*DJ* 16) or lack of resistance (*Widerstandslosigkeit*) to (*DJ* 33). This attraction appears also from the other (Jewish) side, towards what is real (*das Echte*) in what is German (*DJ* 32). This mutual attraction is expressed in the language of spirit (*Geist*), and Schmitt (*DJ* 14, 29, 34) foresees in this respect and himself engages here in a spiritual war (*Geisteskampf*), ultimately against the enemy that we encountered in Chapter 2, Sections A–C above. He contends that under Jewish influence, the German spirit has been falsified by something unspiritual (*Ungeistiges*) (*DJ* 15), which he nevertheless also refers to as a 'spiritual force' (*geistigen Macht*) (*DJ* 15). The German spirit, specifically in the legal field, consequently has to be freed from all 'Jewish falsification', which has extended even to the concept of spirit (*Geist*) (*DJ* 15) and of justice (*DJ* 29). The supposed critical gift of the Jew, he further asserts, springs from a disjunction in respect of everything that is essential (*wesentlich*) and proper (*arteigen*), and contrasts markedly with the mutual critical thinking of German scholars in the legal community (*DJ* 32), who also need to act as legal guardians (*Rechtswahrer*) (*DJ* 28). The danger of the Jew lies for Schmitt in the fact that he 'is unproductive and sterile to the nature of the German spirit' (*DJ* 31), and has a 'parasitical relationship' to such spirit (*DJ* 32). In this respect the Jew engages in an 'atrocious and uncanny changing of masks' (*grauenhafter, unheimlicher Maskenwechsel*), which has a certain 'demonic enigma' (*dämonischer hintergründigkeit*) (*DJ* 32, 33).[40] The Jewish skill in mimicry, Schmitt (*DJ* 33) continues, can be recognised by its consequences, but it cannot be grasped (*begreifen*). This incomprehension is seemingly tied to the fact that, according to Schmitt (*DJ* 32), it is not at all possible to access the 'inner essence of the Jews'.

The description of identity, that is, of the German spirit, that is at stake here shows that the self is constituted by the uncanny return of the absolute stranger

38 For a partial translation, see Rabinbach and Gilman (2013: 216–18).

39 See also Gross (2015: 6–11) who refers to a number of diary entries where the presence of Jewish individuals or Jews in general appears to have caused anxiety, disgust and fear in Schmitt. Bendersky (2015) perhaps gives a somewhat more balanced perspective, particularly relevant for what concerns us here, referring to a 'pervasive existential *Angst*' close to that of Kierkegaard which appears from Schmitt's diary entries and which Bendersky (2015: 5, 7, 30) links to Schmitt's search for security and order in his theories. See also the following elusive remark which Bendersky refers to in the context of a visit to the library by Schmitt and Georg Eisler, the latter reading the book *Psychologie*: 'Amazed and shocked by the power of the Jews. Psychoanalysis is the purest expression of Judaism [*Erstaunt und erschrocken über die Macht der Juden. Die Psychoanalyse ist der reinste Ausdruck des Judentums*]'; see Schmitt (2005c: 314, entry of 9 Feb. 1915).

40 See the remarks above on Friedrich Julius Stahl.

(represented here for Schmitt by the Jew), and which, as we saw above, is replicated in the concept of the state as constructed by Hobbes.[41] What are the implications of this heteronomy? The relation of the mime to the mimed, as we also saw earlier in relation to cinema is not that of the imitated coming before the imitation (*Dis* 203). Instead the imitation (for Schmitt, this refers to the Jew) precedes in a certain way the imitated (the German), and the copy no longer has an *a priori* model. This heteronomy can be understood in view of Schmitt's mention of the strange appearance of Jewish law as the deliverance from chaos, of three polarities that operate in Jewish legal thinking,[42] the difficulty of correlating such thinking with the legal sentiment of the German people[43] and the severe (*stark*, also 'bad') dominance of this thinking over the whole of the legal field (*DJ* 28). At stake in this 'chaos' or demonic force, it is submitted, is the Freudian death drive (Chapter 2, Sections A–C), which the Jewish spirit represents for Schmitt, and which lies at the 'origin' of what Schmitt (*CT* 203/*VL* 165) refers to as the primordial individualistic right (*individualistische Urrecht*): freedom of religion and opinion.

Freedom re-conceptualised

At this point in Schmitt's *Constitutional Theory* we are very close to Derrida's hesitant re-conceptualisation of freedom in *Rogues*. 'Hesitant' because of the associations traditionally coupled to freedom, which were set out above. Freedom is no longer to be simply understood in terms of the liberal model as a sphere of freedom, that is, as mastery or measure, as the autonomy of a subject in control of himself, or even more broadly, in the traditional philosophical sense, as related to power, force, possibility, ability, sovereignty and mastery (*FWT* 48–9; *Rog* 40–4, 54). The above analysis suggests that freedom is instead to be understood in a pre-subjective or pre-cratic sense, as without power, as an exposure beyond mastery, sovereignty and autonomy (*Rog* 47; *FWT* 52). In other words freedom is to be understood as a welcoming of the unforeseeable or incalculable event, of who or what may come or arrive, that is, as a compromising of the self, an opening of the self to its own destruction (*FWT* 45, 49–50, 52; *Rog* 45, 52). We will see below that a close reading of Schmitt's texts suggests the need for a similar re-conceptualisation of equality.

41 The same structure is to be found in the dualistic conception of God that Schmitt adopts in *Political Theology II*, see Chapter 2, Section A and Chapter 3 above.

42 That is, between Jewish chaos and Jewish legality, anarchic nihilism and positivist normativism, raw sensualist materialism and abstract moralism; see *DJ* 28.

43 See in this respect *TTJT* 45/*DARD* 9 where Schmitt remarks that '[t]here are peoples that, without territory, without a state, and without church, exist only in "law" [*Es gibt Völker, die ohne Boden, ohne Staat, ohne Kirche, nur im "Gesetz" existieren*]'.

Equality

The rule-of-law component with freedom at its foundation is, as noted above, not all there is to the modern liberal constitution. Of equal or perhaps even greater importance is equality, which according to Schmitt (*CT* 256) is a principle of democracy, and thus forms part of the political component of the Constitution. Equality for Schmitt (*CT* 258–9) first of all implies an inequality, that is, a certain separation from and exclusion of others so as to form a political unity of equals, or, thought in terms of the concept of the political, of friends (Herrero 2015: 107).[44] According to Schmitt (*CT* 257/*VL* 226), democracy as a specific state form can be grounded (*begründet*) only on a 'precise and substantial concept of equality'. He therefore objects to a conception of equality which is 'general and meaningless [*allgemeine und gleichgültige Gleichheit*]'.[45] As a political concept, Schmitt (*CT* 258) notes, equality requires the drawing of a distinction. The equality of everyone with a human face would mean the dissolution of all distinctions and of the drawing of boundaries (*CT* 257). For Schmitt, equality in this 'substantial' sense is central to the concept of the political itself:

> An equality with no other content than the equality that is common to all human beings [*Menschen*] by itself, would be an unpolitical equality, because it would lack the correlative of a possible inequality. Every equality acquires its meaning and its significance [*ihre Bedeutung und ihren Sinn*] through the correlate of a possible inequality. This equality is the more intensive, the greater the inequality vis-à-vis those that do not belong to the equals. An equality without the possibility of an inequality, an equality that one inherently possesses and that cannot at all be lost, is without value and meaningless.[46]
>
> (*CT* 258/*VL* 227)

This first political principle of equality is for Schmitt (*CT* 259/*VL* 227) the precondition for all other rights to equality to be found in a state, such as the equal right to vote and equal access to employment. The nation thus first distinguishes

44 See also Lindahl (2013: 223) who similarly argues that all claims about equality/inequality are ultimately claims about inclusion/exclusion, i.e. about the 'boundaries, limits and fault lines of legal orders'.

45 Later in *Constitutional Theory*, Husserl is invoked in support of the argument that equality can only be spoken of in respect of members of the same group (or species), otherwise the talk of equality would lose its foundation (*CT* 265/*VL* 236).

46 This sentiment is echoed in *CoP* 54–5 where Schmitt rejects the political nature of the concept of humanity as it makes the friend-enemy distinction impossible. However, as we saw in Chapter 2, Section A, the employment of the concept of humanity at the same time intensifies the political by denying the humanity of the enemy and turning him into a foe that needs to be destroyed. As Schmitt puts it in 'The Age of Neutralizations' (*CoP* 95/*BdP* 94): 'Today we . . . know that the most terrible war is pursued only in the name of peace, the most terrible oppression only in the name of freedom, the most terrible inhumanity only in the name of humanity'.

itself from others, that is, other potential external enemies, but as he does in *The Concept of the Political*,[47] and picking up on the theme broached in the section on 'freedom' above, Schmitt (*CT* 260–1/*VL* 230–1) points out with reference to the Jacobin dictatorship that this political equality/inequality can also find expression *within* a nation where certain opponents are declared to be outlaws or in nations where only those who belong to a certain religion are believed to be deserving of such political equality. Homogeneity is thus a requirement because otherwise peace within the state would be threatened (*CT* 261–2/*VL* 231). Schmitt's notion of homogeneity, as employed in *Constitutional Theory* and elsewhere can easily be misunderstood.[48] In contrast to what some have argued, it is not about the 'sharing of certain physical or moral qualities' and Schmitt makes no claim in *Constitutional Theory* that the members of a polity can 'univocally and uncontroversially identify a set of qualities which defines them as a political unity'.[49] Although Schmitt (*CT* 263/*VL* 234) indeed also speaks about substantial homogeneity (*substantielle Homogenität*) in this context, this should not be understood as implying that a people necessarily is or must be lacking in diversity or plurality.[50] Schmitt is acutely aware that a nation can consist of a diversity of peoples,[51] noting that the belongingness to a nation can be determined 'by very different [*sehr verschiedene*] elements', among which he mentions ideas or representations (*Vorstellungen*) of a common race, a common religion, as well as a shared destiny and tradition (*CT* 258/*VL* 227). Later in the same text he adds to these elements the following: a common language, common historical destinies, traditions and memories, as well as common political goals and hopes (*CT* 262). Although language is no doubt important, Schmitt notes that this is by no means definitive. Decisive is 'the commonality of historical life, conscious willing of this commonality, great events and goals' (*CT* 262/*VL* 231). Real revolutions and victorious wars can furthermore overcome language differences and ground a

47 See *CoP* 32, 37–38, and see Chapter 2, Section A above.

48 See further Minca and Rowan (2016: 110–14); and see Voigt (2015b: 47–8) who points out that Schmitt's contemporaries – e.g. German constitutional scholars like Heller and Kelsen – also believed that homogeneity was a necessary condition for democracy; see likewise Neumann (2015: 63–7). Schmitt's terminology in this respect however changed in the 1930s. In a text such as *SMP* 48/*SBV* 42 Schmitt insists on similarity in kind (*Artgleichheit*) in respect of the German nation, which he specifically ties to race (*der Rasse*); and see also above on the conference *Das Judentum in der Rechtswissenschaft* where Schmitt expresses the view that the German legal system has to be purified of alien elements.

49 See Lindahl (2008a: 13, 14). Schmitt (*CT* 259) actually mentions this kind of similarity (moral and physical) in respect of the Greeks as an example of how substantive equality can differ between different democracies and in different ages; see also *CPD* 9/*GLP* 14.

50 See also Schmitt (2002c: 297/*SGN* 47), noting that the modern state consists of a great diversity in respect of class, interest, culture and religion. It is the task of parliament within the liberal constitutional system to constantly reproduce a political unity, which means bringing about a certain homogeneity (*Homogenität*) or uniformity (*Gleichartigkeit*); see further Chapter 3 above.

51 See also Schmitt (2002d: 306/*PB* 158).

feeling of national belonging (*CT* 262). Schmitt (*CT* 259) also acknowledges that the substance of this equality can be different among different democracies and in different time periods.

Should there be a lack of homogeneity, for example if the state consists of a number of different nations or contain national minorities, there are a number of ways in which such homogeneity can be brought about, such as assimilation or through violent oppression or exile of the heterogeneous sector of the population (*CT* 262). Another solution would be secession. Schmitt (*CT* 262–3/*VL* 232–3) in addition mentions as 'consequences' of the notion of democratic homogeneity: (1) the control and deportation of foreigners; (2) methods of rule of heterogeneous countries by foreign powers in the form of colonies, protectorates or intervention treaties; (3) laws against foreign domination of the economy; (4) the use of denaturalisation and expatriation; and (5) the possibility of enacting a constitution by only a certain section of the population. With these examples, Schmitt seeks to illustrate the inevitability, or perhaps rather necessity, of bringing about substantive or political equality, which unavoidably implies an inequality. The alternative is sketched by Schmitt (*CT* 263/*VL* 233) as follows: 'A democratic state', he notes, 'would deprive itself of its own substance [*sich . . . seiner Substanz berauben*] through a logically consistent recognition of general human equality in the area of public life and of public law'.[52] Political unity, as we saw earlier, requires the continuous reproduction of homogeneity or uniformity. If the state lacks the willingness or capability to do so, it would not be able to 'prevent . . . opposing groups from dissociating to the point of extreme hostility (i.e. to the point of civil war)' (Schmitt 2002d: 307/*PB* 160).

These remarks of Schmitt, which emphasise the link between equality, homogeneity, uniformity and the risk of the heterogeneous (from outside or from within the state), that is, ultimately of state dissolution, should be read together with his criticism expressed earlier in *Constitutional Theory* of the contemporary tendency to extend without limitation the concept of democracy (*grenzenlose Ausdehnung des Begriffes der Demokratie*) so as to include a place for 'everything that is ideal, beautiful and pleasant' (*CT* 257/*VL* 225).[53] In the same context, Schmitt makes the following remark about general, meaningless equality:

> The equality of everything 'that bears a human face [*alles dessen, 'was Menschenantlitzt trägt'*] is incapable of providing a foundation for a state, a state form, or a form of government. No distinctive differentiations and

52 See also *CT* 207/*VL* 169 where Schmitt remarks that the democratic rights of state citizenship 'are dominated by the democratic idea of equality . . . . According to their nature, they are not valid for foreigners (*für Fremde*) because otherwise the political community and unity cease to exist and the essential presupposition of the political existence, the possibility of the distinction between friend and enemy, is eliminated [*entfällt*]'.

53 See also Chapter 3 above.

> delimitations may be derived from it; only the elimination of distinctions and boundaries; no specifically formed institutions can be constituted on its basis, and it can only contribute to the dissolution and elimination of distinctions and institutions that no longer have any force in themselves [*die keine Kraft mehr in sich haben*].
>
> (*CT* 257/*VL* 226)

The concept of equality thus risks suffering the same fate as the concept of democracy, thereby undermining other concepts as well as state institutions. This threat is what motivates Schmitt's attempt to reinvigorate the concept of equality by pointing to its substantive and political dimension. Schmitt (*CPD* 11/*GLP* 16) likewise notes that '[u]ntil now [*Bisher*] there has never been a democracy that did not recognize the concept of the foreign [*des Fremden*] and that could have realized the equality of all men'. Here Schmitt condemns in harsh terms the idea of a democracy of mankind that would realise the equality of all men:

> As much of an injustice as it would be to disregard the human dignity of every single individual human being, it would nevertheless be an irresponsible folly, leading to the most evil formlessness and therefore to even worse injustice [*eine unverantwortliche, zu den schlimmsten Formlosigkeiten und daher zu noch schlimmerem Unrecht führende Torheit*], to deny the specific characteristics of the various spheres [here specifically, of the political].[54]
>
> (*CPD* 11/*GLP* 17)

Such a conception of democracy or of equality would thus entail a denial of the political or a depoliticised understanding of equality; it would deny human nature and the friend/enemy criterion of the political in terms of which people either align themselves with others or stand opposed to them.[55] Such an absolute equality of human beings, Schmitt (*CPD* 12/*GLP* 17) continues, would be an equality which understands itself without risk of or to the self (*die sich ohne Risiko von selbst versteht*). Such an equality, which contains no relation to inequality, Schmitt (*CPD* 12/*GLP* 17) says, would be 'conceptually and practically meaningless, an indifferent equality [*begrifflich und praktisch nichtssagende, gleichgültige Gleichheit*]'. Yet Schmitt does not categorically reject this absolute (conception of) equality; he does so only

> for as long as [*solange*] . . . the various states of the earth distinguish their citizens politically from other human beings and exclude/keep separate [*von sich fernzuhalten wissen*] politically dependent populations that are unwanted,

54 See Campagna (2015: 133) who sees an ambiguity in this passage, though of a different nature than the ambiguity pointed to below.

55 See in this respect also the critique of the notion of humanity in *CoP* 54–5.

on whatever grounds, by combining dependence in international law with constitutional foreignness [*staatsrechtlichen Fremdheit*].

(*CPD* 12/*GLP* 17)

Schmitt seems to suggest that this situation will never change in reality, although colonialism (the second example Schmitt refers to in the quotation above) has in the meantime, at least in a formal sense, come to an end. Were such an absolute equality to be implemented, Schmitt (*CPD* 12/*GLP* 18) further notes, one would not only have robbed political equality of its essence and made it without value for the individual human being (*einzelnen*), but politics would have become without essence (*wesenlos*), as such equality without essence would have been taken seriously within the field (of the political). At stake here is clearly an equality that is divided in itself; with 'substantive equality' as Schmitt conceives of it giving birth to itself by distinguishing itself from what can be called 'meaningless equality'. Schmitt's rhetoric in *The Crisis of Parliamentary Democracy* (1923) is particularly forceful, and he clearly speaks of something he finds threatening. He is looking into the abyss, one could say, and anxiously seeks fixed ground.[56]

As with freedom, at least in some of Schmitt's writings as we saw above, there is clearly something threatening, abyssal, originary perhaps, in equality. This seems to suggest that the seeming inconsistency in Schmitt's views as to whether the rule-of-law component and the political component of the modern constitution exist side by side[57] or whether the political component precedes and determines the rule-of-law component,[58] is to be explained by the haunting presence of something beyond the political, which in a certain way precedes and infuses both these two components. We can see this for example when Schmitt (*CPD* 13/*GLP* 18) distinguishes absolute or limitless equality from democracy ('The equality of all human beings as human beings is not democracy [*Die Gleichheit aller Menschen als Menschen ist nicht Demokratie*]'); yet in doing so he alludes to another 'conception' of democracy, which can with reference to Derrida be referred to as the 'democracy to come', and which would not necessarily be tied to country, state and citizen:

56 Support for this reading can be found in *TL* 81/*DL* 123 where Schmitt notes with reference to Hamann (commenting in turn on Kant) that the 'distance "from transcendental ideas to demonology is not great"'.

57 See in this respect *CT* 93, 101 and 169.

58 See in this respect *CT* 55 and 102, and see Böckenförde (1997: 12). As noted above, in *HdV* 111 Schmitt e.g. points out that the political is unavoidable and ineradicable. It is thus not possible to distinguish politics from science, religion and law. The uniqueness of the political lies in the fact that every possible field of human activity is potentially political and it becomes immediately political when decisive conflicts and questions arise in this field. The political can furthermore combine itself with any matter and gives it a 'new turn'. Everything that is in the public interest is in some or other way political, and nothing which concerns the state can really (*im Ernst*) be depoliticised.

> Until now there has never been a democracy that did not recognise the concept of the foreign and that could have realized the equality of all men [*Bisher hat es noch keine Demokratie gegeben, die den Begriff des Fremden nicht gekannt und die Gleichheit aller Menschen verwirklicht hätte*].
>
> (*CPD* 11/*GLP* 16)

As we saw above, he associates this 'democracy to come' and the incalculable equality associated with it, with irresponsibility, formlessness, injustice (*unrecht*), folly (*Torheit*), meaninglessness and self-destruction. At stake at this point of intersection between Schmitt and Derrida is a *demos* without *kratie* (power),[59] and an equality which does not simply draw no distinctions, but which welcomes the absolute stranger, thereby disrupting the return of the people to itself.[60] The relation between these two forms of equality[61] more precisely raises the question of the drawing or negotiation of a line in relation to who or what comes. In the words of Derrida:

> does this measure of the immeasurable, this democratic equality, end at citizenship, and thus at the borders of the nation-state? Or must we extend it to the whole world of singularities [*à tout le monde des singularités*], to the whole world of humans assumed to be like me, my compeers – or else, even further, to all nonhuman living beings, or again, even beyond that, to all the nonliving, to their memory, spectral or otherwise, to their to-come or to their indifference with regard to what we think we can identify, in an always precipitous, dogmatic, and obscure way, as the life or the living present of living [*la vivance*] in general?
>
> (*Rog* 53/*Voy* 81)

59 See also Chapter 3 above.

60 See also Chapter 5, Section A above. This return of the people to itself, appears most clearly from Schmitt's understanding of the state as the 'identity of the people with itself [*Identität des Volkes mit sich selbst*]' (*CT* 260/*VL* 229–30) and of democracy as 'identity [*Identität*] of ruler and ruled, governing and governed, commander and follower' (*CT* 264/*VL* 234). It expresses the idea that within the democratic state there can be no qualitative difference between those who rule and those who are being ruled. The rulers are in other words in no respect superior to or qualitatively 'better' than those who are being ruled; see also Neumann (2015: 57) who reads this identity as positing an equality between ruler and ruled. Someone who rules thus cannot step out of [*heraustreten*] the general identity and homogeneity of the people (*CT* 264/*VL* 235). This identity between ruler and ruled ultimately gives expression to the democratic idea of the people ruling themselves (*CT* 264). Lindahl (2008a: 13–14), likewise Van der Walt (2010b: 115), reads the above passages in Schmitt as positing the idea of rulers and ruled as 'the same', which he (Lindahl) refers to as co-referential or *idem*-identity, which poses the question 'What am I?' Lindahl in turn argues in favour of a view of identity as 'reflexive', posing the question 'Who am I?'; see further Chapter 3 above.

61 The aporetic structure of equality is elaborated on as follows by Derrida (*Rog* 52/*Voy* 80): equality is 'inadequate to itself, at the same time chance and threat, threat as chance: autoimmune [*inadéquate à elle-même, chance et menace à la fois, menace en tant que chance: autoimmunitaire*]'; see further below.

Living together

The analysis undertaken above of equality and freedom is arguably central to envisaging living together today, whether in a province, region or federal member-state, a nation-state, a federation or union of nation states or in the world. We saw that Schmitt's text stands open to a reading to the effect that both freedom and equality are to be thought beyond subjectivity, mastery, autonomy and consciousness. These concepts are thus to be understood as characterised by a certain unconditionality and incalculability, calling for an absolute welcome of whoever or whatever may come, that is, for a certain irresponsibility beyond reason. Such a reading could have significant implications for the duty of sovereign powers (on the national, transnational and international levels) in their relation to others. This is so both insofar as the singularities (rather than 'subjects' or 'individuals')[62] are concerned to whom freedom and equality are owed and the content of the 'duties' owed to such singularities.[63] The structure at stake here, which we encountered in the analysis above, also appears from a number of Derrida's texts where he speaks of a tension within the concept of democracy between the incalculable singularity of anyone, before any subject, on the one hand, and the universality of rational calculation, equality of citizens before the law, the social bond of being together, on the other.[64] The scope of this duty towards singularities is in principle unlimited, incalculable, that is, a duty beyond duty, law, debt, economy and conditional hospitality (*G&L* 67; 'Auto' 133). This duty is not restricted to those with citizenship, subjectivity or consciousness (*Rog* 86), that is, it goes beyond '[t]he equality of everything "that bears a human face"' that Schmitt (*CT* 257/*VL* 226) speaks of. It is not even restricted to living beings, but extends to those who are dead and to those who are yet to be born (*B&S I* 110). An incalculable or unconditional equality and freedom, which has no regard for the self, is in other words called for.

In somewhat more concrete terms, as Derrida (2013: 37–9; *G&L* 69–72; *B&S I* 109) contends, nothing can justify giving preference to what is regarded as 'our own', rather than to others, for example to those in far-off countries who starve or to what is called 'the animal'. The 'welcome' referred to above calls for the eradication of malnutrition, disease and humiliation, that is, the denial of equality and freedom, throughout the world, to anyone (*Rog* 86).[65] This rethinking of

62 See *Points* 271 for this distinction.

63 Singularity is to be understood in terms of our relation to death, see Derrida (2005a: 140); *Points* 271; *G&L* 52.

64 See 'Auto' 120, 130; *PoF* 22; *Rog* 86; *SoM* 81.

65 The same call can be made via the notion of dignity, which would no longer remain restricted to the recognition of human dignity, but would begin with 'the respectable dignity of the other as the absolute *unlike*, recognized as unrecognizable, indeed as unrecognizable, beyond all knowledge, all cognition and all recognition [*la dignité respectable de l'autre comme l'absolu* dissemblable, *reconnu comme non reconnaissable, voire comme méconnaissable, au-delà de tout savoir, de toute connaissance et de toute reconnaissance*]' (*Rog* 60/*Voy* 90).

equality and of freedom as without autonomy, necessarily requires a reassessment of the notion of (human) rights, which in general is associated with the possession of language, subjectivity, sovereignty, freedom, dignity and moral self-determination, which animals, or, in some versions, *most* animals, are supposed to be lacking in (*FWT* 69; *AR* 246). It is precisely this discourse, including the human rights discourse, which is problematic in many respects (both insofar as the reputed abilities of animals and of humans are concerned),[66] that justifies the violence perpetrated against animals today (Derrida 2008c: 89; *FWT* 74; *B&S I* 111). Simply extending such rights to (some) animals (like primates, because of their seeming proximity to man) would mean keeping the current paradigm and the violence accompanying it, in place. According to Derrida a double strategy is required: on the one hand, support for struggles that seek the extension of human rights to those human beings that are currently deprived thereof, as well as changes in the treatment of animals; and, on the other, 'the most radical questioning possible of all the concepts at work here' ('Auto' 132–3).[67] The notion of human rights is clearly a biased and distorted attempt at domesticating and appropriating the call for absolute hospitality.[68]

The terms of our living together are today mostly spelled out in constitutions, which, as Derrida (2013: 25) points out, provides for a kind of statutory surveillance of such living together or an armed peace or armistice. Yet a living together (in peace) would be impossible without some hospitality or justice beyond the terms of the agreement, that is, a gift beyond the economy of circular return (Derrida 2013: 26, 35). 'Living together (well)' must thus be understood in similar terms to the construction of the self that we encountered above in the analysis of Schmitt. It in other words means that:

> one lives together, well then, only with and as a stranger 'at home,' [*chez soi*] in all the figures of the 'at home' that there is in 'living together' only there where the whole [*ensemble*] is neither formed nor closed, there where the living together (the adverb) contests the completion, the closure, and the cohesiveness of an 'ensemble' (the noun, the substantive), of a substantial, closed ensemble identical to itself; to recognise that there is 'living together'

66 As Derrida (1993b: 35) points out, the animal's relation to death is often disputed, e.g. by Heidegger, whereas *Dasein* is said to have a relation to death. As Derrida shows, the latter is a very problematic assumption. The capability of animals in respect of language, response, society, ethics, etc. is also often unjustifiably disputed. Derrida's contention in this respect is that there is no single limit or threshold between man and animal. No limit furthermore constitutes a solid border and there is more than one limit; see also *B&S I* 309–10, 333–4; and in general, Derrida (2008c).

67 Although Schmitt did not concern himself specifically with the plight of non-human animals, he puts us on guard against the abuse of the notion of the human to deny rights to those (humans) who are denied (human) rights because of a denial of their humanity; see Campagna (2015: 128–33). Schmitt's critique in this respect can easily be extended to non-human animals.

68 See below.

> only there where, in the name of promise and of memory, of the messianic and of mourning without work and without healing, it welcomes dissymmetry, anachrony, nonreciprocity with an other who is greater, at once older and younger, an other who comes or will come perhaps, who has perhaps already come – here is the justice of a law above laws . . . .
>
> (Derrida 2013: 28)

Chapter 7

State, *Großraum*, *nomos*

Introduction

In Chapter 2, Section A above we saw how Schmitt in *The Concept of the Political* seeks to define the enemy with reference to his own ideal description of the *jus publicum Europaeum* as an epoch in which it was possible to tie the concept of the political to the state, despite the independence of these two concepts. War was, in other words, to be understood as a war between states and the enemy as the *external* enemy, who was not to be viewed with hatred, but treated with respect. Schmitt here already observed the demise of the state form as well as the threat of US imperialism and its dehumanisation of the enemy. In Chapter 2, Section B the focus was on the partisan who fights both against a foreign invader in defence of the homeland and as a world revolutionary in an international civil war. In the *Theory of the Partisan* Schmitt seeks to contain this civil war in a way similar to what was achieved with the *jus publicum Europaeum*, through his definition of the partisan as essentially telluric as well as through the idea of great spaces (*Großräume*), an idea which he had developed since the late 1930s with reference to the Monroe Doctrine of 1823 and within the context of Hitler's plans at the time for the expansion of German territory.

In the present chapter, Schmitt's elaboration of the notion of great spaces within the context of an analysis of the so-called *nomos* of the earth will be the main focus point. This will take place by way of an analysis of *Land and Sea* (1942),[1] *The Nomos of the Earth* (1950) and a few smaller publications of Schmitt on the same theme. In these texts Schmitt sketches in broad terms the developments in

1 The mythical nature of *Land and Sea* is often pointed to; see e.g. Dean (2006). It is nonetheless interesting to note that in *GL* 141 Schmitt refers to *Land and Sea* as taking 'a step beyond the mythological into the mythical itself [*ein Schritt über das Mythologische hinaus ins Mythische selber*]'. As we will see in the analysis that follows, Schmitt with this statement appears to be hinting at going beyond the *logos*/*mythos* opposition towards that which gives place to this opposition. See also *ON* 90–1, 100–4, 112–13, 123–4 where a 'myth within the myth . . . an open abyss in the general myth' (*ON* 113) is likewise at stake; see further Chapter 5, Section A above; and see also Spitzer (2011).

international law since Antiquity, showing the movement from a first to a second and ultimately a new *nomos* of the earth in the twentieth century. *Nomos* in Schmitt's reflections has the broad meaning of a law of law or a 'constitution' of the earth as a whole. Schmitt's reflections thus resonate with current debates about the future shape of international law, which Derrida also engaged in, most prominently in *Rogues: Two Essays on Reason*. The intersection between Schmitt and Derrida in this respect will be enquired into here.

The chapter will proceed by first exploring the different meanings of *nomos* in line with Schmitt's analysis. It will be shown that for Schmitt land appropriation is the most original meaning of *nomos*, but that he acknowledges that *nomos* is 'preceded' by what will later in the chapter be referred to as an a-*nomos*, which needs to be overcome in order for *nomos* to be established. This will be followed by an enquiry into the three 'stages' of *nomos* as identified by Schmitt, that is: (1) from Antiquity until the end of the Middle Ages; (2) from around the sixteenth century until the end of the nineteenth century; and (3) from the early twentieth century. The chapter ends with an enquiry into Schmitt's conception of human nature, specifically the manner in which he contrasts land and sea from this point of view, as well as the way in which human nature is linked to *nomos*. The conception of human nature which appears from Schmitt's analysis returns us to the notion of the a-*nomos*, which opens the door to alternative conceptions of *nomos* in contrast with Schmitt's *Großraum* theory.

Nomos

Nomos, as Schmitt (*NoE* 325/*VRA* 489) points out, is usually translated by jurists and historians as law (*Gesetz*), custom (*Sitte*) or tradition (*Gewohnheit*). Schmitt (*NoE* 345/*SGN* 581) wants us to understand it in its original sense as a kind of law of law or original constitution (*Urverfassung*).[2] In Chapter 4 of Part I of *The Nomos of the Earth*, he expresses his understanding of *nomos* as follows:

> The Greek word for the first measurement [*Messung*] of all subsequent measures [*Maßstabe*], for the first land-appropriation [*Landnahme*] understood as the first partition and division of space [*Raum-Teilung und – Einteilung*], for the primeval division [*Ur-Teilung*] and distribution [*Ur-Verteilung*], is *nomos*.
>
> (*NoE* 67/*NdE* 36)

2 In *TTJT* 50–1/*DARD* 14 Schmitt's understanding of *nomos* already hints at such a foundational order when he argues (in a passage which is difficult to translate) for an understanding of Pindar's *nomos basileus* (law as king) as follows: 'One can speak of a true or real *nomos* as true king [*einem wirklichen* Nomos *als wirklichem König*] only if *nomos* means precisely the total, complete or absolute [*den totalen* – Bendersky chose to leave these words untranslated], a concrete order and community with a comprehensive concept of *law* [*umfassenden Begriff von* Recht]'.

With this definition, Schmitt (*NoE* 67/*NdE* 36) wants 'to restore or give back to the word [i.e. *nomos*] its primal force and greatness [*erste Kraft und Größe*]'. He thus seeks to return to the original meaning of *nomos* as derived from the Greek verb *nemein* (German: *nehmen*),[3] that is, taking, appropriation, seizure or the establishment or constitution of radical title (*NoE* 80–1/*NdE* 48–9).[4] Here 'law and order [*Recht und Ordnung*] are one'; 'location and order [*Ortung und Ordnung*]' are inextricably interwoven (*NoE* 81/*NdE* 50). *Nomos* for Schmitt therefore essentially means the constitutive act of taking possession, followed by the other meanings of *nemein*: division or distribution (*teilen*) and pasturage/production (*weiden*).[5] This originary appropriation however tends to be quickly forgotten or suppressed into what he calls the 'semi/half-conscious' (*ins Halbbewußte abgedrängt*) (*NoE* 341/*SGN* 577), in favour of the constituted order. Already in Antiquity, Schmitt (*NoE* 67/*NdE* 36) notes, *nomos* becomes 'a designation for any normative regulation or directive passed or decreed in whatever fashion'. Something of the original meaning nevertheless always remains in place (*NoE* 68).[6] At stake here is a distinction analogous to that found in constitutional theory between constitutive or constituent power, on the one hand, and constituted power, on the other (*NoE* 82).[7] Jurists, Schmitt (*NoE* 82) points out, tend to focus only on constituted power and to regard the process through which such power came about, that is, by way of constitutive/constituent power, as non-legal. They find the source of legality in the constitution or in the will of the state, which is viewed as a person. The origin of the constitution or state itself is regarded as a mere fact (*NoE* 82). Schmitt, as he does in *Constitutional Theory*, insists that the

3 In *NoE* 347/*SGN* 583 Schmitt compares the *nehmen* at stake in land appropriation and the naming which is an inherent part thereof with the *taking* of a wife in marriage, and the wife in turn accepting the (sur)name of her husband: 'In those times, man *took* a wife [nahm *der Mann die Frau*]'. Schmitt also refers here (*NoE* 348/*SGN* 584) to Simon Weil who in her book *Attente de Dieu* reported that as she was reading a beautiful poem, Christ descended upon her and 'took her' (*il m'a prise*). It is perhaps noteworthy that Freud (2001, XV: 156, 158, 162/1991, XI: 158, 160, 165) associates a landscape (*Landschaft*), which appears in dreams, with the female sexual organs. The meaning of *nomos* which Schmitt insists on here, i.e. the taking or appropriation of land, in other words appears to be related to a certain pleasure which we came across in Chapter 5, Section B above; see further below.

4 In exploring the originary meaning of *nomos*, Schmitt (*NoE* 346/*SGN* 582) notes that 'language passes down in its own way [*tradiert auf ihre Weise*] the continuing constitutive processes [*Vorgänge*] and events [*Ereignisse*], also when people have forgotten them. "Language still knows it", says . . . the language philosopher Johann Arnold Kanne'.

5 See *NoE* 326–7/*VRA* 491; and *NoE* 345/*SGN* 581. Lossau (2011: 253–4) contends that for Schmitt land appropriation is ultimately characterised by arbitrariness; see also Minca and Rowan (2016: 220) who speak in this regard of 'the ultimate groundlessness of order' and of historical contingency. This makes the political and the conflict that is inherent in it, inevitable. Schmitt's insistence on bracketed war (also in proposing the idea of great spaces, see below) would thus be an attempt to deal with the inevitability of the political.

6 Ulmen's translation (*NoE* 68) misses out on the always/*immer*.

7 See further Chapter 3 above.

manifestations of constituent power – here understood in an extended sense – also belong within legal discourse.

Nomos is thus to be understood as the foundational order, yet not only of a specific domestic legal order, but, as we will see, of the earth as a whole, that is, of the international legal order. Schmitt (*NoE* 82) points out in this regard that there are two forms of land appropriation from a legal-historical perspective: one kind which takes place within the given order of international law, and another which displaces the whole spatial order, thereby establishing a new *nomos* of the whole spatial sphere for neighbouring peoples and, in so doing, bringing about a radical change for international law. Land appropriation has moreover by no means come to an end after the era of colonialism, as is generally believed; it continues today (*NoE* 346–7).[8] It is important for purposes of our analysis to note that Schmitt (*NoE* 82/*NdE* 50) distinguishes these two forms of land appropriation from instances of invasion or temporary occupation which do not ground a new order but amount to 'mere acts of violence that quickly destroy themselves' or, more literally, 'mere rapidly self-destructive powers/forces [*wenn wir von den bloßen schnell sich selbst zerstörenden Gewalttaten absehen*]'.[9] Schmitt hereby seems to suggest that in order for successful (new) land appropriations to take place within an existing *nomos* or for a new *nomos* of the earth as a whole to come about there has to be an overcoming of self-destructive forces or powers, such as those manifesting themselves in the twentieth century (see below).[10] *Nomos*, in its originary meaning, thus also and perhaps most importantly, involves the surmounting of forces of self-destruction.[11]

The first nomos

According to Schmitt, the first *nomos* lasted from Antiquity to the end of the Middle Ages and land dominates here. The world, as Schmitt (*NoE* 351/*SGN* 518)

8 Schmitt (*NoE* 346–7) refers here specifically to the air and space appropriations of the time, and elsewhere to the attempts by the United States to establish a unified world order under its own dominance (*NoE* 335).

9 See also *NoE* 80/*NdE* 48: 'Not every invasion or temporary occupation is a land-appropriation that founds an order. In world history, there have been many acts of force that have destroyed themselves quickly. [*Selbstverständlich ist nicht jede Invasion oder jede vorübergehende Okkupation schon eine Ordnung begründende Landnahme. Es hat in der Weltgeschichte genug Gewaltakte gegeben, die sich sehr schnell selbst zerstört haben.*]'

10 Schmitt's statement in this regard can be read with his exploration in *NoE* 336/*SGN* 573 of three declarations about power (*Macht*) by P. Erich Przywara, the first of which is that power is the 'secret uncanny ultimate [*geheim unheimlich Letzte*]', which Przywara contrasts with the tendency of power to reveal itself. Schmitt (*NoE* 349/*SGN* 584) later refers to the latter tendency as overpowering the 'satanic temptation [*satanische Versuchung*]' towards a power that remains invisible, anonymous and secret. These passages tie in closely with what was said above about *nomos* having to overcome forces of self-destruction, to which we will return below.

11 See also *Derrida B&S II* 259–60.

points out, was purely terrestrial (*rein terran*). Even though there were also river (potamic) and inland sea cultures (thalassic), the latter ultimately remained terrestrial. Man did not as yet have the audacity to risk sailing across the great oceans. A mythical image of land and sea and of the earth and the heavens dominated here (*NoE* 351). Furthermore, Schmitt (*NoE* 53/*NdE* 23) notes, 'everything remained within the framework and the horizon of a spatial concept of the earth that was neither global nor all-encompassing, of an earth that had not been measured scientifically'.[12] Every powerful nation, such as the Egyptian, Asian, Hellenistic, Roman and even the African and Incan Empires, considered itself to be at the centre of the world and its domain as a place where peace reigned, whereas the space outside was viewed as chaotic (*NoE* 51; *SGN* 518). The outside was furthermore perceived as being without a ruler and thus as 'free' for purposes of conquest, territorial acquisition and colonisation (*NoE* 51/*NdE* 21). In line with his analysis in *The Concept of the Political*, Schmitt (*NoE* 51/*NdE* 21) however rejects the view propagated in the nineteenth century that every stranger was regarded as an enemy, that all foreign territory was enemy territory unless a pact of friendship existed, and that all wars were wars of annihilation. In Roman law for example, a distinction was clearly drawn between the enemy (*hostis*), on the one hand, that is, those that declare war against us, and those against whom we declare war, and thieves and criminals, on the other (*NoE* 51/*NdE* 22).

The second nomos

The second *nomos*, dating from around the sixteenth century, came about due to a 'change' (*Wendung*) in the elements, of which England was in a certain sense the agent. England then took an elementary decision against the land in favour of the sea (*SGN* 396). This was not a methodical plan carried out by one or more persons, Schmitt notes, but rather the consequence of all the 'unleashed maritime energies [*entfesselten maritimen Energien*]', which were inherited by England (*L&S* 49/*L&M* 90; *SGN* 396).[13] The 'decision' of England followed upon the invention of the compass, whale hunting and advancements in ship-building technology, especially by the Dutch, the actions and adventures of pirates,

12 Voigt (2005: 80) summarises the view of Aristotle on space, which, one could say, dominated during the first *nomos*, as follows: 'Space, according to Aristotle, has its own reality, it is a 'receptacle' or 'container' ('*Behälter*'), which assigns to the things contained their specific status (*Stellenwert*). Points (topoi) determine where 'top' and 'bottom' are. They give to space a fixed structure. Space was conceived as limited by fixed stars, as finite space, the centre of which is constituted by the immovable, spherical earth.' See also *L&S* 34.

13 Of interest to our analysis here is a quotation by Schmitt, or Herr Altmann as he calls himself in the essay 'Dialogue on New Space [*Gespräch über den Neuen Raum*]' in *SGN* 561/*DPS* 69 of the English historian Seeley in response to a remark that the developments in England were not consciously planned, and with which Schmitt expresses his agreement: 'In a fit of absence of mind we conquered the world [*In einem Anfall von Geistesabwesenheit haben wir die Welt erobert*]').

privateers, sea traders and other sea roamers (*L&S* 13–26; *SGN* 396), the war against Catholic Spain, the Calvinist notion of predestination[14] and, as we will see below, perhaps most importantly, by changes in the conception of space. England, the strongest sea power since the eighteenth century managed to conquer all the world's oceans (*NoE* 352; *L&S* 21). 'Henceforth' Schmitt (*L&S* 50/*L&M* 92) notes, 'the land would be looked at from the sea, and the island would cease to be seen as a split chipped from the Continent, but as part of the sea, as a ship, or even more clearly, a fish'.[15] This had important consequences for the *nomos* of the earth because the sea as compared to the earth (*die Erde*) 'knows no such sense-perceptible unity of space and law, of order and location [*Ordnung und Ortung*]' (*NoE* 42/*NdE* 13).[16]

The second *nomos* is characterised by the development of the modern state, accompanied by large-scale land appropriation, that is, the colonisation of what was regarded as 'free space', as well as the establishment of colonial protectorates. Schmitt (*NoE* 352) refers in this regard to the discovery and colonisation of a new continent (America) by European powers. In Asia, the Eurocentric structure of *nomos* only partially expressed itself by way of land appropriation; otherwise it found expression in the form of protectorates, leases, trade agreements and spheres of interest (*NoE* 352). Africa, Schmitt (*NoE* 352) notes, was not divided between the European powers until the nineteenth century. A distinction is drawn at this point between the fixed earth, on the one hand, which was divided into state territory, colonies, protectorates and spheres of interest, and the sea, which was free, on the other (*NoE* 352). The sea was open to all states for utilisation without being divided by boundaries, but also, and more importantly, for the waging of war (*NoE* 352). Ultimately, however, the sea belonged to England (*L&S* 46).

The second *nomos* is furthermore characterised by a double balance: between land (powers) and (the only) sea (power), as well as between European land powers, secured by England (*NoE* 172–5, 352–3). According to Schmitt (*NoE* 353), two completely different international orders coexisted here: one for the land and one for the sea. War between land powers was a bracketed war, where the enemy was only the enemy army, not the population. Wars were fought between the armies of European states, not the populations of states (*NoE* 353).[17] The private property of the civil population could not be taken as booty.[18] Sea war however amounted to trade war. Anyone who traded with an opponent/adversary

14 See Palaver (1996: 115–16) who points to the opposition Schmitt posits between Protestantism (specifically the Puritans and Huguenots) and Catholicism, with the latter remaining rooted to the soil, whilst the former 'seem[s] to be able to live on every soil without, however, becoming rooted'.

15 See also *SGN* 395 and 397.

16 Normativism and the *Rechtsstaat* Constitution are in Schmitt's analysis in alliance with the second *nomos*.

17 In 'TP' 7/*TdP* 17 Schmitt acknowledges that the partisan, originating in the early nineteenth century in Spain, constituted an exception to this order.

18 See also *L&S* 47.

was viewed as an enemy (*NoE* 353). The private property of the citizen of a state against which war was waged as well as of neutral states which traded with such states could be taken as booty. On land and sea, completely different concepts of war, enemy and booty thus applied, as if they were two separate worlds (*NoE* 353; *L&S* 47–8). For Schmitt there are also other profound differences between land and sea. In a highly evocative passage to which we will return, Schmitt notes that, although through labour the sea can provide one with many riches,

> fields cannot be planted and firm lines cannot be engraved. Ships that sail across the sea leave no trace. 'On the waves, there is nothing but waves [*Auf den Wellen ist alles Welle*].'[19] The sea has no character, in the original sense of the word, which comes from the Greek *charassein*, meaning to engrave, to scratch, to imprint. The sea is free.
>
> (*NoE* 42–3/*NdE* 13–14)

The open sea moreover and originally knows 'no limits, no boundaries, no consecrated sites, no sacred orientations, no law, and no property' (*NoE* 43/*NdE* 14).[20] The freedom of the sea for Schmitt also means that it is 'state-free'. The modern state, Schmitt (*SGN* 397) points out, developed on the European continent in line with Hobbes's model, rather than in England. The choice for the sea was at the same time a choice against becoming a state (*SGN* 397). England, which as we saw earlier had, according to Schmitt, become a fish (or whale) through its maritime power, was because of the Industrial Revolution and modern technology in the eighteenth and nineteenth centuries, turning from a fish into a machine, thereby laying the basis for the third *nomos* of the earth (*L&S* 54).[21] Technology meant that man was no longer directly engaging with the sea element (*L&S* 54). 'The industrial revolution', Schmitt (*L&S* 54/*L&M* 99) notes, 'has transformed the children of the sea into machine-builders and servants of machines'.

19 A quotation from Schiller's tragedy of 1802–3, *Die Braut von Messina* (2016: 42): 'Auf den Wellen ist alles Welle, Auf dem Meer ist kein Eigentum'.

20 See also *SGN* 564/*DPS* 73: 'the midpoint and core of a terrestrial existence – with all its concrete orders – is the house [*Mittelpunkt und Kern einer terranen Existenz – mit allen ihren konkreten Ordnungen – ist das Haus*]', which Schmitt (in the words of Herr Altmann) opposes to maritime existence where the ship is at the centre. The ship, he notes, is a much more intensive technical means than the house; the ship moves, while the house entails being at rest (*Ruhe*); at stake is a different space in which the ship moves, compared to the landscape in which the house stands. The ship for Schmitt represents 'unleashed technology [*entfesselte Technik*]' (*SGN* 564/*DPS* 74) or 'absolute technology' (*SGN* 541).

21 In *NoE* 178/*NdE* 149 Schmitt notes in this respect that the 'English Isle became the agency of the spatial turn to a new *nomos* of the earth, and, potentially, even the operational base for the later leap into the total rootlessnes of modern technology'. See also *GL* 126–7 where Schmitt notes that 'the transition from sailing ship to machine meant the destruction of this balance [*der Übergang vom Segelschiff zur Maschine war die Zerstörung dieses Gleichgewichts*]', i.e. of land and sea during the second *nomos*.

England can, according to Schmitt, ultimately be said to have won a revolution: the revolution of planetary space (*L&S* 28). With the discovery of the Americas and with the first ship sailing around the earth, a new world was born. It could no longer be denied that the earth was a celestial body which revolved around the sun. Schmitt (*L&S* 34) contends that this was not however the most radical transformation of the age. What was really decisive was the cosmic dimension and the representation of an infinite void (*eines unendlichen leeren Raumes*) (*L&S* 34/*L&M* 65). From Newton's theories a new concept of space comes to the fore. In terms of this conception, '[t]he stars, masses of matter, move while the forces of attraction and repulsion balance each other in an infinite void [*in einem unendlichen, leeren Raum*], by virtue of the laws of gravitation' (*L&S* 34/*L&M* 66). There are no limits to space in this Newtonian conception. It was, according to Schmitt, this changing conception of space which made possible the 'discovery' of new continents and voyages around the world (*L&S* 35/*L&M* 67). Although certain philosophers had previously spoken of the empty or the void,[22] people could now for the first time imagine an empty space. Schmitt (*L&S* 34–5/*L&M* 66) notes that people in earlier times had a fear of emptiness, the void or the abyss (the *horror vacui*). Now people were forgetting their fear and were not concerned about existing in an empty space (*L&S* 35). Some Enlightenment thinkers even mocked this *horror vacui* (*L&S* 35). Yet, comments Schmitt (*L&S* 35), to think a truly empty space is to think absolute nothingness. This 'mocking' was therefore 'probably simply an understandable shudder in the face of the nothing and the emptiness of death [*der Leerheit des Todes*], in the face of a nihilistic idea and in the face of nihilism in general' (*L&S* 35/*L&M* 67). It is important to note that the nothing or nihilism for Schmitt is not simply the void of death.[23] Nihilism for him has a very specific 'meaning', as is evident for example from *The Nomos of the Earth* where Schmitt compares the bracketing of war during the reign of the *jus publicum Europaeum* with its alternative, as manifested in the twentieth century:

> The essence of such [bracketed] wars was a regulated contest of forces gauged by witnesses in a bracketed space. Such wars are the opposite of disorder [*Gegenteil von Unordnung*]. They represent the highest form of order [*Ordnung*] within the scope of human power [*Kraft*]. They are the only protection against a circle of increasing reprisals, that is, against nihilistic acts of hatred and acts of revenge [*nihilistischen Haß- und Racheaktionen*] whose meaningless goal [*sinnloses Ziel*] lies in mutual destruction [*gegenseitigen Vernichtung*].[24]
>
> (*NoE* 187/*NdE* 158–9)

22 Schmitt does not mention any specific philosopher here, but he is most likely alluding to the Atomists, specifically to Democritus.

23 Schmitt (*GL* 165) associates nihilism with the idea of one world state, which for him likewise necessarily involves civil war and self-destruction; see further below.

24 Schmitt (*NoE* 187) furthermore insists on drawing a distinction between anarchy and nihilism (see also *NoE* 56–7, 66). Anarchy, he points out, is not the worst scenario. Anarchy and law do not stand

Schmitt's preferred conception of space, which we will encounter below, clearly aims at overcoming the nothing in this 'sense' of mutual destruction, as also appears from a passage in the *Glossarium*: 'The magnificent sentence of Nietzsche: With sturdy shoulders space stands against the nothing. Where there is space there is Being [*Der herrliche Nietzschesatz: Mit festen Schultern steht der Raum gegen das Nichts. Wo Raum ist, ist Sein*]'.[25] In the *Glossarium* Schmitt (*GL* 318) furthermore links this tension between the nothing and a certain conception of space, with Freud and psychoanalysis. With reference to Gottfried Benn's notion of man as a termite with space neurosis, Schmitt adopts a reading of Freud (of man as having a destructive and ultimately self-destructive drive) which suggests a familiarity with as well as remarkable insight into Freud's contentions concerning the death drive in *Beyond the Pleasure Principle* (Freud 2001, XVIII: 1–64):

> Termites with space-neurosis says expert Gottfried Benn.[26] He seems to view this as fatal. The matter is however different. As long as the termites namely still have space neurosis, they also still have the feeling and the fear of transformation into termites. Only the termites without space-neurosis have become pure termites and insects. And the methods of the Freud-indexed neurosis-therapy indeed have in mind the consummation of this termitisation.[27]
>
> (*GL* 318, entry of 20 July 1951)

The 'ghostly' and 'originary' nature of this truly empty space, the void or the nothing are mentioned in both *Nomos* and the *Glossarium*. Schmitt (*NoE* 178/*NdE* 149) refers to Thomas More's book *Utopia* (1516) which testified to the possibility of a monstrous abolition or upliftment (*einer ungeheuerlichen Aufhebung*) of all

in a mutually exclusive relationship, referring to the right of resistance and self-help as perfectly compatible with (good) law. It is rather international law rules which seek to prohibit all such actions, which risk the 'horrifying nihilistic destruction of all law [*eine grauenhafte, nihilistische Zerstörung allen Rechtes*]' (*NoE* 187/*NdE* 159). Schmitt (*NoE* 66/*NdE* 36) furthermore seeks to restrict nihilism to the nineteenth and twentieth centuries. He sees nihilism as standing in close relationship with utopia (see also *NoE* 178: utopia announces a radical break with *topos*, and see below) and as breaching the inherent relationship between 'order and location [*Ordnung und Ortung*]'. Legal positivism is said to have its origin in the nihilism of the same era; see *NoE* 76.

25 *GL* 317 (entry of 16 Jul 1951), repeated in *SGN* 494 n2.

26 See Benn (1971: 36): 'Stimulus and repression. Today's technology, yesterday's mechanics. The first pirogue had greater sociological consequences than the submarine and the airplane; the first arrow was deadlier than poison gas. The people of Antiquity knew W.C.'s as well as elevators, pulleys, clocks, flying machines, automatons; they had a monomania about tunnels, passages, conduits, aqueducts – termites subject to space neuroses, grip compulsions.'

27 'Termiten mit Raum-Neurose, sagt sachverständig Gottfried Benn. Er scheint das für vernichtend zu halten. Die Sache liegt aber anders. So lange die Termiten nämlich noch Raum-Neurosen haben, so lange haben sie auch noch das Gefühl and die Angst vor der Verwandlung in Termiten. Erst die Termiten ohne Raum-Neurose sind reine Termiten und Insekten geworden. Und die Methoden der Freud-indizierten Neurosentherapie haben ja den Sinn, diese Termitisierung zu vollenden.'

locations (*Ortungen*) on which the first *nomos* of the earth was based. A word such as utopia, Schmitt (*NoE* 178) notes, would have been unthinkable for anyone in Antiquity. Schmitt (*NoE* 178/*NdE* 149–50) further points out that the u- in utopia does not simply negate space (*topos*) as the term a-*topos* would do, but in comparison with the latter term involves 'a still stronger negative relation to *topos* [*noch eine stärkere, negative Beziehung zum Topos*]'. The word foretold, 'as by a shadow [*wie durch einen Schatten*]', the events of the nineteenth century with the replacement of maritime existence by an industrial-technical existence (*NoE* 178/*NdE* 150). Although it appears that Schmitt attaches a negative connotation to such truly empty space, elsewhere the latter takes on more explicitly an 'originary' role. In the *Glossarium*, for example, Schmitt notes that there is no movement without an empty space:

> 'The ocean is free and even more free are sources/springs'[28] . . . . There is no movement without empty space. There is no right without free space. Every rule-like capture and bracketing of space requires an outside, a free space which remains outside of the law . . . . How horrifying is a world in which there is no longer an abroad, and only a domestic; no path to the free; no scope for the free measuring and testing of power.[29]
>
> (*GL* 37)

Although Schmitt can be read as referring here to free space in a phenomenological sense,[30] that is, to the area outside of Europe during the second *nomos*, in view of our analysis above, this passage can also be read in a non-phenomenological sense, that is, as referring to an a-topology, a placeless place which gives place (*Rog* xiv), a spacing beyond metaphysics, as the latter's condition of possibility (Chapter 5, Sections A and B above).

The new nomos

From the sea to air and fire

Towards the end of the nineteenth century, the United States, and in the twentieth century, Russia, become the dominant powers, coupled with the idea of infinite

28 A quotation from Däubler (1910).

29 '"Der Ozean ist frei und freier noch sind Quellen" . . . . Es gibt keine Bewegung ohne leeren Raum. Es gibt auch kein Recht ohne freien Raum. Jede regelhafte Erfassung und Hegung eines Raumes erfordert einen draußen, außerhalb des Rechts verbleibenden freien Raum . . . . Wie ensetzlich ist eine Welt, in der es kein Ausland mehr gibt, und nur noch ein Inland; kein Weg ins freie; kein Spielraum freien Kräftemessens und freier Krafterprobung.' See also Ojakangas (2007: 206); and Minca and Rowan (2016: 223–4).

30 See e.g. Debrix (2011: 223–5).

technological progress. Schmitt (*NoE* 353) points out that the earth is now (temporarily) divided into two parts, East and West, which are purely geographical concepts, and not easily distinguishable. Yet behind this purely geographical opposition (*geographischen Gegensatz*) appears a deeper, more elementary opposition (*ein tieferer, elementarer Gegensatz*) (*NoE* 353/*SGN* 520). Schmitt (*NoE* 353) invokes here the fact that what is referred to as 'the East' is characterised by a huge land mass, whereas 'the West' is characterised by great oceans. The United States can consequently be viewed as the new, bigger island, well-adapted to take the place of England, which had grown too small to be an imperial power in the technological era. Behind the opposition between East and West thus still stands an opposition between a continental and a maritime world, an opposition of land and sea (*NoE* 353; *DPS* 61).[31] In times of the highest tension, as experienced during the Cold War, Schmitt (*NoE* 353) notes, the history of mankind rises to a pure opposition between the elements.

Although the opposition between land and sea thus remained in the twentieth century, modern technology, as we saw above, has robbed the sea of its elemental character (*NoE* 354). Towards the end of *Land and Sea*, Schmitt (*L&S* 57) notes that of the four elements in early Greek philosophy (earth, water, air and fire), the new *nomos* appears to entail a movement towards the dominance of the air.[32] This leads to another spatial revolution (*L&S* 57). Schmitt (*NoE* 316–7/*NdE* 294) further points out that air war is a 'war of pure destruction [*reiner Vernichtungskrieg*]'. Maritime war and land war can likewise be purely destructive, although the latter has a greater chance of being limited in nature because of the mutual relation between obligation and protection (*NoE* 318). Air war is however the furthest removed from this relationship (*NoE* 320). In view of the movement towards airspace, Schmitt (*NoE* 354) notes that many already believe that the whole of the earth is now only an airport or landing place, a storehouse for raw materials and a mother ship for space exploration. Yet we should not be too quick to jump to conclusions concerning the element that is set to dominate in the new *nomos*, Schmitt warns (*L&M* 105).[33] If one takes account of the means and energies employed in exercising human power in airspace, as well as the functioning of the combustion engine through which aeroplanes are propelled, then it seems as if the new element at stake here is fire, which is likewise associated with destruction (*L&M* 105).[34] Schmitt (*L&M* 105)

31 According to Schmitt *L&S* 5–6, maritime and land powers have been engaged in battle against each other throughout history.

32 A third animal (a great bird) is now added to the Behemoth and the Leviathan, representing respectively land and sea; see *L&M* 105.

33 *L&S* 58–9 are not included in the copy of the Draghici translation which I had access to. In what follows, where these pages are at stake, reference will be made only to *L&M*.

34 Zeitlin (2015: lxviii) ascribes this turn to fire in Schmitt's text to the aerial bombardment of Germany at the time.

ultimately decides to leave open the question as to which of these two elements is set to dominate the new *nomos*.

Who or what is coming?

The new *nomos*, Schmitt (*NoE* 354) predicted, could ultimately be characterised by the victory of one power, that is, either the United States or the Soviet Union, leading to world unity. The victorious empire would, in line with the originary meaning of *nomos* explored by Schmitt, appropriate the whole world, including land, sea and air and divide and manage it in line with its own ideas and plans (*NoE* 354). This seemed at the time like the most plausible option in view of the dominant technologically inspired thinking, yet Schmitt (*NoE* 354–5/*SGN* 521) notes that irrespective of the monstrous force of modern technology, it would not be possible to destroy without remainder (*restlos vernichten*) human nature or the violence/power (*Gewalt*) of land and sea, without (technology and/or the land and sea powers) at the same time destroying itself/themselves (*ohne sich gleichzeitig selbst zu vernichten*).[35] Stated in positive terms: world unity can be achieved only by way of total self- or mutual destruction, something which Schmitt likewise cautions against in *The Concept of the Political* (Chapter 2, Section A above).[36] A second possibility would entail something similar to the second *nomos* with its balance of powers, yet adapted in line with contemporary technical means and dimensions. The United States, which as we saw earlier can be referred to as the bigger island (compared to England), would dominate the sea and the air, and would maintain and secure the balance of the rest of the world (*NoE* 355).

A third possibility would likewise copy the balancing of powers of the second *nomos*, but through the recognition of large sovereign spaces of hegemony and non-interference by space-alien powers (*raumfremde Mächte*) (*NoE* 355/*SGN* 521; Schmitt 2011b: 46/*PB* 335).[37] Schmitt prefers the latter option, in view of the

35 The 'sich' is ambiguous here and can refer to either modern technical means or to land and sea (powers). Minca and Rowan (2016: 243 n50) link Schmitt's statement here to the concept of the political as understood with reference to human nature: 'technology could only overcome the inherent conflictual nature of human nature by destroying humanity'.

36 See also *FP* 849: 'When the world and humanity transform themselves through technology into a single unity, graspable with hands, that is to say, into a single person, a "great man" [*magnus homo*], then this "great man can, through the resources of technology, annihilate itself" [*sich . . . selbst auszulöschen*]. The Stoics of antiquity saw in the possibility of philosophical suicide a form of human sacrament. Perhaps it is fantastic, yet not completely unthinkable that humanity deliberately commits this act [*daß die Menschheit diesen Akt vorsätzlich begeht*]. The technical unity of the world also allows the technical death of humanity and this death would be the culmination of universal history, a collective analogue to the Stoic conception, according to which the suicide of the individual represents his freedom and the only sacrament that man himself can administer.'

37 Neumann (2015: 469–71) further notes that only the dominant empire (*Reich*) within each *Großraum* would have a monopoly over the political and thus possess sovereignty; the smaller states or entities within such a *Großraum* would have no sovereignty.

meaning of *nomos* as detailed above (specifically that of division (*Teilung*)),[38] the demise of the nation state in the twentieth century, as well as his own opposition to a certain universalism which authorises the interference of space-alien powers, specifically the United States, into the affairs of Europe.[39] This kind of universalism, typified by the League of Nations, according to Schmitt (2011b: 46/*PB* 335) destroys every reasonable or sensible (*vernünftige*) demarcation and distinction. Schmitt (2011b: 47/*PB* 336) further associates the United States with modern liberal capitalist imperialism, initiated by President Theodore Roosevelt, which, in a space-disregarding manner, transforms the earth into 'an abstract world- and capital-market'. The aim of this imperialism is ultimately world domination by economic means (Schmitt 2011b: 47).[40]

Schmitt concludes *Land and Sea* (*L&M* 107), as well as the later short essay 'The New Nomos of the Earth' (*NoE* 355) by noting that current events do not point to the arrival of the end of the world, but rather to the transition to a new *nomos* which inevitably goes along with the lapsing of inherited measures, concepts and traditions.[41] His last three sentences read as follows:

> However that which is coming is therefore not only boundlessness or a *nomos*-hostile nothing. Also in the fierce[42] struggles of old and new forces, just measures emerge and sensible proportions are shaped.[43]
>
> Also here are Gods and powers
> Vast/great is their measure.[44]
>
> (*L&M* 107)

38 Herrero (2015: 116) points out that *nomos* necessarily supposes limits or borders (see above; and see *NoE* 74–5 where Schmitt refers with reference to Trier to *nomos* as a fence-word) and thus the 'differentiation of spaces'; see also Galli (2015: 114–15). At the time that Schmitt was writing, no new *nomos* was thus in place as both the two major powers (the United States and the Soviet Union) supported a universal order without fences.

39 A number of contemporary thinkers support the notion of great spaces, including Mouffe (2007); Zolo (2007); and Petito (2007); for criticism, see Rowan (2011).

40 In *CoP* 54–5, Schmitt had already spelt out the implications of this universalism – with its reliance on the notion of humanity and the idea of just wars – for the treatment of enemies; see also Odysseos (2007). Compare in this respect *FWT* 98–9 where Derrida seeks a more nuanced approach to the question of the humanitarian.

41 The contemporary relevance of Schmitt's analysis appears from the fact that a battle between these options as outlined by Schmitt has been waging since the end of the Cold War; see Rech (2016: 158); Voigt (2015a: 195–6).

42 In *NoE* 355/*SGN* 522 the word 'grausamen' (cruel/savage) appears.

43 In *NoE* 355/*SGN* 522 this is posited as a possibility: 'können gerechte Maße entstehen und sinnvolle Proportionen sich bilden'.

44 'Aber das Kommende ist darum doch nicht nur Maßlosigkeit oder ein nomosfeindliches Nichts. Auch in dem erbitterten Ringen alter und neuer Kräfte entstehen gerechte Maße und bilden sich sinnvolle Proportionen. Auch hier sind Götter und walten, Groß ist ihr Maß.'

To be noted here are specifically the words 'doch nicht nur' (yet not only). In other words the *nomos* that is coming includes/excludes a lack of measure or the nothing as hostile to *nomos*. The gods and powers or forces of the future can indeed be viewed as a response to a certain lack of measure or to the nothing.[45]

Space as performative

In support of his notion of *Großräume*, Schmitt (*L&M* 106; *WoW* 118/*SGN* 314) insists that, inter alia due to certain developments in the natural sciences, at stake in the twentieth century is no longer empty space but space as a force field of human energy, activity and performance. This new understanding of space, Schmitt (*L&M* 106) notes, only becomes possible in the present age. Schmitt then paraphrases Heidegger (1962: 146/2006: 111) as giving expression to this mode of thinking about space: 'The world is not in space; rather space is in the world' (*L&M* 106).[46] This notion of space is dealt with in more detail in 'The *Großraum* Order' where Schmitt (*WoW* 122–3/*SGN* 318–19) refers to the new conception of space developed in the field of biology which shows that the seemingly eternal 'classical' conception – of empty and neutral space – was simply a reflection of its time:

> According to this theory, 'movement' for purposes of biological cognition does not take place in a pre-existing natural-scientific space, but space-time is rather conversely produced through movement. For this biological reflection, the world is thus not in space, but space is in and upon the world [*die Welt nicht im Raum, sondern der Raum in und an der Welt*].[47]
>
> (*WoW* 123/*SGN* 319)

Schmitt further elaborates on this understanding of space as event as follows:

> The spatial as such [*Das Räumliche*] is produced/generated [*erzeugt*] only along with and in objects, and the spatial and temporal orders are no longer mere entries in the given empty space [*leeren Raum*]; they correspond, rather, to an actual situation, an event [*Ereignis*]. It is only now that the conceptions of an empty dimension of depth [*leeren Tiefendimension*] and a merely formal category of space [*bloß formalen Raumkategorie*] are conclusively overcome. Space becomes a performative space [*Leistungsraum*].[48]
>
> (*WoW* 123/*SGN* 319)

45 See Galli (2015: 107), noting with reference to Schmitt that 'measure is born from what is beyond measure'; and see further above.

46 See also Balakrishnan (2000: 244).

47 This sentence does not appear in the English translation in *WoW* 123.

48 See Tribe (1989) who seeks to develop an approach to constitutional decision-making which relies on a post-Newtonian conception of space, similar to that of Schmitt.

The *Großraum* is similarly a performative space, which, as Schmitt (*WoW* 120/ *SGN* 316) notes somewhat ominously at the time (1939–1941), belongs 'to a historically fulfilled and historically appropriate Reich that brings and bears in itself its own space, inner measures and borders'.[49] The twentieth century conception of space as well as his own notion of *Großräume* (*WoW* 118–20/*SGN* 314–16) seek to overcome in a calculated fashion (performatively, one could perhaps add) the mathematical, natural-scientific and neutral conception of space initiated by Newton which, as we saw earlier, according to Schmitt finds expression in normativism and ultimately determines how the state and its territory are viewed, that is, as an empty space with linear borders).[50]

Man, space, *nomos*

What clearly comes to the fore in Schmitt's analysis of *nomos* as well as his espousal of the idea of great spaces (*Großräume*) is the importance he attaches to man's earth-bound or telluric character.[51] We can see Schmitt's attachment to the telluric dimension perhaps most clearly in the opening words of *Land and Sea*:

> Man is a terrestrial, a grounding. He lives, moves and walks on the firmly grounded earth. It is his standpoint and his base. He derives his points of view from it, which is also to say that his impressions are determined by it and his world outlook is conditioned by it. Earth-born, developing on it, man derives not only his horizon from it, but also his poise, his movements, his figure and his height.[52]
>
> (*L&S* 1/*L&M* 7)

An example of the importance of the telluric dimension in Schmitt's texts is the figure of the partisan, specifically as conceived of by Mao, which Schmitt likewise

49 See similarly *PT II* 65/*PT II* (G) 41: 'The church of Christ is not *of* this world and its history, but it is *in* this world. That means: it takes and gives space [*sie nimmt und gibt Raum*]; and space here means impermeability, visibility and the public sphere'.

50 In *WoW* 122 Schmitt views Kant's conception of space (and time) as an *a priori* form of knowledge, as the philosophical highpoint of the classical conception.

51 See also Dean (2006: 7; 2007: 246); Björk (2016: 123); Ojakangas (2007: 213–14).This telluric force appears to be what also informs Schmitt's insistence on concrete orders in his earlier works in respect of a legal system in general; see further *SGN* 396 where Schmitt notes that all our concepts unconsciously (*unbewußt*) take their point of departure in fixed land; the sea is viewed from the land; and see likewise *L&S* 50–1.

52 See similarly *DPS* 81/*SGN* 569 where Schmitt speaks through Herr Altmann: 'For me, the human is a son of the earth, and so he shall remain as long as he remains human [*Für mich ist der Mensch ein Sohn der Erde, und er wird es bleiben, solange er Mensch bleibt*]'; and see *NoE* 39/*NdE* 6 where Schmitt states in the 'Foreword' that '[h]uman thinking must again be directed towards the elemental orders of its terrestrial being'; and *NoE* 42 where Schmitt speaks of the earth as the mother of law.

analyses in association with the idea of great spaces (Chapter 2, Section B above). The true (autochthonous) partisan, as compared to the world revolutionary partisan, raises the hope in Schmitt that there can ultimately be a return of the political (which is threatened by the universalism of the United States and the Soviet Union) towards a rootedness in the earth in an era in which the state is dissolving. Of the four Greek elements, Schmitt's own preference is thus for the earth. The call of the present also does not come from the cosmos (to be conquered, like the sea by modern technology), but rather from the earth (*DPS* 80). This call entails capturing unbridled technology, binding it (*sie zu bändigen*) and inserting it within a concrete order *(DPS* 80/*SGN* 568).

Yet Schmitt does not fail to acknowledge man's sea-bound nature, with water and sea said to lie at the origin of life, of which he notes 'unconscious memories' (*unbewußten Erinnerungen*) are to be found: 'In people's deepest and often unconscious memories, water and the sea are the mysterious primordial source of all life [*In tiefen, oft unbewußten Erinnerungen der Menschen sind Wasser und Meer der geheimnisvolle Urgrund allen Lebens*]' (*L&S* 2/*L&M* 9).[53] Whereas this passage seems to associate the sea with the Freudian unconscious, we saw earlier that in *The Nomos of the Earth* Schmitt (*NoE* 42–3/*NdE* 13–14) appears to go beyond the unconscious by associating the sea with a 'place' which keeps no memory and which erases all traces (*Auf den Wellen ist alles Welle*).[54] Similarly, in 'Dialogue on New Space' Schmitt, with reference to the New Testament, refers to the sea as something uncanny and evil (*etwas Unheimliches und Böses*) (*DPS* 56/*SGN* 554).[55] Of the four Greek elements, Schmitt chooses consistently for the

53 See also *L&S* 2/*L&M* 9 where Schmitt quotes Goethe: 'Everything is born of water,/Everything is preserved by water,/Ocean, bring us your eternal rule! [*Alles ist aus dem Wasser entsprungen,/Alles wird durch das Wasser erhalten,/Ozean gönn' uns dein ewiges Walten!*]'. Compare in this respect Zeitlin (2015: xlii–xlvi) who reads Schmitt as granting the status of human only to those who are land-based.

54 This passage resonates with Derrida's thinking on the trace; see e.g. *SP* 156/Derrida (1972a: 25): 'The trace has, properly speaking, no place, for effacement belongs to the very structure of the trace [*La trace . . . n'a proprement pas lieu, l'effacement appartient à sa structure*]'; see further Derrida (1982: 65–6; 2002d: 44).

55 In 'Dialogue on New Space' Schmitt (*DPS* 54–5/*SGN* 553) notes (speaking through Herr Altmann) that according to the Bible God gave human beings the land to live on and that this was made possible by repressing or forcing back (*zurückgedrängt*) the sea to the limits of this place of abode (*Wohnsitz*). There it lurks (*lauert es*) as a constant danger and threat to human beings. The sea is to human beings strange and hostile (*fremd und feindlich*). It is not a habitat (*Lebensraum*) for humans. The biblical creation story in other words makes it clear that only the solid earth (*das feste Land*) is the residence (*Wohnung*) or, even better, the home (*das Haus*) of human beings. 'The sea on the other hand, the ocean, is an uncanny monstrosity on the edge of the inhabited world, a chaotic beast, a great serpent, a dragon, a leviathan [*Das Meer dagegen, der Ozean, ist ein unheimliches Ungeheuer am Rande der bewohnten Welt, ein chaotisches Untier, eine große Schlange, ein Drache, ein Leviathan*]' (*DPS* 55/*SGN* 553). Insofar as the New Testament is concerned, Schmitt (*DPS* 56/*SGN* 554) points out that Jesus's walking on the water points to the taming of the Leviathan (*Er hat den Leviathan bezwungen*). Yet precisely from this, Schmitt (*DPS*

earth or land against water (the sea), air and fire, which he associates with (self-) destruction.[56] When Schmitt (*DPS* 80) therefore calls for the capturing or restraining of unbridled technology by way of the new *nomos* of the earth, this is clearly a reactive response to a certain dislocation. This dislocation is not however simply brought about by technology, but by a more originary dislocation, expropriation or deterritorialization,[57] which Schmitt clearly alludes to in his texts.[58] As we saw, in *Land and Sea* Schmitt refers to the Newtonian concept of empty space which for him represents death, absolute nothingness, understood here specifically as self-destruction. In the *Glossarium* we similarly saw that he views man, under the influence of Freud, as a termite without space neurosis. The performative conception of space (*Leistungsraum*) as event (*Ereignis*) which Schmitt endorses in certain of his texts can thus be said to be a reaction to his own recognition of a placeless place, a non-place of another event (*Ereignis*), that is, of the gift without return, a place characterised by expropriation, uprootedness, homelessness, dislocation, dissolution of identity, that is, a total exposure and giving of the self.[59]

Conclusion

What the above analysis shows is that a certain law lies at the foundation of international law. This law does not however simply entail appropriation, division and production, that is, the meanings of *nomos* identified by Schmitt. *Nomos* rather

55/*SGN* 553) notes, we can conclude that also for the New Testament, the sea is 'something uncanny and evil [*etwas Unheimliches und Böses*]'. In the final book of the Bible, Revelation Chapter 21, John sees a new heaven and a new earth, the first heaven and earth had disappeared. With that it is declared that there was no more sea. The disappearance of the sea through the cleansing and transfiguring of the earth is here also associated with sin and evil.

56 See *ECS* 89: 'all destruction is simply self-destruction'; and the discussion in Chapter 2, Section C above.

57 See 'F&K' 45–6; *ET* 79–80; *SoM* 103. The rootlessness which Judaism represents for Schmitt (*WoW* 121–2/*SGN* 317–18; *TTJT* 45/*DARD* 9) is thus not simply the characteristic of a certain nation or culture, but a fundamental structure of man in general; see also Chapter 6 above.

58 See e.g. *GL* 79–80 (entry of 11 Jan 1948) where Schmitt notes in a letter to Pierre Linn that the term 'vagabondage' applied to himself: 'You speak of "vagabondage" and tell me you "detest this style". I somewhat have the impression that this also concerns/looks at me personally [*Vous parlez de "vagabondage" et me dites que vous "detestez ce style". J'ai un peu l'impression que cela me regarde aussi moi même personellement*].' Schmitt furthermore comments that the phenomenon as well as the notion of 'vagabondage' were undergoing existential transformations especially in a place like Germany where the world's opposing forces and tendencies tumultuously converge, or more literally 'give themselves a tumultuous meeting [*se donnent un rendez-vous tumultueux*]'; see further Linder (2015: 6); and *SGN* 541 where Schmitt contends that the old, religious fear of man of the sea could be overcome only through 'a peculiar drive [*eines besonderen Antriebes*]', a technological drive (*technische Antrieb*), which is different from every other technological drive.

59 See Chapter 5, Sections A and B and Chapter 6 above. There is some resonance here with Nancy (1993: 85), who associates *khōra* with the sea, though this cannot be further explored here.

entails a reaction to a certain uncanniness, a pre-originary 'not-at-home-ness', a strangeness, which structures man and all living beings in general.[60] The haunting of what Derrida (*OH* 79) refers to as a 'lawless law, *nomos anomos*, law above the laws and law outside the law'[61] is acknowledged by Schmitt,[62] whilst seeking to ontologise it in outlining a new *nomos* for the earth.[63] An affirmation of this a-*nomos* and its translation into an international or transnational politics should arguably[64] align itself with the current processes of juridification, or perhaps rather of constitutionalisation,[65] as well as calls for the radical transformation of international law[66] rather than with the Schmittian notion of *Großräume*.[67] In both scenarios sovereignty would remain. Yet under constitutionalisation, coupled with the democratisation of international institutions, the disruption of sovereignty (also of global and transnational powers) by the force without power of the a-*nomos* (and thus also justice) arguably stand a better chance than with the Schmittian great spaces.[68] The latter idea cannot however be completely ignored, especially in view of the fact that a number of states are showing signs of asserting

60 See *AR* 399–404; *ON* 104–11; *Adieu* 56.

61 The notion of the a-*nomos*, which is closely tied to the impossible in Derrida's texts (see *OH* 79), can be compared to the notion of the a-legal or of a-legality in Lindahl (2013: 30–8, 156–86), which arguably remains located within the realm of the possible; as well as with Agamben (1998: 36–8) who seeks to establish an inherent link between Schmitt's reliance on *nomos* and the state of exception. The a-*nomos* can indeed be understood in these terms, i.e. as exception, but then in Derrida's sense of the exception as event (*Ereignis*); see further Chapter 2, Section A above.

62 Schmitt (*L&M* 107), as we saw above, calls it 'a *nomos*-hostile nothing [*ein nomosfeindliches Nichts*]'.

63 In *SoM* 102–3/*SdM* 137 a topology of the Schmittian type (of sovereignty, borders, native soil and blood) is referred to as an 'ontopology', which Derrida explains as 'an axiomatic linking indissociably the ontological value of present-being [*on*] to its *location*, to the stable and presentable determination of a locality (the *topos* of territory, soil, city, of the body in general)'.

64 *Cf.* Douzinas (2007: 226–33) who comes to a different conclusion, although his text is partly inspired by Derrida's thinking.

65 Compare Grimm (2012b) and Preuss (2012) for different views on the appropriateness of speaking of a constitution on the international and transnational levels; see also Krisch (2012).

66 See *SoM* 104–7; 'Auto' 114–15; *Rog* 87. This would, as Derrida here and elsewhere (*Neg* 385; *Rog* 97–100) points out, need to include inter alia a restructuring of the United Nations (including the General Assembly and Security Council) with its own power and means of enforcement, also of the decisions of the International Court of Justice.

67 The way in which the concept of a constitution was defined in Chapter 3 and Chapter 5, Sections A and B above with reference to Schmitt, arguably opens the way for the use of this concept on both the transnational and the international levels. Derrida admittedly does not (at least in the texts I know of) speak of an international or transnational constitution, yet he does in *Rog* 87/*Voy* 127 support the 'extension of the democratic beyond nation-state sovereignty, beyond citizenship' by way of what he calls the 'creation of an international juridico-political space'.

68 See further 'Auto' 119–21; Derrida and Caputo (1997: 11–12); and see Chomsky (2011: 25–43; 2016: 10–15, 19–20, 35) on US policy towards Latin and central America in the twentieth century as part of the United States' 'Grand Area' in terms of the Monroe Doctrine.

themselves as such, and in view of the declining powers of the United States.[69] In the event that these developments continue, these great spaces should nonetheless still operate within and be subjected to an international constitution. Although the a-*nomos* as a 'perverformative'[70] cannot be expressly included in an international constitution, it can find indirect expression by seeking to urgently address the causes and consequences of war, oppression, exploitation and inequality around the globe ('Auto' 121–3). National and transnational constitutions should be required to follow its cue.

69 See Voigt (2015a: 224–48); Chomsky (2016: 67–83, 239–58).
70 See De Ville (2011a: 54–6).

Chapter 8

Conclusion

Schmitt 'before' Derrida

A reading of Schmitt in respect of the themes explored above, but without taking account of Derrida's reading of Schmitt in *Politics of Friendship*, may in broad outline be said to entail the following: the concept of the political is the point of departure in Schmitt's thinking (Chapter 2, Sections A–C above). Its determining criterion is the drawing of a distinction between friend and enemy groupings and it finds its extreme limit in war. The latter can, and preferably should, take the form of a war between states rather than civil war, but it can also take the latter form. The political precedes the state, which itself possesses a sovereign personality analogous to that of God.[1] God, who in the Middle Ages was said to have *potestas constituens* and who in Romans 13:1 is designated as the one from whom all power derives, likewise serves as the model for the constituent power of the people (Chapter 3). The people, on the basis of a preceding political unity (the state), and having attained political consciousness of its own power in this regard, takes a sovereign decision about the form and nature of the political unity. The people cannot however exercise this power itself and thus delegates it to a constituent assembly, which exercises a sovereign, but temporary dictatorship. The constituent assembly in other words has to work out the detail of the decision of the people on its own form and nature by drafting and adopting a constitution. Although the constituent assembly exercises a sovereign power in this regard, the power can be revoked at any time by the people and lasts only until the assembly has fulfilled its function.

In line with this understanding of the role of the people as constituent power, Schmitt expresses a preference for the positive concept of the constitution, as

1 In some versions, notably the reading of Schmitt's political theology by Meier (1998), the political is ultimately to be understood in terms of the battle between God and Satan. Schmitt's opposition to liberalism and a world state (where the enemy would disappear) would in line with this reading amount to a battle against the 'hastener' of the rule of the anti-Christ. By contrast, Schmitt's endorsement of the telluric partisan would be in support of the *katechon* or restrainer. The greatest danger for Schmitt would thus lie in the ultimately satanic denial of the political.

opposed to what he refers to as the absolute, relative or ideal concepts (Chapter 5, Section A). The positive concept presupposes a distinction between the constitution, that is, the existential decision about the nature and form of the political unity (for example, to establish a democracy, the rule of law, separation of powers, a representative legislative assembly, a bill of rights and a unitary state), which is often referred to in the preamble of a constitution, as opposed to the secondary constitutional provisions that regulate the detail, which Schmitt terms 'constitutional law(s)'. In accordance with the positive concept, sovereignty does not reside in the constitution itself as is presumed under liberal constitutionalism, but remains with the people as constituent power, even after the adoption of the constitution. The constitution which is adopted by the constituent assembly, today most likely in accordance with the dominant liberal model, will not only have a rule-of-law component, but also a political component, which liberal constitutional thinking as a rule seeks to repress (Chapter 5, Section B). By virtue of the *rule-of-law component*, a separation of powers is established between the legislature, executive and judiciary. These (constituted) state powers are limited in principle in view of individual freedom, with the latter in terms of the rule-of-law component being absolute or unlimited in principle (Chapter 6). The *political component* concerns itself with the state form, that is, a monarchy, aristocracy or democracy, which under liberal constitutionalism is diluted into legislative or executive forms. Whereas democracy is based on the principle of identity, monarchy rests on the principle of representation (Chapter 4). Aristocracy lies somewhere in-between. These two principles of political form nevertheless cannot find expression in their pure form in any state. The democratic concept of equality (in contrast to freedom) also forms part of the political component of the constitution (Chapter 6). As a political concept it includes the possibility of drawing a distinction between those who *do* form part of a particular people, and those who *do not*.

In Schmitt's later thinking, *nomos* plays an important role (Chapter 7). *Nomos* is not to be equated with positive law, but is to be understood in a broader sense as the law of law or original constitution of the earth. It more specifically concerns the appropriation of the earth, as well as its subsequent division and production. In Schmitt's view, *nomos*, similar to the concept of the political, excludes in principle the appropriation of the whole earth by a single empire in the form of a world state. The inherent relation between *nomos* and the earth implies the drawing of boundaries, either in the form of states or, in view of the demise of the state in the twentieth century, *Großräume*. The latter would involve the establishment of large spaces or spheres of influence by dominant powers where interference by other states or empires is not allowed or tolerated.

Derrida reading Schmitt

In *Politics of Friendship* Derrida engages primarily with the concept of the political as Schmitt analyses it in *The Concept of the Political*, 'The Theory of the Partisan' and *Ex Captivitate Salus*. We saw in Chapter 2, Section A above that

Schmitt seeks to identify the enemy as external to the self. He does so by identifying the enemy as in the first place located outside of the body politic. Schmitt furthermore defines the enemy as someone in the public sphere who threatens one's way of life and whom one is prepared to wage war against, but that one nevertheless treats with respect, as opposed to a private enemy that one hates. In view of this definition of the enemy, Schmitt is greatly concerned that in the twentieth century, with the demise of the *jus publicum Europaeum*, the enemy is again becoming a figure of hatred and is no longer respected as an equal. He consequently seeks to contain this absolute hostility, which threatens the whole world with destruction. The enemy concept, as Schmitt seeks to construct it in ideal terms, is in other words in demise, yet this is paradoxically coupled with an intensification of hostility. Derrida seeks to show in his reading that this 'demise' should not be understood in terms of a 'fall' from some ideal purity, but that it instead reveals the paradoxical structure of the political. The distinction which Schmitt seeks to draw between self and other or between the body politic and its other furthermore ultimately breaks down, not only because passion, sentiment and (personal) affect cannot be completely contained, but also because the enemy manifests himself as the brother in the event of civil and partisan warfare.

In his reading of Schmitt's 'The Theory of the Partisan', Derrida shows that the distinction which Schmitt seeks to draw between the real enmity of the defensive, telluric partisan and his degeneration, due to developments in technology, into the rootless, ideologically driven absolute enmity of the global revolutionary partisan likewise breaks down. This is because 'rootlessness' does not involve a 'fall' from some ideal purity, but structures enmity from the start. The war against the brother (partisan) enemy furthermore shows itself to be the most intense form of warfare (Chapter 2, Section B). In Schmitt's analysis, as Derrida shows, the invocation of the brother involves not only a certain ideal doubling of the self, but also a turn against the self. This analysis of the brother enemy is in line with Schmitt's reflections in the prison cell, where he concludes that the enemy ultimately is the brother and/or the self (Chapter 2, Section C). The notion of the enemy as ultimately lodged within the self can be understood via Freud's analysis of the death drive as a drive of self-destruction, Plato's notion of a denaturalisation of nature (*phûsis*), in Gnostic terms as a war by God against himself, or in Heideggerian terms as a 'war' between the gathering of Being and its dissimulation (Chapter 2, Section A). In the political context, these 'metaphors' traditionally manifest themselves either as external or as civil war, and today as international civil war.

The concept of the political is, as we saw, central to Schmitt's constitutional theory. 'After Derrida' it can however no longer be understood simply as the drawing of a distinction between friend and enemy. Behind the destruction which manifests itself in war as the endpoint of the political lies a force of self-destruction which haunts the political, also in its less intensive manifestations. Derrida contends that the latter force should be affirmed as the condition of possibility of the political. This 'force' radically restructures the concept of the political, which is employed in Schmitt's texts. At stake here is a demand for a disproportionate friendship (*aimance*), absolute hospitality or the perfect gift, which calls for a giving without the expectation of a return.

Schmitt 'after' Derrida

The 're-location' of the enemy that takes place in Derrida's reading of Schmitt has important implications for sovereignty, the state, constituent power, identity, representation, the concept of the constitution, human rights, as well as the *nomos* of the earth. Insofar as the state is concerned, Chapter 3 engaged with Schmitt's positing in *Constitutional Theory* of the political unity of the people as a precondition for the exercise of constituent power. At stake here is however no fixed identity, because the state is established and maintained through an uncanny fear of the beast within the self, coupled with a love of this fear. This insight into the 'nature' of the state ties in closely with Schmitt's description in *Constitutional Theory* of the people. The latter, in its role as the subject of constituent power, is defined as *natura naturans*, formless and unorganised. When read with Schmitt's adoption of the Gnostic conception of God in *Political Theology II*, it appears that the people can by analogy be said to be divided within itself, rendered asunder by a force of self-destruction. This means that the sovereign, existential and self-preserving decision which finds expression in constituent power is necessarily derivative. It is always preceded by a law of absolute hospitality, from which a return to the self is sought. This law needs to be affirmed in the exercise of constituent power as well as of constituted powers. Decisions taken by such powers need to arrive as closely as possible at the impossible demand for absolute hospitality even though the decision will always only take the form of conditional hospitality. This reading of Schmitt arguably takes us beyond the so-called paradox of constituent power, without reverting back to sovereignty. It furthermore adds a hyper-political and hyper-ethical dimension to notions such as the crowd, the multitude and the people. The door is moreover opened for an understanding of the people as the *demos* without *kratos* and for a *demos* beyond the nation state.

In Chapter 4 the relationship between identity and representation was explored in more detail. It appeared that Schmitt does not understand the concept of representation as the simple doubling of some pre-existing entity, but as an enhancement thereof. Furthermore, for representation to establish itself, what Schmitt refers to as 'unbridled prophetism' has to be 'repressed' and 'overcome'. Prophetism can consequently be understood as the 'representation' of what Schmitt says cannot in fact be represented, that is, something that is dead, weak, lowly and valueless. The un-representable in this way shows itself as a structural part of the concept of representation and places the same demand as outlined above with reference to constituent power, on constituted powers. In respect of the concept of the constitution, Chapter 5, Sections A and B showed that Schmitt's text stands open to a reading to the effect that the modern constitution should in the first place be understood in terms of *khōra*, that is, as the unconditional giving of place, and secondly as incorporating within itself a crypt from which issues a law of absolute hospitality. At stake in the concept of the constitution is thus a gift without return to the *demos*. A move here in other words takes place beyond conceptions of the constitution as absolute or relative, as well as beyond the Schmittian positive concept of the constitution, which returns to the subject of constituent power. In respect of freedom and equality, Chapter 6 showed that these concepts do not in all respects stand opposed in Schmitt's thinking. In line with his thinking on a certain beyond to the political (Chapter 2, Sections A–C above), Schmitt recognises a freedom and an equality which are unconditional, and which precede liberal freedom and democratic equality. Freedom and equality in this unconditional sense impose a demand upon those placed in charge of ensuring their fulfilment (whether a state or a transnational or international organisation), to seek the welcoming and radical equality of everyone everywhere without exception or limitation.

In considering finally the relation between national, transnational and international legal orders in Chapter 7, it appeared that the *nomos* of the earth is a response to a certain a-*nomo*s, which like *khōra* and the crypt calls for a gift without return, and points to a place characterised by expropriation, uprootedness, homelessness, dislocation and a dissolution of identity, that is, a total exposure and giving of the self. Schmitt's texts on the *nomos* thus allow for an alternative conception of international law, which is not founded on the sovereignty of states or of *Großräume*, but which in the name of the gift without return, seeks to urgently address the causes and consequences of war, oppression, exploitation and inequality around the globe.

In response to the question posed in Chapter 1, the reading of Schmitt given here cannot provide a foundation for constitutional theory as it undermines the whole discourse of foundations. This does not however mean that constitutional theory remains unaffected. All the Schmittian concepts explored above show themselves to be divided and to explode or self-destruct on closer inspection. The 'concepts' which arise from this self-destruction are no longer tied in the first place to the concrete, the land and the earth as they would be in a reading of Schmitt 'before' Derrida. They instead point to the impossible as the condition of possibility for constitutional theory, and thereby open the door to a transformed understanding of the obligations placed upon constituent and constituted powers on the national, transnational and international levels in providing food and water, education, health, better working conditions, as well as in addressing in a just manner inequality and poverty, migration, violence and terror.

Bibliography

Abraham, N. and Torok, M. (1976) *Cryptonomie: Le Verbier de l'Homme aux Loups*, Paris: Éditions Aubier Flammarion.

——— (1986) *The Wolf Man's Magic Word: A Cryptonomy*, trans. N. Rand, Minneapolis: University of Minnesota Press.

——— (1987) *L'Écorce et le Noyau*, Paris: Flammarion.

——— (1994) *The Shell and the Kernel: Renewals of Psychoanalysis,* vol. I, trans. N. Rand, Chicago and London: The University of Chicago Press.

Agamben, G. (1998) *Homo Sacer: Sovereign Power and Bare Life*, trans. D. Heller-Roazen, Stanford, CA: Stanford University Press.

——— (1999) *Potentialities: Collected Essays in Philosophy*, ed. and trans. D. Heller-Roazen, Stanford, CA: Stanford University Press.

——— (2000) *Means without End: Notes on Politics*, trans. V. Binetti and C. Casarino, Minneapolis: University of Minnesota Press.

——— (2005) *State of Exception*, trans. K. Attell, Chicago and London: The University of Chicago Press.

——— (2011) *The Kingdom and the Glory: For a Theological Genealogy of Economy and Government*, trans. L. Chiesa, Stanford, CA: Stanford University Press.

Arato, A. (2010) 'Post-sovereign constitution-making in Hungary: after success, partial failure, and now what?', *South African Journal on Human Rights*, 26(1): 19–44.

Ashe, M. (2003) 'Limits of tolerance: law and religion after the Anti-Christ', *Cardozo Law Review*, 24(2): 587–620.

Balakrishnan, G. (2000) *The Enemy: An Intellectual Portrait of Carl Schmitt*, London: Verso.

Bargu, B. (2010) 'Unleashing the Acheron: sacrificial partisanship, sovereignty, and history', *Theory & Event*, 13(1): 1–23.

Bendersky, J.W. (1987) 'Carl Schmitt at Nuremberg', *Telos*, 72: 91–6.

——— (2000) 'Schmitt and Freud: anthropology, enemies and the state', pp. 623–35, in D. Murswiek, U. Storost and H.A Wolff (eds), *Staat – Souveränität – Verfassung: Festschrift für Helmut Quaritsch zum 70. Geburtstag*, Berlin: Duncker & Humblot.

——— (2005) 'New evidence, old contradictions: Carl Schmitt and the Jewish question', *Telos*, 132: 64–82.

——— (2007) 'Carl Schmitt's path to Nuremberg: a sixty-year reassessment', *Telos*, 139: 6–34.

——— (2015) 'Schmitt's Diaries', pp. 1–36, in J. Meierhenrich and O. Simons (eds), *The Oxford Handbook of Carl Schmitt*, Oxford: Oxford University Press. Available from *Oxford Handbooks Online*, at www.oxfordhandbooks.com (accessed 20 July 2016).

Benn, G. (1971) *Primal Vision: Selected Writings of Gottfried Benn*, New York: New Directions.

Bennington, G. (2011) *Not Half No End: Militantly Melancholic Essays in Memory of Jacques Derrida*, Edinburgh: Edinburgh University Press.

Benveniste, E. (1973) *Indo-European Language and Society*, Coral Gables, FL: University of Miami Press. Available at http://chs.harvard.edu/CHS/article/display/4308 (accessed 7 July 2016).

Bernstein, R.J. (2011) 'The aporias of Carl Schmitt', *Constellations*, 18(3): 403–30.

Björk, M. (2016) 'Representation and the unrepresentable', pp. 120–33, in M. Arvidsson, L. Brännström, and P. Minkkinen (eds), *The Contemporary Relevance of Carl Schmitt: Law, Politics, Theology*, Abingdon and New York: Routledge.

Böckenförde, E.-W. (1994) 'Die Verfassunggebende Gewalt des Volkes – Ein Grenzbegriff des Verfassungsrecht', pp. 58–80, in U.K. Preuss (ed.), *Zum Begriff der Verfassung: Die Ordnung des Politischen*, Frankfurt am Main: Fischer Taschenbuch Verlag.

——— (1997) 'The concept of the political: a key to understanding Carl Schmitt's Constitutional Theory', *Canadian Journal of Law and Jurisprudence*, 10(1): 5–19.

Botha, H. (2010) 'Instituting public freedom or extinguishing constituent power? Reflections on South Africa's constitution-making experiment', *South African Journal on Human Rights*, 26(1): 66–84.

Brännström L. (2016) 'Carl Schmitt's definition of sovereignty as authorized leadership', pp. 19–33, in M. Arvidsson, L. Brännström, and P. Minkkinen (eds), *The Contemporary Relevance of Carl Schmitt: Law, Politics, Theology*, Abingdon and New York: Routledge.

Briggs, R. (2015) 'Teletechnology', pp. 58–67, in C. Colebrook (ed.), *Jacques Derrida: Key Concepts*, London and New York: Routledge.

Campagna, N. (2015) 'Carl Schmitt und Zwei Mythen des Liberalismus', pp. 115–36, in R. Voigt (ed.), *Mythos Staat*, 2nd edn, Baden-Baden: Nomos.

Caruth, C. (1996) *Unclaimed Experience: Trauma, Narrative and History*, Baltimore, MD and London: The John Hopkins University Press.

Cheah, P. (2014) 'Second-generation rights as biopolitical rights', pp. 215–232, in C. Douzinas and C. Gearty (eds), *The Meaning of Human Rights: The Philosophy and Social Theory of Human Rights*, Cambridge: Cambridge University Press.

Chomsky, N. (2011) *How the World Works*, Berkeley, CA: Soft Skull Press.

——— (2016) *Who Rules the World?* London: Penguin.

Connors, C. (2011) 'Derrida and the friendship of rhyme', *The Oxford Literary Review*, 33(2): 139–49.

Cortes, D. (1879) *Essays on Catholicism, Liberalism and Socialism: Considered in their Fundamental Principles*, Dublin: MH Gill & Son.

Däubler, T. (1910) *Das Nordlicht*. Available at www.zeno.org/Literatur/M/D%C3%A4ubler,+Theodor/Versepos/Das+Nordlicht+(Florentiner+Ausgabe) (accessed 10 July 2016).

——— (1916) 'Grünes Elysium', in *Die Deutsche Gedichtebibliothek*. Available at http://gedichte.xbib.de/D%E4ubler_gedicht_Gr%FCnes+Elysium.htm (accessed 15 November 2016).

——— (1919) *Hymne an Italien*, Insel-Verlag, Leipzig. Available at https://babel.hathitrust.org/cgi/pt?id=wu.89018346619;view=1up;seq=9 (accessed 10 July 2016).

Dean, M. (2006) 'A political mythology of world order: Carl Schmitt's *Nomos*', *Theory, Culture & Society*, 23(5): 1–22.

——— (2007) '*Nomos*: word and myth', pp. 242–58, in L. Odysseos and F. Petito (eds), *The International Political Thought of Carl Schmitt*, London and New York: Routledge.

De Benoist, A. (2013) *Carl Schmitt Today: Terrorism, 'Just' War, and the State of Emergency*, London: Arktos.

Debrix, F. (2011) 'The virtual nomos?', pp. 220–6, in S. Legg (ed.), *Spatiality, Sovereignty and Carl Schmitt*, London and New York: Routledge.

Deleuze, G. and Guattari, F. (2004) *A Thousand Plateaus: Capitalism and Schizophrenia*, trans. B. Massumi, London and New York: Continuum.

Derrida, J. (1967) *L'Écriture et la Différence*, Paris: Éditions du Seuil.

——— (1972a) *Marges de la Philosophie*, Paris: Éditions de Minuit.

——— (1972b) *La Dissémination*, Paris: Éditions du Seuil.

——— (1972c) *Positions*, Paris: Éditions de Minuit.

——— (1973) *Speech and Phenomena and Other Essays on Husserl's Theory of Signs*, trans. D.B. Allison, Evanston, IL: Northwestern University Press.

——— (1974) *Glas*, Paris: Éditions Galilée.

——— (1976a) *Of Grammatology*, trans. G.C. Spivak, Baltimore, MD and London: John Hopkins University Press.

——— (1976b) 'Fors: Les mots anglés de Nicolas Abraham et Maria Torok', pp. 7–73, in N. Abraham and M. Torok, *Cryptonomie: Le Verbier de l'Homme aux Loups*, Paris: Éditions Aubier Flammarion.

——— (1978) *Writing and Difference*, trans. A. Bass, New York and London: Routledge.

——— (1979) *Spurs: Nietzsche's Styles/Éperons: Les Styles de Nietzsche*, trans. B. Harlow, Chicago and London: The University of Chicago Press.

——— (1980) *La Carte Postale: de Socrate à Freud et au-delà*, Paris: Flammarion.

——— (1981) *Positions*, 2nd edn, trans. A. Bass, London: Continuum.

——— (1982) *Margins of Philosophy*, trans. A. Bass, Chicago: The University of Chicago Press.

——— (1984) *Signéponge/Signsponge*, trans. R. Rand, New York: Columbia University Press.

——— (1986a) *Glas*, trans. J.P. Leavey, Jr. and R. Rand, Lincoln and London: University of Nebraska Press.

——— (1986b) 'Foreword: *Fors*: the anglish words of Nicolas Abraham and Maria Torok', trans. B. Johnson, pp. xi–xlviii, in N. Abraham and M. Torok, *The Wolf Man's Magic Word: A Cryptonomy*, Minneapolis: University of Minnesota Press.

——— (1986c) *Parages*, Paris: Éditions Galilée.

——— (1987) *The Post Card: From Socrates to Freud and Beyond*, trans. A. Bass, Chicago and London: The University of Chicago Press.

——— (1988a) *Limited Inc*, trans. S. Weber, J. Mehlman, and A. Bass, Evanston, IL: Northwestern University Press.

——— (1988b), 'Ein Gespräch mit Jacques Derrida', pp. 83–93, in J. Altwegg (ed.), *Die Heidegger Kontroverse*, Frankfurt am Main: Athenäum Verlag.

——— (1988c) *The Ear of the Other*, trans. P. Kamuf, Lincoln: University of Nebraska Press.

——— (1989) *Of Spirit: Heidegger and the Question*, trans. G. Bennington and R. Bowlby, Chicago and London: The University of Chicago Press.

——— (1991) *Donner le Temps: 1. La Fausse Monnaie*, Paris: Éditions Galilée.

——— (1992a) *Given Time: I. Counterfeit Money*, trans. P. Kamuf, Chicago: The University of Chicago Press.

——— (1992b) *The Other Heading: Reflections on Today's Europe*, trans. P.-A. Brault and M.B. Naas, Bloomington and Indianapolis: Indiana University Press.

——— (1992c) *Points de Suspension: Entretiens*, Paris: Éditions Galilée.

——— (1993a) 'Heidegger's ear: philopolemology (*Geschlecht* IV)', trans. J.P. Leavey, Jr., pp. 163–218, in J. Sallis (ed.), *Reading Heidegger: Commemorations*, Bloomington and Indianapolis: Indiana University Press.

——— (1993b) *Aporias*, trans. T. Dutoit, Stanford, CA: Stanford University Press.

——— (1993c) *Spectres de Marx: L'État de la Dette, le Travail du Deuil et la Nouvelle Internationale*, Paris: Galilée.

——— (1993d) *Khôra*, Paris: Galilée.

——— (1994) *Politiques de l'amitié: Suivi de l'Oreille de Heidegger*, Paris: Galilée.

——— (1995a) *Points . . . Interviews, 1974–1994*, E. Weber (ed.), Stanford, CA: Stanford University Press.

——— (1995b) *Archive Fever: A Freudian Impression*, trans. E. Prenowitz, Chicago and London: The University of Chicago Press.

——— (1995c) *On the Name*, T. Dutoit (ed.), Stanford, CA: Stanford University Press.

____ (1996) *Le Monolinguisme de l'Autre: ou la Prothèse d'Origine*, Paris: Éditions Galilée.

——— (1997a) *Politics of Friendship*, trans. G. Collins, London and New York: Verso.

——— (1997b) 'The Villanova roundtable: a conversation with Jacques Derrida', pp. 3–28, in J.D. Caputo, *Deconstruction in a Nutshell: A Conversation with Jacques Derrida*, New York: Fordham University Press.

——— (1998a) 'Faith and knowledge: the two sources of "religion" at the limits of reason alone', trans. S. Weber, pp. 1–78, in J. Derrida and G. Vattimo (eds) *Religion*, Stanford, CA: Stanford University Press.

——— (1998b) *Resistances of Psychoanalysis*, trans. P. Kamuf, P.-A. Brault and M. Naas, Stanford, CA: Stanford University Press.

——— (1998c) *Monolingualism of the Other; or, the Prosthesis of Origin*, trans. P. Mensah, Stanford, CA: Stanford University Press.

——— (1998d) 'The retrait of metaphor', pp. 102–29, in J. Wolfreys (ed.), *The Derrida Reader: Writing Performances*, Lincoln: University of Nebraska Press.

——— (1999a) 'On the gift: a discussion between Jacques Derrida and Jean-Luc Marion', pp. 54–78, in J.D. Caputo and M.J. Scanlon (eds), *God, the Gift and Postmodernism*, Bloomington: Indiana University Press.

——— (1999b) *Adieu: to Emmanuel Levinas*, trans. P.-A. Brault and M. Naas, Stanford, CA: Stanford University Press.

——— (1999c) 'Marx & sons', pp. 213–69, in M. Sprinker (ed.), *Ghostly Demarcations: A Symposium on Jacques Derrida's Specters of Marx*, London and New York: Verso.

——— (2001a) *The Work of Mourning*, P.-A. Brault and M. Naas (eds), Chicago and London: The University of Chicago Press.

——— (2001b) *Foi et Savoir: Suivi de le Siècle et le Pardon*, Paris: Éditions du Seuil.

——— (2001c) *On Cosmopolitanism and Forgiveness*, London and New York: Routledge.

——— (2002a) *Acts of Religion*, G. Anidjar (ed.), New York and London: Routledge.

——— (2002b) *Negotiations: Interventions and Interviews 1971–2001*, E. Rottenberg (ed.), Stanford, CA: Stanford University Press.

——— (2002c) *Without Alibi*, trans. P. Kamuf, Stanford, CA: Stanford University Press.

——— (2002d) 'Archive fever in South Africa', pp. 38–80, in C. Hamilton, V. Harris, J. Taylor, M. Pickover, G. Reid and R. Saleh (eds), *Refiguring the Archive*, Cape Town: David Philip.

——— (2003a) 'Autoimmunity: real and symbolic suicides – a dialogue with Jacques Derrida', in G. Borradori, *Philosophy in a Time of Terror: Dialogues with Jürgen Habermas and Jacques Derrida*, Chicago and London: The University of Chicago Press.
——— (2003b) *Voyous: Deux Essais sur la Raison*, Paris: Éditions Galilée.
——— (2003c) *Psyché: Inventions de l'Autre,* vol. II, Paris Galilée.
——— (2003d) *Derrida: A Film by Kirby Dick and Amy Ziering Kofman*, New York: Zeitgeist Films.
——— (2004a) *Dissemination*, trans. B. Johnson, London: Continuum.
——— (2004b) 'A testimony given', pp. 39–58, in *Questioning Judaism: Interviews by Elisabeth Weber*, trans. R. Bowlby, Stanford, CA: Stanford University Press.
——— (2005a) *Sovereignties in Question: The Poetics of Paul Celan*, T. Dutoit and O. Pasanen (eds), New York: Fordham University Press.
——— (2005b) *Rogues: Two Essays on Reason*, trans. P.-A. Brault and M. Naas, Stanford, CA: Stanford University Press.
——— (2005c) *Force de Loi: Le 'Fondament Mystique de l'Autorité'*, Paris: Éditions Galilée.
——— (2006a) *Specters of Marx: The State of Debt, the Work of Mourning, and the New International*, trans. P. Kamuf, New York and London: Routledge.
——— (2006b) 'Hostipitality', pp. 208–30, in L. Thomassen (ed.), *The Derrida-Habermas Reader*, Chicago: The University of Chicago Press.
——— (2007a) *Psyche: Inventions of the Other,* vol. I, P. Kamuf and E. Rottenberg (eds), Stanford, CA: Stanford University Press.
——— (2007b) 'A certain impossible possibility of saying the event', *Critical Inquiry*, 33: 441–61.
——— (2007c) 'Abraham, the other', pp. 1–35, in B. Bergo, J. Cohen and R. Zagury-Orly (eds), *Judeities: Questions for Jacques Derrida*, New York: Fordham University Press.
——— (2008a) *The Gift of Death, & Literature in Secret*, trans. D. Wills, Chicago and London: The University of Chicago Press.
——— (2008b) *Psyche: Inventions of the Other,* vol. II, P. Kamuf and E. Rottenberg (eds), Stanford, CA: Stanford University Press.
——— (2008c) *The Animal that Therefore I Am*, trans. D. Wills, New York: Fordham University Press.
——— (2008d) *Séminaire: La Bête et le Souverain,* vol. I *(2001–2002)*, Paris: Éditions Galilée.
——— (2009) *The Beast & the Sovereign,* vol. I, trans. G. Bennington, Chicago and London: The University of Chicago Press.
——— (2010) *Séminaire: La Bête et le Souverain,* vol. II *(2002–2003)*, Paris: Éditions Galilée.
——— (2011a) *The Beast & the Sovereign,* vol. II, trans. G. Bennington, Chicago and London: The University of Chicago Press.
——— (2011b) *Parages*, trans. T. Conley, J. Hulbert, J.P. Leavey and A. Ronell, Stanford, CA: Stanford University Press.
——— (2013) 'Avowing – the impossible: "returns," repentance, and reconciliation', trans. G. Anidjar, pp. 18–41, in E. Weber (ed.), *Living Together: Jacques Derrida's Communities of Violence and Peace*, New York: Fordham University Press.
——— (2014) *The Death Penalty,* vol. I, trans. G. Bennington, Chicago and London: The University of Chicago Press.

——— (2016) *Heidegger: The Question of Being & History*, trans. G. Bennington, Chicago and London: The University of Chicago Press.

Derrida J. and Caputo, J.D. (1997) *Deconstruction in a Nutshell: A Conversation with Jacques Derrida*, New York: Fordham University Press.

Derrida, J. and Dufourmantelle, A. (2000) *Of Hospitality*, trans. R. Bowlby, Stanford, CA: Stanford University Press.

Derrida, J. and Eisenman, P. (1997) *Chora L Works*, New York: The Monacelli Press.

Derrida, J. and Ferraris, M. (2001) *A Taste for the Secret*, G. Donis and D. Webb (eds), Cambridge: Polity Press.

Derrida, J. and Roudinesco, E. (2004) *For What Tomorrow . . . A Dialogue*, trans. J. Fort, Stanford, CA: Stanford University Press.

Derrida, J. and Stiegler, M. (2002) *Echographies of Television*, trans. J. Bajorek, Cambridge: Polity Press.

Derrida, J. and Thévenin, P. (1998) *The Secret Art of Antonin Artaud*, trans. M.A. Caws, Cambridge, MA and London: The MIT Press.

Descartes, R. (1968) *Discourse on Method and the Meditations*, trans. F.E. Sutcliffe, London: Penguin Books.

Deuber-Mankowsky, A. (2008) 'Nothing is political, everything can be politicized: on the concept of the political in Michel Foucault and Carl Schmitt', *Telos*, 142: 135–61.

De Ville, J. (2008) 'Derrida's *The Purveyor of Truth* and Constitutional Reading', *International Journal for the Semiotics of Law*, 21(2): 117–37.

——— (2010) 'Revisiting *Plato's Pharmacy*', *International Journal for the Semiotics of Law*, 23(3): 315–38.

——— (2011a) *Jacques Derrida: Law as Absolute Hospitality*, Abingdon and New York: Routledge.

——— (2011b) 'Mythology and the images of justice', *Law and Literature*, 23(3): 324–64.

——— (2012) 'Deconstructing the Leviathan: Derrida's *The Beast and the Sovereign*', *Societies*, 2(4): 357–71.

De Vries, H. (1999) *Philosophy and the Turn to Religion*, Baltimore, MD: The John Hopkins University Press.

Diamantides, M. (2015) 'Constitutional theory and its limits – reflections on comparative political theologies', *Law, Culture and the Humanities*, 11(1): 109–46.

Douzinas (2007) *Human Rights and Empire: The Political Philosophy of Cosmopolitanism*, London and New York: Routledge-Cavendish.

——— (2013) *Philosophy and Resistance in the Crisis: Greece and the Future of Europe*, Cambridge: Polity Press.

Dyzenhaus, D. (1994) 'Now the machine runs itself: Carl Schmitt on Hobbes and Kelsen', *Cardozo Law Review*, 16(1): 1–19.

——— (1997) *Legality and Legitimacy: Carl Schmitt, Hans Kelsen and Hermann Heller in Weimar*, Oxford: Oxford University Press.

Ellmann, M. (2000) 'Deconstruction and psychoanalysis', pp. 211–37, in N. Royle (ed.), *Deconstructions: A User's Guide*, New York: Palgrave.

Engels, F. (1894) *Herr Eugen Dühring's Revolution in Science (Anti-Dühring)*, trans. E. Burns, New York: New York International Publishers. Available at https://archive.org/details/antidhringherr00enge (accessed 10 July 2016).

Filmer, H. (2007) *Derridas Kritik an Carl Schmitts Begriff des Politischen in 'Politik der Freundschaft'*, Norderstedt: GRIN Verlag.

Freud, S. (1925) *Gesammelte Schriften III: Ergänzungen zur Traumlehre*. Available at http://archive.org/details/GesammelteSchriftenIiiErgnzungenZurTraumlehre (accessed 22 July 2016).

——— (1985) *The Complete Letters of Sigmund Freud to Wilhelm Fliess, 1887–1904*, trans. J.M. Masson, Cambridge, MA and London: Harvard University Press.

——— (1991) *Gesammelte Werke: Chronologisch Geordnet*, Bd. I–XVIII, London: Imago.

——— (2001) *The Standard Edition of the Complete Psychological Works of Sigmund Freud*, Bd. I–XXIV, J. Strachey (ed.), London: Vintage.

Fues, W.M. (2010) 'The foe. The radical evil. Political theology in Immanuel Kant and Carl Schmitt', *The Philosophical Forum*, 41(1–2): 181–204.

Galli, C. (2015) *Janus's Gaze: Essays on Carl Schmitt*, trans. A. Minervini, Durham, NC and London: Duke University Press.

Gardiner, M.M. (1964) 'The Wolf Man grows older', *Bulletin/Journal of the American Psychoanalytic Association*, 12(1): 80–92.

——— (1983) 'The Wolf Man's last years', *Bulletin/Journal of the American Psychoanalytical Association*, 31(4): 867–97.

——— (1991) *The Wolf Man by the Wolf Man: The Double Story of Freud's Most Famous Case*, New York: The Noonday Press.

Gasché, R. (1986) *The Tain of the Mirror: Derrida and the Philosophy of Reflection*, Cambridge, MA and London: Harvard University Press.

——— (2004) 'The partisan and the philosopher', *NCR*, 4(3): 9–34.

Glenn, C. (2015) 'Al Qaeda v ISIS: leaders & structure', Wilson Center. Available at www.wilsoncenter.org/article/al-qaeda-v-isis-leaders-structure (accessed 29 July 2016).

Grear, A. (2006) 'Human rights – human bodies? Some reflections on corporate human rights distortion, the legal subject, embodiment and human rights theory', *Law and Critique*, 17(2): 171–99.

Grimm, D. (2012a) 'Types of constitutions', pp. 98–132, in *The Oxford Handbook of Comparative Constitutional Law*, Oxford: Oxford University Press.

——— (2012b) 'The achievement of constitutionalism and its prospects in a changed world', pp. 3–22, in P. Dobner and M. Loughlin (eds), *The Twilight of Constitutionalism?*, Oxford: Oxford University Press.

Groh, R. (1998) *Arbeit an der Heillosigkeit der Welt: Zur politisch-theologischen Mythologie und Anthropologie Carl Schmitts*, Frankfurt am Main: Suhrkamp.

——— (2014) *Carl Schmitts gnostischer Dualismus*, Berlin: LIT Verlag.

Gross, R. (2015) 'The "true enemy": antisemitism in Carl Schmitt's life and work', pp. 1–26, in J. Meierhenrich and O. Simons (eds), *The Oxford Handbook of Carl Schmitt*, Oxford: Oxford University Press. Available from *Oxford Handbooks Online*, at www.oxfordhandbooks.com (accessed 20 July 2016).

Grosz, E. (1994) 'Women, *chora*, dwelling', *Architecture New York*, 4 (January/February): 22–7.

Hacking, I. (1995) *Rewriting the Soul: Multiple Personality and the Sciences of Memory*, Princeton, NJ: Princeton University Press.

——— (2004) *Historical Ontology*, Cambridge, MA and London: Harvard University Press.

Hardt, M. and Negri, A. (2000) *Empire*, Cambridge, MA and London: Harvard University Press.

——— (2004) *Multitude: War and Democracy in the Age of Empire*, New York: The Penguin Press.

——— (2011) 'The fight for "real democracy" at the heart of Occupy Wall Street', *Foreign Affairs*, 11 October 2011. Available at www.foreignaffairs.com/articles/north-america/2011-10-11/fight-real-democracy-heart-occupy-wall-street (accessed 13 July 2016).

Hegel, G.W.F. (1977) *Phenomenology of Spirit*, trans. A.V. Miller, Oxford: Oxford University Press.

——— (1986) *Phänomenologie des Geistes*, Werke 3, Frankfurt am Main: Suhrkamp.

Heidegger, M. (1962) *Being and Time*, trans. J. Macquarrie and E. Robinson, San Francisco: Harper & Row.

——— (1982) *Vom Wesen der menschlichen Freiheit*, Gesamtausgabe Bd. 31, Frankfurt am Main: Vittorio Klostermann.

——— (1983) *Einführung in die Metaphysik*, Gesamtausgabe Bd. 40, Frankfurt am Main: Vittorio Klostermann.

——— (2000) *Introduction to Metaphysics*, trans. G. Fried and R. Polt, New Haven, CT and London: Yale University Press.

——— (2005) *The Essence of Human Freedom: An Introduction to Philosophy*, trans. T. Sadler, London: Continuum.

——— (2006) *Sein und Zeit*, 19th edn, Tübingen: Max Niemeyer Verlag.

Herrero, M. (2015) *The Political Discourse of Carl Schmitt: A Mystic of Order*, London and New York: Rowman & Littlefield.

Hirst, P. (1987) 'Carl Schmitt's decisionism', *Telos*, 72: 15–26.

Hitschler, D. (2010) *Zwischen Liberalismus und Existentialismus: Carl Schmitt im englischsprachigen Schrifttum*, Baden-Baden: Nomos.

Hobson, M. (2001) 'Derrida and representation: mimesis, presentation and representation', pp. 132–51, in T. Cohen (ed.), *Jacques Derrida and the Humanities: A Critical Reader*, Cambridge: Cambridge University Press.

Hohendahl, P. (2008) 'Political theology revisited: Carl Schmitt's postwar reassessment', *Konturen*, 1: 1–28.

Hooker, W. (2009) *Carl Schmitt's International Thought: Order and Orientation*, Cambridge: Cambridge University Press.

Horn, E. (2004) '"Waldgänger," traitor, partisan: figures of political irregularity in West German postwar thought', *New Centennial Review*, 4(3): 125–43.

Hyppolite, J. (1974) *Genesis and Structure of Hegel's Phenomenology of Spirit*, trans. S. Cherniak and J. Heckman, Evanston, IL: Northwestern University Press.

Isensee, J. (1995) *Das Volk als Grund der Verfassung*, Düsseldorf: Westdeutscher Verlag.

——— (2004) 'Staat und Verfassung', pp. 3–106, in J. Isensee and P. Kirchhof (eds), *Handbuch des Staatsrechts*, Bd. II, 3rd edn, Heidelberg: CF Müller.

Jameson, F. (1999) 'Marx's purloined letter', pp. 26–67, in M. Sprinker (ed.), *Ghostly Demarcations: A Symposium on Jacques Derrida's Specters of Marx*, London and New York: Verso.

Johnson, L. (2011) *The Wolf Man's Burden*, Ithaca, NY and London: Cornell University Press.

Kaldor, M. (2006) *New and Old Wars*, 2nd edn, Cambridge: Polity Press.

Kalyvas, A. (2000) 'Carl Schmitt and the three moments of democracy', *Cardozo Law Review*, 21(5): 1525–65.

——— (2009) *Democracy and the Politics of the Extraordinary: Max Weber, Carl Schmitt and Hannah Arendt*, Cambridge: Cambridge University Press.

Kennedy, E. (2004) *Constitutional Failure: Carl Schmitt in Weimar*, Durham, NC and London: Duke University Press.

Kirkby, J. (2006) '"Remembrance of the future": Derrida on mourning', *Social Semiotics*, 16(3): 461–72.

Kistner, U. (2009) 'Sovereignty in question: Agamben, Schmitt, and some consequences' *SA Public Law*, 24(2): 239–68.

——— (2011) 'The exception and the rule: fictive, real, critical', *Telos*, 157: 43–59.

Kochi, T. (2006a) 'The partisan: Carl Schmitt and terrorism', *Law and Critique*, 17(3): 267–95.

——— (2006b) 'Terror in the name of human rights', *Melbourne Journal of International Law*, 7(1): 127–54.

Kreuder-Sonnen, C. (2013) 'Die Entgrenzung des Ausnahmezustands: global und permanent?', pp. 163–84, in R. Voigt (ed.), *Ausnahmezustand: Carl Schmitts Lehre von der kommissarischen Diktatur*, Baden-Baden: Nomos.

Krisch, N. (2012) *Beyond Constitutionalism: The Pluralist Structure of Postnational Law*, Oxford: Oxford University Press.

Kristeva, J. (1984) *Revolution in Poetic Language*, New York: Columbia University Press.

Laplanche, J. and Pontalis, J.-B. (1973) *The Language of Psychoanalysis*, trans. D. Nicholson-Smith, New York and London: W.W. Norton and Co.

Leavey, J.P. (1986) *Glassary*, Lincoln and London: University of Nebraska Press.

Lievens, M. (2013) 'Carl Schmitt's metapolitics', *Constellations*, 20(1): 121–37.

Lindahl, H. (2003) 'Acquiring a community: the *Acquis* and the institution of European legal order', *European Law Journal*, 9(4): 433–50.

——— (2007) 'The paradox of constituent power', *Ratio Juris*, 20(4): 485–505.

——— (2008a) 'Constituent power and reflexive identity: towards an ontology of collective selfhood', pp. 9–24, in M. Loughlin and N. Walker (eds), *The Paradox of Constitutionalism*, Oxford: Oxford University Press.

——— (2008b) 'Collective self-legislation as an *Actus Impurus*: a response to Heidegger's critique of European nihilism', *Continental Philosophy Review*, 41(3): 323–42.

——— (2013) *Fault Lines of Globalization: Legal Order and the Politics of A-Legality*, Oxford: Oxford University Press.

——— (2015) 'Possibility, actuality, rupture: constituent power and the ontology of change', *Constellations*, 22(2): 163–74.

Linder, C. (2015) 'Carl Schmitt in Plettenberg', pp. 1–29, in J. Meierhenrich and O. Simons (eds), *The Oxford Handbook of Carl Schmitt*, Oxford: Oxford University Press. Available from *Oxford Handbooks Online*, at www.oxfordhandbooks.com (accessed 20 July 2016).

Lock, P. (1982) 'Text crypt', *MLN*, 97(4): 872–89.

Loraux, N. (2006) *The Invention of Athens: The Funeral Oration in the Classical City*, trans. A. Sheridan, New York: Zone Books.

Lossau, J. (2011) 'Postcolonialism', pp. 251–9, in S. Legg (ed.), *Spatiality, Sovereignty and Carl Schmitt: Geographies of the Nomos*, London and New York: Routledge.

Loughlin, M. (2010) *Foundations of Public Law*, Oxford: Oxford University Press.

——— (2014) 'The concept of constituent power', *European Journal of Political Theory*, 13(2): 218–37.

Mack Brunswick, R. (1928) 'A supplement to Freud's "History of an Infantile Neurosis"', *International Journal of Psycho-Analysis*, 9(4): 439–76.

Malpas, J. (2016) 'On the philosophical reading of Heidegger: situating the *Black Notebooks*', pp. 3–22, in I. Farin and J. Malpas (eds), *Reading Heidegger's Black Notebooks 1931–1941*, Cambridge, MA and London: The MIT Press.

Marder, E. (2008) 'Mourning, magic and telepathy', *Oxford Literary Review*, 30(2): 181–200.

Marder, M. (2010) *Groundless Existence: The Political Ontology of Carl Schmitt*, New York: Continuum.

McCormick, J.P. (1999) *Carl Schmitt's Critique of Liberalism: Against Politics as Technology*, Cambridge: Cambridge University Press.

——— (2007) 'Irrational choice and mortal combat as political destiny: the essential Carl Schmitt', *Annual Review of Political Science*, 10: 315–39.

Meier, H. (1998) *The Lesson of Carl Schmitt: Four Chapters on the Distinction between Political Theology and Political Philosophy*, trans. M. Brainard, Chicago and London: The University of Chicago Press.

——— (2013) *Carl Schmitt, Leo Strauss und 'Der Begriff des Politischen'*, 3rd edn, Stuttgart: Verlag J.B. Metzler.

Minca, C. and Rowan R. (2016) *On Schmitt and Space*, London and New York: Routledge.

Mouffe, C. (2007) 'Carl Schmitt's warning on the dangers of a unipolar world', pp. 147–53, in L. Odysseos and F. Petito (eds), *The International Political Thought of Carl Schmitt*, London and New York: Routledge.

Müller, J.-W. (2003) *A Dangerous Mind: Carl Schmitt in Post-War European Thought*, New Haven, CT: Yale University Press.

——— (2006) '"An irregularity that cannot be regulated": Carl Schmitt's theory of the partisan and the "war on terror"'. Available at www.princeton.edu/~jmueller/Schmitt-WarTerror-JWMueller-March2007.pdf (accessed 22 July 2016).

Münkler, H. (2005) *The New Wars*, trans. P. Camiller, Malden, MA: Polity Press.

Naas, M. (2003) *Taking on the Tradition: Jacques Derrida and the Legacies of Deconstruction*, Stanford, CA: Stanford University Press.

Nancy, J.-L. (1993) *The Experience of Freedom*, Stanford, CA: Stanford University Press.

Negri, A. (2009) *Insurgencies: Constituent Power and the Modern State*, trans. M. Boscagli, Minneapolis and London: University of Minnesota Press.

Neumann, V. (2000) 'Introduction', pp. 280–90, in A.J. Jacobson and B. Schlink (eds), *Weimar: A Jurisprudence of Crisis*, Berkeley: University of California Press.

——— (2015) *Carl Schmitt als Jurist*, Tübingen: Mohr Siebeck.

Newman, E. (2004) 'The "new wars" debate: a historical perspective is needed', *Security Dialogue*, 35(2): 173–89.

Ng, A.H.S. (2008) 'Introduction: reading the double', pp. 1–13, in A.H.S. Ng (ed.), *The Poetics of Shadows: The Double in Literature and Philosophy*, Stuttgart: Ibidem Verlag.

Nietzsche, F. (1989) *Beyond Good and Evil: Prelude to a Philosophy of the Future*, New York: Vintage Books.

Nitschke, P. (2011) 'Oswald Spengler und Carl Schmitt: zur Morphologie des Kampfes', pp. 131–47, in R. Voigt (ed.), *Freund-Feind-Denken: Carl Schmitts Kategorie des Politischen*, Stuttgart: Franz Steiner Verlag.

Odysseos, L. (2007) 'Crossing the line? Carl Schmitt on the 'spaceless universalism' of cosmopolitanism and the war on terror', pp. 124–43, in L. Odysseos and F. Petito (eds), *The International Political Thought of Carl Schmitt*, London and New York: Routledge.

Ojakangas, M. (2007) 'A terrifying world without an exterior: Carl Schmitt and the metaphysics of international (dis)order', pp. 205–21, in L. Odysseos and F. Petito (eds), *The International Political Thought of Carl Schmitt*, London and New York: Routledge.

Ottmann, H. (1993/94) 'Hegel und Carl Schmitt', *Hegel Jahrbuch*, 19–24.

Ovid (1951) *Metamorphoses*, trans. F.J. Miller, Cambridge, MA: Harvard University Press.

Palaver, W. (1996) 'Carl Schmitt on *nomos* and space', *Telos*, 106: 105–27.

Pan, D. (2013) 'Carl Schmitt's *Theory of the Partisan* and the stability of the nation-state', *TELOSscope*, 2 January 2013. Available at www.telospress.com/carl-schmitts-theory-of-the-partisan-and-the-stability-of-the-nation-state (accessed 8 July 2016).

Pasquino, P. (1988) 'Die Lehre vom "pouvoir constituant" bei Emmanuel Sieyès and Carl Schmitt', pp. 371–85, in H. Quaritsch (ed.), *Complexio Oppositorum: Über Carl Schmitt*, Berlin: Duncker & Humblot.

Patočka, J. (1996) *Heretical Essays in the Philosophy of History*, trans. E. Kohák, Chicago and La Salle, IL: Open Court.

Petito, F. (2007) 'Against world unity: Carl Schmitt and the Western-centric and liberal global order', pp. 166–84, in L. Odysseos and F. Petito (eds), *The International Political Thought of Carl Schmitt*, London and New York: Routledge.

Phemister, P. (2006) *The Rationalists: Descartes, Spinoza and Leibniz*, Cambridge: Polity Press.

Plato (1955) *The Republic*, Harmondsworth: Penguin Books.

——— (1997) *Complete Works*, ed. John M. Cooper, Indianapolis, IN and Cambridge: Hackett Publishing Co.

Plotkin-Amrami, G. and Brunner, J. (2015) 'Making up "national trauma" in Israel: from collective identity to collective vulnerability', *Social Studies of Science*, 45(4): 525–45.

Poe, E.A. (1845) *The Purloined Letter*. Available at http://xroads.virginia.edu/~hyper/poe/purloine.html (accessed 8 July 2016).

Preuss, U.K. (1999) 'Political order and democracy: Carl Schmitt and his influence', pp. 155–79, in C. Mouffe (ed.), *The Challenge of Carl Schmitt*, London and New York: Verso.

——— (2012) 'Disconnecting constitutions from statehood: is global constitutionalism a viable concept?', pp. 23–46, in P. Dobner and M. Loughlin (eds), *The Twilight of Constitutionalism?*, Oxford: Oxford University Press.

——— (2015a) 'Carl Schmitt and the Weimar Constitution', pp. 1–24, in J. Meierhenrich and O. Simons (eds), *The Oxford Handbook of Carl Schmitt*, Oxford: Oxford University Press. Available from *Oxford Handbooks Online*, at www.oxfordhandbooks.com (accessed 20 July 2016).

——— (2015b) 'Carl Schmitt – Die Bändigung oder die Entfesselung des Politischen?', pp. 137–62, in R. Voigt (ed.), *Mythos Staat*, 2nd edn, Baden-Baden: Nomos.

Rabinbach, A. and Gilman, S.L. (2013) *The Third Reich Sourcebook*, Berkeley: University of California Press.

Rancière, J. (1999) *Dis-agreement: Politics and Philosophy*, trans. J. Rose, Minneapolis and London: University of Minnesota Press.

Rank, O. (1925) *Der Doppelgänger: Eine Psychoanalytische Studie*, Leipzig, Vienna and Zürich: Internationaler Psychoanalytischer Verlag.

——— (1971) *The Double: A Psychoanalytical Study*, Chapel Hill: The University of North Carolina Press.

Rashkin, E. (1992) *Family Secrets and the Psychoanalysis of Narrative*, Princeton, NJ: Princeton University Press.

Rech, W. (2016) 'Eschatology and existentialism: Carl Schmitt's historical understanding of international law and politics', pp. 147–64, in M. Arvidsson, L. Brännström, and P. Minkkinen (eds), *The Contemporary Relevance of Carl Schmitt: Law, Politics, Theology*, Abingdon and New York: Routledge.

Rissing, M. and Rissing T. (2009) *Politische Theologie: Schmitt – Derrida – Metz*, München: Wilhelm Fink Verlag.

Römer, P. (1990) 'Tod und Verklärung des Carl Schmitt', *Archiv für Rechts- und Sozialphilosophie*, 76(3): 373–99.

Rowan, R. (2011) 'A new nomos of post-nomos? Multipolarity, space, and constituent power', pp. 143–62, in S. Legg (ed.), *Spatiality, Sovereignty and Carl Schmitt*, London and New York: Routledge.

Saddad, S. (2013) *Derrida and the Inheritance of Democracy*, Bloomington and Indianapolis: Indiana University Press.

Saghafi, K. (2010) *Apparitions – Of Derrida's Other*, New York: Fordham University Press.

——— (2011) 'The chase: rivalry and conjuration', *Parallax*, 17(1): 34–42.

Sallis, J. (1999) *Chronology: On Beginning in Plato's Timaeus*, Bloomington and Indianapolis: Indiana University Press.

Salter, M.G. (2012) *Carl Schmitt: Law as Politics, Ideology and Strategic Myth*, Abingdon and New York: Routledge.

Schiller, F. (2016) *Die Braut von Messina oder die feindliche Brüder: Ein Trauerspiel mit Chören*, Berlin: Verlag der Contumax.

Schmitt, C. (1933) *Der Begriff des Politischen*, Hamburg: Hanseatische Verlagsanstalt.

——— (1934) *Staat, Bewegung, Volk: Die Dreigliederung der politischen Einheit*, Hamburg: Hanseatische Verlagsanstalt.

——— (1935a) 'Was bedeutet der Streit um den "Rechtsstaat"?', *Zeitschrift für die gesamte Staatswissenschaft*, 95(2): 189–201.

——— (1935b) 'Die Verfassung der Freiheit', *Deutsche Juristen-Zeitung*, 40(19): 1133–5.

——— (1936a) 'Eröffnung der wissenschaftliche Vorträge', pp. 14–17, in *Das Judentum in der Rechtswissenschaft, Bd. 1: Die deutsche Rechtswissenschaft im Kampf gegen den jüdischen Geist*. Available at https://archive.org/details/DasJudentumInDerRechtswissenschaftBandDieDeutscheRechtswissenschaft (accessed 17 July 2016).

——— (1936b) 'Schlußwort', pp. 28–34, in *Das Judentum in der Rechtswissenschaft, Bd. 1: Die deutsche Rechtswissenschaft im Kampf gegen den jüdischen Geist*. Available at https://archive.org/details/DasJudentumInDerRechtswissenschaftBandDieDeutscheRechtswissenschaft (accessed 17 July 2016).

——— (1940) 'Das "Allgemeine Deutsche Staatsrecht" als Beispiel Rechtswissenschaftlicher Systembildung', *Zeitschrift für die gesamte Staatswissenschaft*, 100(1/2): 5–24.

——— (1969) *Gesetz und Urteil: Eine Untersuchung zum Problem der Rechtspraxis*, 2nd edn, Münich: Verlag CH Beck.

——— (1987) 'Interrogation of Carl Schmitt by Robert Kempner (I–III)', *Telos*, 72: 97–129.

——— (1988a) *The Crisis of Parliamentary Democracy*, trans. E. Kennedy, Cambridge, MA and London: The MIT Press.

——— (1988b) 'Der Begriff des Politischen. Vorwort von 1971 zur italienischen Ausgabe', pp. 269–73, in H. Quaritsch (ed.), *Complexio Oppositorum: Über Carl Schmitt*, Berlin: Duncker & Humblot.

——— (1991) *Glossarium: Aufzeichnungen der Jahre 1947–1951*, Berlin: Duncker & Humblot.
——— (1994) *Positionen und Begriffe im Kampf mit Weimar – Genf – Versailles 1923–1939*, 3rd edn, Berlin: Duncker & Humblot.
——— (1995) *Staat, Großraum, Nomos: Arbeiten aus den Jahren 1916–1969*, Berlin: Duncker & Humblot.
——— (1996a) *Der Hüter der Verfassung*, 4th edn, Berlin: Duncker & Humblot.
——— (1996b) *Roman Catholicism and Political Form*, trans. G.L. Ulmen, Westport and London: Greenwood Press.
——— (1997) *Land and Sea*, trans. S. Draghici, Washington, DC: Plutarch Press.
——— (1999) *Four Articles: 1931–1938*, trans. S. Draghici, Corvallis: Plutarch Press.
——— (2001) *State, Movement, People: The Triadic Structure of the Political Unity*, ed. and trans. S. Draghici, Corvallis, OR: Plutarch Press.
——— (2002a) *Der Begriff des Politischen. Text von 1932 mit einem Vorwort und drei Collarien*, 7th edn, Berlin: Duncker & Humblot.
——— (2002b) 'A pan-European interpretation of Donoso Cortés', trans. M. Grzeskowiak, *Telos*, 125: 100–15.
——— (2002c) 'The liberal rule of law', pp. 294–300, in A.J. Jacobson and B. Schlink (eds), *Weimar: A Jurisprudence of Crisis*, Berkeley: University of California Press.
——— (2002d) 'State ethics and the pluralist state', pp. 300–12, in A.J. Jacobson and B. Schlink (eds), *Weimar: A Jurisprudence of Crisis*, Berkeley: University of California Press.
——— (2003) *Verfassungsrechtliche Aufsätze aus den Jahren 1924–1954: Materialien zu einer Verfassungslehre,* Berlin: Duncker & Humblot.
——— (2004a) 'The Theory of the Partisan: a commentary/remark on the concept of the political', trans. A.C. Goodson, *The New Centennial Review*, 4(3): 1–78.
——— (2004b) *On the Three Types of Juristic Thought*, trans. J. Bendersky, Westport, CT and London: Praeger.
——— (2004c) *Legality and Legitimacy*, trans. and ed. J. Seitzer, Durham, NC and London: Duke University Press.
——— (2004d) *Politische Theologie: Vier Kapitel zur Lehre von der Souveränität*, 8th edn, Berlin: Duncker & Humblot.
——— (2005a) *Frieden oder Pazifismus? Arbeiten zum Volkerrecht und zur internationalen Politik 1924–1978*, G. Maschke (ed.), Berlin: Duncker & Humblot.
——— (2005b) *Political Theology: Four Chapters on the Concept of Sovereignty*, trans. G. Schwab, Cambridge, MA and London: The University of Chicago Press.
——— (2005c) *Tagebücher Oktober 1912 bis Februar 1915*, E. Hüsmert (ed.), 2nd revised edn, Berlin: Akademie Verlag.
——— (2006a) *The Nomos of the Earth in the International Law of the Jus Publicum Europaeum*, trans. G.L. Ulmen, New York: Telos Press.
——— (2006b) *Die Diktatur: Von den Anfängen des modernen Souveranitätsgedankens bis zum proletarischen Klassenkampf*, 7th edn, Berlin: Duncker & Humblot.
——— (2006c) *Über die drei Arten des rechtswissenschaftlichen Denkens*, 3rd edn, Berlin: Duncker & Humblot.
——— (2007a) *The Concept of the Political,* expanded edn, trans. G. Schwab, Chicago and London: The University of Chicago Press.

——— (2007b) 'The "fourth" (second) interrogation of Carl Schmitt at Nuremberg', *Telos*, 139: 35–43.

——— (2007c) *Theory of the Partisan: Intermediate Commentary on the Concept of the Political*, trans. G.L. Ulmen, New York: Telos Press.

——— (2008a) *Constitutional Theory*, trans. and ed. J. Seitzer, Durham, NC and London: Duke University Press.

——— (2008b) *Politische Theologie II: Die Legende von der Erledigung jeder Politischen Theologie*, 5th edn, Berlin: Duncker & Humblot.

——— (2008c) *Political Theology II: The Myth of the Closure of Any Political Theology*, trans. M. Hoelzl and G. Ward, Cambridge: Polity Press.

——— (2008d) *The Leviathan in the State Theory of Thomas Hobbes: Meaning and Failure of a Political Symbol,* trans. G. Schwab and E. Hilfstein, Chicago and London: The University of Chicago Press.

——— (2008e) *Land und Meer: Eine weltgeschichtliche Betrachtung,* 6th edn, Stuttgart: Klett-Cota.

——— (2008f) *Romischer Katholizismus und politische Form*, 5th edn, Stuttgart: Klett-Cotta.

——— (2008g) *Gespräch über die Macht und den Zugang zum Machthaber*, Stuttgart: Klett-Cotta.

——— (2009a) *Donoso Cortés in gesamteuropäischer Interpretation: Vier Aufsätze*, 2nd edn, Berlin: Duncker & Humblot.

——— (2009b) *Theodor Däublers 'Nordlicht': Drei Studien iiber die Elemente, den Geist und die Aktualität des Werkes*, 3rd edn, Berlin: Duncker & Humblot.

——— (2009c) *Hamlet or Hecuba: The Intrusion of the Time into the Play*, trans. D. Pan and J. Rust, New York: Telos Press Publishing.

——— (2010a) *Theorie des Partisanen: Zwischenbemerkung zum Begriff des Politischen*, 7th edn, Berlin: Duncker & Humblot.

——— (2010b) *Verfassungslehre*,10th edn, Berlin: Duncker & Humblot.

——— (2010c) *Ex Captivitate Salus: Erfahrungen der Zeit 1945/47*, 3rd edn, Berlin: Duncker & Humblot.

——— (2010d) *Die geistesgeschichtliche Lage des heutigen Parlamentarismus*, 9th edn, Berlin: Duncker & Humblot.

——— (2011a) *Der Nomos der Erde im Völkerrecht des Jus Publicum Europaeum*, 5th edn, Berlin: Duncker & Humblot.

——— (2011b) '*Großraum* versus universalism: the international legal struggle over the Monroe Doctrine', trans. M. Hannah, pp. 46–54, in S. Legg (ed.), *Spatiality, Sovereignty and Carl Schmitt*, London and New York: Routledge.

——— (2011c) *Writings on War*, trans. T. Nunan, Cambridge and Malden, MA: Polity Press.

——— (2012a) *Der Leviathan in der Staatslehre des Thomas Hobbes: Sinn und Fehlschlag eines politischen Symbols*, 4th edn, Stuttgart: Klett-Cotta.

——— (2012b) *Legalität und Legitimität*, 8th edn, Berlin: Duncker & Humblot.

——— (2014a) *Dictatorship: From the Origin of the Modern Concept of Sovereignty to Proletarian Class Struggle*, trans. M. Hoelzl and G. Ward, Cambridge: Polity Press.

——— (2014b) *Volksentscheid und Volksbegehren: Ein Beitrag zur Auslegung der Weimarer Verfassung und zur Lehre von der unmittelbare Demokratie*, Berlin: Duncker & Humblot.

——— (2014c) *Die Militärzeit 1915 bis 1919*: *Tagebuch Februar bis Dezember 1915: Aufsätze und Materialien*, eds E. Husmert and G. Giesler, Berlin: Akademie Verlag.

——— (2015) *Dialogues on Power and Space*, Cambridge and Malden, MA: Polity Press.

Schmitt, C. and Schickel, J. (1970) 'Gespräch über den Partisanen', pp. 9–29, in J. Schickel (ed.), *Guerrilleros, Partisanen: Theorie und Praxis*, München: Carl Hanser Verlag.

Schneider, P. (1957) *Ausnahmezustand und Norm: Eine Studie zur Rechtslehre von Carl Schmitt*, Stuttgart: Deutsche Verlags-Anstalt.

Schuppert, G.F. (2003) *Staatswissenschaft*, Baden-Baden: Nomos.

Schwab, G. (1987) 'Enemy or Foe: A Conflict of Modern Politics', *Telos*, 72: 194–201.

——— (1989) *The Challenge of the Exception: An Introduction to the Political Ideas of Carl Schmitt between 1921 and 1936*, 2nd edn, New York: Greenwood Press.

Shamai, M. (2016) *Systemic Interventions for National and Collective Trauma: Theory, Practice, and Evaluation*, New York and Abingdon: Routledge.

Sieyès, E.J. (2003) *Political Writings*, ed. M. Sonenscher, Indianapolis, IN and Cambridge: Hackett Publishing Company.

Simon, R. (2008) *Die Begriffe des Politischen bei Carl Schmitt und Jacques Derrida*, Frankfurt am Main: Peter Lang.

Slomp, G. (2009) *Carl Schmitt and the Politics of Hostility, Violence and Terror*, New York: Palgrave Macmillan.

Sokhi-Bulley, B. (2011) 'Government(ality) by experts: human rights as governance', *Law and Critique*, 22(3): 251–71.

Spang, M. (2014) *Constituent Power and Constitutional Order: Above, Within and Beside the Constitution*, Basingstoke: Palgrave Macmillan.

Spitzer, A.N. (2011) *Derrida, Myth and the Impossibility of Philosophy*, London and New York: Continuum.

Stern, K. (1984) *Das Staatsrecht der Bundesrepublik Deutschland*, Bd. I, 2nd edn, München: Verlag CH Beck.

Stirner, M. (1845) *Der Einzige und sein Eigentum*, Leipzig: Otto Wigand. Available at www.lsr-projekt.de/msee.html (accessed 29 July 2016).

——— (2006) *The Ego and Its Own*, Cambridge: Cambridge University Press.

Strauss, L. (2007) 'Notes on Carl Schmitt, *The Concept of the Political*', trans. J.H. Lomax, pp. 97–122, in C. Schmitt, *The Concept of the Political*, Chicago: The University of Chicago Press.

Taubes, J. (2013) *To Carl Schmitt: Letters and Reflections*, trans. K. Tribe, New York: Columbia University Press.

Thiele, U. (2011) '"Der Feind ist unsere eigene Frage als Gestalt": Zur Problematik negativistischer Identitätskonstruktionen', pp. 151–72, in R. Voigt (ed.) *Freund-Feind-Denken: Carl Schmitts Kategorie des Politischen*, Stuttgart: Franz Steiner Verlag.

Thomson, A.J.P. (2005) *Deconstruction and Democracy: Derrida's Politics of Friendship*, New York: Continuum.

Tormey, S. (2012) 'Occupy Wall Street: from representation to post-representation', *Journal of Critical Globalisation Studies*, 5: 132–7.

——— (2015) *The End of Representative Politics*, Cambridge: Polity Press.

Tribe, L.H. (1989) 'The curvature of constitutional space: what lawyers can learn from modern physics', *Harvard Law Review*, 103(1): 1–39.

Tschumi, B. (2005) 'Derrida: an ally et un ami', *Log*, 4 (Winter): 117–19.

Van der Walt, J. (2009) 'The shadow and its shade: a response to Ulrike Kistner's paper "Sovereignty in question"', *SA Public Law*, 24(2): 269–96.

——— (2010a) 'Constitution-making as a learning process: Andrew Arato's model of post-sovereign constitution-making: editor's introduction', *South African Journal on Human Rights*, 26(1): 1–18.

——— (2010b) 'Vertical sovereignty, horizontal constitutionalism: a case of competing retroactivities', *South African Journal on Human Rights*, 26(1): 102–29.

——— (2012a) '*Timeo Danais Dona Ferre* and the constitution that Europeans may one day have given themselves', pp. 267–308, in J. van der Walt and J. Ellsworth (eds), *Constitutional Sovereignty and Social Solidarity in Europe*, Baden-Baden: Nomos.

——— (2012b) 'Mandela, Merkel and the courage to give'. Available at http://papers.ssrn.com/sol3/papers.cfm?abstract_id=2127122 (accessed 13 July 2016).

——— (2014) *The Horizontal Effect Revolution and the Question of Sovereignty*, Berlin and Boston: Walter de Gruyter.

Vardoulakis, D. (2006) 'The return of negation: the Doppelganger in Freud's "The 'Uncanny'"', *SubStance*, 35(2): 100–16.

——— (2009) 'Stasis: beyond political theology?', *Cultural Critique*, 73 (Fall): 125–47.

Vatter, M. (2015) 'The political theology of Carl Schmitt', pp. 1–31, in J. Meierhenrich and O. Simons (eds), *The Oxford Handbook of Carl Schmitt*, Oxford: Oxford University Press. Available from *Oxford Handbooks Online*, at www.oxfordhandbooks.com (accessed 20 July 2016).

Virgil (2002) *The Aeneid*, trans. A.S. Kline. Available at www.poetryintranslation.com/PITBR/Latin/Virgilhome.htm (accessed 22 July 2016).

Virno, P. (2004) *A Grammar of the Multitude: For an Analysis of Contemporary Forms of Life*, trans. I. Bertoletti, J. Cascaito, A. Casson, South Pasadena, CA: Semiotext(e).

Voigt, R. (2005) *Weltordnungspolitik*, Wiesbaden: Verlag für Sozialwissenschaften.

——— (2015a) *Denken in Widersprüchen: Carl Schmitt wider den Zeitgeist*, Baden-Baden: Nomos.

——— (2015b) 'Zwischen Mythos und Wirklichkeit: zur Staatskonzeption von Carl Schmitt', pp. 35–57, in R. Voigt (ed.), *Mythos Staat*, 2nd edn, Baden-Baden: Nomos.

Wagner, R. (1876) *Götterdämmerung*. Available at www.rwagner.net/libretti/gotterd/e-t-gott.html (accessed 9 July 2016).

Wall, I. (2012a) *Human Rights and Constituent Power: Without Model or Warranty*, London and New York: Routledge.

——— (2012b) 'A different constituent power: Agamben and Tunisia', pp. 46–66, in M. Stone, I. rua Wall and C. Douzinas (eds), *New Critical Legal Thinking: Law and the Political*, Abingdon and New York: Routledge.

Wigley, M. (1995) *The Architecture of Deconstruction: Derrida's Haunt*, Cambridge, MA and London: The MIT Press.

Wolfreys, J. (1998) 'Justifying the unjustifiable: a supplementary introduction, of sorts', pp. 1–49, in J. Wolfreys (ed.), *The Derrida Reader: Writing Performances*, Lincoln: University of Nebraska Press.

Wood, S. (2009) *Derrida's Writing and Difference: A Reader's Guide*, London and New York: Continuum.

Zakin, E. (2011) 'The image of the people: Freud and Schmitt's political anti-progressivism', *Telos*, 157: 84–107.

Zeitlin, S.G. (2015) 'Propaganda and critique: an introduction to *Land and Sea*', pp. xxxi–lxix, in C. Schmitt, *Land and Sea: A World-Historical Meditation*, trans. S.G. Zeitlin, New York: Telos Press.

Žižek, S. (2000) *The Ticklish Subject: The Absent Centre of Political Ontology*, London and New York: Verso.

Zolo, D. (2007) 'The re-emerging notion of Empire and the influence of Carl Schmitt's thought', pp. 154–65, in L. Odysseos and F. Petito (eds), *The International Political Thought of Carl Schmitt*, London and New York: Routledge.

Zweig, E. (1909) *Die Lehre vom Pouvoir Constituant: Ein Beitrag zum Staatsrecht der französischen Revolution*, Tübingen: Verlag von JCB Mohr.

Index

For Product Safety Concerns and Information please contact our EU representative GPSR@taylorandfrancis.com Taylor & Francis Verlag GmbH, Kaufingerstraße 24, 80331 München, Germany

Batch number: 10725973

Printed by Printforce, the Netherlands